A Mosaic of Corpus Linguistics

Studien zur romanischen Sprachwissenschaft und interkulturellen Kommunikation

Herausgegeben von Gerd Wotjak

Band 66

PETER LANG

Frankfurt am Main · Berlin · Bern · Bruxelles · New York · Oxford · Wien

Aquilino Sánchez / Moisés Almela (eds.)

A Mosaic of Corpus Linguistics

Selected Approaches

PETER LANG
Internationaler Verlag der Wissenschaften

Bibliographic Information published by the Deutsche Nationalbibliothek
The Deutsche Nationalbibliothek lists this publication in the Deutsche Nationalbibliografie; detailed bibliographic data is available in the internet at http://dnb.d-nb.de.

Gratefully acknowledging financial support by

Asociación Española de Lingüística de Corpus

AELINCO

GOBIERNO DE ESPAÑA
MINISTERIO DE EDUCACIÓN

and

REGIÓN DE MURCIA
fundaciónséneca
AGENCIA REGIONAL DE CIENCIA Y TECNOLOGÍA

ISSN 1436-1914
ISBN 978-3-631-58789-8

www.peterlang.de

Contents

Why a monograph on corpus linguistics?

Moisés Almela
Aquilino Sánchez
LACELL[1], Universidad de Murcia

1. The trouble with defining corpus linguistics

The task of compiling a monograph on corpus linguistics must be faced up with the problem that there is at present no consensus among linguists as to what corpus linguistics actually is. Several years ago, when the corpus linguist was still a rara avis, and the idea of a prototypal linguist was still identified with the figure of an "armchair scholar," the publication of books having corpus linguistics as a subject matter responded to a pressing need. It was necessary to spread the knowledge of a nascent research framework and persuade other members of the academic community of its advantages. Now that the discipline has achieved relevance and popularity among linguists, a different problem has emerged, namely, the difficulty of ascertaining what is exactly "corpus linguistics."

It is generally admitted that the mere fact of quoting authentic examples of language use is not a sufficient condition for a piece of research to qualify as corpus linguistic. This raises the question of which methodological, epistemological, or even theoretical requirements are necessary conditions for declaring this or that study in full compliance with the expectations raised by the epithet "corpus linguistic." The reader will probably be acquainted with Sinclair's (2001) and Tognini-Bonelli's (2001) disquisitions about this issue. Their opinion, as is well known, favours a clear-cut divide between "corpus-based" and "corpus-driven" approaches to work with corpora. However, the question remains open of whether there is a core common ground to both approaches which could justify a superordinate use of the label "corpus linguistics" as a cover term for both "corpus-based" and "corpus-driven" approaches. And if so, how do they oppose to non-corpus linguistics.

We shall make no pretence of answering this question here. For the time being, let us be contended with pointing out some of the intricacies involved in any attempt at advancing a consensual definition of corpus linguistics. This introduction does not contend either for a narrow or for a broad conception of the discipline; the aim is rather to reflect on some of the issues that need to be addressed when it comes to drawing the outer boundaries of corpus linguis-

1 Grupo LACELL (*Lingüística Aplicada a la Computación, Enseñanza de Lenguas y Lexicografía*) is a Research Group (EO20-02) within the English Department at the University of Murcia (http://www.um.es/grupos/grupo-lacell/quees.php).

tics—that is, when it comes to deciding what lies within its remit and what lies outside of it. After all, the variety of issues addressed in this book is in need of an adequate rationale behind.

2. Between methodology and theory: broader and narrower notions of corpus linguistics

The major bone of contention between conflicting versions of corpus linguistics concerns the relationship between methodological and theoretical parameters. The following two claims stand in sharp contrast to one another:

(*i*) Corpus linguistics is a theory-independent methodology or set of methodologies. The decision to rely on corpus techniques does not entail embracing any particular theoretical statement about language. This means that the discipline of corpus linguistics remains largely neutral to theoretical controversies on the nature of language. The question of how empirical language data is best obtained does not have implications for the question of what is language.

(*ii*) The methodological aspects of corpus linguistics are wedded to a number of theoretical assumptions about what language is. Any methodology must be adjusted to the inherent properties of the object under investigation, and such properties must be formulated in theoretical statements. The fact that corpus techniques lead to relevant discoveries about language structure and use is itself an indication that some linguistic theories are sounder than others. Thus, not all theories are able to explain why some properties of language structure reveal themselves through quantitative analysis of authentic textual data, and not through introspection.

Meyer (2002) has argued boldly for the first option above. For him, corpus linguistics is only a methodology, a mere "way of doing linguistics" (Ibid., p. xi), thereby emphasizing that it is not a research paradigm on par with sociolinguistics or psycholinguistics. This view is diametrically opposed to Tognini-Bonelli's (2001: 1) contention that "corpus linguistics has [...] a theoretical status," as well as to Teubert's (2005: 2) description of corpus linguistics as "a theoretical approach to the study of language." Other authors opt for a more eclectic position, a middle way between those who see corpus linguistics as nothing more than a methodology, and those who regard it as an approach impregnated with theoretical content:

> "Corpus linguistics is viewed primarily as a methodology, not a theory. However, this should not be understood simply to imply that corpus linguistics is theory-free. The focus and method of research, as well as the type of corpus selected for a study, is influenced by the theoretical orientation of the researchers, explicit or implicit" (McEnery and Gabrielatos 2006: 35).

McEnery and Gabrielatos go on to identify the relation between theory and data as one of "the main points of tension in corpus linguistics" (Ibid.), an issue interconnected with further controversies such as the role of intuitions or the utility of corpus annotation. After all, a system of annotation necessarily embodies a theory of language. It is thus easy to understand why the controversy between the two main competing centres for leadership in British corpus linguistics, namely Lancaster and Birmingham, has so often revolved around the issue of annotation. The argument advanced by the detractors of annotation – traditionally associated with the Sinclair/Cobuild line of research at Birmingham – is that corpus-based approaches, by relying on a previously designed framework of categories, do not permit detection of the clashes and mismatches existing between mainstream theories of language and actual corpus data.

Indeed, the relationships among the observables, the methods of observation, and the theoretical constructs have come to represent a significant battleground between different approaches to corpus research. One of the issues at stake is the possibility of a "theoretically innocuous" method in science—that is, the question of whether there exists any such thing as a direct observation which leaves no imprint on representations of the observed phenomena. In this sense, the debate between different versions of corpus linguistics is not unconcerned by the more general epistemological problem of induction, long and lively discussed among philosophers of science. Sinclair (1992: 6) warns that "it is impossible to study patterned data without some theory, however primitive." This reflection reproduces an on-going, unresolved conflict in the philosophy of science. In discussing the concept of corpus-driven linguistics, one cannot avoid engaging in the debate between deductive and inductive epistemologies. K. Popper's criticism of inductive reasoning has not lost its topicality.[2]

> "[T]he epistemology of induction breaks down even before taking its first step. It cannot start from sense data or perceptions and build our theories upon them, since there are no such things as sense data or perceptions which are not built upon theories [...] Thus the 'data' are no basis of, no guarantee for, the theories: they are not more secure than any of our theories or 'prejudices' but, if anything, less so" (Popper 1972: 146).

For corpus linguists, the problem of induction is twofold. To the general problem stated above, we must add a second, more specific difficulty affecting the

2 Similar worries about the flaws of inductive reasoning have been expressed by linguists from outside the tradition of corpus linguistics. This critical position is formulated by Bernárdez (2008: 104) as follows: "Los datos con los que se trabaja no existen de forma puramente objetiva, como es sabido: toda recogida de datos es *theory-driven*, está impulsada por la teoría y no puede ser de otro modo". The same view had been held by Alcaraz Varó (1990: 19): "un dato, es decir, el producto de una observación lingüística, está condicionado por orientaciones teóricas o tendencias pre-teóricas [...], y la obtención y selección de datos que hagamos estarán basadas en premisas teóricas."

programme of corpus-driven linguistics in particular. Supposing that a linguistic epistemology of induction were possible, would it be consistent with the commitment to theory that corpus-driven linguistics has so insistently claimed for itself? Tognini-Bonelli (2001) characterizes corpus-driven linguistics both as a theoretically specific and as a primarily inductive approach. But is this not an oxymoron, a contradiction in terms? On the one hand, corpus-driven linguistics is attributed a specific theoretical content, while on the other hand, it is associated with an epistemology that forbids commitment to theoretical assumptions or received views.

Such contradiction can only be resolved if the two terms involved (theory and induction) are interpreted in their laxer sense. Assuming that the application of vague hypotheses to the data counts as an instance of inductive methodology, it makes sense to conclude that corpus linguistics can be inductive and theoretically biased at the same time. By definition, the starting point of corpus-driven research is not a fully-fledged model, as would befit a deductive procedure, but rather a set of fuzzy assumptions, i.e. "loose and flexible frameworks," as Sinclair (1992: 18) would call them, that allow the linguist to "accommodate the new information that will come from the text." The theoretical background to corpus-driven linguistics seems to comply with this requirement of fuzziness and flexibility. Such background is generally identified with British Contextualism and the Firthian tradition, but Firth, as Stubbs (1993: 28) observes, "did not leave a tidy and consistent body of writings." To the extent that Firth's contribution to linguistic theory was rather sketchy and ambiguous, we can consider that the application of this framework to corpus data does not blatantly fail to comply with the dictates of an epistemology of induction sensu lato.

By the concept of "induction sensu lato," or "impure induction," we may understand the minimization and flexibilization of all the theoretical assumptions applied to the data. This practice is opposed not only to the analytic-deductive operation of inferring particular statements from a priori propositions, but also to the naive attempts at depriving empirical observations from absolutely all kinds of previous assumptions or biases. It is essential to warn against the pitfalls of a strict formulation of induction, such as the one put forward by Tognini-Bonelli below:

> "Corpus work can be seen as an *empirical approach* in that, like all types of scientific enquiry, the starting point is actual authentic data. The procedure to describe the data that makes use of a corpus is therefore *inductive* in that it is statements of a theoretical nature about the language or the culture which are derived at from observations of the actual instances. The observation of language facts leads to the formulation of a hypothesis to account for these facts; this in turn leads to a generalisation based on the evidence of the repeated patterns in the concordance; the last step is the unification of these observations in a theoretical statement" (Tognini-Bonelli 2001: 2).

Two objections can be levelled at Tognini-Bonelli's definition of corpus-linguistic methodology in the excerpt quoted above. Firstly, it is misleading to suggest that the starting point is the actual data as such, because claims of pure induction ("induction sensu stricto") are chimerical. In fact, corpus linguists have not always been ignorant of the fallacy of pure induction: "the concept of corpus-driven linguistics must confront the classic problem that there is no such thing as pure induction [...] the linguist always approaches data with hypotheses and hunches, however vague" (Stubbs 1993: 25). The second objection is that Tognini-Bonelli's claim of pure induction for corpus-driven linguistics is at odds with her own recourse to neo-Firthian contextual theory of meaning in order to underpin the necessary distinction between the concept of a "text" and the concept of a "corpus."

"Working within a contextual theory of meaning, we can say that a text exists in a unique communicative context as a single, unified language event mediated between two (sets of) participants; the corpus, on the other hand, brings together many different texts and therefore cannot be identified with a unique and coherent communicative event" (Tognini-Bonelli 2001: 2).

Implicitly, this quotation illustrates how the adoption of a corpus-linguistic methodology must be justified with reference to some theoretical grounds, however rudimentary. Corpus linguistics works on the assumption that the distinction between a text and a corpus depends on the property of coherence (i.e. unity). For all that the interests and underpinnings of corpus linguistics intersect in various ways with those of text linguistics, there are some methodological practices of the former that are not applicable to the latter. Thus, many of the statistical techniques utilized in corpus linguistics enable the researcher to detect co-occurrence patterns whose distribution in the discourse is widely spread throughout a tapestry of registers and discourse types. The corpus linguist is justified in focusing his/her attention on such patterns, because they reflect language structure, even if they have little bearing on the internal unity of individual texts or in the identification of text types. It follows that a corpus-linguistic approach to language relies on theoretic-conceptual categories that pre-exist the methodological framework itself.

The fact is that, in practice, research processes involve a permanent dialectic between theory and observation, as Coseriu remarked more than three decades ago, in 1973, even before the surge of corpus linguistics (cf. Coseriu 1981: 58). More recently, Allan (2007) advocates a similar view by arguing that induction and deduction play complementary roles and are integrated with each another in actual research:

"Linguistic theorizing needs both the macro-paradigms of linguistics in order to achieve its proper end. The bottom-up data-gathering and preliminary classification from inductivism (preceded by abduction), and the top-down hypothesis construction from hypothetico-deductivism cannot be related in neat temporal sequence: experience tells us that the linguistic researcher must expect to go to and fro between them, reviewing the data to intuit hypotheses, and then checking the hypothesis against the data [...] classification and taxonomy deal with abstract objects that are no less than theoretical constructs of a hypothetico-deductive system. It follows that inductivists' choice of data, indeed their very perception of the data, involves a categorial process which cannot, in the end, be satisfactorily distinguished from hypothetico-deductivism" (Allan 2007: 295).

In the corpus-linguistic community, some scholars have invoked the paradox of the observer to suggest the inevitability of associating the method of observation with a characteristic theoretical content, however minimum. Partington (1998) concedes that the treatment of collocation as a structurally central form of linguistic patterning has been "the direct result of the availability of a new research tool" (Ibid., p. 144), but he adds that the paradox of the observer is a common problem to all empirical sciences. The object of study "is very much defined by the tools available to it" (Ibid.). This means that the methodological framework employed always exerts some kind of effect on the theoretical generalizations the corpus linguist arrives at—or, to put it another way, the statements always bear some kind of trace of the method.

The acknowledgement that theory and method are intertwined is implicit in Sinclair's famous comment that "the language looks rather different when you look at a lot of it at once" (Sinclair 1991: 100), a very elegant and straightforward way of arguing that empirical findings from quantitative analyses can lead to qualitatively different models of language. This view dovetails with Stubbs (1996: 232) remark that "when new quantitative methods are applied to very large amounts of data, they always do more than provide a mere summary. By transforming the data, they can generate insight." In a similar vein, Hunston and Francis (2000) explain that in corpus linguistics – as in other disciplines – theoretical and methodological developments feed back on each other:

> "[B]oth facts and theories are, in a sense, constructed by methods; every description of grammar is dependent upon the methods employed to arrived at it [...] New methods, in any field of enquiry, lead not only to more data, but to data of a different kind, and this in turn can inspire new theories" (Francis and Hunston 2000: 250).

It is therefore possible to draw a distinction between "broader" and "narrower" definitions of corpus linguistics, depending on the type of relationship they establish between methodology and theory. Meyer's position is favourable to broadening the scope of corpus linguistics. On the view that corpus methodologies are not committed to any specific theory of language, the array of approaches qualifying as corpus-linguistic will be considerably wide. In principle, a broad concept of corpus linguistics leaves room for the adoption of corpus techniques of analysis in the context of theoretical frameworks as diverse from one another as can be neo-Firthian linguistics, cognitive linguistics, generative linguistics, or structural linguistics, among others. Conversely, the claim that genuine corpus linguistics has a theoretical dimension involves a drastic reduction in the range of studies associated with the discipline.

3. Corpus linguistics and language theories

In a sense, the distinction we have drawn above between broader and narrower definitions of corpus linguistics runs parallel to the one established by Tognini-Bonelli (2001) between corpus-driven and corpus-based research, since one of the differences between them, apart from the degree of commitment to the data, is the theoretical specificity of the former, as opposed to the neutrality of the latter. The broader the notion of corpus linguistics, the wider the range of different theoretical frameworks and linguistic paradigms that are deemed to be compatible with corpus methodologies.

This prompts the question of what are the main theoretical issues that articulate the corpus-based/corpus-driven controversy, as well as the strife between broader and narrower notions of corpus linguistics. The question cannot be tackled here in depth, but suffice it to say that the corpus-driven approach lays special emphasis on the social aspect of language, while a corpus-based approach is not biased towards either a sociological or a psychological/cognitive perspective on language phenomena. For some scholars, the techniques of corpus linguistics are no less suited to discovering the inner mechanisms of the human mind than they are to describing discursive formations of a particular language community. For other scholars, however, a universal theory of language cannot be at home with corpus-linguistic techniques of analysis, because there is at present no available methodology to find a direct connection between what is observed in a text (i.e. what language data the speaker has produced) and what goes on in the mind of speakers during the processes of text generation or interpretation. There is a chasm between these two views, as can be gathered from a comparison between the two quotations below.

> "Because corpus linguistics is a methodology, all linguists – even generativists – could in principle use corpora in their studies of language. However, most generativists feel that a corpus enables one to study performance, not competence; as a result, they continue to use introspection as the primary source of their data" (Meyer 2002: 28):

> "Corpus linguistics looks at language from a social perspective. It is not concerned with the psychological aspects of language. It claims no privileged knowledge of the workings of the mind or of an innate language faculty" (Teubert 2005: 2-3).

Meyer leaves the door open to combining a psychologicist approach to language with a corpus-linguistic methodology. On his view, the low popularity of corpus techniques among adherents to generativism is only a matter of fact, not a matter of principle. It follows that corpus linguistics is not by definition incompatible with generative grammar, or with any other universalist, psycholinguistic or cognitive approach. Teubert, by contrast, has long insisted on denying corpus data any potential for granting access to mental processes (Teubert and Kervio-Berthou 2000; Teubert 2005).

The use of corpus methodology in the framework of psychologicist approaches to language, notably Chomskyan linguistics and cognitive linguistics, has been controversial. Doubts have been raised concerning the possibility of accessing the individual speaker's mind through descriptions of discourse, which is a social phenomenon. The Sinclair/Cobuild school in particular has been famous for decrying attempts at crossing the boundaries between empirical observation of external textual data and speculation about I-language. In general, the British tradition in corpus linguistics has remained reluctant to extrapolate facts about the mind from facts about the discourse. Stubbs (2002: 221) defines corpus linguistics as "inherently sociolinguistic" and underlines the idea that its sole object of study are "acts of communication used in a discourse community." Much in the line of thinking of the London School championed by Firth, the mainstream of corpus linguistics in Britain has drawn a thick dividing line between the patterns produced by an entire linguistic community, on the one hand, and the mental processes going on inside each individual speaker, on the other.

The sociolinguistic orientation of British corpus linguistics is clearly illustrated in the first and the last of the list of eight principles put forward by Stubbs, which are respectively formulated as follows: "linguistics is essentially a social science," and "language in use transmits culture" (Stubbs 1993: 2). There appears to be in the literature a twofold motivation for this exclusive focus on the social aspects of language. The first kind of motivation is purely epistemological. British corpus linguistics is characterized by a strong empiricist stance on linguistic epistemology, which in turn leads to a considerable scepticism about inferences. British corpus linguists are very cautious about taking steps from descriptions of observable facts (e.g. repetitions in the discourse) to guesses about non-observable entities (e.g. mental structures and mechanisms). The second kind of motivation for adopting a sociolinguistic bias has been theoretical. The seventh principle of British Contextualism, following Stubbs (1993: 2), claims that "much language use is routine." This implies that a substantial part of linguistic performance by individuals can be explained on the grounds of imitative behaviour, which is a function of social factors such as the pressure to converge with collective behaviour, among other determinants. What follows from this is not a negation of individual creativity but rather a conferral of explanatory power on the force of repetition:

> "Repeated events are significant. The first task of corpus linguistics is to describe what is usual and typical. Unique events certainly occur, but can be described only against the background of what is normal and expected" (Stubbs 2002: 221).

The sociological bias of British corpus linguistics is deeply rooted in Firth's ideas about the nature of verbal behaviour, more specifically in his equation of speech with social structure, as can be easily gathered from the quotation below:

> "Conversation is much more of a roughly prescribed ritual than most people think. Once someone speaks to you, you are in a relatively determined context and you are not free just to say what you please. We are born individuals. But to satisfy our needs we have to become social persons, and every social person is a bundle of roles and personae, so that the situational and linguistic categories would not be unmanageable" (Firth 1957: 28).

In a later passage of the same paper, Firth goes on to add that "it is here [in the study of conversation] we shall find the key to a better understanding of what language really is and how it works" (Ibid., p. 32). After having described conversation as a "prescribed ritual," this remark is to be interpreted as a clear suggestion that it is in the nature of language to be highly ritualistic, an aspect of language that can be better captured from a sociolinguistic perspective than from a psycholinguistic one.

In sum, the advent of corpus linguistics has fuelled the old strife between psychological/biologistic and sociological perspectives in linguistics. Although this debate is not specific to corpus linguistics, the rise of this discipline has certainly contributed to invigorating the discussion. On one side of debate are those linguists – both inside and outside corpus linguistics – who think that the analysis of the linguistic performance by individuals could shed light on the cognitive and neurological basis underlying linguistic knowledge and processing. On the other side are those linguists – both inside and outside corpus linguistics – who think that language structures can be studied independently of how they are represented and processed inside the mind/brain of individual speakers.

At present, the debate remains unresolved. On the one hand, cognitive science enjoys considerable popularity, and this is reflected, among other things, in the range of empirical methods employed for investigating the relationship between observable behaviour and underlying mental machinery (or neural processes). There are more and more cognitive linguists who adhere to the corpus-based research framework, in the belief that introspection, psycholinguistic tests, and neuro-imaging are not the only valid strategies for accessing the mind/brain of speakers, and that quantitative analysis of performance data is at least as adequate a methodology for gaining insights into cognitive processes and representations.

On the other hand, the tendency to locate language inside the individual speaker is encountering growing opposition from scholars who lay more emphasis on the external rather than on the internal aspect of language. This implies the view that psychological reality is not an ontological condition for linguistic categories. That is, language data has an objective structure which can be described and formalised in linguistic statements independently of how the same data is stored and processed by human subjects. On this opinion, the main task of linguistics is not to bring speaker-internal processes to light but rather to study the structure and use of language objects that exist "out there," both in the ether and in written documents. To quote Allan (2007: 292), "neither a model of language processing ability nor a model of a cognitive state is a model of language."

Logically, the fact that language is produced by and for human beings, and that human beings have a mind/brain, does not necessarily imply that a model of language is a model of the mind brain. Food, too, is produced by and for human beings, but that does not render it an object of psychology or neurology instead of gastronomy. We know that recipes are invented by humans in order to meet human demands; we also know positively that humans have brains (what we cannot be sure of is whether they also have minds) and that consumption of food brings about specific effects on parts of our body, including our nerves. Does it follow from this that gastronomy is only a branch of cognitive science, that there are no objective properties of recipes which could be studied independently of the effects that food has on the nervous system of human consumers? It is difficult to argue that every object produced and used by human beings can be reduced to mental states or neural processes. The study of how a particular dish or a particular natural language is made is not by definition a study of the mind/brain, even though dishes and languages are both created and used by living beings with a mind/brain. Language is both a human artefact and a stimulus to the nervous system of human beings, but it is important to remember that the study of an artefact is not identical with the study of its creator, and that the study of stimulus data cannot be reduced to the study of nervous systems.

It is not our goal in this monograph – let alone in the Introduction – to resolve the question of whether corpus linguistics is wedded to a sociolinguistic approach, or whether it is also compatible with psycholinguistic inquiry. The issue is further developed by W. Teubert in his contribution to this book. Our task as editors is simply to introduce the two sides of the debate and present the reader with a range of materials representing different approaches and aspirations. The collection of papers included in this monograph encompasses different attitudes towards the relationship between corpus linguistics and language theory. Some of them reflect an optimistic stance on the possibility of conducting psycholinguistic/cognitive/neurolinguistic inquiry with the empirical aid of corpus data; some other contributions denote a more sceptical attitude, typically manifested in a "retreat" within the confines of the observable. It is up to each reader to decide whether the first option is too audacious, or whether the second one is too cautious.

4. The structure of this book

Formally, the structure of this book is divided into six parts. The first one is devoted to reflection on what are the defining characteristics of corpus research. **W. Teubert** takes up the issue raised in this Introduction, namely, the difficulty of ascertaining what corpus linguistics is, and develops his own position on the matter. Especially thought-provoking is his view that corpus linguistics should not be seen as an opportunity for linguistics to incorporate or imitate the methods of the "hard" scientific disciplines. Rather, Teubert maintains that, because corpus linguistics is essentially an interpretive practice, it should be seen as primarily a hermeneutic, and consequently, it falls entirely within the realm of the humanities, as opposed to the sciences.

By providing comments on contributions by other authors, Teubert's paper also serves as a frame for next section of the book. The diversity of notions of corpus linguistics is particularly palpable in the field of discourse analysis. Different approaches to discourse reflect different ways of doing and conceiving of corpus linguistics. Therefore, Teubert was invited to illustrate his discussion of approaches to corpus linguistics with specific references to the papers selected for the "discourse analysis" section. Thus the reader will note that there is a dialectic relation between Part One and Part Two. In this way, the debate between different conceptions of corpus research has been built into the structure of the book itself.

Part Two is composed of four papers representing an array of approaches to the role of corpora in linguistic research. The compilation ranges from the strictly corpus-driven approach of T. Bastow's paper to the corpus-based cognitive approach of I. Zulaica, through L. Hồ-Đắc's combination of concepts from traditional, systemic-functional and cognitive linguistics.

T. Bastow widens the perspective of analysis of modal adverbs to include discursive properties that fail to be accounted for by grammars and dictionaries. He contends that the expressions *of course*, *clearly*, *obviously* and *certainly* serve complex rhetorical functions concerning both the internal organization of text and the regulation of speaker-hearer interaction. Especially interesting in T. Bastow's contribution is the insight that lexical and grammatical analyses will not exhaust the description of properties of a lexical item — or, at least, of certain kinds of lexical items. Apart from the much studied 'discourse markers,' there are also other words and expressions with properties and functions that lie beyond the scope of lexical and grammatical semantic classes, and whose description can be legitimately approached from a broader text-linguistic and discourse-analytical perspective.

J. Rivas and E. Brown analyse the phrase *No sé* ('I don't know') as a discourse marker. Previous research has shown that discourse markers proceed along the following grammaticalization cline: non-subjective > subjective > intersubjective uses. J. Rivas and E. Brown look for evidence of this grammaticalization cline using a previously unexamined discourse marker in Spanish (*no sé*). In line with Bybee and Sheibman (1999), they show that *no sé* seems to be stored in lexical representation as a single item in Spanish. Such an analysis is based on phonological reduction and measures of string frequency and transitional probability of the word combination. Further, following Company Company (2002), a cross-dialectal comparison of relative frequency of use of *no sé* reveals differing degrees of intersubjectification of this discourse marker.

One of the main difficulties with which corpus linguistic approaches to discourse analysis must be confronted resides in the level of detail required. The study of text organization often calls for more specific observations than those accessible to the quantitative methods usually employed in the corpus linguistic literature. The chapter contributed by **L. Hồ-Đắc** is motivated by the same concern that has driven some of the research conducted by D. Biber over the last few years, namely, the need to bridge the gap between the level of generalization inherent in quantitative corpus-linguistic techniques, on the one hand, and the level of specificity demanded by studies of discourse organization, on the other. L. Hồ-Đắc puts forward a highly sophisticated method for capturing the characteristic discourse-organizational strategies of different text types. The method is based on automatic analysis of the distribution of specific features.

This part of the book closes with the paper written by **I. Zulaica Hernández**. As anaphoric elements, demonstratives are widely used by speakers to refer to first, second and third order (intensional) entities. In this sense, demonstratives are said to co-refer with individuals, events, situations and propositions thus greatly contributing to discourse cohesion. I. Zulaica Hernández considers that for some authors, the distinctive behaviour of referential expressions like demonstratives, definite, indefinite articles, etc. lies in their capability to 'mark' the cognitive status of their antecedents. Thus, for example, demonstratives (this/that) would differ from the neuter pronoun (*it*) in that the former mark their antecedents as cognitively activated vs. the cognitive status in-focus of the latter. This chapter focuses on Spanish demonstratives and the theoretical notion of cognitive status and argues in favour of a reconsideration of the status activated for these elements in Spanish based on empirical data from a corpus study that analyzes the factor 'recency of mention of the antecedent' as a determining factor.

Part Three is devoted to corpus research that is oriented to applications in disciplines beyond linguistics. The research conducted by **P. Fuertes-Olivera and J. Rodrigues Rodrigues** has ultimately a pedagogical goal. It is aimed at improving dictionaries for students of specific technical and scientific fields.

Their article focuses on some three-word lexical bundles that have over 200 occurrences in academic prose (Biber et al. 1999). The results confirm Hyland's (2002) hypothesis that the discourse of the academy does not form an undifferentiated, unitary mass but a variety of subject-field literacies. The article also performs a qualitative analysis on two three-word lexical bundles: *in order to*; *the fact that*. In this occasion, they obtained mixed results. On the one hand, these two lexical bundles behave syntactically as described in corpus-based grammars. On the other hand, they show a strong preference for some clusters and uses and are therefore ideal candidates for being explained in detail to students.

The second paper of this section is geared towards applications in the field of natural language processing. Research on word sense disambiguation has been rather intensive in the last quarter of the twentieth century. Difficulties for a successful disambiguation algorithm lie mainly in polysemous words with high granularity. The research conducted by **A. Sanchez and P. Cantos**, which applies a supervised WSD method, indicates that the success rate is clearly lower in words with high granularity, compared to the percentage of success in words with poor semantic granularity. The analysis of the results reveals that failure in the identification of the meaningful contextual features is the main reason leading to disambiguation errors. The authors conclude that the model of meaning organization used by most sense disambiguation algorithms is not adequate to successfully deal with fine-grained semantic granularity. The model of lexical constellation is advanced and sketched as a possibility to initiate a break through in the field. Its non-linear character and three dimensionality fits better the non-linear and hierarchical structure of meaning organization in real language.

Part Four explores a relatively untrodden territory, namely, the application of corpus linguistics in the field of clinical investigation. The various stages of cognitive decline in patients with Alzheimer's disease include a linguistic deterioration. **P. Cantos** describes the case study of former British Prime Minister Harold Wilson's speeches transcripts in order to explore possible effects of AD process at the earliest stage on his language use. The author analyses (i) a selection of two time periods: 1964 (first year of office) and 1976 (year of resignation) and (ii) the use of additional language parameters: punctuation variables, lexical distribution measures, POS distribution, noun counts, person and spatial deixis, use of indefinite words and two readability indexes (*Automated Readability Index* and *Coleman-Liau Index*). According to Cantos, the data suggest changes in Wilson's mental lexicon, vocabulary, and personality (speaker-addressee involvement and the perception of the reference to the location of the participant in the speech event).

Part Five of the book is entirely devoted to historical corpus linguistics, a field which has traditionally favoured the adoption of sociolinguistic rather psycholinguistic perspectives on performance data. The article by **J. Pérez Guerra** and **A. Martínez Insua** epitomizes the benefits of interdisciplinary cooperation between historical linguistics and (corpus-based) discourse analysis. This paper, which combines the study of diachronic and synchronic language variation, tests whether structural complexity in noun phrases evolves differently across text types. In this way, the authors explore the reliability of structural complexity as a criterion for detecting differences among registers. Moreover, the paper provides valuable insights into the interface between syntax and text/discourse, because it examines the principles governing the relationship between length and position of clause constituents (i.e. end-weight and end-focus).

The goal of **J. Ruano-García**'s paper is to fill a gap in the study of regional dialect variation in Early Modern English. The author claims that scholars have shown a widespread concern for phonological or orthographical issues, while lexis has not deserved any particular attention. This article presents a preliminary analysis of suffixation in Early Modern northern English by means of a selection of literary samples extracted from The Salamanca Corpus. He attempts, firstly, to provide insight into the word-formation patterns of sixteenth- and seventeenth-century northern speech, and secondly, to shed light upon the chronology of certain suffixal derivatives that have been inadequately documented in historical and dialect dictionaries.

For all that quantitative analysis is central to corpus-based and corpus-driven methodologies, many descriptive tasks remain which make it impossible to do away with arduous, painstaking qualitative analysis of individual examples. This is illustrated by **F. Alonso-Almeida and N. Vázquez**'s study on usages of modal verbs in recipes from the early modern period of English. It takes a thorough analysis in broad linguistic context to determine which specific type of modality is conveyed by each instance of these verbs in a corpus. One of the main objectives of this chapter is to assess the degree of systematicity (or randomness) with which different functions are assigned to modal verbs in the corpus, and this goal requires a previous process of zooming in on text passages one by one. Thus, this chapter – like T. Bastow's – exemplifies the fact that corpus linguistics involves complementation of quantitative analysis with qualitative analysis, or conversely, but not substitution of the former for the latter.

The topic of Part Six is implementation and methodology. **P. Valverde Ibáñez and E. Bick** present a rule-based role labelling system for Spanish. The system has been applied to an Internet corpus of more than 11 million words, and the results, according to preliminary evaluation, give cause for optimism. The success rate is around 80%, and the authors see room for improvement. The success of automatic annotators of semantic roles is indeed good news for grammarians and corpus linguists in general, because it renders corpora even more suitable tools for studying the interface between syntax and semantics. With few exceptions – such as Stefanowitsch and Gries' Collostructional Analysis – the study of interactions between verb meaning and syntactic structure has relied more on introspective judgement than on corpus data. To some extent, this situation was understandable, due to the impossibility of retrieving deep semantic information. Shallow parsers do not assign semantic roles to the arguments of a verb. Therefore, role labelling systems are welcome to remove one of the main obstacles that once stood in the way of corpus-based grammar.

As editors, we thought that the best way to close the book would be with a warning and a recommendation to future research. It has to be conceded that the statistical techniques employed in corpus research are often below scientific standards. To improve this situation is the main rationale for **S. Gries**' contribution to this volume.

Over the last decade, the work conducted by S. Gries on statistical methods has been fulfilling an important mission in the program of corpus linguistics. In principle, one of the main advantages of corpus research over other methodological frameworks in linguistics is the possibility to render empirical generalizations more precise, ambitious, and reliable. However, this potential remains underutilized as a consequence of the low level of statistical sophistication of many corpus-linguistic analyses. The paper written S. Gries offers solutions to this problem. Two aspects of this paper are worth highlighting. First, the topic concentrates on the particular kind of statistical data that is usually more relevant to the specific demands of corpus research, viz. distributional data. Second, the author leads a critical discussion of state-of-the-art methods of analysis. In sum, we are confident that S. Gries' chapter will be helpful to all those corpus linguists who wish to be updated on methodological developments.

References

Alcaraz Varó, E. (1990): *Paradigmas de la investigación lingüística*, Alcoy, Marfil.

Allan, K. (2007): *The Western Classical Tradition in Linguistics*, London / Oakville, Equinox.

Bernárdez, E. (2008): *El lenguaje como cultura. Una crítica del discurso sobre el lenguaje*, Madrid, Alianza Editorial.

Coseriu, E. (1981 [1973]): *Lecciones de lingüística general*, Madrid, Gredos.

Firth, J. R. (1957): *Papers in Linguistics. 1934 – 1951*, London/New York/ Toronto, Oxford University Press.

Hunston, S. and G. Francis (2000): *Pattern Grammar. A Corpus-Driven Approach to the Lexical Grammar of English*, Amsterdam/Philadelphia, John Benjamins.

McEnery, T. and C. Gabrielatos (2006): "English corpus linguistics," in B. Aarts and A. McMahon (eds.), *The Handbook of English Linguistics*, Oxford, Blackwell, 33-71.

Meyer, C. F. (2002): *English Corpus Linguistics. An Introduction*, Cambridge, Cambridge University Press.

Partington, A. (1998): *Patterns and Meanings. Using Corpora for English Language Research and Teaching*, Amsterdam/Philadelphia: John Benjamins.

Sinclair, J. (1992): "Trust the text," in M. Davies and L. Ravelli (eds.), *Advances in Systemic Linguistics: Recent Theory and Practice*, London, Pinter, 5-19.

Sinclair, J. (2001): [Review of: Biber, D., S. Johansson, G. Leech, S. Conrad and E. Finegan (1999): *The Longman Grammar of Spoken and Written English*, London, Pearson Education]. *International Journal of Corpus Linguistics*, 6, 2, 339-359.

Stubbs, M. (1993): "British traditions in text analysis. From Firth to Sinclair," in M. Baker, G. Francis and E. Tognini-Bonelli (eds.), *Text and Technology: In Honour of John Sinclair*, Philadelphia/Amsterdam, John Benjamins, 2-33.

Stubbs, M. (1996): *Text and Corpus Analysis*, Oxford/Cambridge, Mass., Blackwell.

Stubbs, M. (2002): *Words and Phrases. Corpus Studies of Lexical Semantics*, Oxford/Malden, Mass./Melbourne/Berlin, Blackwell.

Teubert, W. (2005): "My version of corpus linguistics," *International Journal of Corpus Linguistics*, 10, 1, 1-13.

Teubert, W. and V. Kervio-Berthou (2000): "Linguistique de corpus et lexicographie," *Cahiers de Lexicologie*, 77, 137-163.

Tognini-Bonelli, E. (2001): *Corpus Linguistics at Work.* Amsterdam/Philadelphia, John Benjamins.

PART ONE

On the Nature of the Discipline

Rethinking corpus linguistics

Wolfgang Teubert
University of Birmingham

1. Introduction

I have been asked by the editors to comment on four papers in this collection, papers by Tony Bastow, by Lydia-Mai Hồ-Đắc, by Javier Rivas and Esther Brown, and by Iker Zulaica Hernández. As three of these papers attempt an integration of corpus research into a cognitive framework, this task gives me a welcome opportunity to reassess my view of the relationship between these two paradigms which I have often enough claimed to be incompatible. As I grow older, I am afraid I have to accept that I belong to the old guard, and I shouldn't continue to fight lost battles. Instead, engaging in a serious discussion would open the chance to resolve apparent differences through collaborative reflection. Why should I not acknowledge that there are more ways to do corpus linguistics than we in our Birmingham citadel have acknowledged? Why should we not let ourselves be inspired by these fertile seeds that we now see cropping up all over the world? Should we not be happy about this multitude of studies that have come to agree that linguistic research should be based not just on any empirical evidence but very definitely on real language data? As we can see, this must not keep scholars like Tony Bastow from strictly avoiding the c-word 'cognition'. Interpreting linguistic research using real language data will engender new ideas and, we may hope, resolve antithetical stances on a more elevated level.

2. Defining corpus linguistics

Over the summer of 2008 there was, on the Corpora-List under the name of 'Bootcamp', a lengthy and quite controversial discussion about the role of corpus linguistics within the discipline of linguistics (corpora-bounces@uib.no). It does not matter that the differences were not resolved; what is important about this dispute is that it demonstrates the co-existence of different conceptions of what is called corpus linguistics. It quickly became clear that those of us who insisted that corpus linguistics is a theoretical paradigm in its own right, incompatible with other mainstream approaches such as Chomskyan mentalism or the many schools of cognitive linguistics, are in a minority. Here I present are some of the voices representing the majority view, namely that corpus linguistics should be viewed primarily as a way to provide corpus evidence for claims made by these mainstream paradigms:

ANDREW HARDIE: As a corpus linguist I consider myself primarily a methodologist and CL primarily a methodology, to be applied to whatever theory seems most appropriate for the task at hand - cognitive or typological or literary or political or whatever. Though I won't speak for anyone else I know I am not alone in this. This tradition of CL-as-method is, contrary to what WT suggests, equally as venerable as the CL-as-theory. It is unnecessarily divisive to suggest that "old-fashioned" corpus linguists must subscribe to CL-as-theory, or that the CL-as-method view is in some way a degeneration or a hijacking of CL-as-theory.

TONY MCENERY: [Lita Taylor] clearly shows that scholars simply disagree with regard to what they think corpus linguistics is: a discipline, a paradigm, a framework, and more importantly, a theory or a method. Some regard it a theory - some, [like] [Richard] Xiao, [Yukio] Tono, [Charles] Meyer, [Andrew] Hardie and myself consider it a method(ology). It is the remarkable diversity of the uses of corpus data - and the diversity of viewpoints that their use has promoted - that is utterly refreshing. Linguistics is so diminished when it narrows to doctrinaire positions as, sadly, it so often has in the past. I enjoy and value a wide range of views and works. ... The conjunctions and disjunctions in their positions will promote debate - I accept and welcome that. I think that this position, the position of open minded enquiry, is the one that the great majority of self identified corpus linguists share.

YORICK WILKS: Some of my friends are corpus linguists, ... but what I have never seen able to see is what corpus linguistics is FOR, except the production of better dictionaries, and that is a fine and worthy end, except, paradoxically of course for the corpus linguist, dictionaries are never more than compendia of intuitions! The low-level anti-representational empiricism of corpling must, it has always seemed to me, inhibit it from really carrying out any other task, in the sense in which CL/NLP does carry out many tasks with corpora on a vast scale ... The debate so far has not convinced me that many corplingers know much about CL/NLP: I think they are a bit frightened of it as real computation and prefer to tinker with small "toolboxes" to no clear end, while muttering the incantation "trust the text". Whatever that phrase meant to John Sinclair, or to corplingers now, it can only have sense with respect to small "viewable" texts, since it plainly comes from the tradition of literary criticism... What can "trust the text" mean of a corpus of 1.8 billion words (our standard reference corpus for English experiments) let alone the whole accessible English web?! I was a great admirer of John ... but I have to say I do not believe that mantra has any precise sense at all beyond mere commonsense--except perhaps "beware of theory"!

KHURSHID AHMAD: It is not easy to answer the (rhetorical?) question 'what corpus linguistics is for?'. But the iconoclastic nature of the enterprise, going against the grain of cognitivism, was very apparent from the very beginning. History of science tells us that the progress of science is sometimes facilitated by an iconoclastic attitude. ... Corpus linguistics then is another way of looking at language and its digression from the main-stream, and the reminiscences of its early protagonists, is very welcome. If the results of the research in a subject are being applied, and if some of our colleagues manage to get themselves in mega projects, then it is all to the greater good of corpus linguistics.

MARTIN WYNNE: My immediate impression of this discussion is that we have people from different academic disciplines discussing together theory, methods, resources - and of course that's great, we all love that, it's interdisciplinary, cross-disciplinary, multi-disciplinary, innit. ... However, I find it somewhat problematic that many of the contributions seem to labour under the misapprehension that we are all from one discipline, with one goal. What academic community we might constitute, I'm not sure. Subscribers to the corpora list? Certainly. Corpus linguists? I'm not sure. So we seem to have an attempt at a discussion involving literary critics, mathematicians, sociolinguists, data providers, computer scientists, and language teachers about the nature of 'their' discipline. From this perspective, it seems to me highly unlikely that we will find common cause in what we think corpora and corpus analysis are FOR, how we should use them, or what a course in using corpora should include. That does not mean that there is no such thing as corpus linguistics. So what might it be? I don't think that we should be deceived into believing that the necessity of the use of computers and electronic resources makes it somehow a branch of computer science (any more than the fact that the producers of language have minds should make linguistics a branch of cognitive science). I believe that corpus linguistics is a branch of linguistics, a humanistic discipline examining and analysing the nature and role of language in human communication and society.

It is obvious that those advocating corpus linguistics as a methodology, not a theory, do not all call themselves cognitive linguists. But they all would argue that they are working within a scientific framework on par with that of the natural sciences. This seems to be the case even if they regard themselves less as scientists and more as engineers, their aim being NLP, natural language processing, i.e. developing language technology applications such as machine translation or artificial intelligence. Language engineering, like any other kind of engineering, is commonly understood as the application of scientific results for practical purposes. Indeed we can observe throughout the 20th century a persistently reiterated 'mantra' that the study of language or languages has its place in the 'hard' sciences. But what exactly are the 'scientific' results, the undeniable 'facts' about language that theoretical linguistics, the linguistics of the language system, have taught us? How does corpus linguistics compare to this invocation of 'hard' science?

3. The long way to establish linguistics as a science

My own position in the Bootcamp discussion was to insist that corpus linguistics is more than the application of corpus tools to corpora. Corpus linguistics, as I understand it, is a way to make sense of what is said. This focus on the discourse and the texts of which it consists rather than on the language system is what sets it, as I see it, fundamentally apart from the main paradigms we find in the 20th century. In spite of obvious and very important differences, paradigms such as Saussurean structuralism and its further developments, e.g. the Prague School and Roman Jakobson, Louis Hjelmslev, formal semantics in various guises including those of Algirdas Julien Greimas and Bernard Pottier, the valence theory developed by Lucien Tesnière, and, probably in their impact more relevant, Chomskyan linguistics underpinned by Jerry Fodor's language philosophy, and lastly all those linguistic schools that sprang up after the cognitive sciences took over from behaviourism and began to dominate our perspective on language; all these schools shared the ambition to lay bare the system, the mechanism that determines what we can say and how we can say it. They see it as the task of linguistics, as a 'hard' science, to describe language as a system similar to that of mechanics or meteorology, i.e. a system based on laws outside of the reach of the speakers themselves, laws determining the way all languages work and would hold even if there were no one actually using a language. Such laws control Chomsky's language faculty, for him a universal, permanent and inalterable biological mechanism which cannot be explained as the result of evolutionary adaptation. Saussure, on the other hand, excluded the issue of permanency by opting for a strictly synchronic approach, and his focus was not language in general, but a natural language such as French. He described it not as a biological but as a social system, echoing Emile Durkheim's stance that the workings of society are governed by laws over which the people making up society have no power.

For a linguistics that aims to be recognised as a 'hard' science, the focus has to be on the language system, not the discourse, just as meteorology is more than collecting weather data; it is about modelling a system that can predict what is happening next by applying a rule-based mechanism to the data. Applied meteorology is about forecasting; theoretical meteorology is about modelling the mechanism in ever finer detail that makes forecasts possible. Applied linguistics, on the other hand, is not about what the next text will be about; it is about telling people what they have to do if they want to avoid breaking rules, if they want to be understood. The open question is how to find these rules. Corpus linguists hope to obtain them by looking for structures and patterns in the data, in the discourse, in the corpus. Mainstream theoretical linguists believe that these data will never suffice to tell us why certain things can be said and other things cannot. Cognitive linguists believe that it is the mechanism of the mind, perhaps even a special language module in a mind understood as a distributed processing system.

Neither mainstream linguistic theories of the 20th century nor 'classical' corpus linguistics can ever give us the whole story. What is missing is the diachronic dimension of language, a dimension very much in the foreground of 19th century philology, is the fact that everything said now may impact what can be said in the future. Languages do undergo change. What is possible today may not have been part of the system a hundred years ago. The same spoken Spanish language expresses intersubjectivity differently in Madrid, New Mexico or Puerto Rico, as Javier Rivas and Esther Brown have found out. How is language change possible if the language system is governed by eternal laws that do not change? Chomsky's answer used to be that we have to distinguish between the deep structure, which is inalterable and universal, and the surface structure specific to a given language at a given time. Apparently, however, we do not have immediate or conscious access to this deep structure, the language of thought, as Fodor (1975) called it, or mentalese, which seems to be the more common term now (Pinker 1994). While we may all think in a universal language of thought (even though so far no one could give us any concrete account of it), we need a natural language if we want to make ourselves aware of what we are thinking. The surface structure, the natural language we use to make ourselves aware of our thoughts and to communicate, can undergo change. The universal innate mechanism, though, remains unaffected of such change.

Over time many alleged language universals (hypothetical properties of the underlying deep structure and the rules for its conversion into the pertaining surface structure) have been repudiated, and the language faculty today seems more like a switchboard, detailing a finite list of options between which individual languages, but not individual speakers, can choose. What is switched on or off in an individual's language system is automatically determined by a child's being exposed to this or that input, it is, Chomsky and his followers maintain, not something that could consciously be learned. Saussure preferred a different perspective. His language system, the *langue*, is the mechanism of a language at a given time, existing within a given language community. The individual members of this community have no power over it. Saussure's model is that of an ideal situation. It does not deal with language change, and it does not deal with different varieties of a language.

As we all know, Chomskyan linguistics is interested less in the language as a surface phenomenon, as sets of natural language data, and more in commonalities between languages. It is not so much concerned about man-made rules, which can after all be changed (may infinitives be split or not?) as in the biological laws determining a universal innate language faculty. This is why the community of mentalist (and also of cognitive) linguists was so shaken when confronted with the claim that the language of **the Pirahãs**, a small remote tribe along the Amazon river, differs from all other languages by not practising recursion, the last remaining uncontested language universal in the eyes of Hauser, Chomsky and Fitch (2002). That all languages allow their users to embed more or less complex elements in a sentence structure has been thought to be a key property of what distinguishes our human language faculty from all other communication systems we find in nature. In the Chomskyan language model, recursion has the status of a natural law.

For Saussure, with his philological training, things were more difficult. His *langue* is not the universal language faculty but the system of the French language, which, as he well knew, was constantly undergoing change, just like all other languages. To speak French properly, speakers have to obey rules. Rules, however, differ from the laws of nature in that they can be violated and that they can be changed. Unlike natural laws, rules are contingent. Human laws, for instance constitutions, also are contingent. They are rules we must obey. They can be listed, they can be categorised, they can be discussed and interpreted, they can be called a system. But they cannot be the object of a 'hard' science, a science that tells us in terms of cause and effect that the data we analyse can be explained by natural laws. Saussure's trick to save the idea of an inalterable language system was to exclude the diachronic dimension. From a synchronic perspective, there is no language change; at most there is the co-existence of mutually exclusive rules: regional or social varieties. From a synchronic perspective, there is a mechanistic language system as long as we find for everything that is said an underlying rule, if necessary a rule that applies only to one single instance, or as long as we claim that whatever does not conform to the rules are violations of the language system. How the rules themselves come about, must not concern us from a synchronic perspective. In Saussure's view, the language system was just one of the systems making up society. The workings of society, and thus also of its various sub-systems, were seen as subject to permanent universal unchangeable laws. In the end it is these laws that determine the rules the language system. Thus Saussurean linguistics, too, has established itself as a hard science.

4. How does corpus linguistics fit in?

John Sinclair, the doyen of corpus linguistics, did little to establish himself as a prominent member of the theoretical linguistics community. He did not look for confrontation there. As far as I know, he was not really interested in the question whether corpus linguistics belongs somehow to the 'hard' sciences or the interpretive sciences, what the French and Germans call the *sciences humaines* or *Geisteswissenschaften*. In his modesty, he always described himself as an applied linguist. But he insisted that corpus linguistics is more than just a bunch of methods or a toolkit to extract linguistic facts from a corpus. For him, it was a new and different way to look at language. What did he mean?

His goal was certainly not to invent yet another mechanistic model of the language system. Indeed, he was not concerned about inherent laws underlying all languages. His aim was, on the contrary, to find out what is specific to the discourse represented by the corpus. He did not want to correlate the words of English with mental representations, universal or not, we may have or not in our minds. His aim was to tell people how the words he found in the corpus that would, years later, become the Bank of English, had been used and what one had to do to use them properly. The Cobuild dictionary project was one of his major achievements. As he came to realise, existing dictionaries were based only to a small degree on real language data. They did not objectively record how words were actually used in the discourse. Rather, a new edition of a dictionary would update the previous edition by editing out a few obsolete words, replacing them with scores of neologisms many of which would not survive the subsequent edition. He considered his own corpus-based or corpus-driven approach more scientific, and by applying it he managed to create a new paradigm in lexicography. Today there is no serious monolingual dictionary for English that does not profess to be based on corpus evidence.

Yet Sinclair's aspiration went much further. Taking some pleasure in iconoclasm, he frequently made short shrift of many of those categories linguists were using as if they were ontological realities. As he saw it, any serious approach had to be based on the analysis of real language data, on what Saussure had called *la parole*, on the discourse, as we would say today. To analyse language, Sinclair insisted, we have to start with real language data, compiled in a corpus in a principled way, and then proceed from scratch, carrying out an unprejudiced analysis of the data. We must be willing to throw overboard all we have inherited from questionable traditions. If the approach of theoretical linguistics has been mostly top-down, starting with categories often inherited from Latin grammars of former centuries (e.g. the parts of speech), and searching for evidence of them in the data, corpus linguists tend to favour a bottom-up approach, starting with real language data and developing categories to describe them from scratch. In a famous paper, Sinclair contested even the received wisdom which classified the lexical item *of* as a preposition. For an appraisal, see Owen (2007).

For Sinclair, the starting point of any analysis had to be to observe how elements, crucially words, co-occur with each other. Words, he knew, are mostly fuzzy and ambiguous; in isolation, decontextualised, they rarely display a concrete meaning. Yet once we find them embedded in the concrete context, this fuzziness and ambiguity tends to appear. As node words in conjunction with the words on the left and the right of a fairly narrow window, they turn into monosemous units of meaning. A statistical co-occurrence analysis would reveal underlying patterns, collocations on the lexical level and colligations on the syntactic level. Statistics was for Sinclair the means to achieve an unbiased, objective view. The magic word is significance. When two words within close contextual vicinity co-occur more frequently in a reasonably large corpus than they would under random conditions, then this co-occurrence rate must mean something, it must be significant. The question that Sinclair never fully answered was whether a statistical significance in the rate of co-occurrence of two or more words actually tells us that these elements form a unit of meaning, or whether it only draws our attention to them, and that additional evidence is needed to ascertain their status. Be that as it may, the introduction of statistics into linguistics and the striking results achieved in many cases enhanced the scientific credibility of the corpus linguistics approach, in spite of the arbitrariness of the statistical methods used and the divergence of the results they yield. Applying statistical tools to real language data was seen as the best way to verify the claims made concerning the laws or rules that determine the elusive language system.

5. Is corpus linguistics a 'hard' science?

Linguistics tries to answer many questions. It looks at syntactic structures, it distinguishes language varieties, it looks at discourse structures, to name but a few objectives. Yet behind all language studies looms the issue of meaning. After all, we use language in order to communicate. A text, a text segment, a lexical item has a meaning. A large part of our verbal interactions are devoted to making sense of what has been said, to endorsing, modifying rejecting, in any case interpreting previous enunciations. Interpretation, though, always involves making conscious decisions, making a choice between several options. Decisions are, of necessity, arbitrary acts; they are not the necessary consequences of applying a scientific methodology. Corpus linguistics can analyse the corpus as deeply as its methods and tools allow; it can never tell us how we have to interpret what has been said.

Meaning is different. The meaning of a word, a lexical item, a text segment is the entirety of what has been said about it in the discourse, in the corpus. The meaning of an item such as *globalisation* is the entirety of the contexts in which it occurs, no more and no less. This is what corpus linguistics can find out. Meaning is, in limits, a scientific concept. What is scientific about it is that each time someone applies certain appropriate tools accepted by the peer community on the same corpus, the same result will show up. That is like running the same experiments in a chemical lab and consistently obtaining identical results. But the findings as such do not tell us anything. The date extracted, the compilation of all contexts in a corpus in which the word *globalisation* is found, has to be interpreted to become meaningful. In chemistry, this would mean that the results fit in with predictions made on a theoretical model. But meaning is not the property of a language model. Meaning is constructed in the discourse and therefore contingent, it is the result of negotiations between the members of a discourse community, negotiations whose results are arbitrary. To make sense of what is said it takes an interpretive community that will discuss it. Interpretation is the very opposite of hard science. It is at the core of the humanities.

As long as language studies explore phenomena connected with meaning (and are not content to point out type-token-ratios or the results of statistical co-occurrence tests such as T-score, Mutual Information, log-likelihood etc.) they can never approximate the ideal of the 'hard' sciences, namely that the facts speak for themselves. How could it be different? The meaning of a sign is something that needs to be negotiated between those who actively or passively use this sign. Such negotiations are always provisional and they often lead to quite different results. Different people have different ideas of the meaning of a given sign. Meaning is not a neat formula, it is not a finite and accessible mental concept waiting to be described, it is not a complex construct of a finite list of observable universal semantic primitives and it does not correspond to the ontological reality of a cluster of neurons. Things as such do not mean, only signs do. What turns a thing (e.g. a phonetic string) into a sign is that someone suggests to someone else that this thing should function as a sign, meaning this or that, and that his or her audience accepts this meaning. It works as long as ongoing re-uses of this sign among the members of a discourse community by and large honour such an agreement. But anyone can challenge it, and if they are just a wee bit successful in their modifications they have succeeded in installing a slightly deviant way to use this sign. Different groups may use the same sign in different ways. Instead of stability there is fuzziness and ambiguity, and at any time everyone within this discourse community is free to re-interpret the sign according to their whims. All we can say is that meaning is nowhere but in the discourse. But we cannot make sense of a sign without interpreting it. Interpretations, however, are contingent and provisional, and never factual.

I am afraid we have to accept that language studies, to the extent they deal with meaning, can never be all 'scientific.' Without interpretation, their findings are empty and meaningless. But this interpretation is a collaborative activity in which every member of the discourse community, not just linguists, can participate. Linguists are in no position to know better than a normal language user what a sign means. There is no such thing as a 'true' meaning. Any new interpretation is a re-negotiation of what has been said so far about the meaning. The discourse, at least a healthy discourse, should be democratic and plurivocal. Everyone can contribute to the question what *globalisation*, the word and the discourse object for which it stands, means. The task of linguists is to present the evidence, evidence they extract from the discourse, and thus provide the 'factual' basis for an interpretation.

Meaning is symbolic. Only what people have declared to be a sign has a meaning. It takes at least two people to turn a material thing, a sound sequence or a visual image or a sequence of alphabetic characters or (a combination of) ideograms into a sign, by jointly assigning a meaning to it. People may then come up with mental representations of a sign, but whatever these may be (and so far cognitive linguistics has failed to ascertain their existence) these are secondary. Meaning is always socially, collaboratively constructed. All that matters are the negotiations which determine how someone wants someone else to 'read' a sign. What people think without entering their thoughts into the discourse, what mental (or neural) representations may loom in the depths of their minds and brains remains irrelevant as long as it has not been said, as long as it has not become a part of the discourse. This is why I think corpus linguistics has a better grip on meaning than cognitive linguistics. What we would find in someone's mind, if only we could gain direct access to it, can never be more than a duplication of the part of the discourse to which this person has been exposed.

Cognitive linguists, of course, have a different perspective. What a corpus linguist looks at is only the surface, they would claim, is comparable to the data of temperature, pressure, wind or precipitation a meteorologist would record. Forecasting needs such data, but it needs more than that: There must be a theoretical model, a system behind it that tells the meteorologist to predict how the weather is going to develop on the basis of such data. Likewise for language, a cognitivist would claim, there must be some mechanism, partly innate and partly acquired, that enables people to say certain things but not others. Only if we can obtain a better grasp of this mechanism, we have begun to understand the idea of language. To a lesser or larger extent, the four papers on which I comment, attempt to fuse the two approaches. It is up to us, the peer group, the interpretive community, to negotiate to which extent they have succeeded.

6. The four papers under review

6.1. "Modal adverbials in a corpus of US defence speeches"

Tony Bastow discusses in his paper 'Some discourse functions of the modal adverbs *of course*, *clearly*, *obviously*, and *certainly* in a corpus of US defence speeches' the impact these elements have on the meaning of what is said. Bastow is an experienced corpus linguist, and he knows what he is doing. He begins his paper by reviewing the relevant literature on his chosen adverbs, Quirk et al.'s *Comprehensive Grammar* in particular, who divide them up into the categories conjuncts' and 'disjuncts,' further distinguishing between 'style disjuncts' and 'content disjuncts,' and finally subdividing the content disjuncts into ''degree of truth' disjuncts' and ''value judgment' disjuncts.' Such categories are part of a theoretical framework, and even though examples are given for them, Bastow wonders to which extent they are borne out by a thorough corpus analysis. Quirk et al.'s strategy is clearly top-down, setting up the categorical pigeonholes before sorting the phenomena. Bastow, on the other hand, starts with the evidence and leaves it initially open if he will use those categories, or if he comes up with different ones.

His corpus, a compilation of scores of speeches by a variety of people belonging to the US Department of Defense (DoD) and addressed to diverse audiences, consists, true enough, of real language data. It is an adequate sample of a discourse that has been so defined that we can say of any text whether it belongs to this discourse or not. But it was Bastow's free decision to unite these texts under a corpus umbrella. There is no 'natural kind' of a DoD text. What makes this corpus viable is the contingent and provisional endorsement by the peer community of (corpus) linguists.

Bastow then carries out a stringent, thorough analysis of his four adverbs. He knows well that we have to look for contrasts to discern their salient points. This is why he compares the DoD corpus to the Bank of English as a more general reference corpus. He shows that the adverb *clearly* is significantly more frequent in the DoD corpus, while *obviously* is (to my surprise) more frequent in the Bank of English. Of course Bastow is selective. For reasons of space and time it is virtually impossible for him to analyse the co-occurrence particulars for each of the, say, top twenty collocates of the node *clearly*, ranked by their level of statistical significance. But if such arbitrariness is not what hard science asks us to do, it is a display of common sense. Being selective has the consequence that one has to find arguments supporting the selection one has made. He therefore not only presents his findings, but he also contrasts his reading of the evidence with that of other (corpus) linguists. In short, he interprets his results, adding his own interpretation to that of his colleagues, thus providing all the relevant information the peer group / the interpretive community needs to make up their own minds. Interpretations, though, are not cogent. They are never a scientifically necessary result, as convincing they may be. Thus Bastow alerts us to the finding that there is a set of cases in his DoD corpus in which *obviously* precedes a *but*, and he claims that in these cases "*obvious* precedes a 'call for action statement.'" I would rather see it as a call for more reflection, a suggestion that whatever seems too obvious may not quite be as what it appears. The point is that there is no right or wrong here. Interpretations are there to alert us to alternative views. Scientifically obtained results do not promote innovation. Only interpretation does that.

Then why should we need pure corpus linguistics? We need it because it teaches us that language is never so simplistic that we can sort the phenomena into clear-cut categories. The labels found in these top-down approaches are "insufficient"; they neglect that the context analysis of the adverbs in question "reveal multiple (and often overlapping) functions." Corpus linguistic teaches us humbleness.

6.2. "Variable development of intersubjectivity in Spanish"

In their paper, Javier Rivas and Esther Brown analyse spoken language, more exactly the varieties found in New Mexico, Puerto Rico and Madrid. Their focus is the previously unexamined discourse marker *no sé* ('I don't know'). Lexical items turn into discourse markers of this kind when they "relate to the speaker's attitude towards the message," a phenomenon called subjectification. The authors cite Elizabeth Traugott's definition of intersubjectivity, "the development of meanings that encode speaker/writers' attention to the cognitive stances and social identities of the addressees." In the words of the authors, they function as hedges, softening the conveyed message. The aim of the paper is to establish *no sé* as a single lexical item, to "determine the forms and functions" of this item and to compare its use in the three different dialects.

The paper distinguishes three functions of the marker, subjective, textual and a combination of the two. 'Subjective' means that the speaker uses it "to soften the strength of their propositions, to avoid face-threatening acts, or to attenuate disagreeing statements." 'Textual' means speakers use it "for turn management and/or topical development." The distinction is clearly a matter of interpretation and not something computers can do. Consequently, all occurrences were annotated manually.

In the corpus linguistics community the issue of annotation or tagging is very controversial, even more so if tagging is carried out manually rather than automatically. It is easy to see why this conflict cannot easily be resolved. Whether an occurrence of *no sé* as a discourse marker is 'subjective' or 'textual' is a matter of interpretation; there is no corresponding overt structure a computer program could parse. Would we be able to find an statistically significant correlation between form and content if we analyse the syntactic features of a sufficiently high number of instances which have been manually tagged as 'subjective' or 'textual', respectively? A corpus linguist from Birmingham would object that notions of this kind are questionable top-down categories, and that any annotation therefore only mirrors the potentially unfounded bias the annotator has.

The comparison between the three dialects reveals interestingly that people in Madrid use *no sé* not so very differently from those in Puerto Rico, while it is much less frequent with New Mexican speakers. Could the reason be the interference of English in diglossic New Mexico?

Javier Rivas and Esther Brown's paper is, like Bastow's paper, a pleasantly straightforward study within the framework of corpus linguistics. There are only two references to cognitive linguistics, both without impact on the argumentation. One of them is contained in the quotation of Traugott, who speaks of a 'cognitive stance'. The other reads "If *no sé* is stored as a single lexical unit, this implies it is not necessarily analyzed as a negative particle (*no*) + verb (*sé*), but rather is a prime candidate to be adopted as a discourse marker." Stored where and how?, I would like to ask. It is up to the linguists whether they describe *no sé* as one or two or even three distinct lexical items, and such a decision (which is not the result of applying a certain methodology, but a matter of interpretation), should be based on what we find in the discourse, not on unverifiable assumptions on the workings of the mind. If we had ready access to people's minds and their mental representations, we would not need to argue the case in a linguistic paper; we only would have to take a look inside people's heads.

6.3. "Data-driven analysis for describing discourse organisation"

Like Tony Bastow, and like Javier Rivas and Ester Brown, Hồ-Đắc, too, looks at discourse markers. The title of her paper is 'An exploratory data-driven analysis for describing discourse organisation.' Data-driven reads like a half-explicit reference to the concept of 'corpus-driven,' as opposed to 'corpus-based,' as the distinction was introduced a decade ago by Elena Tognini Bonelli (2001). The corpus-driven approach is characterised as being bottom-up; all the categories used have to be derived, or at least verified, by corpus evidence, by results obtained through the application of corpus tools on the corpus. Hồ-Đắc's interest lies in the ways elements preceding the finite verb (of the first main clause) help to organise a text. Right at the beginning she introduces a venerable concept, namely the opposition between theme and rheme, evoking the idea that each textual unit, sentences or paragraphs in particular, can be divided up into theme or topic (what the unit is about) and rheme or comment (what is said about the theme). The theme-rheme dichotomy has provoked many inspired and contentious discussions, from the times of philology in the 19th century up to the present day, whether in the structuralism of the Prague School, or in the work of Jean-Marie Zemb at the Collège de France (Zemb 1982), or in Halliday's systemic functional grammar (Halliday 1968). If we take the theme-rheme distinction as part of the semantic (not syntactic) structure of a textual unit, then we cannot rely on an objective scientific method to extract themes from a corpus. Take the sentence "It was pouring when the train arrived," that I just found on the internet. I really cannot make up my mind what is topic and what is comment. The *it*, of course, has no meaning at all; it is a syntactically necessary, but semantically void placeholder. So is it the whole clause, namely *it was pouring*? Would the sentence have a somehow different semantic structure, and would its theme be *when the train arrived*, if I turned it around: "When the train arrived it was pouring."? In the end we have to ask the interpretive community, and I am afraid the jury is still out on this matter.

The alternative is to follow Halliday, and to define theme not as part of the semantic but of the syntactic structure: whatever precedes the first finite verb of the main clause of a sentence. Halliday also distinguishes between what he calls the marked theme, usually a connector or an adverbial, sometimes an apposition, called the 'detached element' by Hồ-Đắc, and the unmarked theme, the syntactic subject of a sentence. This is something a computational tool can easily deal with, and this is what Hồ-Đắc sets out to analyse in her three small corpora, one consisting of texts dealing with social geography, one of texts dealing with international relations, and one consisting of biographies. She concludes that her "methodology shows that we cannot speak about the structuring power of a lexical marker [detached element or subject] by itself." The problem, I believe, is caused by the assumption that there is a direct correlation between a syntactically defined theme and the semantic role it is supposed to play in structuring and organising a text.

More interesting is what Hồ-Đắc has to say about another parameter, namely accessibility. In addition to a linguistic and a textual level of discourse (I would say: text) structure she assumes a third level, the 'cognitive level,' which "sees the writer's mental representation as structured by the basic strategies of continuity and discontinuity." The cognitive level, she claims, cannot be isomorphic with the two other levels, which are of course linear, while she, as many other cognitive linguists, seems to know that mental representations are not. Accessibility describes how easily a cognitive process can cope with a referent in a given text. The more abstract and indefinite they are, the less 'accessible' they will be. Also if some referent is newly introduced, then this referent will be less accessible than later anaphoric references to this referent. Her data have been (manually) annotated concerning various degrees of accessibility according to Mira Ariel's scale, using grammatical definitions. But the results obtained apparently did not make much sense: "The use of degrees of accessibility in order to represent the instructional meaning of grammatical subjects must certainly be reassessed."

It seems that in many cases a marked theme, e.g. a space adverbial, will provide an orientation that should increase 'accessibility', while they are frequently followed by a new proper name indicating very low 'accessibility.' This is certainly an important finding, but it does not provide an answer to the question of how cognitive accessibility could be measured except by relying on what has been defined as their textual correlates, marked themes or grammatical subjects. We cannot look into people's heads, and we have no model of the mind explaining how quickly new textual information is absorbed, at least not a model that can be put to test. What can be analysed is the text and its features. As long as accessibility is defined in terms of such features, it can be measured. How this measurement corresponds to accessibility as a cognitive parameter must remain an open question. We may believe that mental representations are holistic and non-linear. But how can we be sure that thoughts do not have a beginning and an end? As long as we know so little about the correlation between the syntactic and the semantic structure of a text (one of which can be decoded by a computer, while the other one needs to be interpreted by humans), we should be wary of isomorphisms between texts and their mental representations.

6.4. "Testing accessibility and givenness in a corpus of Spanish"

Accessibility, together with saliency and cognitive focus, is also the topic of Zulaica's paper 'Testing accessibility and givenness in a corpus of Spanish'. He wants to find out how these notions correlate with textual phenomena. Thus he investigates the anaphoric force of the three so-called neuter pronominal demonstratives *este*, *eso* and *aquello*. For him, the three notions saliency, accessibility and cognitive focus are "different ways of conceptualising one single phenomenon: *focus attention of the addressee*." While *este* and the less frequent *eso* are more proximal demonstratives (roughly corresponding to 'this' in English), the least frequent *aquello* is more distal ('that').

The corpus linguistics part of Zulaica's study looks into the span between the anaphorically used demonstratives and the preceding referent, measured in clauses. These referents have been tagged manually. The corpus consists of a sample of 193 examples taken from the CREA corpus. The results show that in 78% of cases, the referent is one clause away, while only in 1% the referent occurs five clauses or more back. The differences between the three demonstratives appear to be rather random and from a statistical perspective not very significant.

These findings are confronted with Mira Ariel's notions of accessibility, with Jeannette Gundel's notion of givenness or cognitive focus and with saliency, a concept "deeply rooted in cognitive sciences." What do we learn about these notions (which I refrain from further distinguishing)? "Language users would have more difficulty in retrieving past events." "*Aquello* would indicate a higher processing effort … to retrieve the referent from memory." "Different cognitive statuses stand for the memory or attention status that the intended referent is assumed to have in the mind of the addressee." "[T]he main role of demonstratives … is actually bringing entities into the current focus of attention of the participants." "Demonstratives thus contribute to communication by establishing a joint focus of attention between the participants."

The problem I have with cognitive linguistics is that it provides an interpretation of what I would like to call introspection. As so much research into folk psychology has shown, introspection can very easily be deceptive (cf. Christensen and Turner 1993). What we find looking into our minds is only too often what the discourse has taught us to expect. Of course there is also psycholinguistic experimentation. In the seventies of last century, such experiments 'proved' that the processing speed of the mind was strictly correlated to the number of transformations needed to turn a Chomskyan deep structure into a surface structure. It took years to defeat these claims.

When people use these pronominal demonstratives, do we have to imagine them to make assumptions about the addressees' memory status? How conscious are they of the strategies they employ? Do speakers expect that it will take hearers longer to process a sentence with *aquello* than with *este*? What is the referent in their mental representation to which the demonstrative refers? Is it a mental concept of the noun phrase or of the discourse-external entity which stands for it? Zulaica's paper alerts us to these issues in cognitive linguistics. He is not content to accept that accessibility, givenness and saliency are supposed to be distinguishable concepts, and he shows the shortcomings of these notions.

In the end, his paper demonstrates that there is not very much concrete essence when it comes to our knowledge of the workings of the mind to which his corpus evidence could be correlated. The link between the two is rather tenuous.

7. Outlook: Linguistics reconsidered

At the beginning of these remarks I have talked a lot about the attempts to establish linguistics as being on par with the 'hard' sciences. Theories were developed positing a language system that, we were told, is governed by laws similar to the natural laws we find in physics. The language system is a mechanism ruling what can be said. Admittedly, we do find in *la parole*, or in Chomsky's 'performance,' irregular utterances. But in the eyes of many theoretical linguists these are due to interferences from outside the system. It is the system that tells us whether any sentence conforms to the rules and thus is 'grammatical.' The one major handicap of these mainstream theories of the 20th century is that much of what we 'know' about the language system is based on intuition (what Germans call the 'Sprachgefühl'), on introspection (often confounded by common notions of 'folk psychology') and on an arbitrary presentation of select examples that ignores the overall evidence.

Corpus linguistics was meant to be a corrective. The corpus was hoped to be a fair representation of the discourse at large, or a special discourse under investigation. Tools, many of them based on statistics, were introduced, discussed and accepted by the corpus linguistics community. Their findings were considered incontrovertible, scientific evidence. One question, though, was never quite resolved. How reliable, appropriate and useful are the categories on which query procedures and the resulting findings were based? Some of them seemed formal enough: there is in written (or transcribed) texts, for languages using the Roman alphabet, a standard indicating, for each language, a finite number of vowels and consonants, diacritics allowing for language specific differences; there is such a thing as words defined as alphabetical chains between spaces; and there are visible punctuation marks rendering larger structural entities such as sentences, clauses and the like. It is this methodology that makes corpus linguistics so attractive to theories of the language system. Properly applied, it would 'objectively' test the claims made by a given approach; it might give linguists a more direct access to the rules defining the underlying system.

Not all categories, however, are quite so obvious. Parts of speech, for instance, are more controversial, and cannot directly be identified in the corpus. Taggers are needed, and different taggers reflect different conceptions and therefore bring about different results. People disagree, for instance, on what should be called a particle. Rules, however, presuppose categories. One cannot describe a sentence without classifying the elements it consists of. Categories are essential for building theories. No language model could do without them. The Birmingham brand of corpus linguistics considers itself as corpus-driven. It would never accept the 'particle' tag of anyone's tagger as sufficient evidence that a given word is a particle. A particle, John Sinclair would say, needs to be defined in strict terms of collocation and colligation, of language-inherent patternings revealed by computational discovery procedures. Not all corpus linguists would go so far. Lancastrian corpus linguists have a much more engaging attitude towards annotation. Are they wrong? Does not the notion of colligation, used by Sinclair, Stubbs and Louw, among others, presuppose the existence of categories? McEnery et al. (2006) point out in their introduction to corpus linguistics that any claims about the colligation pattern of a lexical item presuppose a tagged or a parsed corpus.

Take, for instance, the notion of 'sentence' that I have already addressed above as featuring in the concept of 'recursion,' the last remaining universal in Chomskyan linguistics. How data-based is it? Linguists often take it for granted that there is such a thing as a sentence because the data they are working with normally shows it, data which is in almost all cases written or otherwise recorded language, even in the case of transcripts of spoken language. Sentences are linear arrangements of words to which a syntactic structure can be assigned and which feature, in most western languages, Indo-European languages in particular, a finite verb in their main clause. Is such a scenario also realistic for languages in oral societies? Do people there, or in typical pub talk in Britain, really speak in complete sentences? When I was attending primary school in Germany, we were constantly reminded by our teachers not just to throw in a word or a phrase, but to respond in such 'full' sentences.

The notion of sentence is, I believe, a very good example for the fact that what we call language indeed incorporates numerous acculturated features, features often owing themselves to the introduction of writing. Writing presupposes standardisation much more than an oral language because a written text must stand for itself, it must be interpretable even in the absence of the writer. When I cannot 'read' the mumblings of the person next to me just before closing time of my pub, I can ask her what she means. Yet when I receive a similarly unstructured chain of words in writing (e.g. a cable) I must fill in virtual punctuation marks to make sense of the text, and I can only do that if there is a standard way of arranging words which has been followed by the writer. These standards can change over time, and they can differ from language to language. Chinese, for instance, does not have finite verb forms. This has implications for the definition of a sentence in Chinese.

The contingent socio-cultural construct of a sentence is crucial to Chomskyan linguistics. In their joint paper mentioned above, Marc Hauser, Noam Chomsky and Tecumseh Fitch argue: "The core property of discrete infinity is intuitively familiar to every language user. Sentences are built up of discrete units: There are 6-word sentences and 7-word sentences, but no 6.5-word sentences." Would that be also true for people in oral societies? Would they intuitively know what a word or what a sentence is? These days we find in the linguistic community a lot of discussion of the Pirahãs and their seemingly so unique language, which is, according to its foremost expert, Dan Everett, the only one which does not know recursion. Everett, who has, initially as a missionary, lived among the Pirahãs off and on for three decades, has received his linguistic training within the Chomskyan framework. Recursion is explained by Frederick Newmeyer in his paper 'Cognitive and functional factors in the evolution of language' in these words: "Every language on earth allows for the possibility of recursion, that is, sentences embedded inside of sentences inside of sentences, ad infinitum". According to John Colapinto in his article in the *New Yorker* 'The interpreter', two other eminent linguists, Steven Pinker, a Chomskyan, and Ray Jackendoff, belonging to the cognitive field, "cited Pirahã as an example of a language that has 'phonology, morphology, syntax, and sentences,' but no recursion." How do they define the notion of sentence?

The Pirahãs probably have no idea whether they have sentences in their languages or not. Indeed, before the arrival of westerners insisting on discussing their language with them, they may not even have been aware that there is such a thing as language, just as we are normally not conscious that we are communicating also with our facial expressions, gestures, body language, odours and probably a lot of other devices which have not yet been discovered by popular science writers. Pirahãs learn to communicate through language by imitating their carers and their peers; but we can hardly expect them to undergo the kind of pronunciation training children in literate societies receive. Whatever the Pirahã language has to offer in terms of vowels and consonants is about as fuzzy as the facial expressions we present to our partners in communication. Linguistically minded anthropologists or missionaries taking stock of an oral language have to align what they hear to the phonetic alphabets they are using. What Everett found for Pirahã are the three vowels /a/, /i/ and /o/. In terms of consonants, he is sure there are /p/, /b/, /t/, /s/, /g/, /h/ and /ʔ / (the glottal stop); perhaps also /k/. This is not very much, compared to western languages. What is more problematic is that we cannot be sure that these sounds can be taken for phonemes, that they serve to distinguish one word from another. Keren Everett, Dan's (now divorced) wife and former missionary partner, now thinks that her and Dan's original approach to this language, using the categories they had learned at college such as sentence and vowels and consonants, was all wrong. She told John Colapinto: "The key to learning the language is the tribe's singing, the way that the group can drop consonants and vowels altogether and communicate purely by variations in pitch, stress, and rhythm—what linguists call 'prosody.' This language uses prosody much more than any other language I know of. It's not the kind of thing that you can write, and capture, and go back to; you have to watch, and you have to feel it. It's like someone singing a song." Could it be that Pirahã is a kind of an extreme tonal language, much more extreme than Chinese or Vietnamese, a language that has done away with phonemes realised as consonants and vowels altogether and replaced them by a multitude of tones?

The case of Pirahã illustrates quite well, I believe, why I should not have jumped to the conclusion that the bottom-up approach of corpus linguistics is preferable to the top-down approach that most theories of the language system tend to use. Cognitive linguistics makes categorical assumptions about the way the mind processes language. But while corpus linguistics may resist the temptation to use categories such as theme and rheme, it is still stuck with the letters of the alphabet, punctuation marks and spaces, and, in its assumptions about colligation, it also presupposes that there are syntactic categories which can be disambiguated through their distribution features. Cognitive linguists believe there is such a thing as the mind, even though it seems hard to know how this entity should be more ontologically real than the soul that caught the imagination of former centuries. Corpus linguists believe there is such a thing as language that exists as an ontological reality, a collection of real language data exhibiting properties at least as real as those ascribed to nuclear particles.

Neither the mind nor language as such are objects we can find outside of the discourse. It is us, the members of the discourse community, who find these objects constructed in the discourses in which we participate. We talk about the mind just like our ancestors have talked about the soul. People offer ideas about it. We learn that it is the home of our memory, of our reasoning power, our emotive givenness, our intuitions, and also of our ability to entertain ideas and to share them with others. The reality of the mind is a reality that has been constructed within the discourse, by endless contributions of uncountable participants. It is not the reality we assume to find outside of the discourse, of the 'real' world. Without people talking about it, there is no such thing as a mind. The minds we find constructed in the cognitive sciences or in the philosophy of mind are contingent, constructed as the unicorns and the fairies in children's fiction. They could be constructed differently, and if we look closely enough, we find that the mind of today is not any more quite the same mind that was discussed ten years ago. Different discourses will construct minds in different ways over time.

Perhaps we should extend such a perspective to language as well. Paradoxical as it may sound, we could take language to be a construct of the discourse. The real language data I have talked about above are no more real, no more pieces of linguistic communication than to the extent they are interpreted as such within the discourse. For the Pirahãs using their vocal chords is certainly a way to interact. But they do not see such an act of communication as a sequence of sentences consisting of words which in turn consist of phonemes. They are not aware that they are using signs whose meaning has been negotiated and renegotiated by generation after generation. Language is not a reality of their discourse. For them, talking to each other is not symbolic. For them, there is no system of rules for producing grammatical utterances. Consequently they do not train their offspring to carefully distinguish between phonemes such as /p/ and /b/.

Language as we, in our western world, know it, is less a thing of a discourse-external 'real' world than a construct of our discourse. Some basic categories, like that of 'sentence', of 'word', of the parts of speech, date back to Greek and Latin antiquity. Many more rules, rules telling us how to write proper English (or Spanish, or Irish), have been introduced over the 19th century, created by language teachers in the interest of a standardised language fitting the recent notion of the nation state. Other aspects have been added on by linguists of all feathers. Some like to build models of the universal language system, focussing on what might be common to all natural languages. Others look at language as a social practice. To cognitive linguists we owe the idea that the concept of language covers the whole distance from turning thoughts into utterances and utterances into thoughts. The discourse of academic linguistics is linked to the general discourse. Ideas may find their way from a journalist's essay into a linguist's conference contribution and back into the public discourse, undergoing change along the way. There is an interdependence between the language we use and what we say about it.

The four papers that I have discussed above all appeal to our introspection, to the ways we have learnt to think about language. They intend to change our conceptions. Their aim to re-construct our notions of the discourse object 'language.' Tony Bastow suggests new interpretations of the 'adverbials of high epistemic value.' If they find their way back to the US Department of Defense, they may impact on future speeches. Javier Rivas and Esther Brown look at differences in the use of discourse markers in three varieties of Spanish. They add new notions to the existing construct of the Spanish language. Lydia-Mai Hồ-Đắc correlates the traditional linguistic notion of theme versus rheme to cognitive notions of accessibility, thus throwing doubt on the ways this relationship has been constructed before. Similarly, Iker Zulaica Hernández questions the ways in which different demonstrative pronouns correlate with 'accessibility', thus suggesting to re-construct the discourse object 'language' as we find it in cognitive linguistics.

Thinking about language, however, is not restricted to the academic ivory tower. Unlike oral societies, literate societies seem to be keen to talk about this topic. An academic discipline of linguistics became possible a hundred years ago because it was supported by public opinion. A large part of any discourse in literate societies is devoted to discussing the meaning of what is said in the other part. Our discourse keeps reflecting itself. The more academic linguistics interacts with the discourse at large concerning the construction of the discourse object 'language', the more relevant it will become.

What these four papers have shown me is a need to rethink linguistics as the discipline whose remit is 'language'. The notion of the natural sciences, constructed and re-constructed continually ever since the beginning of the enlightenment, has made us accept that there is a 'real' world outside of the discourse, a reality which is subject to unchangeable laws of nature and that describing this reality in appropriate categories will reveal its systematic properties. But outside of the discourse there is no object 'language'. Language, it seems, keeps (re-) creating itself, in a never-ending bootstrapping operation. There is no language system that still would be there once no one talked about it. Language is a human artefact, subject only to the contingency of human action. I fully agree with Roland Barthes (1981: 149): "System, as we know it, is the declared enemy of man and art."

There is, however, a different kind of system, the kind of self-generating, self-organising system we find in Niklas Luhmann's systems theory. For him, the discourse, or what he calls 'communication,' is such a system. His social theory, 'antihumanistic' as he calls it, does not pretend it can look into people's heads. His discourse is what happens within the discourse community, between people. It consists of a continuous stream of input, adding more or less random new stuff to all that has already been said. Some of it may be successful: it may have an impact on what is subsequently said. It is a discourse that creates itself; it is auto-poietic. What is already there in the discourse determines in quite unpredictable ways subsequent input, in that much of what is said refers back to things said before. This discourse is self-referential; it does not necessarily refer to anything outside the discourse even if we all believe it does. It has, of necessity, a diachronic dimension. It keeps changing. We can study it. But once we take away all the references of a text, a text segment or a lexica item to all other occurrences in previous and subsequent texts there is nothing left. Meaning is only in the discourse. Language is no more than our notion of language, of everything that has been said about it. There is nothing systematic about language except what we have constructed as our language system. We, the linguists, find it by making sense of the discourse at large. Applying a strictly 'scientific' method as offered by corpus linguistics can never be more than a first step.

The four papers discussed here have given me much food for thought. I have to retract a key point I made in many earlier papers, namely that corpus linguistics, being bottom up, can give us a more objective way to look at language that the theories of the language system working with top-down categories. This is not such an important distinction as I have made it out to be. Instead we should aim to describe language as a construct of the discourse. Our starting point should be what has been said about language, not as an objective image of what language 'really' is, but as a constantly re-negotiated construct that could have been constructed differently. The ideas, notions, conceptualisations we find in the discourse about language should be compared not so much to what corpus linguists have called real language data but to our interpretations of these data, which are, of necessity, again a part of the discourse. Our task thus is to add layer after layer of interpretation to the discourse object 'language.' The more such interpretations will be based on data we agree to share, the more they will be acceptable to the interpretive community. It is in this rather limited sense that corpus linguistics may have an advantage over other ways to look at language.

References

Barthes, R. (1981): *The Responsibility of Forms*, Berkeley, The University of California Press.

Bootcamp, (corpora-bounces@uib.no [corpora-bounces@uib.no])

Christensen, S. M. and D. R. Turner (eds.) (1993): *Folk Psychology and the Philosophy of Mind*, Hillsdale, New Jersey, Lawrence Erlbaum.

Colapinto, J. (2007): "The interpreter", (*The New Yorker*, April 16, 2007, http://www.newyorker.com/reporting/2007/04/16/070416fa_fact_colapinto?).

Fodor, J. (1975): *The Language of Thought*, Cambridge, Mass., Harvard University Press.

Halliday, M. A. K. (1968): "Notes on transitivity and theme in English (part 3)", *Journal of Linguistics*, 4, 2, 179-215.

Hauser, M., N. Chomsky and T. Fitch (2002): "The faculty of language: what it is, who has it, and how did it evolve?", *Science*, 298, 1569-1579.

Luhmann, N. (1998): "Die Gesellschaft der Gesellschaft", Frankfurt am Main, Suhrkamp.

McEnery, T., R. Xiao and Y. Tono (2006): *Corpus-based Language Studies: An Advanced Resource Book*, London, Routledge.

Newmeyer, F.: "Cognitive and functional factors in the evolution of language", (http://www.interdisciplines.org/coevolution/papers/3/5).

Owen, C. (2007): "Notes of the ofness of *of* – Sinclair and grammar", *International Journal of Corpus Linguistics*, 12, 201-221.

Pinker, S. (1994): *The Language Instinct*, New York, Harper Collins.

Quirk, R., S. Greenbaum, G. Leech, J. Svartvik (1985): A *Comprehensive Grammar of the English Language*, London, Longman.

Tognini Bonelli, E. (2001): *Corpus Linguistics at Work*, Amsterdam, John Benjamins.

Zemb, J. M. (1982): "Les occurrences phématiques, rhématiques et thématiques des archilexèmes modaux", in: *La notion sémantico-logique de modalité*, Metz, Univ. de Metz & Klincksieck, Recherches linguistiques VIII, 75-116.

PART TWO

A Kaleidoscope of Discourse Analysis

Some discourse functions of the modal adverbs *of course*, *clearly*, *obviously*, and *certainly* in a corpus of US defence speeches

Tony Bastow
University of East London

1. Introduction

The aim of this paper is to explore how four adverbials of 'high epistemic value' – *of course, clearly, obviously,* and *certainly* – not only have a function in persuading the reader or listener that the proposition they *directly* introduce is highly warrantable or unassailable, but also how they have an important rhetorical function in the wider discourse.

In this paper I will be drawing upon examples from a specially created corpus of US defence speeches, which I will henceforth refer to as the DoD corpus. This corpus consists of one million words from speeches covering the years 1995-2001 given by senior defence officials (Chiefs of Staff, generals, etc.) downloaded from the US Department of Defence website at www.defenselink.mil/speeches. It will be shown from this corpus that, while such 'certainty' adverbials are apparently synonymous, they may have different rhetorical functions in their contexts of use. Where appropriate, I will also be drawing on comparative data from a large, general, or 'reference' corpus, namely Cobuild's Bank of English.

Before discussing these functions, a few remarks should be made concerning a grammatical distinction that is sometimes made between 'conjuncts' and 'disjuncts', one which is challenged by some theorists and by the corpus evidence I will provide here.

2. Conjuncts and disjuncts

Quirk et al. (1985: 631-632), indeed, draw a clear distinction between conjuncts and disjuncts in the following statement: 'Whereas, in the case of disjuncts, we relate them to the speaker's "authority" for (or the speaker's comment on) the accompanying clause, we relate conjuncts to the speaker's comment in one quite specific respect: his assessment of how he views the connection between two linguistic units.' Thus, while conjuncts (*however, in addition*, etc.) function primarily as cohesive (textual) devices in the discourse, disjuncts (*obviously, clearly*) are to be interpreted primarily as items reflecting speaker stance. Within Quirk et al.'s (1985: 612-31) category of disjuncts, the authors distinguish between 'style disjuncts' (*frankly, generally, personally*) and 'content disjuncts' (*undoubtedly, perhaps*). 'Content disjuncts' make observations on the actual content of the utterance and its truth conditions, and are, according to Quirk et al's (ibid: 620-23) taxonomy, of two types: (a) 'Degree of truth' disjuncts and (b) 'Value judgment' disjuncts. Value judgement disjuncts 'convey some evaluation of or attitude towards what is said' (ibid: 621), and include such items as cleverly, sensibly and rightly.

'Degree of truth' disjuncts, on the other hand, with which this paper is specifically concerned, 'present a comment on the *truth* value of what is said, expressing the extent to which, and the conditions under which, the speaker believes what he is saying is true' (ibid: 620; emphasis added). These may express conviction (*obviously*), a degree of doubt (*presumably*), or speaker judgement on the truth value of the proposition (*actually*). In the case of conviction, the following correspondences apply:

> *Clearly*, he's mistaken.
> *It is clear (that)* he doesn't object.
> That he doesn't object *is clear.*

But not necessarily: he's *clearly* mistaken (which may be classified as a 'subjunct', modifying 'mistaken').

Other theorists (e.g. Thompson and Zhou 2000: 121-141) have challenged this, suggesting that disjuncts also have an important *conjunctive* function. In their argument, they invoke the notion of 'evaluative coherence' to claim that disjuncts are *not* just concerned with exhibiting attitudes, but play an important cohesive function; they are thus more properly 'conjuncts with attitude'.

For example, in the following example (reproduced from Thompson and Zhou 2000: 125), *certainly* concedes a proposition (which can be seen as a 'sidestep' to the main argument), while *yet* asserts an unexpected proposition, which focuses attention on the main point that the author wishes to make:

> Before the war, it was always the working class which bore the brunt [of economic sacrifices]. Since the war the outcome has been quite different...*Certainly* the middle classes have come off distinctly better under the Tories. *Yet* a repetition of 1921 or 1931 is unthinkable even now; the national shift to the Left, with all its implications for the balance of power, may be accepted as permanent.

Quirk et al. (1985: 639) do discuss the same phenomenon, but only with regard to *of course*, which they label as a 'concessive conjunct', concerning which they say: 'Where one unit is seen as unexpected in the light of the other, we have the use of concessive conjuncts...concessive *of course* makes a conjoin resemble a subordinate clause: "*Of course* he's a bit lazy; all the same I'd like to give him the job." (="Although he's a bit lazy, I'd like to give him the job all the same").'

3. Corpus evidence

In examining four adverbials from my special corpus, namely *of course*, *clearly*, *obviously*, and *certainly* - I will argue that, although they may be equivalent at a denotational level (they all express 'conviction'), they may also have distinct discourse and rhetorical properties, for which labels such as 'conjunct' and 'disjunct' do not fully apply.

Before taking a closer look at these adverbs in this special corpus, a few words should be said about their relative frequency in this corpus and the reference corpus, the Bank of English.

Table 1 shows the frequency of these adverbs per one million words in the two corpora:

Adverbial	**DoD corpus** (per one million words)	**Bank of English** (per one million words)
of course	253	209
certainly	182	157
clearly	161	100
obviously	58	97

Table 1. Relative frequency of *of course, certainly, clearly* and *obviously* in the DoD corpus and the Bank of English

It can be seen from the table that, with the exception of *obviously*, the adverbials under discussion are significantly more frequent (ranging from 20% to 50% more frequent) in the DoD corpus than in the language as a whole, as evidenced by the general (reference) corpus. This finding may be predicted, given the highly rhetorical nature of the DoD speeches. In the case of *obviously*, the evidence shows a contrary indication, possibly indicating its 'interactional functions in conveying solidarity' (Simon-Vandenbergen and Aijmer 2007:199) in everyday speech.

3.1. Of course

Of course is the most frequent of the adverbials (occurring 253 times in the DoD corpus), and can be paraphrased as 'unsurprising', 'generally known'. The Cobuild Learner's Dictionary (1996) states: 'You say *of course* to suggest that something is normal, obvious, or well-known, and should therefore not surprise the person you are talking to.'

Quirk et al. (1985) regard *of course* as a conjunct, in which the *of course* clause presents a 'commonsense' statement or comment which is textually cohesive with its preceding and succeeding clause(s). However, its function is more than merely conjunctive. Biber and Finegan (1988: 21) suggest it has an additional *politeness* function, in that it 'acknowledges those addressees who already know the information being asserted, while it incidentally supplies the information for those who don't know it.'

It has also a number of other rhetorical functions which I shall call 'topic focussing' and 'self-validatory', which will be discussed now.

Textual and semantic function	**Instances**
Conjunct (='naturally')	105
Topic-focusing: 'external'	67
Topic-focusing: 'internal'	53
Concessive	12
Self-validation	8
Response to questions	8

Table 2. Functions of *of course* in the DoD corpus

Of course as a 'topic-focuser' serves to signal that a new topic (or a new aspect of a current topic) is about to be discussed. It is used by the speaker as a means to control the direction of the discourse. As shown in Table 2, 67 of the 120 instances of 'topic-focusing' *of course* are concerned with America's (often problematic) relations with other countries (which are indicated as 'external' in the table). For example, in the following extracts, the topic is introduced by *of course* and then elaborated in the subsequent clauses:

> ...of the scourge of illegal narcotics, both the supply and the demand, which feed habits of crime and corruption, endanger our streets and poison our children. And *of course*, compounding all of these problems are the more traditional concerns of *regional aggression by rogue regimes* that threaten peace in places such as the murky waters of the Persian Gulf...

> There is so much promise in the dynamism that's coming back to the Middle East countries, and yet they live in a neighborhood in which the terror is equally tangible and palpable. This brings me, *of course*, to talk about *Iran and Iraq*. Much of the future security of that region will depend upon what kind of actions they undertake...

In the first example above, the speaker uses *of course* to direct the topic under discussion from 'crime and corruption on our streets' to 'regional aggression by rogue states', despite the questionable link between them. In the second example, *of course* links 'Middle East countries' and 'terror' to 'Iran and Iraq' as if by default, the implication being that hearers need hardly consider other countries. Their introduction by *of course* then allows the speaker to elaborate further on the topic.

Of course also serves as 'topic-focuser' for *internal* defense matters, usually relating to force readiness and modernization issues:

> NATO must have the capability to conduct up to three major operations, including two corps-sized crisis response operations, which implies *of course* that we *must* maintain a quite robust planning capability…

> The Marines are revolutionizing their capabilities by honing their skills in urban warfare. And, *of course*, the Army has embarked on a historic transformation to dramatically enhance the speed, mobility, and firepower of our soldiers.

In the first example, the two modal elements of *of course* and *must* not only reinforce the speaker's endorsement of a strategy he sees as shared by the community on whose behalf he speaks, but also allows him to elaborate on it. In the second example, *of course* reminds the audience of something they are *presumed* to know, while again opening the way for the speaker to detail more precisely the nature of that modernization.

The fourth category concerns the use of *of course* to express *concessive* relations between clauses. In the first extract here, the speaker concedes that September 11 was a surprise, while at the same time asserting the need to prepare for similar surprises; in the second extract, the speaker concedes that problems of diversity exist, but asserts his belief in the principles of law and order (X is true, but Y is also true):

> A second emphasis in this Quadrennial Defense Review is to emphasize the importance of uncertainty and surprise in our defense planning. *Of course* September 11th was a surprise, *but* it wasn't the first surprise and it won't be the last one.

> *Of course*, it would be wrong to say we don't have problems that arise from our diversity, and at times these problems can get ugly. *But* in general, the principles of law and order and tolerance and freedom have won out in the end.

As Biber and Finegan (1988: 29) remark, the writers 'anticipate objections from potential readers and concede obvious *opposing* points as beyond dispute, in order to demonstrate emphatically that the author's argument is not diminished by those points', while Hoye (1997: 191) suggests more directly 'that the speaker is reluctant to accept the truth of what is being said.'

The next use of *of course* is as a marker of 'self-validation'. Here the US presents itself as the unquestioned leader on the world stage, at liberty to pursue policies which it 'knows' to be right. The US imperialistic agenda is far from being construed as undesirable or immoral – on the contrary, it is good and natural. As Chomsky (2004: 43) remarks: 'US hegemony is the realization of history's purpose, and what it achieves is for the common good, the merest truism, so that empirical evaluation is unnecessary, if not faintly ridiculous':

> As the world's leading and most influential nation, that [forming a new world order] must be a primary issue for our policy and for our military forces. *The simple fact is, of course, that no other nation in the world has the power or the reach to perform this role.*

> Why are we deployed anywhere in a new world? *The answer to that, of course, is that we are a superpower.*

Finally, there are a few uses of *of course* concerned with speaker face. Firstly, it can be used to assert authority, by introducing a proposition which may not immediately come to the mind of even the informed listener. Burchfield (1999: 188) quotes Fowler (1926) in advising against this use of *of course,* which appears to herald 'an out-of-the-way fact that one has just unearthed from a book or reference.' The effect of *of course* in such cases (albeit rare in this corpus) is apparently to emphasize a gap between speaker and hearer knowledge. In presenting complex information as though it were wholly evident, the speaker marks out his authority as 'expert':

> I have in mind, *of course*, the "Berlin-plus" decisions at the Washington Summit, wherein our heads of state and government pledged assured EU access to NATO planning capabilities able to contribute to military planning for EU-led operations.

Secondly, in contrast to the above, *of course* is used to mitigate threat to speaker face (again rare in this corpus). Biber and Finegan (1989: 115) remark that 'whenever speakers…are put on the spot, they begin using frequent certainty adverbs, in marked contrast to the *actual* certainty of their discourse' (emphasis added). This function is similar to the concessive function, in that it acknowledges a deficit in speaker knowledge or competence:

> speaker had to say - while I am sure that he was very eloquent and wise – I can't remember a single word that he said. And *of course, I guess that's a warning to me*, for undoubtedly my own thoughts will prove equally perishable and fleeting!

> of finding ways to see that the ability to track transactions is improved. The problem here - and, *of course, needless to say, I don't know about the specific instance you're describing.*

In general, there is a tendency for *of course* in the DoD corpus to be associated more with facts, events and concepts (frequently instantiated in relational and existential processes), while *of course* in the Bank of English is frequently followed by the pronouns *I/you/we,* suggesting a closer, more interactional engagement between speaker and hearer :

> and Palmer: (In unison) Of course *we* trust *you.* <p> B. Ziff: OK, then
> x on top of that which, of course, *you* double for the tip if you're o
> u can switch each year. Of course, *you* must confine your switches to
> y most substances. Now, of course, *we* know that many ingredients make
> nd pencils and erasers. Of course *I* expect *your* penmanship to be at i
> way from childhood. <p> Of course, *we* all had to grow up, but did we
> inese burn, though. <p> Of course, *you* realise everyone is going to h
> he international scene. Of course, *I*'m pleased *he*'s fit and he had a
> e other end and scored. Of course *we* can still win the league. We're

In conclusion, it can be said that *of course* in the DoD corpus has a text-cohesive function in offering a new perspective on a topic being discussed, while, for the most part, assuming a parity in speaker and listener knowledge. It marks the speaker's intention to present information in such a way that the listener shares in the assumptions being expressed. It also has an important role in allowing the speaker to control the direction of the discourse (its 'topic-focusing' function), but can also be used concessively and as a means of self-validation. As we have just seen, in the Bank of English, it has a greater role in interactional discourse, collocating with items such as *then, but,* and *yes,* as well as the pronouns *I, we* and *you.*

3.2. Certainly

Now to my second adverbial, *certainly*. In their support of Halliday, Thompson and Zhou (2000: 130) remark: '*Certainly*...might appear simply to be a comment on the truth value of the proposition. However, as has frequently been pointed out, we do not normally find it necessary to proclaim explicitly the truth value of a proposition unless that value is in some way in question. As Halliday (1994: 89) puts it: "you only say you are certain when you are not" – or, in broader and perhaps more accurate wording, saying explicitly that you believe something to be true admits the possibility of it not being believed to be true by everyone.'

Table 3 represents the four main functions of *certainly* in the DoD corpus (which I will shortly discuss), with their frequency and grammatical realizations:

Function	**Frequency (percentage of total)**	**Grammatical realization**
Emphatic	138 (76%)	subjuncts and disjuncts
'bad news'	21 (11.5%)	subjuncts
Concession	14 (7.5%)	disjuncts
Evasion	9 (5%)	disjuncts (some subjuncts)

Table 3. Functions of *certainly* in the DoD corpus

Out of a total of 182 instances of *certainly* in the DoD corpus, 138 have the emphatic function of 'definitely', and are both subjuncts and disjuncts:

> in many respects. It's *certainly* a personal safety and human issue
> developed. And I would *certainly* appreciate it very much, Mr.Presid
> something which we are *certainly* dedicated to. President Clinton
> nd elsewhere. We would *certainly* consult closely with Allies were th
> tion Panel, stated, "I *certainly* consider the DD-21 and CVNX to be t
> ning, your talent, and *certainly* your determination. We watch what's
> profound consequences, *certainly* for us, but for millions of people

In approximately 14 lines, however, the writer uses *certainly* to concede ground to the reader or listener, anticipating or acknowledging a tacit objection that the reader may have. By forestalling any such objection, the speaker is effectively warding off criticism that - in the following examples - he might not 'take full cognizance' of the legislation, openly debate national defence, or address the concerns of accidental launch. By the use of *certainly,* he is limiting possible damage to face. In this sense, it is comparable to *of course*:

> And I *certainly agree with you that* before anything else is done, we have to take full cognizance of the legislation and of you and your associates and your interest, and consult.

> Yes, we can always do better, and national defense is *certainly a subject matter that is open to debate* and improvement. Hopefully that will be the case whatever administration comes in next year.

> I think there is a concern, legitimate concern, about accidental launch. *I think these are certainly things that we do need to take into account.*

As mentioned before, such concessive disjuncts represent a 'side step' to the author's main argument, which is brought back into focus by counter-assertions introduced by conjunctive items such as *but* and *that said* and *at the same time*. While recognizing that listeners may have objections (sometimes made explicit in rhetorical questions), the speaker, in using items such as *certainly*, at the same time avoids the need to address them:

> Both carriers coordinated well alongside a third carrier, the Foch, on station to conduct its own national mission requirements in the Adriatic. *A complicated picture, certainly.* Could the operations have been streamlined by a more coherent, political backdrop? Of course. *But reality continues to dictate political complexity among our nations. The good news is that* the operation in the Adriatic was ultimately successful…

> Given that we have the opportunity, *there is certainly a moral imperative to* stop the bloodshed and violence in Bosnia-Herzegovina, *but it is the danger of a wider war that is the most significant threat to U.S. interests.*

> And *we certainly have a humanitarian interest in mitigating the violence*. So in my view, walking away is not an option. *At the same time, we are not going to take sides in the war as a combatant.*

Related to this, in 21 of the lines, *certainly* signals 'bad news' or unpalatable truths which the speaker trusts his listeners will accept:

> We *certainly will be targeted* overseas as terrorists try to make a political statement like at Khobar Towers

> Intervention of U.S. forces would not necessarily have been effective, but *certainly would have involved very large casualties.*

> *Certainly, ethnic hatred and related disputes* still dominate life there.

> The unintended consequence could be to rule out, or *certainly to make more difficult*, a cooperative solution, and perhaps leave the president no choice but to withdraw from the treaty unilaterally.

Finally, Jacobson (1978: 16) argues that there are some cases where the pragmatic function of *certainly* 'totally disregards the inherent content.' He gives the example of a Minister of Finance who diverts attention away from the imminence of a proposed action when he states *we are certainly not going to devalue*, adding: 'Normally *certainly* expresses certainty, but both the speaker and his hearers [in the above case] know that a Minister of Finance cannot be expected to tell journalists about his *real* intentions as regards devaluation. The pragmatic function, then, of *certainly* [here] is not to underline the *certainty* of what is said, but to increase the possibility of the *lie being taken as truth.*' (ibid: 16; emphasis added).

In the DoD corpus there are possibly six examples of *certainly not* suggesting the possibility of a contrary position. In the last example, something that is *certainly not imminent* is almost certainly on the agenda in the long run:

So *the intention is certainly not to* throw a lot of – we don't have money to throw away at things that don't provide us a real capability.

Before I am accused of misplaced optimism, I must say that I am *certainly not suggesting* that our naval cooperation be a method to subordinate our national interests.

That would just be one of the many hundreds of decisions that have to be made about how the architecture develops in an incremental way. That is *certainly not imminent* in our program right now.

This 'evasive' use of *certainly* accounted for 21 instances in the DoD corpus. In a sample 100 lines from the Bank of English, there were no apparent examples of 'inherent content being disregarded'. Rather, *certainly* is serving to emphasize the negativity of the proposition, to show how categorically certain the writer is in stating something is, indeed, *not* the case:

was accidental. It *was certainly not deliberate* <p> Hull coach Royce
to almost a fiver *will certainly not impress* British drinkers. Howev
red it personally - and *certainly not in exchange for money* or other
s you're staying there, *certainly not without advertising* his presenc
r principal artists are *certainly not going to thank you for* casting
(BoE data)

Negativity associated with the word *certainly* is as evident in the Bank of English as it is in the DoD corpus, as the following lines attest:

nomy a success. *It will certainly be tough for them* at first, as the
t that to fire *it would certainly cause fatal casualties* amongst the
t Indian go-slow *almost certainly cost England the wicket* of Graham T
that Karen would *almost certainly die from the condition,* called acut
orge Ndah, United *would certainly have been dead and buried.* In fact,
Harford said. Ferguson *certainly inflamed* the situation. I have seen

In conclusion, in both the DoD corpus and the Bank of English, *certainly* is both a positive and negative signal of evaluation. In its positive function, it collocates with items such as *appreciate*, *help, improve,* etc. In its negative role, it concedes the possibility of 'bad news', and (in political discourse, at least) may even mask the genuine thoughts or intentions of the speaker. *Certainly* also pretends to consider the ideas offered by other people, only to reject them.

3.3. Clearly

Now let us turn to *clearly*. On the use of *clearly*, Hunston and Thompson (2000: 23) remark that it 'indicates not only how certain the writer is of what is to follow, but how obvious it is to the reader, or expected by the reader…in the case of *clearly* it is the discourse itself that is being evaluated as obvious or expected, as well as the information in the discourse.' It is therefore perhaps not surprising to find *clearly* used (sometimes ambiguously) as disjunct, subjunct and intensifier.

Clearly (which occurs 161 times in the DoD corpus, 61% more frequently than in the Bank of the English) has three principal uses in the DoD corpus. Firstly, it may be used as a disjunct to express conviction, either as direct claim or from general perception of evidence, although these are not always easy to disambiguate (e.g. *Clearly, the Asian-Pacific region is making tremendous advances...*). This was the largest category in the DoD corpus, accounting for 52% of all instances (Table 2), where "the presence of *clearly* creates an expectation that the grounds for the claim will follow" (Lewis 1999: 371).

Its second most common use in the DoD corpus is as a manner adverb (e.g. *it stated clearly that*; 24% of all instances), while its third use is as a subjunct 'emphasizer' (e.g. *they would clearly benefit* – 21%):

Semantic function	**Frequency (percentage of total)**	**Functional category**
conviction	83 (52%)	disjuncts
manner	38 (24%)	verb modifiers
emphasizer	34 (21%)	subjuncts
intensifier	5 (3%)	adj/adv. modifiers

Table 4. Functions of *clearly* in the DoD corpus

Clearly as a manner adverbial (which can be paraphrased as 'unambiguously', 'comprehensibly', 'accurately'), typically involves verbal processes of saying, stating, and defining, and accounts for 38 instances in the corpus:

and local agencies. And *it clearly acknowledges* the essential
t, and we want to *state it clearly and fully*. But we also und
ee. I *expressed my concern clearly*, and I hope forcibly, to th
s *registering our concerns clearly and emphatically* any time R
rity. Let me *state this as clearly as I can* and directly and d

That said, however, the first line above is functionally ambiguous. Is the sense here 'accurately', or 'it's clear to you and me?' This functional indeterminacy, which may or may not be consciously exploited by the writer, is also shared by *obviously*. 15 instances in this category are concerned with 'seeing' or 'comprehending' complex historical processes, with the first person plural pronoun *we* as frequent collocate:

ape the world; *we see most clearly how* the U.S. is he
arly. But *what we see less clearly* is what our leadership could mean
d *if we all look at Bosnia clearly*, not through a rose-colored glass
is country against *what we clearly see* now are actual threats. Secr
erize history that *you can clearly see* after the fact, I think we ca

For Lakoff and Johnson (1980: 48), such examples are, of course, realizations of the conceptual metaphor UNDERSTANDING IS SEEING.

Turning now to 'clearly' meaning 'obviously', where potentially contentious propositions are presented as if they were self-evident, White (2003: 28) notes that such usages are 'highly contractive dialogistically, in that for anyone to challenge such a view, they are positioned as going against the 'accepted view' as what is generally accepted.' In other words, *clearly* suggests unchallengeable consensus between the participants of a discourse community.

This might suggest that *clearly* has the same functionality as *of course* in the DoD corpus, but the data presents a more complex picture. *Clearly* would seem to be rhetorically more forceful, in that it frequently signals a highly controversial proposition which the speaker knows may well be opposed by other communities:

> To begin with, despite our significant military power, we are welcome in Central Europe because we carry no historical baggage and *clearly have no territorial aspirations* on the Continent.

> It is *clearly important that all allies take steps to improve our nuclear, chemical and biological defenses*; both their protection and detection capabilities.

> But nowhere has the argument for our leadership been more *clearly justified than in the struggle to stop or prevent war and civil violence*. From Iraq to Haiti, from South Africa to Korea, from the Middle East to Northern Island, we have stood up for peace and freedom because it is the right thing to do.

In the examples above, America's claim to have no territorial aspirations on the Continent might not persuade everyone (and may imply, for some, that America has territorial aspirations *elsewhere*). Similarly, opponents of US foreign policy may disagree with the proposition that nuclear, chemical and biological defences should be enhanced, and that America is entitled to intervene in the affairs of other countries simply because 'it is the right thing to do'. Partington (2003) notes in his study that *clearly* is used 'as a rhetorical instrument to make an argument, perhaps even to pass off as uncontroversial parts of the argument that are not necessarily so' (ibid: 205).

In some instances, *clearly* signals a subsequent concessive clause:

> The central ones in the examples I mentioned have to do with the question of whether the development of a testbed, which would *clearly* be legal under the treaty, *becomes illegal if you harbor the intention or the plan or the possibility of turning that testbed into an operational capability.*

> While the pace and extent of China's strategic modernization *clearly* indicates deterrent rather than first strike intentions, *the number of Chinese strategic missiles capable of hitting the United Slates will increase significantly during the next two decades.*

> *Clearly* the United States military and in particular the U.S. European Command are not and should not be the world's policeman. *But U.S. leadership is required in creating the conditions which will reinforce our ideals and values and assure our security and that of our allies into the 21st century.*

In a few instances, *clearly* introduces a proposition which is not necessarily a consequent of the preceding one. In the following examples, democratization in the Ukraine is used as a pretext for the US to bring the country under its sphere of influence. It does not necessarily follow that *because* the Ukraine is freer and more stable it is ready to join NATO:

> Our relationship with Ukraine is also critical. Ukraine has made great strides against tremendous odds toward freedom and stability. *It is clearly ready to play its part in building a secure and undivided trans-Atlantic community.* We should strive to have a NATO-Ukraine agreement ready for signature in Madrid.

In the Bank of English, by contrast, *clearly* plays only a minor role in contentious propositions - indeed there was no evidence of it in a random sample of 100 lines I examined. Instead, it tends to function as an intensifier (pre-modifying adjectives or adverbs), or as a disjunct in propositions expressing conviction:

he eighth green. Kite was *clearly ashamed* of the attitude of his coun
on the jagged rocks were *clearly audible*. Each second their boom gre
ed that many callers were *clearly frightened by* what was happening to
p> He also claimed it was *clearly unconstitutional* and breached a rec
down of left-handers, was *clearly unimpressed* when Muster was sick in
and's reserve hooker, was *clearly upset* but confirmed he had used a f
eye, but others should be *clearly visible*. Air Force geophysicist Ed

ubject for a play? Whelan *clearly believes* it is, if only because bot
<p> This is a place which *clearly cares passionately about* its food.
m cradle to grave, and he *clearly doesn't have a lot of time for* the
g the military leadership *clearly had even less difficulty than usual*

> untrue. His sharp retort *clearly made an impact.* When delegates were
> pplies and services. *This clearly meant the continuation of* rationing

In conclusion, in the DoD corpus *clearly* is frequently used to mask the contentious nature of subsequent propositions, or to express a direct claim. In the Bank of English, on the other hand, the rhetorical function of *clearly* to signal a contentious proposition is much less prominent.

3.4. Obviously

Now let us consider *obviously*. Quirk et al. (1985: 623) remark that 'just as the verb *see* can be used for both visual and mental perception (cf. *I see* ['understand'] *what you mean*), so adverbs as disjuncts can be used for both types of perception. In: *Obviously, he doesn't want to help him*, the speaker's conviction may well be based on what the person has said rather than anything that has been perceived visually. On the other hand, in: *Obviously, he is in very poor health*, it may be based largely on the person's appearance.' In this respect, it shows similarities with *clearly.*

Obviously occurs 58 times in the DoD corpus, nearly all of them disjuncts of mental perception. There were arguably 7 instances of 'visual perception':

> g for his troops. *It's obviously cold* and he's praying for his troop
> m older and grayer and *obviously slower than I was* back in those da
> that? Some of you are *obviously very young*. We have people as youn

In these instances, it would acceptable to replace *obviously* with *clearly,* where the item is premodifying the predicative adjective. Placing the modal *obviously* in initial or final position (*Obviously, it's cold* and *It's cold, obviously*) might lead to the interpretation of *obviously* as 'of course' or 'it goes without saying'.

But there are cases where the sense of *obviously* cannot be conclusively interpreted as either visual or mental perception:

> tion, and I'm going to try to make two points, first, using that question as an opportunity to appeal to this audience, which has *obviously* got a lot of influential opinion makers in it.

Is it from *empirical evidence* that the speaker concludes that there are influential opinion makers in the audience, or is he saying that it *goes without saying* that such an audience would have influential opinion makers in it?

These examples are ambiguous, but rare. Most instances of the adverb are of the inferential type, namely 'it goes without saying.' The use of *obviously* here is to make the reader or listener who does not find the comments obvious suspect his or her own judgement; in other words, missing the 'obvious' is a sign of poor judgement or intelligence. In the examples below, for example, *obviously* is coupled with either vague referents (*Middle East **and elsewhere***), or technical matters that can only reasonably be expected to be 'obvious' to the experts concerned:

> That's especially important in Asia and *obviously* in the Middle East and elsewhere, and I'm delighted that you and your colleagues will be going on a mission over the next week or two to convince skeptical elements about the merits of the proposal.
>
> We considered several approaches for fielding a boost-phase intercept capability against theater ballistic missiles. *Obviously*, it is desirable, if possible, to intercept an enemy missile while it is still boosting.

There are several instances where the 'obvious' statement precedes a 'call for action' statement (signalled by *but*). *Obviously*, like *of course*, may signal concessive clausal relations:

> *Obviously*, the Russian people, the Russian government must do whatever possible they can in order to solve their own economic system. *But we have to be concerned about it and we have to work with them.*
>
> It's *obviously* passé now to refer to the sarin attack in Tokyo. *But, if ever there were a wake up call, it was that.*
>
> We will be spending a lot of time on those questions at a later hearing, and *obviously* today people will comment on that, and you already have. *But* what I want to focus on today has to do with the testing which is now being requested…
>
> Obviously, Osama bin Laden and his organization -- or organizations, I should say -- are high on the list of suspects, as are others. *But there has been no definitive assessment of responsibility at this point.*
> (BoE data)

Finally, there is one case where *obviously* co-occurs with the modal 'I think'. The effect of *obviously* here is to negate any tentativeness or uncertainty suggested by 'I think', such that, in the example below, the Chinese *will* challenge America in the future:

> *I think* China *obviously* will have its own foreign policy agenda. *I think* they will seek to challenge us at points in the future, as any other power would. *I think* we have to deal with them on that basis.

In the Bank of English, *obviously* most frequently co-occurs with the pronouns *I* and *you* and in existential clauses beginning *there is/are.* With the personal pronouns, *obviously* does not so much convey the meaning of 'empirically valid' or imply shared knowledge; rather they serve an interpersonal function in engaging the listener in the speaker's thought processes:

who will take care of it. *Obviously* I know the exact spot where she i
got a clue to do with it. *Obviously* I will want to look after all the
it was anyway erm she had *obviously* I should think already said well
ing going I mean you know *obviously* I don't know <ZF1> what <ZF0> wha

y confused and angry man. *Obviously* you're a glutton for punishment,
> <M01> Can I ask you and *obviously* you see <ZF1> I <ZF0> I've only e
hat work er this term? Or *obviously* you're still not you've another h
riety. And you know <ZGY> *Obviously* you've got to start from a point

In the existential clauses, *obviously* serves to qualify previous statements or provide additional information to support previous propositions. This is similar to some of the usages found in the DoD corpus:

imply to rise above them. *Obviously*, there's more than a dash of smi
ting a little bit better. *Obviously* there are certain companies who a
ing. <F0X> Because I mean *obviously* there's <ZF1> a sort of ongoing
from four to eight. So *obviously* there are headings deemed not to

In summary, *obviously* in the DoD corpus is used as a modal of both mental and visual perception, and frequently has a rhetorical function in introducing vague details and concepts as if they were 'obvious' when they may not be. It may also function concessively. In the Bank of English, *obviously* seems to have a greater interpersonal function in the negotiation of discourse, with its more frequent collocation with *I* and *you.*

4. Conclusion

In this paper I have attempted to argue that grammatical labels such as 'conjunct' and 'disjunct' are insufficient in accounting for the discourse functions of the adverbs *of course*, *certainly, clearly,* and *obviously* in the DoD corpus. These items are not merely limited to either a linking function or an attitudinal function, but have complex rhetorical functions which may be exploited by the speaker. These functions are summarized below

Let us start with *of course.* The function of *of course* is more than merely conjunctive. Its main function, indeed, would seem to be to allow the speaker to control the direction of the discourse, focusing the reader's attention on a particular topic, or introducing a new angle on a topic under discussion. At the same time, as Biber and Finegan (1988: 21) say, 'it acknowledges those addressees who already know the information being asserted, while it incidentally supplies the information for those who don't' (*Complementing our alliance with Japan in regional security matters, of course, is the U.S. and South Korea military alliance. This alliance continues to be rock solid...)*. *Of course* may also be used concessively, where the adverbial 'serves to reduce the status of the idea expressed by its host clause and to turn that clause into a satellite of the following nucleus' (Lewis 1999: 368) (***Of course** it would wrong to say...**but** in general...*). Finally, it may be used as a marker of self-validation, to present 'truisms' which are not expected to be challenged (*The answer to that, of course, is that we are a superpower*).

Clearly, a modal of mental and visual perception, on the other hand, is the most 'dialogistically contractive' (White 2003: 28), in that it presents information which is categorically not expected to be challenged by the reader/ listener (*what we clearly see now are actual threats*). It may also function as a means of diverting attention away from potentially contentious propositions (*Clearly, the US military should not be the world's policeman).*

Obviously, another modal of mental and/or visual perception, is sometimes used in the DoD corpus as a means of introducing imprecise details and concepts as if they were 'obvious' to the listener when they may not be (*Obviously, it is desirable, if possible, to intercept an enemy missile while it is still boosting).*

Similar to *of course*, it may also signal concessive relations between clauses. *Certainly* may be used both positively and negatively. In its negative sense, it concedes the possibility of 'bad news' (*We certainly will be targeted overseas*), and may mask the genuine thoughts or intentions of the speaker (*That is certainly not imminent in our program*).

In conclusion, this study has attempted to show how an examination of the contexts surrounding four recurrent modal adverbs in a special corpus of rhetorical speeches can reveal multiple (and often overlapping) functions. Such items are considered worthy of investigation, since, as Corum (1975: 134) quite rightly observes, they are used 'in precisely those areas where speakers have something to gain or lose by their addressee's acceptance or rejection of what they are saying.'

References

Biber, D. and Finegan, E. (1988): "Adverbial stance types in English", *Discourse Processes,* 11, 1-34.

Biber, D. and Finegan, E. (1989): "Styles of stance in English: lexical and grammatical marking of evidentiality and affect", *Text*, 9, 1, 93-124.

Burchfield, R. W. (1999): *The New Fowler's Modern English Usage.* Oxford: Oxford University Press.

Chomsky, N. (2004): *Hegemony or Survival: America's Quest for Gobal Dominance*, London, Penguin.

Cobuild Learner's Dictionary (1996), Glasgow: HarperCollins.

Corum, C. (1975): "A pragmatic analysis of parenthetic adjuncts", in R.E. Grossman et al. (eds), *Papers from the Eleventh Regional Meeting of the Chicago Linguistic Society*, Chicago, University of Chicago, 131-141.

Fowler, H. W. (1926): *Dictionary of Modern English Usage*, Oxford, Oxford University Press.

Halliday, M. A. K. (1994): *An Introduction to Functional Grammar.* 2nd ed., London, Edward Arnold.

Hoye, L. (1997): *Adverbs and Modality in English*, London, Longman.

Hunston, S. E. and G. Thompson (eds.) (2000): *Evaluation in Text: Authorial Stance and the Construction of Discourse*, Oxford, Oxford University Press.

Jacobson, S. (1978): *On the Use, Meaning, and Syntax of English Preverbal Adverbs*, Stockholm, Almqvist and Wiksell.

Lakoff, G. and M. Johnson (1980): *Metaphors We Live By*, Chicago, Chicago University Press.

Lewis, D. (1999): "From modal adverbial to discourse connective: some rhetorical effects in present-day English", in J. Verschueren (ed.), *Pragmatics in 1998: Selected papers from the 6th International Pragmatics Conference*, Vol. 2, Antwerp, International Pragmatics Association, 363-375.

Partington, A. (2003): *The Linguistics of Political Argument: the spin-doctor and the wolf-pack at the White House*, London, Routledge.

Quirk, R., S. Greenbaum, G. Leech, and J. Svartvik (1985): *A Comprehensive Grammar of the English Language*, London, Longman.

Simon-Vandenbergen, A-M. and K. Aijmer (2007): *The Semantic Field of Modal Certainty: A Corpus-Based Study of English Adverbs*, Berlin, Mouton de Gruyter.

Thompson, G. and J. Zhou (2000): "Evaluation and organization in text: the structuring role of evaluative disjuncts", in S. Hunston and G. Thompson (eds.), *Evaluation in Text: Authorial Stance and the Construction of Discourse*, Oxford, Oxford University Press, 121-141.

White, P. (2003): "Engagement", at www.grammatics.com/appraisal (accessed 20 June 2008).

Variable development of intersubjectivity in Spanish

Javier Rivas
Esther Brown
University of Colorado at Boulder

1. Introduction

Grammaticalization is a gradual process whereby a lexical item or construction becomes a grammatical item or a grammatical item becomes even more grammatical. Grammaticalization processes start in very specific pragmatic and syntactic contexts of use, which, by means of reanalysis, allow the lexical item to acquire grammatical functions. As a result, the grammaticizing element typically undergoes decategorialization, phonological reduction and semantic bleaching (Brinton and Traugott 2005; Lehmann 1995; Hopper and Traugott 2003). In addition, as is noted by Bybee (2003), grammaticalized forms are more frequent than their original lexical source; they increase their productivity because they undergo syntactic expansion, that is to say, they progressively co-occur with different unit types. This, in turn, increases the text frequency of the forms undergoing grammaticalization.

Lexical items participating in grammaticalization processes generally undergo a shift from a more concrete/specific meaning to a more abstract/general meaning that typically relates to the speaker's attitude towards the message. This phenomenon, known as subjectification (Traugott 1995a: 31), manifests itself in the development of grammatical forms that explicitly refer to the speaker's perspective. Subjectification plays an important role in many grammaticalization processes, such as for example, the development of discourse markers, as is shown by Traugott (1982, 1995a, 1995b, 2003) and Traugott and Dasher (2002) regarding, among others, markers such as *in fact, indeed, actually* and *well.*

Discourse markers are items that connect portions of discourse by simultaneously referring anaphorically to the previous discourse and cataphorically to the subsequent discourse by imposing some type of relationship between them. Traugott (2003: 125) points out that discourse markers are subjective because they express the speaker or writer´s viewpoint towards the connectivity between clauses. Furthermore, discourse markers are also subjective in that they are concerned with the speaker's degree of knowledge of or involvement in the message s/he is conveying. The rise of these epistemic uses may eventually lead to intersubjectification, that is to say, "the development of meanings that encode speaker/writers' attention to the cognitive stances and social identities of addressees" (Traugott 2003: 124). Discourse markers acquire these intersubjective uses because they serve as hedges in the utterance and are used to soften the strength of the proposition.

Discourse markers may have different lexical and/or syntagmatic sources. *I don't know,* for example, arises from the construction 1ST PERSON SINGULAR SUBJECT PRONOUN *I* + CONTRACTED NEGATED AUXILIARY *don't* + VERB *know*. Bybee and Scheibman (1999) and Scheibman (2000) suggest that *I don't know* is a chunk in lexical representation, and is in reality, stored in the lexicon as any morphologically complex word would be. These authors based this hypothesis on the frequent repetition of the construction, which, consequently, undergoes phonological reduction. In fact, phonological reduction is almost the norm when *I don't know* is used pragmatically to express subjective and/or textual meanings.

Although some studies (for example, Bravo Caldera 2003; Cuenca and Marín 2009; Davidson 1996) identify *no sé*, the translation equivalent of *I don't know*, as an example of a discourse marker, there are no studies dedicated to the analysis of this construction exclusively. The purpose of the present paper is to determine the forms and functions of *no sé* through a large-scale quantitative analysis. We analyze 828 tokens that we extract from three corpora of spoken Spanish in New Mexico, Puerto Rico, and Madrid, Spain. As is the case with *I don't know*, we will show that *no sé* seems to have lexical status as a chunk in Spanish. We will base this analysis on phonological reduction and measures of the frequency of occurrence of *no sé*, such as the string frequency and the transitional probability of the combination. In addition, the analysis of the three varieties of Spanish mentioned above will allow us to show that the extent of intersubjective uses of *no sé* as a discourse marker varies according to dialect.

2. Background

In the last decades, there has been a growing interest in academic research on discourse markers (also known as *muletillas, pragmatic markers, discourse connectives, discourse operators*, *discourse particles,* among others). Research on these items has been undertaken from different perspectives by scholars such as Cortés Rodríguez (1991), Fraser (1990, 1999), Martín Zorraquino (1994), Portolés (1998), Schiffrin (1987), Traugott (1982, 1995), and Travis (2005), *inter alia.* Discourse markers are considered to be "sequentially dependent elements which bracket units of talk" (Schiffrin 1987: 31). Fraser (1999: 938) elaborates that discourse markers "impose a relationship between some aspect of the discourse segment they are a part of [...] and some aspect of a prior discourse segment." Typically, as noted by Portolés (1998: 26), the function of discourse markers is "guiar, de acuerdo con sus distintas propiedades morfosintácticas, semánticas y pragmáticas, las inferencias que se realizan en la comunicación [guide the inferences that take place in communication according to their different morphosyntactic, semantic, and pragmatic properties]."

The morphosyntactic sources of discourse markers are heterogeneous. In Spanish, they include invariable classes such as adverbs (*bien* 'well'), prepositions (*hasta* 'until') and conjunctions (*pero* ′but′), but also nouns (*¡hombre!* 'man!') and verbs (*mira* 'look'). In their development, they lose morphological and syntactic autonomy, and typically behave as independent elements. Concurrently their word frequency increases and the meaning becomes more general without fully losing its original semantic content (Hopper 1991; Schwenter 1996: 858). In those cases in which discourse markers come from more than one word — for example, *o sea*, which consists of the adversative conjunction *o* 'or' and the third person present subjunctive of *ser* 'be' — they form lexically cohesive elements.

Particular discourse markers previously analyzed in Spanish include *o sea* (Schwenter 1996), *bueno* (Serrano 1999), and *pues* (Garcés Gómez 1992), to name a few. Examples of these discourse markers found in our corpus follow:

(1) Puerto Rico
I: D. R. a cada rato va a allí.
E: Pero esos son, **o sea**, son permisos especiales, digo de turista.
′I: D. R. goes there all the time
E: But those are, I mean, they are special permits, I mean, tourist permits′

(2) Puerto Rico
E: ¿Y quiénes quedan en la compañía, P., que tú conozcas?
I: **Bueno**, todavía quedan dos o tres de los muchachos. J. creo que se va a retirar ahora.
′E: And who is still in the company, P., that you know?
I: Well, there are still two or three guys. J., I think he′s going to retire now'.

(3) Puerto Rico
E: Yo tengo que saber de dónde viene mi familia.
I: **Pues**, pregúntale a A. cuando lo veas a ver si él sabe más que yo de eso.
′E: I have to know where my family comes from.
I: Well, ask A. when you see him. He may know about that more than I do′

These and other discourse markers have been shown to possess certain linguistic characteristics which set them apart from other non discourse / pragmatic elements. They are prosodically independent. That is to say, they tend to occur either between pauses or intonation breaks, though not exclusively. Furthermore, they are invariable elements. They display no inflectional or derivational variation. For instance, *bueno*, as a discourse marker never reflects gender or number as the adjectival counterpart would (*bueno, buena, buenos, buenas*). Another characteristic of discourse markers is that they lie outside the limits of the clause. In fact, their scope often includes several clause combinations.

Much research has been conducted in English on the forms and functions of *I don′t know* (Bybee and Scheibman 1999; Pichler 2007; Scheibman 2000; Tsui 1991). These studies have shown that *I don′t know* conveys two main functions as a discourse marker: subjective and textual. In these uses, the construction departs from its original verbal meaning of 'lacking knowledge about something' to express subjective meanings relating to the epistemic stance of the speaker and textual meanings regarding turn management, topic development, and repair, *inter alia*. In addition, Bybee and Scheibman (1999: 303) find that, when *I don't know* performs a discourse function, it systematically undergoes phonological reduction; the vowel of the auxiliary *don't* is typically reduced to schwa, and, furthermore, in most cases the initial consonant may also be reduced to a flap. This phonological reduction is due to the high frequency of co-occurrence of the construction. This evidence suggest that *I don't know* constitutes a chunk in lexical representation. In line with the Exemplar Model of Lexical Representation (Bybee 2001; Pierrehumbert 2001), these authors suggest that this construction is stored in the lexicon as if it were a morphologically complex word.

In contrast to *I don't know*, its translation equivalent *no sé* has not been the subject of any previous analysis. In what follows, we will account for the forms and functions of *no sé* through the analysis of three Spanish dialects; New Mexico, Puerto Rico, and Madrid.

3. Data and methods

In order to determine the extent to which *no sé* is used as a discourse marker in Spanish, we use three separate corpora for our quantitative analyses. We relied upon transcriptions of sociolinguistic interviews conducted with native speakers from three different varieties of Spanish; New Mexican Spanish, Puerto Rican Spanish, and the Spanish of Madrid. We chose New Mexican data in order to investigate the role phonological reduction has (if any) in the occurrence of *no sé* as a discourse marker. In the traditional Spanish spoken in New Mexico and Southern Colorado, there is considerable phonological reduction of word and syllable initial /s/ (Brown 2005), making it possible to test for reduction within the *no sé* word pair. We also chose another American variety (the Puerto Rican data) and a European variety (Madrid, Spain) to enable cross-dialectal comparison.

The New Mexico data in this analysis comes from the New Mexico and Southern Colorado Linguistic Atlas Project (Bills and Vigil 2008). The NMCOSS project, initiated in 1991, documents, via interviews with 350 native speakers, the traditional language spoken throughout the state of New Mexico and the sixteen counties of southern Colorado by descendents of the first settlers to the region (Bills and Vigil 1999). The NMCOSS data was collected by trained field workers who tape-recorded interviews involving both controlled elicitation and guided conversation (Vigil 1989). The data reported upon in this study are taken solely from the free conversation portion of interviews with 18 males and 6 females, ranging in age from 36-90 years old and residing predominantly in rural regions of New Mexico (with 2 speakers coming from Albuquerque). From New Mexico we analyze 133 examples of *no sé* in approximately 97,000 words.

The Puerto Rican data are taken from transcriptions representing roughly 27 hours of conversation with eighteen native speakers. These conversations were collected and transcribed by a native speaker in Caguas, Cayey, and San Juan, Puerto Rico in 2000 (Cortés-Torres 2005). Speakers range in age from 24-90 years old. Interviews ranged in duration from one half hour to three hours in length. The corpus of Puerto Rican Spanish, which consists of approximately 370,000 words, contains 501 examples of *no sé.*

The analysis of *no sé* tokens in Madrid was conducted using a portion of the Corpus del Español (Davies 2002) online. We limit our coding to the first 194 occurrences of *no sé* in 'Habla Culta de Madrid.' There are 487 tokens of *no sé* in the total 140,000 number of words in Habla Culta de Madrid. We do not control for cross-corpora differences of size or for topic of conversation or sociolinguistic factors.

In both the American varieties of Spanish, the frequency of occurrence of *no sé* overall is very similar. In New Mexico, *no sé* has a text frequency of approximately 1,371 per million, and in Puerto Rico, the word pair has a text frequency of approximately 1,354 per million. In contrast, in Madrid the text frequency for *no sé* is more than twice that of the non-European dialects (approximately 3,474 per million). Based on this word frequency, we could predict that the Spanish variety would be the one to be more likely to have more developed discourse / pragmatic uses.

In order to determine the discourse / pragmatic and verbal functions of *no sé* in these varieties of Spanish we isolated all occurrences of the words *no* and *sé* contiguously. Across the three corpora of spontaneous conversational data this yielded 828 instances of *no sé*. We first identified lexical uses of *no sé*, which are cases in which its use only indicates a lack of knowledge of something on the part of the speaker. To do this, we considered both grammatical and semantic content. For example, instances in which *no sé* takes either a nominal or a clausal direct object are coded as verbal uses. Examples are found in (4) and (5).[1]

1 Thompson (2002) argues against the subordinate status of so-called complement clauses such as "si le pedí su nombre" in (5). Rather, examples such as (5) are "combinations of (i) CTP [Complement-Taking Predicate]-phrases, serving specific epistemic, evidential, and evaluative frames for the clauses they occur with, and (ii) finite indicative clauses, both declarative and interrogative" (Thompson 2002: 136). According to this analysis, *no sé* conveys similar semantic / pragmatic functions regardless of grammatical context. However, in line with Thompson (2002: 143), we have considered *no sé* as a discourse marker only in those contexts in which it does not occur with a so-called complement clause.

(4) Madrid (*no sé* + NP)
A. - Y es cierto, que...pero, la verdad, que yo **no sé** las dificultades que habrá, pero que no se hace.
´A: And it is true, that....but, to be honest, I don´t know about the dificulties that we will have, but that is not acceptable´

(5) New Mexico (*no sé* + *si* – clause)
E: Y **no sé** si le pedí su nombre, ¿cómo era, cómo se llamaba ella?
´E: And I don´t know if I asked her name, what was it, what was her name?
´

Lack of a complement did not automatically lead to a token being considered as a discourse marker. We also regarded as lexical those cases in which *no sé* only indicated lack of knowledge. This can be seen exemplified in (6).

(6) Puerto Rico
E: ¿Fue a todas las casas?
I: Yo **no sé**. Por lo menos vino a esta.
´E: Did he visit all the houses?
J: I don't know. He at least came to this one´

Overall, these methods allowed us to identify 616 lexical uses of *no sé*. The remaining 212 tokens were all coded as discourse markers.

Following Bybee and Scheibman (1999), Pichler (2007), Scheibman (2000), and Tsui (1991), we classified the discourse / pragmatic functions into three distinct categories: subjective, textual, or a combination of the two (both). Tokens were coded as 'subjective' when they were used by the speaker in order to soften the strength of their propositions, to avoid face-threatening acts, or attenuate disagreeing statements. In many cases the subjective uses of *no sé* co-occur with other discourse markers of epistemic stance like *yo creo* and *pues* in (7), or *o sea* and *como,* as in (8).

(7) New Mexico
M: *yo creo* que la mujer, *pues* **no sé**, se le fue con otro, pero *yo creo* que tenía problemas con el alcohol también.
´M: I think that his wife, well I don't know, he ran away with another man, but I think that she had alcohol problems too´

(8) Madrid
I: por esto, *o sea*, porque **no sé**, siempre estás *como* más acompañada.
'I: ´for that reason, [I mean?], because I don't know, you're always like not alone´

Tokens were coded as 'textual' when they were used by the speaker for turn management and/or topical development. Textual functions also include cases of hesitation and repair. Examples are given in (9) and (10).

(9) Madrid

I: Es que a mí me da muchísimo miedo el... el **no sé**, el... por una tontería, porque realmente cuando pasan esas cosas suelen ser por una tontería

´I: The thing is that I'm afraid of the…the I don't know, the…for something silly because when things like that happen it is generally for something silly´

(10) Madrid

B: Bueno, pues mira es que [...] a mí, la narrativa me gusta...estoy leyendo, pero eso ya no es novela, sino que es ensayo, es un libro de, de John Wilson, "El lenguaje y la búsqueda de la verdad" y después, novela, pues **no sé** y... ¿ tú qué tal?

A: Claro, lo que pasa es que yo veo, que a ti te interesa mucho más el ensayo...

´B: Well, look, the thing is... I like narrative...I´m reading, but this is not a novel but an essay, it´s a book by, by John Wilson, "Language and the search of truth", and then novel, well I don't know and…. how are you?

A: Sure, the thing is that I can see that you are much more interested in essays...´

In excerpt (9) *no sé* acts as a "filler" repair (Fox, Hayashi and Jasperson 1996: 204). The speaker placed *no sé* in the structural slot of the head noun of the subject NP of *dar miedo* 'frighten' as a means to delay the production of a next noun due during what appears to be a word search. In excerpt (10) *no sé* is used in an attempt to close a topic and leave the floor to the interlocutor.

Not all cases are either clearly subjective or textual, but rather seem to perform both functions simultaneously, as noted by Pichler (2007: 180). Examples are provided in (11) and (12).

(11) Puerto Rico

E: Yo le dije que yo no tenía, yo no tenía ganas de salir porque a mí no me gusta salir en despedida de año, pero, no me gusta, porque aquí la gente es muy salvaje guiando, no me quiero imaginar el día de despedida de año con dos o tres palos encima la gente guiando por ahí.

B: Pues hasta ahora-

E: Así que **no sé**, **no sé**, **no sé**. ¿Y qué hicieron el día de Navidad?

´E: I told him that I didn´t feel, I didn´t feel like going out because I don´t like going out on New Year´s Eve, because people here drive very aggressively, I can´t imagine on New Year´s Eve, people driving after having two or three drinks under their belt

B: Well, up to now-

E: So I don´t know, I don´t know, I don´t know. And what did you do on Christmas day?´

(12) Madrid

I: Es verdad que la preparación técnica es fundamental, es decir, el avance de... técnico creo que es fundamental para... para el progreso , pero creo que más fundamental todavía es el... **no sé**, las ideas, el mundo de las ideas

'I: It is true that technical training is essential, that is to say, technical advancement I think it is essential for progress, but I think that even more important yet is the...I don't know, ideology, the world of ideas'

In excerpt (11) it appears the speaker would like to close a topic, but at the same time could wish to soften the strong statement that she made in her previous turn, and hence the repetition of *no sé*. Excerpt (12) has another example of *no sé* as a filler repair (cf. with (9)) but at the same time the speaker seems to want to attenuate the previous utterance (which also includes the epistemic use of *creo*).

4. Results

The results of our quantitative analyses reveal that *no sé* has discourse functions in the three varieties. This word pair is used 194 times in the Madrid data that we analyzed, with 60% of the uses being pragmatic. This is summarized in Table 1. In Puerto Rico, of the 501 instances of *no sé*, 17% are used with a discourse / pragmatic function. In New Mexico, 10% of the tokens have a pragmatic function.

	N	%
Madrid	116/194	60
Puerto Rico	83/501	17
New Mexico	13/133	10

Table 1. Percent of pragmatic uses in three dialects

As we mention before, Bybee and Scheibman (1999) and Scheibman (2000) discuss phonological reduction and frequency of co-occurrence of the individual lexical items that make up the construction *I don't know*. They suggest this reduction is an indicator of its discourse marker status differentiating its use from other (non-pragmatic) uses of *I don't know*. Results of our analyses suggest that *no sé* behaves significantly differently than the lexical combination of *no* + other 1st person singular high frequency verbs. This can be seen summarized in Table 2.

	Madrid	Puerto Rico	New Mexico
no sé	487	501	133
no puedo	25	83	17
no quiero	8	34	8
no tengo	52	70	12
no soy	15	13	1
no voy	15	42	4
no estoy	24	21	5
no creo	37	19	5

Table 2. String frequency of high frequency verbs (1st person singular indicative)

The tokens of use for *no sé* listed in Table 2 reflect an interesting fact. In all three varieties, the string frequency (the token frequency of a multiword combination) of *no* + *sé* is quite high. In Madrid, it occurs 487 times, in Puerto Rico 501, and in New Mexico 133 times. This word combination frequency can be compared to the other verbs of high frequency listed in the Table. In Madrid, the 'no + verb' combination with the next highest text frequency is *no tengo* with 52 occurrences. In Puerto Rico it is *no puedo* with 83 occurrences, and in New Mexico it is also *no puedo* with 17 occurrences. These are all significant differences in string frequency (*no sé* vs. *no tengo* Madrid p = 0.0000, Chi-square = 4321.407, *no sé* vs. *no puedo* Puerto Rico p = 0.0000, Chi-square = 299.8766, *no sé* vs. *no puedo* New Mexico p = 0.0000, Chi-square = 89.90075).

Another difference to highlight between *no sé* and the other verb combinations is the strikingly high transitional probability (Jurafsky et al. 2001) of the combination. The transitional probability (or conditional probability) of a particular target word (*sé* in this case) given a previous word (*no*) is calculated from our corpus by calculating the number of occurrences of *no sé* and dividing by the number of times the word *sé* occurs. This calculation controls for the frequency of the previous word. Some word dyads can have a high string frequency simply as a result of being two highly frequent words (e.g.; *es el*). As Jurafsky et al. (2001: 272) note, however, unlike string frequency, "the conditional probability would be high only if the second word was particularly likely to follow the first."

The transitional probability of *no sé* is quite high, as can be seen summarized in Table 3. Of all the tokens of *sé* in the corpus (N = 565 in Madrid, for example), 86% appear after *no*, yielding the construction *no sé*. A similarly high transitional probability is found for *no sé* in the Puerto Rican and New Mexican data (64% and 88% respectively). The implication of such a high transitional probability, and high string frequency as discussed in the preceding paragraph, is the increased likelihood of lexical storage as a chunk in all three dialects (Bybee 2001:163; Bush 2001: 269).

	Madrid	Puerto Rico	New Mexico
no sé	487/565 = 86%	501/776 = 64%	133/151 = 88%
no puedo	25/77 = 32%	83/181 = 46%	17/50 = 34%
no quiero	8/44 = 18%	34/173 = 20%	8/41 = 20%
no tengo	52/280 = 19%	70/498 = 14%	12/98 = 12%
no soy	15/90 = 17%	13/123 = 11%	1/10 = 10%
no voy	15/133 = 11%	42/493 = 9%	4/43 = 1%
no estoy	24/157 = 15%	21/318 = 7%	5/23 = 22%
no creo	37/512 = 7%	19/358 = 5%	5/127 = 4%

Table 3. Percentage of high frequency verbs (1st person singular indicative) directly preceded by lexical item *no*

As a chunk, does *no sé* exhibit phonological reduction as *I don't know* was shown to do in Bybee and Scheibman (1999). This is testable in the New Mexican data in which syllable and word-initial /s/ has been shown to variably aspirate or delete. Word-initial /s/ reduces in this variety at a rate of 16% overall and at a rate of 30% overall in word-medial, syllable-initial position (Brown 2005: 815). If *no sé* were stored as two distinct words, we might expect reduction of the /s/ in *sé* to reflect rates found for other word-initial /s/ tokens. However, reduction in the word-initial /s/ of the form *sé* in the combination *no sé* is 36% (N = 116), as can be seen summarized in Table 4. This reduction rate more closely reflects reduction of the word-medial, syllable-initial /s/ tokens. Further, reduction of the /s/ of *sé* outside the combination *no sé* (in combinations such as *yo sé, sí sé*, etc.) is significantly lower at 6% (N = 32, p = .0021, X2 = 10.49417). This result is suggestive that *no sé* has lexical status as a chunk.

	N	% Reduction
word-initial /s/	415/2594	16
word-medial, syllable initial /s/	928/3048	30
/s/ reduction in *no sé* dyad	43/116	36
/s/ reduction in *sé* (outside of dyad)	2/32	6

Table 4. Percentage of syllable-initial /s/ reduction in New Mexico

Interesting, however, is the result obtained by just examining the phonological reduction of the very few tokens of *no sé* as a discourse marker in New Mexico. Following Bybee and Scheibman (1999), we might predict higher reduction when used with a pragmatic meaning as these authors find for *I don't know*. However, our findings do not bear this out, as Table 5 summarizes.[2]

2 We have very low token numbers for this analysis and all conclusions are thus tentative.

	Lexical / Verbal Uses	Discourse / Pragmatic Uses
Non-reduced ([s])	75	6
Reduced ([h], [ø])	43	1
Percent reduction	36%	14%

Table 5. Phonological reduction of *no sé* in New Mexican Spanish

Initial /s/ reduction is greater (36%) in lexical uses than in discourse / pragmatic uses (14%). This may suggest that phonological reduction is not characteristic of this particular discourse marker in Spanish and/or may simply reflect the lower degree of entrenchment of *no sé* as a discourse marker in New Mexico which we outline in the discussion.

The item *no sé* appears to have chunk status based upon its usage (Tables 2 and 3) and on the higher than average reduction rate in the word combination (36%) (Table 4). If *no sé* is stored as a single lexical unit, this implies it is not necessarily analyzed as a negative particle (*no*) + verb (*sé*), but rather is a prime candidate to be adopted as a discourse marker (with no morphological variation and lack of complementation).

As a discourse marker, we could predict that *no sé* would demonstrate different linguistic behavior from the lexical uses (for example, regarding co-occurrence with subject pronouns) because it no longer performs true verbal functions. We analyze co-occurrence of *no sé* with the subject pronoun *yo* for both lexical and pragmatic uses (as summarized in Table 6). On the left we list uses of *yo* with the discourse / pragmatic function of *no sé* and on the right uses of the subject pronoun with the verbal function of *no sé*.

	Discourse Markers			Verbs		
	yo no sé	*no sé*	% *yo*	*yo no sé*	*no sé*	% *yo*
Madrid	5	111	4	13	65	17
Puerto Rico	30	53	36	211	206	51
New Mexico	9	4	69	49	71	41

Table 6. Use of subject pronoun yo with discourse/pragmatic vs. verbal uses of *no sé* in three varieties of Spanish

In Madrid, when used with a discourse function, the subject pronoun appears in just 4% of the cases. Conversely, when used with a verbal function in Madrid, subject pronoun usage is significantly higher at 17% (p = .0036, X2 = 8.459556). Puerto Rico is a variety of Spanish with high overt subject pronoun usage (Cameron 1993: 306, Hochberg 1986: 615, Morales 1997: 155), and rates of *yo* usage are, perhaps not surprisingly, higher. A similar pattern of *no sé* usage is found in this variety however. When *no sé* functions as a discourse marker, the subject pronoun co-occurs at a rate of 36%. With true verbal function, the subject pronoun is used significantly more, in 51% of the cases ($p = .0161$, $X2 = 5.792954$).

In the New Mexican data, we see a different pattern of pronominal usage.[3] Despite frequency per million of *yo* being lower in New Mexico (10,927) than in Puerto Rico (15,056), when *no sé* functions as a discourse marker, overt *yo* usage is quite high (69%). In fact, subject pronoun usage for the discourse marker is significantly higher than the usage with lexical meaning ($p < .05$, $X2 = 3.846318$). We will comment on this in our discussion below.

Further results of our quantitative analyses are summarized in Table 7. Through an analysis of *no sé* tokens that perform a pragmatic function, it is apparent that it fulfills the same discourse functions in the three varieties of Spanish we analyze. This can be seen by the fact that in all three dialects, *no sé* performs the three functions that we examined; subjective, textual, and both. In all three varieties, the most frequent use of *no sé* is the subjective function (Madrid 59%, New Mexico 85%, Puerto Rico 76%). In both New Mexico and Puerto Rico, however, the number of textual uses (NM 8%, PR 18%) is considerably lower than that found in Madrid (28%). Subjective~textual uses are the least frequent in all three dialects as Table 7 makes evident.

	Madrid	New Mexico	Puerto Rico
Subjective	69 (59 %)	11 (85%)	63 (76%)
Textual	32 (28 %)	1 (8%)	15 (18 %)
Subjective~Textual	15 (12%)	1 (8%)	5 (6%)
	N = 116	N = 13	N = 83

Table 7. Discourse / pragmatic functions of *no sé* in three varieties of Spanish.[4]

5. Discussion

As a discourse marker, *no sé* has limited use in the New Mexican variety. This is evident in Table 1, where we can see that out of the 133 tokens of *no sé* we found in the corpus, only 10% (N = 13) are used discursively. Despite the low number of examples, we nevertheless see a similar pattern of usage to the other two dialects (Table 2, Table 3, Table 7). It appears, however, that when compared to the other varieties of Spanish, *no sé* is a less preferred discourse marker in New Mexico.

This lack of subjective strength of *no sé* as a discourse marker is perhaps reflected in the result we obtained regarding subject pronoun usage (Table 6). Overall in New Mexican Spanish, the average rate of the subject pronoun *yo* expression is 34% (Torres Cacoullos and Travis, forthcoming). Contrary to the other varieties of Spanish, in New Mexico when *no sé* is used pragmatically,

3 This result is tentative owing to the low token number (N = 13).

4 Percentage Subjective use Madrid vs. PR: $p < .05$, $X2 = 5.841602$.

there is a strikingly high occurrence of *yo* (69%). As has been noted by Davidson (1996: 551), the subject pronoun when used explicitly adds 'pragmatic weight' to an utterance, and specifically can trigger more abstract readings of certain verbs. We interpret this result in Table 6, therefore, as indicative of the fact that *no sé* does not have a strong subjective or textual use in this variety without the added weight of the subject pronoun.

The Puerto Rican variety of Spanish appears to hold an intermediary position between the other two varieties we study. As seen in Table 1, the number of uses as a discourse marker is higher than in New Mexico, at a rate of 17%, yet does not reach the high usage seen in Madrid. As in New Mexico, the preferred pragmatic use of *no sé* is subjective (as seen in Table 7). The number of textual uses is higher than in New Mexico - 18%. It may be the case that the textual function is taken up by other discourse markers in Puerto Rico and New Mexico [e.g. *so* or *entonces* (Aaron 2004)].

The results of our analysis on the Madrid data reveal an important difference between the American dialects and the European variety. Firstly, in the Peninsular variety, the proportion of *no sé* tokens that are pragmatic as opposed to lexical is significantly higher. In Madrid, 60% of uses have a discourse / pragmatic function (Table 1). Further, just looking at pragmatic uses of *no sé*, in Madrid it is used with textual functions significantly more than in the Puerto Rican variety (Table 7), revealing significant differences in usage between the varieties.[5] The dialectal differences we find between America and Spain may reveal similar, but divergent, diachronic pathways.

Traugott (1982, 1995b) and Traugott and Dasher (2002) have argued that the development of discourse markers depends upon changes towards subjectivity. There is a pathway of change in which items that become discourse markers change from a more objective/propositional/non-subjective use to a more subjective, pragmatic use. Traugott and Dasher (2002: 155) point out that discourse markers are subjective because they "indicate the SP[speaker]/W[riter]'s rhetorical, metatextual, stance towards the cohesiveness of the discourse being developed" by means of the way the speaker chooses to deal with the preceding information: s/he may choose to develop, qualify, background, or foreground it. Furthermore, discourse markers are subjective in that they reflect the degree of knowledge a speaker has regarding his/her message. In the case of *no sé*, we have evidence of this subjective stance in cases in which *no sé* co-occurs with other epistemic markers such as *yo creo, me parece, pues, bueno, o sea,* etc. The function of these uses of *no sé* is to attenuate disagreeing statements, avoid face-threatening acts, and soften the propositional stance. In so doing it acquires *inter*subjective uses, not just subjective (Traugott and Dasher 2002: 155) in that they take into consideration the interlocutor.

---

5 It does not achieve statistical significance for the New Mexican variety perhaps as a result of the low token numbers we have for the New Mexico data.

Intersubjectivity is also a key element of textual uses in that these uses encompass issues such as turn management. As we mentioned previously, textual instances of *no sé* include functions such as closing of a topic and turn-closing. This seems to suggest to us that *no sé* could proceed along the following grammaticalization cline (adapted from Traugott and Dasher 2002: 187): non-subjective/propositional uses > epistemic/subjective uses > intersubjective uses. As we noted in our analyses, there are more textual uses in Madrid than in other the other varieties we analyze (Table 7) suggesting that this discourse marker has extended its use further in Spain than in America. In fact, Traugott (2003: 130) points out that the development from subjectification to intersubjectification is unidirectional, that is to say, intersubjectification can only exist after some degree of subjectification.

The dialectal division we find between America and Spain in the use of *no sé* may reflect a diachronic pathway. An alternate explanation may be found in the argument put forth in Company Company (2002). Through an analysis of relative frequencies of four distinct syntactic forms (nominal possession, diminutives, leismo, present perfect), Company Company (2002: 43) outlines a dialect division between Mexican and Peninsular Spanish, noting that the:

> "español de España y español de México gramaticalizan varias zonas de sus respectivos sistemas siguiendo dos pautas distintas de gramaticalización, las cuales obedecen a una distinta selección o perfilamiento de un mismo complejo semántico – los rasgos externos o referenciales el primer dialecto, los rasgos internos, relacionales o valorativos el segundo."
>
> [Spanish of Spain and Spanish of Mexico grammaticalize different areas of the respective systems following two different grammaticalization processes which respond to a different selection or outline of a similar semantic complex – external or referential features the former, internal, relational or evaluative traits the latter.]

In Mexico the syntactic phenomena Company Company (2002) highlights have developed primarily subjective uses, whereas in Spain, these same syntactic phenomena are used referentially. Company Company (2002:65) proposes a dialect split, therefore, based on the fact that the four independent syntactic phenomena she outlines behave in similar ways. We lack, in our current analysis, historical data that will help determine if the synchronic data we present, are in fact representative of a unified diachronic pathway of change, with Madrid leading the way, or rather whether each variety basically selects different discourse markers to perform these textual functions.

Acknowledgements

We are indebted to the New Mexico and Southern Colorado Linguistic Atlas directors Neddy Vigil and Garland Bills for allowing us use of their data. We would also like to express our gratitude to Mayra Cortés-Torres for sharing with us the interviews that she transcribed and collected in Puerto Rico. We would like to acknowledge helpful comments we received on an earlier version of this work by Ivo Sánchez and by audience members at CILC 09 in Murcia, Spain.

References

Aaron, J. (2004): " 'So respetamos un tradición del uno al otro': so and entonces in New Mexican Bilingual Discourse", *Spanish in Context* 1, 2, 161-179.

Bills, G. and N. Vigil (1999): "Ashes to ashes: the historical basis for dialect variation in New Mexican Spanish", *Romance Philology*, 53, 43-67.

Bills, G. and N. Vigil (2008): *The Spanish Language of New Mexico and Southern Colorado. A Linguistic Atlas*, Albuquerque, NM, The University of New Mexico Press.

Blecua, J. et al. (eds.) (1994): *Actas del Congreso de la Lengua Española. Sevilla, 7 al 10 de Octubre de* 1992, Madrid, Instituto Cervantes.

Bravo Cladera, N. (2003). "Un estudio de los marcadores del discurso y su distribución en interacciones diádicas de jóvenes bilingües", in F. Sánchez Miret, (ed.), vol. II, 126-133.

Brinton, L. and E. Traugott (2005): *Lexicalization and Language Change*, Cambridge, Cambridge University Press.

Brown, E. (2005): "New Mexican Spanish: insight into the variable reduction of 'la ehe inihial' (/s-/)", *Hispania* 88, 4, 813-824.

Bush, N. (2001): "Frequency effects and word-boundary palatalization in English", in J. Bybee and P. Hopper (eds.), 255-280.

Bybee, J. (2001): *Phonology and Language Use*, Cambridge, Cambridge University Press.

Bybee, J. (2003): "Mechanisms of change in grammaticalization: the role of frequency", in B. Joseph and R. Janda (eds.), 602-623.

Bybee, J. (2007): *Frequency of Use and the Organization of Language*, Cambridge, Cambridge University Press.

Bybee, J. and J. Scheibman (1999): "The effect of usage on degree of constituency: the reduction of don't in English", *Linguistics*, 37, 4, 575-596. [Reed. in J. Bybee, 294-311].

Bybee, J. and P. Hopper (eds.) (2001): *Frequency and the Emergence of Linguistic Structure*, Amsterdam/Philadelphia, John Benjamins.

Cameron, R. (1993): "Ambiguous agreement, functional compensation, and nonspecific tú in the Spanish of San Juan, Puerto Rico and Madrid, Spain", *Language Variation and Change*, 5, 305-334.

Company Company, C. (2002): "Gramaticalización y dialectología comparada. Una isoglosa sintáctico-semántica del español", *Dicenda. Cuadernos de Filología Hispánica*, 20, 39-71.

Cortés Rodríguez, L. (1991): *Sobre Conectores, Expletivos y Muletillas en Español*, Málaga, Editorial Librería Ágora.

Cortés-Torres, M. (2005): *La Perífrasis Estar + -Ndo en el Español Puertorriqueño: Variación Dialectal o Contacto Lingüístico?* Unpublished PhD dissertation, University of New Mexico, Albuquerque, New Mexico, USA.

Cuenca, M. and M. Marín (2009): "Co-occurrence of discourse markers in Catalan and Spanish oral narrative", *Journal of Pragmatics*, 41, 899-914.

Davidson, B. (1996): " 'Pragmatic weight' and Spanish subject pronouns: the pragmatic and discourse uses of 'tú' and 'yo' in spoken Madrid Spanish", *Journal of Pragmatics*, 26, 543-565.

Davies, M. (2002-): *Corpus del Español (100 million words, 1200s-1900s)*, (http://www.corpusdelespanol.org).

Fox. B., M. Hayashi and R. Jasperson (1996): "Resources and repair: a cross-linguistic study of syntax and repair", in E. Ochs, E. Schegloff and S. Thompson (eds.), 185-237.

Fraser, B. (1990): "An approach to discourse markers", *Journal of Pragmatics*, 14, 383-395.

Fraser, B. (1999): "What are discourse markers?", *Journal of Pragmatics*, 31, 931-952.

Garcés Gómez, M. (1992): "El operador discursivo pues en el español hablado", *Romantistisches Jahrbuch*, 43, 261-276.

Hickey, R. (ed.) (2003): *Motives for language change*, Cambridge, Cambridge University Press.

Hochberg, J. (1986): "Functional compensation for /s/ deletion in Puerto Rican Spanish", *Language* 62, 3, 609-621.

Hopper, P. (1991): "On some principles of grammaticalization", in E. Traugott E. and B. Heine (eds.), 17-36.

Hopper, P. and E. Traugott (2003): *Grammaticalization*, Cambridge, Cambridge University Press.

Joseph, B. and R. Janda (eds.) (2003): *The Handbook of Historical Linguistics*, Oxford/New York, Blackwell.

Jurafsky, D., A. Bell, M. Gregory and W. Raymond (2001): "Probabilistic relations between words: evidence from reduction in lexical production", in J. Bybee and P. Hopper (eds.), 309–335.

Lehmann, C. (1995): *Thoughts on Grammaticalization*, Munich, LINCOM EUROPA.

Lehmann, W. and Y. Malkiel (eds.) (1982): *Perspectives on Historical Linguistics*, Amsterdam/Philadelphia, John Benjamins.

Martín Zorraquino, M. (1994): "Gramática del discurso: los llamados marcadores del discurso", in J. Blecua et al. (eds.), 709-720.

Morales, A. (1997): "La hipótesis funcional y la aparición de sujeto no nominal: el español de Puerto Rico", *Hispania*, 80, 1, 153-165.

Ochs, E., E. Schegloff and S. Thompson (eds.) (1996): *Interaction and Grammar*, Cambridge, Cambridge University Press.

Pichler, H. (2007): "Form-function relations in discourse: the case of I DON'T KNOW", *Newcastle Working Papers in Linguistics*, 13, 174-187.

Pierrehumbert, J. (2001): "Exemplar dynamics: word frequency, lenition and contrast", in J. Bybee and P. Hopper (eds.), 123-136.

Portolés, J. (1998): *Marcadores del Discurso*, Barcelona, Ariel.

Rivera-Mills, S. and D. Villa (forthcoming): *Spanish of the Southwest: A Language in Transition*, Frankfurt, Iberoamericana/Vervuert.

Sánchez Miret, F. (ed.) (2003): *Actas del XXIII Congreso Internacional de Lingüística y Filología Románica. Salamanca 24-30 de Septiembre de 2001*, Tubingen, Max Niemeyer Verlag.

Scheibman, J. (2000): "*I dunno*: a usage-based account of the phonological reduction of don´t in American English conversation", *Journal of Pragmatics*, 32, 105-124.

Schiffrin, D. (1987): *Discourse Markers*, Cambridge, Cambridge University Press.

Schwenter, S. (1996): "Some reflections on o sea: a discourse marker in Spanish", *Journal of Pragmatics*, 25, 855-874.

Sedano, M., A. Bolívar and M. Shiro (eds.) (2006): *Haciendo Lingüística. Homenaje a Paola Bentivoglio*, Caracas, Universidad Central de Venezuela.

Serrano, M. (1999): "*Bueno* como marcador de inicio de turno y contraposición: estudio sociolingüístico", *International Journal of the Sociology of Language*, 82, 115-133.

Stein, D. and S. Wright (1995): *Subjectivity and Subjectivisation: Linguistic Perspectives*, Cambridge, Cambridge University Press.

Thompson, S. (2002): "Object complements and conversation: Towards a realistic account", *Studies in language*, 26, 1, 125-163 [Reed. as "Hacia una explicación de los 'complementos objeto' y la conversación", in M. Sedano, A. Bolívar and M. Shiro (eds.), 347-392].

Torres Cacoullos, R. and C. Travis (forthcoming): "Variable *yo* expression in New Mexico: English influence?", in S. Rivera-Mills and D. Villa (eds.).

Traugott, E. (1982): "From prepositional to textual and expressive meanings: some semantic-pragmatic aspects of grammaticalization", in W. Lehmann and Y. Malkiel (eds.), 245-271.

Traugott, E. (1995a): "Subjectification in grammaticalization", in D. Stein, and S. Wright (eds.), 31-54.

Traugott, E. (1995b): "The role of the development of discourse markers in a theory of grammaticalization" (http://www.stanford.edu/~traugott/papers/discourse.pdf).

Traugott, E. (2003): "From subjectification to intersubjectification", in R. Hickey, R. (ed.), 124-139.

Traugott, E. and B. Heine (eds.) (1991): *Approaches to Grammaticalization*, Amsterdam/Philadelphia, John Benjamins.

Traugott, E. and R. Dasher (2002): *Regularity in Semantic Change*, Cambridge, Cambridge University Press.

Travis, C. (2005): *Discourse Markers in Colombian Spanish: A Study in Polysemy*, Berlin/New York, Mouton de Gruyter.

Tsui, A. (1991): "The pragmatic functions of *I don't know*", *Text*, 11, 4, 607-622.

Vigil, N. (1989): "Database for a linguistic atlas of the Spanish of New Mexico and Southern Colorado, computer methods in dialectology", *Journal of English Linguistics Special Issue*, 1, 69-75.

An exploratory data-driven analysis for describing discourse organization

Lydia-Mai Hồ-Đắc
Université de Toulouse-UTM

1. Introduction

Discourse or text organization is usually difficult to study with corpus linguistics methods because of the apparent incompatibility between the qualitative nature of discourse analysis and the quantitative requirements of corpus linguistics:

> "[I]t has been much less common to study discourse organization from a corpus perspective. In fact, these two subfields have research goals and methods that might be considered incompatible: The study of discourse organization – linguistic structure 'beyond the sentence' – is usually based on detailed analysis of a single text, resulting in qualitative linguistic description of the textual organization. In contrast, corpus studies are based on analysis of all texts in a corpus, utilizing quantitative analysis measures to identify typical distributional patterns that occur across texts." (Biber et al. 2007: 2)

The methodology we present here on a French corpus provides an alternative solution to this incompatibility, allowing a data-driven approach to discourse organization. It aims at describing high-level discourse structures (beyond the sentence) and discourse markers via a quantitative analysis based on automatic and systematic marking of linguistic features in a fairly large corpus of long written texts (c. 700.000 words in total). Three basic principles govern the methodology: it applies to long expository texts where discourse organization is necessary; it is based on the premise that discourse signalling results from an interaction between several forces and may also concern extra-linguistic features; finally, only elements occurring in sentence-initial, paragraph-initial and section-initial position are taken into account.

Section 2 situates our research question, which is the signalling of discourse organization and the discourse function of elements in initial position. Section 3 then exposes the range of cues taken into account. Section 4 details each step of the methodology that we need in order to describe the data configurations in section 5.

2. Discourse organization viewed through initial position

2.1. Discourse organization, text segmentation and sequentiality

The object of this study concerns 'discourse organization' or 'text organization.' These terms – considered here as synonymous – convey the idea that text is not a bag of words, a bag of sentences, a bag of paragraphs but should be seen as a structured object. Discourse organization is seen as the consequence of the "linearization problem" (Levelt 1981). Although the representation we have in our mind is not linear (similar to a picture, a form, a scene, etc.), the text (either written or oral) must be linear. Text is a succession of sentences because sentences must appear one after the other in time. This lack of isomorphism between mental representations and what we must produce or what we have to interpret constitutes a major problematic in the study of discourse organization.

The issue of sequentiality in text as defined in Goutsos (1996: 501) proposes a solution by seeing text as a "periodic alternation of transition and continuation spans." His model of sequentiality distinguishes three levels of discourse structure. The cognitive level sees the writer's mental representation as structured by the basic strategies of continuity and discontinuity. The linguistic level is concerned with the techniques available to realize these strategies. The textual level is the material result of these strategies and techniques. Text segmentation into continuation and transition spans pertains to the textual level.

Text segmentation can be viewed from the continuity angle and the discontinuity angle. From the continuity angle, linguistic units cluster around a specific interpretation criterion. From the discontinuity angle, text is divided into segments or spans (in Goutsos' terminology). Although Goutsos considers only thematic (dis)continuity, we argue that the specific interpretation criteria which bind text units together may concern different levels of organization: concerning part of the subject matter (e.g. thematic continuity but also space/time reference) or the presentation process (e.g. rhetorical or document structure). A shift between two segments may be a referential break, the end or opening of a discourse frame, a rhetorical articulation or the end or beginning of a paragraph or section.

Example 1[1] constitutes a good illustration of multi-level discourse sequentiality. In this extract, a string of cohesive devices establishes continuity around the topic of "debate between specialists of transatlantic relations." All these devices (in italics) may be interpreted as cues helping the reader understand that the writer keeps referring to the same thing, i.e. that there is a main continuation span constructed around a topical continuity.

(1) ***Since the end of the cold war***, *the debate between specialists of transatlantic relations has tended to be satisfied with worthy pronouncements and much simplification. It has not shown sufficient concern for the breadth of the changes taking place [...].*

More recently, *the discussion* has been focusing on a supposed gap in social values between the two shores of the Atlantic, an idea to which the events of 9/11 have put an end. *This debate* is ongoing, but it is now limited to the domain of social analysis. **In foreign policy terms**, *this discussion* on continental shift

[1] We have translated examples from our French-language corpus to help comprehension.

has turned into an opposition between the unilateralism of America's policy and the multilateralism of its European partners.

At the same time, example 1 has three shift cues opening new circumstance frames (in bold type). First a temporal frame is introduced via an adverbial setting a time reference (*Since the end of the cold war*). This time reference remains valid all through the first paragraph. This scope effect builds, at the textual level, a first (sub-)continuation span.

The second paragraph begins with another time adverbial *(More recently*) expressing another time reference. This adverbial introduces a new temporal frame and signals a shift. As previously, this frame covers the entire paragraph. There is also a third frame – a "notional" frame this time –, introduced with the adverbial *In foreign policy terms,* fitting inside the temporal frame introduced with *More recently*.

Figure 1 gives a representation of this complex sequentiality: a continuation span containing several other (sub-)continuation spans associated with a different component of the process (e.g. topics and circumstances). The Gestalt figure/ground distinction helps us define the different components of the process. The participants or the topics of the process are seen as "figure" whereas the circumstances of the process have to do with "ground" (by setting the scene in which the figure appears).

In this example, transition spans are minimal, consisting in the space between two sentences or two paragraphs. All the continuity cues (cohesive devices) and the discontinuity cues (initial adverbials) mentioned occur in sentence-initial position. This positioning is not a coincidence but a correlation between initial position and the signalling of sequentiality in discourse—that is, the indication of whether there is discontinuity or continuity.

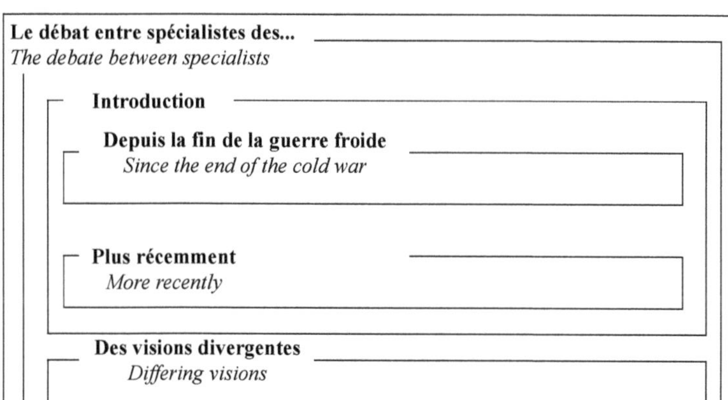

Figure 1. Representation of sequentiality in example 1

2.2. The role of elements in initial position in discourse organization

Some cognitive studies (e.g. Enkvist 1989; Givón 1995) claim that what the writer expresses first corresponds to 'crucial' information, i.e. information necessary to the correct interpretation of the purpose of a given message. This concept is derived from the *crucial information first* principle (CIF) defined by Enkvist (1989) as a counterpart of the *old information first* principle. According to information flow, crucial information can correspond to old information or to new information: either the writer wants to indicate that incoming information is in continuation with preceding information; or he wants to indicate that there is a shift or a break. In both cases, this indication is given by the elements coming first in the message. In the case of continuation, these first elements may correspond to given information. In the case of shift, the first elements express information which provides an orientation with respect to what comes next, for example, setting new circumstances. In other words, elements in initial position participate in the management of discourse organization by fulfilling a dual function: orientation and connection. These two functions define what is called *theme* in Systemic Functional Linguistics (Halliday 1985).

The first function associated with elements in initial position consists in a backward-looking connection: elements in initial position connect the rest of the message to the preceding discourse by expressing elements that allow the reader to integrate incoming information in a coherent way into the mental model in construction. As Halliday (1970: 161) states: "Theme is the peg on which the message is hung."

In this way, elements in initial position are cohesive devices. For example, a common strategy used to indicate that incoming information is linked to the preceding information is to express given information in theme position and new information in rheme position (this is the old information first principle). In example 1, all grammatical subjects (except the first) connect the sentence to the preceding one, creating a topical continuity in this continuation span. Sentence-initial time adverbials also connect the first paragraph to the second paragraph by establishing a temporal organization between them.

At the same time as they establish a connection, elements in initial position orient discourse by setting preliminary interpretation criteria for the incoming message. Because they have been read first, they have a stronger influence on the interpretation of the incoming message than later elements (see Thompson 1985; Hasselgård 1996; Le Draoulec and Péry-Woodley 2003). If we focus particularly on initial elements occurring before the grammatical subject (detached elements), we find elements that may set a discourse frame for the interpretation, as stated by Chafe (1976: 53): "[elements in initial position] limit the domain of applicability of the main predication to a certain restricted domain [...] set[ting] the spatial, temporal or individual framework within which the predication holds."

Orientation is typically the case with the three initial adverbials in example 1. Grammatical subjects may also function as orienters for the rest of the message. In example 1, the first subject establishes the main topic of the entire paragraph (and even of the section).

Initial position is a good starting point for the study of discourse organization: from a linguistic perspective, it allows us to approach the complexity of discourse organization (by taking into account initial adverbials and grammatical subjects) and, from a computational perspective, it makes it possible, thanks to a precise definition of the unit under analysis, to carry out a comparative quantitative analysis based on automatic marking.

3. Configurations of cues for signalling discourse organization

Recent linguistic studies (Jacques and Rebeyrolle 2006; Péry-Woodley 2005) state that discourse organization is signalled by configurations of cues rather than by single markers. Writers and readers have to manage several levels of organization which include not only thematic continuity but also time and space reference, rhetorical articulation and document structure. Discourse cues may simultaneously contribute to several of these interdependent levels. Strong markers (i.e. lexical expressions absolutely correlated with a designed discourse function) are not as common as are interactions of soft cues. A global view of discourse organization is needed in order to discover these interactions. Such a global view may be achieved by combining three kinds of cues: lexico-syntactic elements, text position and text-type.

3.1. Lexico-syntactic elements

The set of lexico-syntactic elements taken into account corresponds to all the elements occurring in initial position. In this study, initial position is delimited to the preverbal zone of the first sentence of the different textual units (sections, paragraphs, sentences). Figure 2 represents the variety of elements found in this position in French.

A first distinction is made between special and canonical constructions. Special constructions correspond to sentences where the grammatical subject has no referential meaning. These constructions may be used to focus on one part of the sentence (as in cleft constructions or left dislocations), to introduce new referents (e.g. presentational constructions) or to indirectly express an evaluation of the process being expressed (e.g. *it*-extraposition). In canonical constructions, the grammatical subject has referential meaning and may constitute the topic of the sentence.

A second distinction related to syntactic integration is made between detached elements and integrated elements. Detached elements are those which occur before the grammatical subject, separated or not by a comma (e.g. adverbials, appositions, fronted adjuncts). Integrated elements correspond to grammatical subjects.

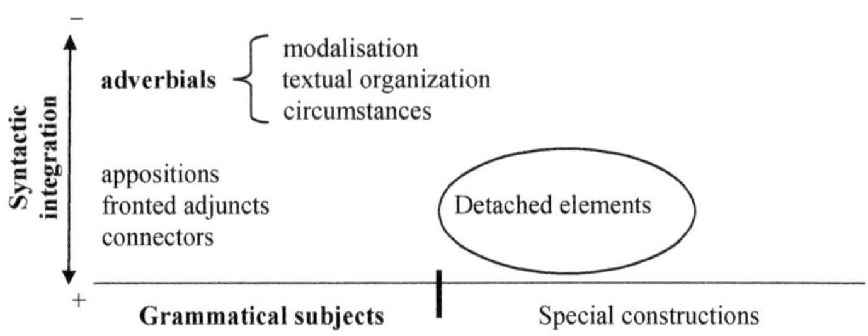

Figure 2. Lexico-Syntactic elements in preverbal zone

3.2. Text-type

Textual variation is a feature that must be taken into account in the description of sequentiality. Discourse organization is different depending on whether the text is narrative, descriptive, argumentative, etc. The notion of text-type is defined here following Biber's view: types are determined by linguistic characteristics, in contrast to genres, which are identified on the basis of extra-linguistic parameters such as social function (Biber 1988). In other words, text producers (and readers too) use strategies designed for the different text types. These strategies depend on discourse organization itself rather than on genre. For example, a sub-part of the corpus is composed of texts that have a mono-referential quality in common (they revolve around a single topic). Conversely, there are pluri-referential texts which abound with space and time references. This criterion of text-type characterisation is further explained below, in section 4, which also describes the corpus.

3.3. Text position

The last feature which forms the basis of our methodology is text position. Text position is linked to the level of organization that is marked by the document structure. Orientation and connection processes are likely to vary according to the level of organization: elements in initial position may function differently depending on whether they start a new section, a new paragraph, or merely a new sentence inside a paragraph.

This hypothesis is based on the idea that document structure strongly participates in the construction of the meaning of a text (for further details, see Power et al. 2003). From the reader's point of view, the beginning of a new section or a new paragraph triggers specific discourse processes that orient the interpretation.

The choice of three text positions follows a common (and quite intuitive) association between discontinuity and section or paragraph break. Therefore, the three exclusive text positions taken into account are:

S1 = section initial position;
P1 = paragraph initial position;
P2 = paragraph internal position.

Through 'playing' with the three text positions in three text-types, relevant configurations of cues will be discovered.

3.4. Some assumptions about these cues

According to the morpho-syntactic categories of grammatical subjects, the syntactic function of detached elements, and the different text positions, potential correlations can be derived between these cues and their contribution in indicating continuity or discontinuity in discourse organization. Although our approach is essentially data-driven, it is strongly shaped by a number of hypotheses which are also tested through this study. The main assumptions are presented in Table 1.

Correlation with	discontinuity	continuity
at experiential level		
figure	Grammatical subjects with a low degree of accessibility, paragraph breaks (P1), headings and new sections (S1)	Grammatical subjects with a high degree of accessibility, paragraph-internal position (P2)
ground	Circumstance adverbials, paragraph breaks (P1), headings and new sections (S1)	Apposition, fronted adjuncts, initial connectors
at rhetorical level		
	Textual adverbials, initial connectors, paragraph breaks (P1), headings and new sections (S1)	Paragraph-internal position (P2)

Table 1. Potential correlations between cues and their contribution in indicating discourse organization

Grammatical subjects are represented here in terms of their degree of accessibility as in the scale devised by Ariel (1990). Accessibility models such as those of Ariel (1990), Gundel et al. (1993) or Centering Theory (Walker et al. 1998) aim to explain cognitive processes involved in the activation of discourse referents. One of these processes is concerned with the continued activation of a given referent. In Ariel's work, one way to keep a referent activated is to use morpho-syntactic elements that are correlated with a high degree of accessibility (e.g. pronouns). Conversely, the introduction of a new referent must be accomplished via elements correlated with low accessibility (e.g. indefinite NP). Although Ariel's accessibility scale is not specifically designed to classify referential expressions in a way that corresponds to the notions of continuity or discontinuity, it provides a model that can be adapted and applied to automatic marking. The adopted correspondences are given in Table 2.

If we look back on example 1, we can see that in the first sentence, the complete definite description introducing the main topic correlates with a middle-low degree of accessibility (DA = 2). In subsequent sentences, several cues of topical continuity occur: an anaphoric pronoun (DA = 7), a reduced co-referential definite description (DA = 3), a reduced co-referential demonstrative description (DA = 6) and finally a complete demonstrative description (DA = 5).

indefinite description of special construction	0	low acc.
proper name without lexical reiteration	1	↑
long definite description without lexical reiteration	2	
definite description with lexical reiteration or short	3	
reiteration of a proper name ("redenomination")	4	
long demonstrative description without lexical reiteration	5	
demonstrative description with lexical reiteration or short	6	↓
pronoun or possessive NP	7	high acc.

Table 1: Scale of accessibility adapted from Ariel's
Theory of Accessibility (1990)

In example 2 extracted from texts of another text-type, anaphoric pronouns are seen to be more frequent. This frequent use indicates a strong topical continuity in this type of text.

(2) ***Florence-Milan, 1500 - 1513** [heading]*
In 1500, *Leonardo* goes to Mantova, where he draws Isabella d'Este's portrait, [...], to Venice, [...], and to Florence, where -[...]- he will stay till 1506. *He* shares his time between painting [...], and military engineering projects in the Arno valley and in Piombino. *Leonardo* resumes work on the Trattato started between 1487 and 1792, and continues until around 1513. **From 1506**, *he* divides his time between Milan where [...], and Florence where [...]. *He* returns to his equestrian statue project, [...]. *He* deploys an intense scientific activity: anatomy, mathematics, and produces architectural and decoration projects for Charles d'Amboise. But, **in 1513**, *he* leaves Milan for good as the city is reclaimed by the anti-French coalition.

> ***Rome-Ambroise, 1513-1519*** *[heading]*
> **In Rome**, where *he* has his lodgings in the Belvedere, *Leonardo* finds himself [...]

Examples 1 and 2 are both organized, as regards figure, around a main continuation span and, as regards ground, around different temporal frames. Curiously, the elements in section or paragraph initial position always express a circumstantial reference and the topic of the segment. In example 1, each paragraph begins with a time adverbial and a referring expression related to the topic. In example 2, the first section (not divided into paragraphs) begins with a time adverbial and the second with a space adverbial. The first grammatical subject of each section is the repeated proper name Leonardo. These configurations of cues are meant to indicate the organization of the section rather than a coincidence. It is this kind of configuration of cues that the methodology we propose attempts to detect.

4. A data-driven approach

The choice of a data-driven approach, necessarily based on an exhaustive analysis, aims to let the data "do the talking" and to "trust the text" (cf. Sinclair 2004) contrary to a hypothesis-driven approach. As a result, all the elements in the preverbal zone are analyzed (and not just a selection of elements for which there are assumptions). After describing the corpus, and setting out the automatic marking, various relevant quantitative analyses will be explained.

4.1. Corpus description

The methodology is applied on a French corpus designed for the study and determined by three choices. The first choice concerns a general category of texts that seem the most relevant ones: long written texts which need a more complex discourse organization than short texts or oral texts. Oral texts strike us as completely different as far as construction and interpretation are concerned. It is possible for short texts to work around a single topical continuity or around the default continuity established by human interpretation. For example, in texts under 2 pages, headings and section divisions are not need. The texts in the corpus are always over 10 pages in length and divided into sections.

The second choice follows from the first and concerns genre: here expository texts. Expository texts are topic centered, unlike narrative texts where organization is participant and event centered. In expository texts, there is no relation of succession (as happens by default in narratives) or action structure that motivates implicit organization. Moreover, the use of headings and subsections is rare in narratives.

The third choice concerns the parameter of textual variation. The corpus is composed of three sub-corpora representing three text-types distinguished by subject-matter and presentational organization.

a) ATLAS (~205,000 words), composed of 3 descriptive social geography texts;
b) GEOPO (~250,000 words), a collection of 32 argumentative texts in the domain of international relations;
c) PEOPL (~220,000 words), 30 descriptive biographies.

Texts in ATLAS are much longer than in GEOPO and PEOPL. They are mostly organized in terms of space and time references acting as settings for large spans of text, with no strong topical continuity. Conversely, texts in PEOPL are organized around a strong topical continuity (the topic being the subject of the biography). All texts include parts structured around time, but temporal organization is not the norm and never extends to the whole text. GEOPO is more difficult to characterize, with an occasional temporal organization and rather weak topical continuities.

If we count the frequency of nouns in each text, GEOPO and ATLAS show a wider variety of frequent nouns than in PEOPL. This difference could be interpreted as a cue to pluri-referentiality (many frequent nouns) and mono-referentiality (few frequent nouns). Concerning spatial reference, ATLAS has many more basic space adverbials[2] (e.g. *In Europe*) which, moreover, occur more often in initial position than elsewhere. Concerning temporal reference, ATLAS and PEOPL both display a high frequency of basic time adverbials in initial position (e.g. *In 1900*), much more so than in GEOPO.

4.2. Automatic cue tagging

In order to perform an exhaustive analysis without selecting specific cues, all elements appearing in the preverbal zone of every sentence in the corpus are systematically marked. This marking is performed automatically for all the elements carried out in figure 2.

For each of the 23.000 sentences in the corpus, the following features are annotated:

- text position
- sub-corpus
- presence of a detached connective (e.g. *But, And, Nevertheless...*)

- presence of one or more detached elements
- canonical/special syntactic construction

Each detached element (there are 7022 in total) is characterized in terms of:

---

2 As this analysis is mostly based on automatic marking, a basic expression must also be an expression which lends itself to automatic extraction.

- part of speech
- function (circumstance adverbial, textual adverbial, apposition, etc.)
- semantic meaning for circumstance adverbials (temporal, spatial, notional)

Finally, grammatical subjects are characterized in terms of four properties:

- part of speech
- length (a distinction is made between short NP, consisting of less than four words, and long NP, consisting of more than three words)
- reiteration, i.e. the fact that the NP's head repeats a noun already mentioned in the current section
- degree of accessibility in accordance with the accessibility scale of Ariel (1990) as indicated in Table 2.

These features are automatically detected using a set of regular expressions based on the results of Treetagger and the parser Syntex (Bourigault 2007).

4.3. Measurement of variations

The data are systematically explored in search for configurations of cues via two main measures: deviations in the use of different linguistic elements in initial position, and degree of association between detached elements and grammatical subjects.

The first step of the analysis consists in extracting lexico-syntactic cues which vary according to text-type and text position. For each lexico-syntactic element, the following variations are measured:

a) distributions in each corpus are compared with overall distributions;
b) distributions in each text position are compared with overall distributions.

The significance of variations is given in terms of z-score. We regard as significant positive deviations above +2.5 and negative deviations below -2.5.

The second step consists in measuring:

a) variations in subject position according to the presence of a particular detached element;
b) variations in detached position according to the presence of a particular type of grammatical subject.

These variations are measured in the host sentence and in the following sentence, considering each text-type and each text position.

5. Results and interpretation

Through this exploratory method, a number of results are obtained and presented in Hồ-Đắc (2007). After presenting an overview of the results obtained and their interpretation, the second sub-section illustrates in more detail the method with a step by step account of the study of variations concerning time and space adverbials.

5.1. Organization and text-types

The first set of results presented in figure 3 indicates the general associations showing a significant deviation according to text position. Figure 3 displays all the elements occurring in the preverbal zone for which the z-score test shows a significant association (/z/ > +2.5) with S1, P1 or P2. The label of all the elements that occur significantly more in section-initial or paragraph-initial and significantly less in paragraph-internal position is indicated above the horizontal line. Conversely, below the line are indicated all the elements occurring significantly more in paragraph-internal position and less in section and paragraph initial position.

Detached element		***Grammatical Subject***		
apposition	Temporal adv.	Proper name	Long definite NP	S1
	Spatial adv.	Lexical reiteration		P1
No detached element		Pronoun and possessive	Short definite NP (without reiteration)	P2

Figure 3. Significant general associations between lexico-syntactic elements and text-position

If we focus on grammatical subjects, we find well-known associations. Categories that strongly mark continuity such as pronouns and possessives occur significantly more in paragraph-internal position (P2). On the other side of the horizontal line, there are elements traditionally linked to discontinuity such as:

a) in S1, full definite descriptions and new proper names that may mark discontinuity by introducing a low accessible referent;
b) in P1, lexical reiteration that may be used to emphasize a topical continuity when there is a shift in ground information or in rhetorical structure.

No significant variations according to text position are measured for special constructions. It seems that special constructions play a role in information structure rather than in global organization.

For detached elements, there are associations between (i) absence of detached elements and paragraph-internal position (P2), and (ii) presence of detached elements and the beginning of document structure segments (S1 and P1). Appositions and time adverbials are significantly more associated to S1 in all corpora.

In P1, there are significant variations according to text-type: paragraphs seem to be organized around space references in ATLAS and around time references in GEOPO. In PEOPL, appositions, which signal topical continuity, occur significantly more in P1. Only the strongest deviation, concerning space adverbials in ATLAS, is reported with general variations indicated in figure 3.

Table 3 summarizes the different significant variations measured for detached elements according to text-position in each sub-corpus. The same measures for grammatical subjects are indicated in Table 4.

	S1 -----------------------> P1 ---------------------> P2		
GEOPO	apposition time adv.	time adv.	no detached element
ATLAS		circumstantial adv. space adv.	
PEOPL	time adv. (apposition)	apposition	

Table 3. Detached elements: significant variations according to text position in each text-type.

	S1 ------------------> P1 ------------------> P2		
GEOPO	definite NP	long (definite) NP	pronoun possessive NP short NP
ATLAS	definite NP long NP	lexical reiteration	
PEOPL	definite NP long NP proper name	repeated proper name	repeated proper name pronoun possessive NP

Table 4. Grammatical subjects: significant variations according to text position in each text-type

Variations measured for grammatical subjects may be interpreted with respect to the management of referential continuities in these three text-types. Whereas continuity seems to be achieved with lexical reiteration in ATLAS, GEOPO relies on reduced description. In PEOPL, the majority of proper names and pronouns signal strong topical continuity around a single topic (the famous person whose life story the text tells). Repeated proper names are associated here with high accessibility despite the fact that they are located in the middle of the accessibility scale. In fact, the status of repeated proper names is very characteristic in PEOPL. As Schnedecker (2005) showed, repeated proper names in biographies function more as alternatives to pronouns than as shift markers. This hypothesis is effectively supported by the significant association with P2 and means that we must pay attention to the correlation between degree of accessibility and signals of (dis)continuity.

Space and the methodological orientation of the present paper prevent us from discussing this point further here or from delving deeper into the detailed analysis of each feature taken into account in this study. We choose to illustrate the methodology we have just outlined by describing the case of space and time adverbials, as they give a good overview of the processes involved in this data-driven approach.

5. An illustration: variations associated with time and space adverbials

5.1. Step 1: variations according to text-type and text position

Time adverbials are frequent in detached initial position. They constitute 21% of all initial elements in our corpus (1466 occ.). Space adverbials are less frequent (7% of all initial elements, 500 occ.). Time adverbials are regularly distributed across text-types: 31% are found in ATLAS, 36% in GEOPO and 34% in PEOPL. This is not the case of space adverbials: 66% are found in ATLAS, 21% in GEOPO and 13% in PEOPL. Figure 4 compares the distribution of these adverbials in each text-type and their overall distribution. The statistical measure employed is z-score.

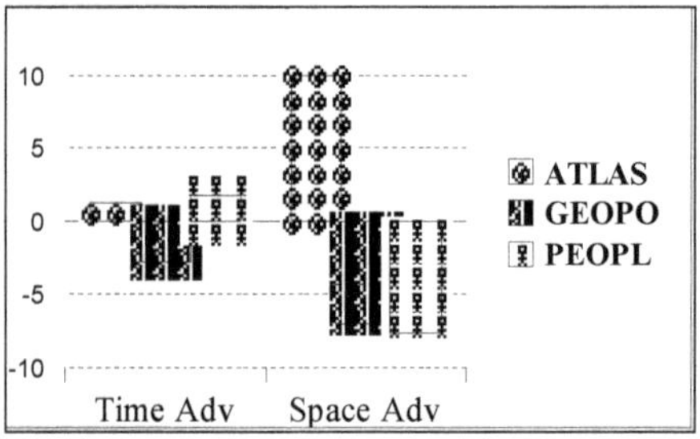

Figure 4. Time and space adverbials: deviations according to text-type

It appears clearly that time adverbials are not specific to one corpus (there is no positive significant deviation in one or more sub-corpora). In GEOPO, which is the least specific sub-corpus, there is a weakly significant negative /z/. This lower incidence means that there is a wider variety of initial elements in

GEOPO rather than fewer time adverbials. In fact GEOPO has the highest number of occurrences of time adverbials: 522 compare to 452 in ATLAS and 492 in PEOPL.

Conversely, space adverbials characterize ATLAS as shown by the strong positive deviation for ATLAS and the two negative deviations for GEOPO and PEOPL.

Variations concerning text positions (S1: section-initial; P1: paragraph-initial; P2: paragraph-internal) are given in Figure 5. Here, the z-score test compares the distribution of elements in each text position with their overall distribution.

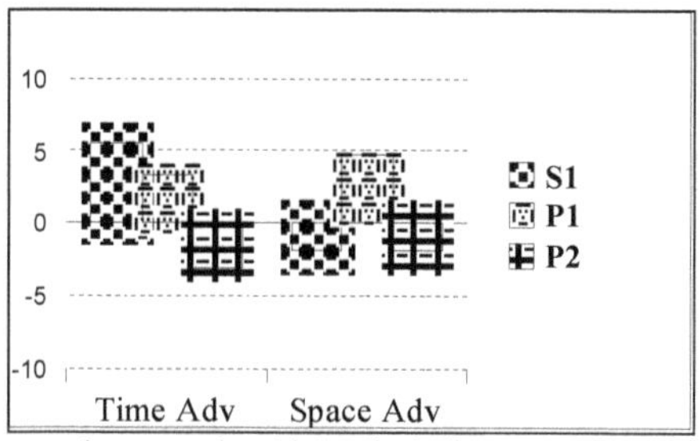

Figure 3. Time and space adverbials: deviations according to text position

Time adverbials can be seen to occur significantly more in S1 and in P1, while space adverbials occur significantly more in P1 only. Conversely, there are significantly fewer time adverbials in intraparagraphic sentences (P2).

The difference between space and time adverbials may be explained in terms of the comparison between local discourse function and global discourse function. Space adverbials are associated with paragraph-initial position but not with section-initial position. Moreover, the deviation is not significant in the case of space adverbials occurring in P2. In contrast to time adverbials, space adverbials are not unlikely to occur in paragraph-internal position. These results may indicate that space adverbials fulfill a more local discourse function than time adverbials. These observations are confirmed by the results below.

Figure 6 displays the results of the same z-score test applied in each sub-corpus. The aim is to discover whether such associations with text positions remain stable across the three text-types.

Deviations associated with time adverbials are found in all three corpora. There are more time adverbials in S1 and P1 and fewer in P2. The z-score in P1 for GEOPO and PEOPL, though not in ATLAS, may be accepted as statistically significant. It is only in comparison with time adverbials that we can find significant deviations affecting the use space adverbials in ATLAS. The discourse function of circumstance adverbials seems to be more definite in this sub-corpus. Time adverbials begin sections while space adverbials begin paragraphs. This role distribution is facilitated by the fact that sections in ATLAS are very short and hierarchically embedded, compared to PEOPL or GEOPO.

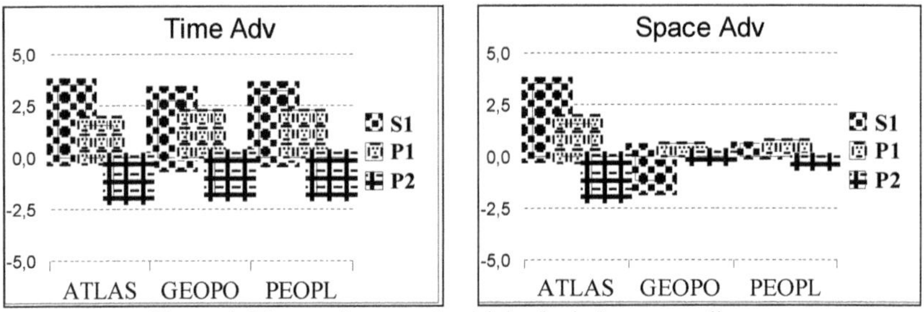

Figure 4. Time and space adverbials: deviations according to text position in each sub-corpus

These first results lead us to conclude that adverbials may constitute good discontinuity markers because of their strong association with the starting point of document structure segments. However, this interpretation must be qualified. Firstly, it is important to take into account text-type (time adverbials appear to be less specific of a text-type than space adverbials). Secondly, this association does not mean that adverbials signal discontinuity on their own, as for example when they appear in a location other than section-initial or paragraph-initial position. The analysis of the lexico-syntactic environment of adverbials will clarify this last point.

5.2. Step 2: variations in grammatical subject preceded by an adverbial

The second stage of the analysis measures the variations in subject position relative to the presence of an adverbial in detached position. Here, the reader will find only a summary of the most important results (for a complete description, see Hồ-Đắc and Péry-Woodley 2008).

Firstly, the discourse function of space/time adverbials seems to be highly sensitive to text position. Space/time adverbials seem to be good segmentation markers when they occur in S1 or P1. In P2, their discourse function would appear to depend on the textual strategy used in the text: text may be organized around a dominant topical continuity or a dominant space/time structure.

Variations measured for grammatical subjects according to text-type and text position indicate that PEOPL is organized around a strong topical continuity—unlike ATLAS and GEOPO, as was seen in the previous sub-section. The power of this topical continuity is also relevant in variations observed in host and following sentences of space/time adverbials and may explain the strong difference which opposes ATLAS and GEOPO to PEOPL.

In ATLAS and GEOPO, space/time adverbials may indicate discontinuity but only in specific configurations. Space/time adverbials collocate significantly more with reiterations that correlate with medium accessibility. This kind of subject may be used to emphasize a topical continuity when there is a shift in the setting (i.e. ground) or in the rhetorical structure, but not in thematic structure (i.e. figure). Space/time adverbials also collocate significantly more with new proper names that correlate with lower accessibility. This collocation may indicate that there is simultaneously a ground and a figure discontinuity. But variations in the following sentences do not support this suggestion. If the opening of a new time or space continuation span corresponds to the opening of a new thematic continuation span, the subject in the following sentence should correlate with high accessibility. However, the data show that it is not the case.

Grammatical subjects of sentences that follow a P2 sentence introduced with a space/time adverbial are significantly more associated with the bottom or the middle of the accessibility scale. We can also notice a significant association with demonstrative NPs. Demonstrative NPs correlate with high accessibility, but they mean more than just referential accessibility. The preferential use of demonstrative NPs in comparison to the use of pronouns is often associated, in French, with "reclassification." Reclassification consists in expressing a known referent stripped of its initial circumstances (De Mulder 1997). The referent's reclassification negates the possibility of an extension of the adverbial's scope (for more details, see Hồ-Đắc and Péry-Woodley 2008).

The significant positive variations observed in the sentence following a space/time adverbial's host sentence may be a sign that space/time adverbials do not open a new continuation span at ground level. They merely locate the process of the host-sentence. Configurations where the host sentence's subject is a new proper name and the following sentence's subject is a demonstrative NP may indicate a discontinuity to do with the figure but not with the ground.

The case of PEOPL is very different. The topical continuity is so strong in this text-type that time adverbials seem to align their behaviour with the organization established by topical continuity. In PEOPL, time adverbials co-occur significantly more with high accessibility co-referential expressions, such as pronouns, possessive NPs and repeated proper names.

These associations in PEOPL are in agreement with the general model: in P2 subject referents present a remarkably high degree of accessibility, indicating topical continuity. This continuity is not in the least disturbed by the presence of a time adverbial in initial position. The power of topical continuity is so strong that it is possible to have such associations in section-initial or paragraph-initial positions. This result agrees with observations presented in Le Draoulec and Péry-Woodley (2003) whereby, in narrative texts, time adverbials do not open a discourse frame but rather locate the chronological starting point for a succession of events. This is exactly what we have with the first time adverbial in example 2: *In 1500* does not really extend its semantic scope until the second time adverbial. The semantic criterion of the first temporal frame is *from 1500 to 1506* instead.

Nevertheless, we may state that in example 2, time adverbials structure the text by indicating the boundaries of the three periods of Leonardo's life between 1500 and 1513. But this structuring power would certainly be less strong without this heading and if the section did not begin with a time adverbial predicting a time organization for the rest of the document structure segment.

6. Conclusion

The data-driven approach presented here provides really interesting new insights. It has proved to be an effective tool for processing data. The z-score test is very simple to manipulate and enables us to test the structuring power of each feature that may interact in the signalling of discourse organization. It offers new perspectives for the study of discourse organization and enables us to identify the textual characteristics of global organization: for example, the fact that ATLAS is characterized by a strong spatio-temporal organization while the discourse organization in PEOPL is clearly topic centred.

Now concerning advances in the study of discourse organization, the hypothesis concerning the marking of discourse organization has been partially validated. By testing the discourse function of specific lexico-syntactic elements such as time adverbials, this methodology shows that we cannot speak about the structuring power of a lexical marker by itself. It is rather a matter of complex configurations of cues where lexico-syntactic elements play a role. This validation shows also that discourse organization is strongly sensitive to text-type. In this study, the treatment of text-types takes into account the shape of a document and the textual strategies used in it. A promising future direction would be to test the use of the configurations of cues discovered in this study in automatic text-type profiling.

Some aspects of this methodology need further refinement. First, the use of degrees of accessibility to represent the instructional meaning of grammatical subjects must certainly be reassessed. Second, a necessary step to evaluate this methodology will be to apply it to other corpora and other languages in other contexts. We plan to do this in the framework of a project (ARC project – Catholic University of Leuven) aiming to study "The transformation of the relationship with information in multimedia communication" by exploring variations across newspapers on line and on paper.

7. References

Allén, J. (ed.) (1989): *Possible Worlds in Humanities, Arts and Sciences*, Berlin, New-York, Walter de Gruyter.

Ariel, M. (1990): *Accessing noun phrase antecedents*, London, Routledge.

Berry, M. (1995): "Thematic options and success in writing," in M. Ghadessy (ed.), 55-84.

Biber, D., U. Connor and T. A. Upton (2007): *Discourse on the move: using corpus analysis to describe discourse structure*, Amsterdam, John Benjamins.

Biber, D. (1998): *Variation across speech and writing*, Cambridge, Cambridge University Press.

Chafe, W.L. (1976): "Giveness, contrastiveness, definiteness, subjects, topics, and point of view," in C.N.Li (ed.), 25-55.

Condamines, A. (ed.) (2005): *Sémantique et corpus*, Paris, Hermès.

De Mulder, W. (1997) : « Les démonstratifs: des indices de changement de contexte, " in N. Flaux, D. Van de Velde and W. de Mulder (eds.), 137-200.

Enkvist, N.E. (1989): "Connexity, interpretability, universes of discourse, and text worlds," in J. Allén (ed.), 162-186.

Flaux, N., D. van de Velde and W. de Mulder (eds.) (1997) : *Entre général et particulier: les déterminants*, Besançon, Artois Press Université.

Fries, P.H. (1995) : "Themes, methods of development, and texts. In R. Hasan and P. H. Fries (eds.), 317-360.

Ghadessy, M. (ed.) (1995): *Thematic Development in English Texts*, London, Pinter.

Givón, T. (1995): *Functionalism and Grammar*, Amsterdam/Philadelphia: John Benjamins.

Goutsos, D. (1996): "A model of sequential relations in expository text," *Text*, 16, 4, 501-533.

Gundel, J.K., N. Hedberg and R. Zacharski (1993): "Cognitive status and the form of referring expressions in discourse," *Language*, 69, 2, 274-307.

Halliday, M.A.K. (1985): *An introduction to Functional Grammar*, London, Edward Arnold.

Halliday, M.A.K. (1970): "Language structure and language function," in R. Hasan and P. H. Fries (eds.), 140-164.

Hasan, R. and P. H. Fries (eds.) (1970): *New horizons in Linguistics*, Harmondsworth, Penguin.

Hasan, R. and P. H. Fries (eds.) (1995): *On Subject and Theme. A Discourse Functional Perspective*, Amsterdam, John Benjamins.

Hasselgård H. (1996): *Where and When: Positional and functional conventions for sequences of time and space adverbials in present-day English*, Oslo, Scandinavian University Press, Acta Humaniora.

Hồ-Đắc, L.-M (2007): *Exploration en corpus de la position initiale dans l'organisation du discours*, Unpublished PhD Dissertation, University of Toulouse-UTM, France.

Hồ-Đắc, L.-M. and M.-P. Péry-Woodley (2009): "A data-driven study of temporal adverbials as discourse segmentation markers," *Discours*, Special issue on Linearisation and Segmentation in Discourse [online].

Jacques M.-P. and J. Rebeyrolle (2006): "Titres et structuration des documents," *Proceedings of the International Symposium: DISCOURSE and DOCUMENT (ISDD'06),* 1-12.

Lagerwerf, L., W. Spooren and L. Degand (eds.) (2003): *Determination of Information and Tenor in Texts : MAD 2003*, Amsterdam / Münster, Stichting Neerlandistiek & Nodus Publikationen.

Le Draoulec, A. and M.-P. Péry-Woodley (2003): "Time travel in text: temporal framing in narratives and non-narratives," in L. Lagerwerf, W. Spooren and L. Degand (eds.), 267-275.

Levelt, W. J. M. (1981): "The speaker's linearization problem," *Philosophical Transactions of the Royal Society of London*, B295, 305-315.

Li C.N. (ed.) (1976): *Subject and Topic*, New York, Academic Press.

Matthiessen, C. (1995): "THEME as an enabling resource in ideational 'knowledge' construction," in M. Ghadessy (ed.), 20-54.

Péry-Woodley, M.-P. (2005): "Discours, corpus, traitements automatiques," in A. Condamines (ed.), 177-210.

Power, R., D. Scott and N. Bouayad-Agha (2003): "Document structure," *Computational Linguistics*, 29, 2, 211-260.

Schnedecker, C. (2005): Les chaînes de référence dans les portraits journalistiques: éléments de description," *Travaux de Linguistique*, 5, 85-133.

Sinclair, J. (2004): *Trust the Text: Language Corpus and Discourse*, London, Routledge.

Thompson, S. (1985): "Grammar and written discourse: initial vs. final purpose clauses in English," *Text*, 5, 55-84.

Walker, M.A., A. Joshi and E. Prince (1998): "Centering in naturally occurring discourse: an overview," in M. A. Walker et al. (eds.), 1-28.

Walker, M. A., A. Joshi and E. Prince (eds) (1998): *Centering Theory of Discourse*, Oxford, Calendron Press.

Testing accessibility and givenness in a corpus of Spanish

Iker Zulaica Hernández
The Ohio State University

1. Introduction

The emergence of electronic corpora a few decades ago brought about a new way of testing important theoretical issues in linguistics. Indisputably, the main advantage of the use of language corpora for linguistic research is their suitability to confirm or refute hypothesis based on a source of fully objective, empirical data. In this respect, today corpora are for linguists what labs mean for physicists or electronic microscopes for biologists. In addition, language corpora also allowed many linguists to get rid of a long-lasting dependency on constructed, sometimes even artificial, examples to illustrate and support their arguments. Last but not least, these tools have also provided us with the material supply needed to give shape to elusive theoretical constructs. A property that proves particularly important when it comes to dealing with notions like *givenness*, *saliency* or *focus* in natural languages. Unfortunately, these concepts, widely used in psycholinguistics and the cognitive sciences, have not been given a satisfactory textual characterization so far.

In this paper, I present a critical review of the notions of *accessibility*, *saliency* and *cognitive focus* as they have been profusely employed to explain the semantic and pragmatic differences of the range of referential expressions across languages. The primary goal is to test the appropriateness of these concepts to explain the peculiar pragmatic behavior shown by demonstratives in discourse. The focus is put on Spanish demonstrative anaphors and, more specifically, on the three so-called neuter pronominal demonstratives *esto*, *eso* and *aquello*. To this aim I carried out a corpus study and analyzed the recency of mention of the antecedent as a way of measuring the degree of saliency of the referent for the addressee. I will argue that saliency, accessibility and cognitive focus are three different ways of conceptualizing one single phenomenon: *focus of attention of the addressee*. By elaborating on this idea, I will defend that previous attempts to account for the cognitive status of the referent of demonstrative anaphors do not seem adequate given the evidence from naturally occurring examples in Spanish. Instead, I will argue that demonstrative anaphors should be better viewed as pragmatic focus markers whose primary role is that of helping the hearer or addressee direct his/her attention towards a particular discourse referent by making it salient enough in the speech situation. In this respect, demonstrative anaphors do not differ much from the basic role of deictic demonstratives.

The study of demonstratives must be framed within the widest scope of referential expressions. Referential expressions include all those linguistic elements whose primary role is to help identify a physical object or a conceptual entity in the speech situation. Thus, for example, the use of a deictic demonstrative (probably accompanied by a deictic gesture like a pointing finger) serves to uniquely identify an object in the physical domain of the speech situation. But the referent of a linguistic expression does not need to be tangible (e.g. having substance or material existence). The referent can be a purely mental or conceptual entity (e.g. *remember those school days*). Pronouns, definite descriptions, demonstratives or even null objects constitute referential expressions. Consider the following example:

(1) a. *Juan* es lingüista.
John is a linguist.
b. *Él* es lingüista.
He is a linguist.
c. *Pro* es lingüista.
(He) is a linguist.
d. *El novio de María* es lingüista.
Mary's boyfriend is a linguist.
e. *Ese chico* es lingüísta.
That guy is a linguist.

The proper name *Juan* in (1a), the third person pronoun *él* (he) in (1b), the empty syntactic position or *pro* in (1c)[1], the definite description headed by the definite article *el* (the) in (1d) and the demonstrative expression *ese chico* (that guy) in (1e) all refer to the same individual *Juan*. Note the varying degree of descriptive information that all these expressions embody (e.g. from the null descriptive content of *pro* to the property expressed by the definite description *Mary's boyfriend* that clearly helps the addressee to uniquely identify the entity referred to). Having situated demonstrative anaphors within the frame of referential expressions, the rest of the paper will be divided as follows. The notions of accessibility, cognitive focus and saliency will be presented and examined in sections 2.1-2.3. Section 3 will be entirely devoted to presenting the methodology and results of the corpus study that is the basis of this paper. Finally, the corpus results will be discussed in section 4 in addition to present an alternative hypothesis to account for the referential behavior of Spanish demonstrative anaphors and some future prospects on the topic.

---

1 Spanish is a pro-drop language. Grammatical information relative to the subject of a sentence (person and number) is embodied in the tensed verb hence the syntactic subject can be easily omitted without comprehension being affected at all.

2. Givenness, saliency and the degree of accessibility

2.1. Accessibility

The different distribution and behavior shown by referential expressions in discourse has been explained on the basis of the degree of givenness[2] of the referent for the addressee. The lack of a precise and clear-cut definition for the notion of givenness led several scholars to elaborate on this notion and characterize it in cognitive and linguistic terms. Thus, Ariel's *Accessibility Theory* (1988, 1990) proposed a reformulation of the notion of givenness of a referent in terms of a varying degree of accessibility. In Ariel's theory, accessibility can be defined as the relative ease with which the addressee can identify the referent of a referring expression or, alternatively, the ease with which the addressee can retrieve the referent from memory. The *Scale of Accessibility* (henceforth SoA) is shown in (2):

(2) Extremely High Accessibility Markers (gaps, including pro, PRO and *wh* traces, reflexives and Agreement) > Unstressed pronoun > Cliticized pronoun > Stressed pronoun + gesture > Stressed pronoun > Proximal demonstrative (+ NP) > Distal demonstrative (+NP) > Proximal demonstrative + modifier > Distal demonstrative + modifier > First name > Last name > Short definite description > Long definite description > Full ('namy') name > Full name

According to the scale, demonstratives occupy an intermediate position in terms of the degree of accessibility they confer to their referents. The scale indicates that proximal demonstratives mark higher accessibility than distal demonstratives. Note that the amount of extra information that is attached to a demonstrative results in the demonstrative marking lower accessibility. Thus, when a modifier accompanies demonstratives they rank lower in the scale (e.g. *that house* vs *that house next to the bus stop*). This is explained for the more accessible a referent the lesser information is needed to for the addressee to identify it. As the scale clearly indicates, the less informative (null) forms (gaps, PRO, etc) occupy the highest position, that is, they are high accessibility markers. Whenever the speaker uses one of these markers, he would be (in)-directly communicating the addressee that the referent can be easily accessed and there is no need to give further unnecessary information. It is important to keep in mind that the SoA was primarily intended to account for English referential expressions.

Besides questioning the middle position in the scale occupied by demonstratives, a subsidiary question arises regarding the degree of accessibility conferred to different demonstratives in the SoA, namely, why does the proximal demonstrative signal a higher accessibility than the distal demonstrative? For Ariel, this can be explained for the English proximal demonstrative (this) correlates with

---

2 Givenness is defined in dictionaries of English as the quality of being granted as a supposition; of being acknowledged or assumed.

present tenses and the distal demonstrative (that) with past tenses in discourse. Present tenses are semantically conceived as closer to the speech time (the 'now' of the utterance situation) than past tenses, which in a Reichenbachian (1947) conception of time occur at a time that is distant to the speech time. The rationale behind this idea originally proposed by Fillmore (1975) is that present events, which are closer to the speech time, are more accessible than past events, which are distant from the speech time. The correlation tense-demonstration as suggested by Fillmore and supported by Ariel finds support in Spanish. As pointed out in Zulaica-Hernández (2008), Spanish demonstrative pronouns strongly correlate with past and present tenses. In a corpus study, this author showed that distal demonstrative *aquello* shows a strong preference to be accompanied by past tenses when reference to events is made in written and oral discourse. On the other hand, figures showed that proximal and medial demonstratives *esto* and *eso* are indistinctively used along with past and present tenses. This fact was first observed by Fernández-Ramírez (1951) but it was never put to test and confirmed until recently. Whether the parallelism tense-demonstration observed in various languages should be explained in terms of the TIME-IS-SPACE metaphor or in terms of the varying degree of accessibility conveyed by past/present tenses and distal/proximal demonstratives is an issue that is far beyond the purpose of this paper. It is nevertheless an interesting question that clearly deserves future research. For the time being, the suggestion that entities close to the speech time are more accessible than entities distant from the speech time will remain as a purely speculative proposal until there is some psycholinguistic evidence to support it. In my opinion, this idea should be better characterized in terms of access to memory storage. Thus, language users would have more difficulty in retrieving past events from memory than present or closer events as the former would have been stored in the long-term memory storage whereas the latter would still be located in short-term or an intermediate memory state. Accessing entities from the long-term memory storage would then be more costly in terms of processing effort than accessing more 'recent' entities. Demonstratives would thus reflect the different memory state of their referents and of the past/present tenses that co-occur with them in discourse. A possible characterization is given in (3):

(3) a. PAST TENSE > DISTAL w.r.t. Speech time >
Long Term Memory Storage **entails** LOWER ACCESSIBILITY
b. PRESENT TENSE > PROXIMAL w.r.t. Speech time >
Short Term Memory Storage **entails** HIGHER ACCESSIBILITY

Now, the most difficult part would be to integrate demonstratives into the picture presented in (3) or, in other words, provide a suitable explanation for the source of the correlation tense-demonstration observed across many languages. Technically, tenses are not referential expressions but according to Davidson

(1980) natural language tenses convey events as a primary feature of their meaning. A verb like, for example, *comer* (eat) would thus convey an eating event (*e*-eat) in Davidson's theory of tense and it is this event what is more difficult for a hearer to retrieve from memory when the verb that denotes it is a past tense. The correlation tense-demonstration could then be conceived as a sort of 'matching' in the degree of memory retrieval effort whereby Spanish distal demonstrative *aquello* would also indicate a higher processing effort (lower referential accessibility) by part of the hearer to retrieve the referent from memory. On the other hand, demonstratives *esto* and *eso* would indicate a lower processing effort or higher referential accessibility. In any case, this would leave unexplained why English demonstratives occupy a medial position in Ariel's SoA and to exactly what degree past and present tenses mark higher and lower accessibility for if present tenses, by virtue of being closer to the speech time, indicate a higher accessibility they should strongly correlate with referential expressions that rank higher in the scale but, to my knowledge, this has not been proved so far.

For Piwek and Cremers, additional factors like topichood or saliency contribute to increase referential accessibility (1996: 837). For Ariel, there are up to four different factors, which may influence the accessibility of the referent of a discourse anaphor. These factors are described in (4a-d).

(4) a. Distance: the textual distance between the antecedent and the anaphor.
b. Competition: as the number of suitable referents increases, the harder will be for the addressee to pick up a particular referent. According to Ariel, competition cancels the accessibility of all referents involved.
c. Saliency: some referents stand out more than others, for example when the referent is the discourse topic.
d. Unity: antecedents that are within the same frame/world/point of view/segment or paragraph as the anaphor are easier to access than those that are not.

Whereas factors (4a) and (4c) are easier to characterize formally and, therefore, tested against an electronic corpus, factors (4b) and (4d) are truly hard to model in a corpus based study for various reasons. On the one hand, *Competition* refers to the number of potential competing suitable referents for the addressee to interpret. As this number increases, the harder will be for the addressee to find the unique referent intended by the speaker. Crucially, as stated in (4b), this factor eventually cancels the accessibility of all referents involved. In discourse anaphoric processes though, it is not uncommon at all to find a considerable amount of intervening material (potential competing suitable referents) between the intended antecedent and the anaphor. Consider examples (5)[3] and (6)[4]. Note the antecedent is indicated in talics and the demonstrative anaphor in small caps.

---

3 Source: CREA. *Operación Ópera*, 1991.

(5) Y al fín y al cabo, si ustedes están aquí es porque quieren que les hable de *la Operación Opera*, claro. ¡Me cuesta tanto volver al pasado! Ya comprenderán, aquí el tiempo transcurre de otra manera...Y todo AQUELLO sucedió en el 92, hace ya... ¡Pero sea! No voy a defraudarles: les contaré la historia tal y como sucedió.

[After all, if you are here is only because you want me to tell you about *the Opera Operation,* that is for sure. It's so hard to me to go back in time! You'll see, time goes by differently here ... And all THAT happened in 1992, about ... But well! I won't disappoint you: I'll tell you the story exactly as it happened.]

(6) *Tener una relación con un hombre* no está en mis planes por el momento ya que debo esperar a que primero sanen mis heridas. Pero mis amigas que lo conocen me dicen que no sea boba, que me dé la oportunidad ya que ESO pasa sólo una vez en la vida.

[*Having a relation with a man* is not in my plans for the moment, as I must first wait until my heart heals. But my friends tell me not to be stupid, that I should give myself a chance as THAT only happens once in a lifetime.]

In both examples, there is some intervening text between the most likely antecedent and the anaphor. The antecedent in (5) is the NP *la Operación Opera*, but there are three additional potentially competing NPs in the Spanish original version, namely, *el pasado*, *el tiempo* and the null subject (*ustedes*) of the verb *comprenderán* (you'll see). In (6), the number of competing NPs is still higher (*mis planes*, *el momento*, *mis heridas*, *mis amigas*, *lo*, *la oportunidad* and several null subjects.) But these NPs do not exhaust the list of potential antecedents for both pieces of discourse. The antecedent of the medial demonstrative anaphor *eso* in (6) is a clause headed by a non-finite verb form *tener* (having a relation with a man). The three Spanish demonstrative anaphors *esto*, *eso* and *aquello* (this, that, that yonder) are commonly used in discourse to refer to a range of discourse entities that show a high degree of syntactic polymorphism and semantic variation. The three so-called 'neuter' demonstrative pronouns are, in fact, not neuter as no such grammatical gender actually exists in Spanish. Most likely, they are commonly referred to as 'neuter' in the grammatical tradition for their peculiar referential properties, namely, they are capable of referring to genderless semantic entities like propositions, eventualities, factual information, discourse topics, etc (Asher 1993). But not only pronominal demonstratives are licensed to refer to such high-order, non-tangible entities. Demonstrative adjectives can also be used to refer to abstract entities in combinations like the following, where the denotation of the noun clearly indicates its abstract reference: *ese hecho* (that fact), *aquel evento* (that event), *esta situación* (this situation), etc. From a syntactic point of view, abstract referents adopt various

---

[4] Source: CREA. *Vea on line*, nº 1761 from 17/05/2003. San Juan de Puerto Rico.

forms, i.e. entire sentences, subordinate clauses, infinitival clauses as in (6), NPs, or combinations of more than one sentence. For this reason, not only NPs are available as potential antecedents for demonstrative anaphors. In consequence, the intervening material that is found between the intended antecedent and the demonstrative anaphors in (5) and (6) is larger than what we initially proposed. This fact has clear implications for the competition factor as defined in (4b). Now the question arises as to what is the necessary number of competing suitable antecedents for accessibility to be cancelled. Intuitively at least, the antecedents in our two examples should not be accessible for the hearer/reader due the considerable amount of suitable textual antecedents in clear competition with the intended one. Nevertheless, the demonstrative can be perfectly interpreted regardless the amount of intervening material between antecedent and anaphor.

The *Unity* factor (4d) appeals to thematic harmony as a way of explaining the distinctive accessibility marking of referential expressions. Thus, Ariel talks about antecedent and anaphor sharing the same discourse frame, world or point of view. It is well known that the topic or topics of a particular discourse persist across sentences in a way such as to maintain discourse coherence. Several proposals have been developed from different linguistics fields to explain topic continuity or persistence across discourse (see for example Givón (1983) and Grosz et al. (1995) for a semantic/pragmatic and a computational approach, respectively). As discourse topics are supposed to be more salient than other discourse entities, it makes sense to suggest that topics are more accessible than other, non-topical referents. The problem with unity as proposed by Ariel lies in the vagueness of the term, as it does not accurately explain what she understands by point of view, world or frame. Segment and paragraph, on the other hand, are more concrete notions yet still a bit too general. The size of a paragraph can vary considerably across discourse and the notion 'segment' is a bit confusing as it may refer to textual segments like paragraphs, sentences, clauses, etc. Purely textual notions like segment and paragraph clearly indicate that this factor is directly dependent on textual distance between antecedent and anaphor.

In summary, we are left with *Distance* (4a) and *Saliency* (4c) as factors, which are easier to control, model and test against a corpus. To these factors we will devote the rest of this paper. Our corpus study will be entirely devoted to test the textual distance of antecedents relative to their anaphors and observe the effect that this factor may have on the general referential properties of Spanish demonstrative anaphors. We will see that textual distance and saliency are also intimately connected to one another and that the degree of referential accessibility marked by Spanish demonstrative anaphors crucially depends on these two linguistic notions.

2.2. The Givenness Hierarchy

In a series of papers, Gundel et al. (1993, 2001, 2005) fleshed out a hierarchy of referential expressions and cognitive statuses to account for the different distribution that these expressions show in languages like English and Spanish. There are six different cognitive states in the hierarchy (*in focus*, *activated*, *familiar*, *uniquely identifiable*, *referential* and *type identifiable*) that reflect the degree of givenness of the referents of the various referential expressions that exist in those languages. Thus, for example, the English weak pronoun 'it' differs from the definite article 'the' in that the referent of the former is supposed to be in focus whereas that of the latter is only uniquely identifiable. Likewise, the Spanish null or zero pronoun Ø marks its referent as being into the current focus of attention (in focus) whereas the Spanish definite article marks the same status as its English counterpart, namely, uniquely identifiable. The Givenness Hierarchy, (henceforth GH), is shown in table 1.

	In focus >	Activated >	Familiar >	Uniquely > identifiable	Referential >	Type Identifiable
English	*it*	*HE, this that, this N*	*That N*	*The N*	*Indefinite this N*	*a N*
Spanish	*Ø, él*	*El, este, ese, aquel, este N*	*Ese N Aquel N*	*El N*	*ØN Un N*	

Table 1. The Givenness Hierarchy

For the purposes of this paper, we will only deal with the first three cognitive statuses (in focus, activated and familiar) as these are the ones that directly affect demonstratives in some way. In focus entities occupy the highest position on the hierarchy whereas activated entities rank one step lower in the scale. In turn, familiar entities rank lower than activated ones. The statuses are in a unidirectional entailment relation (top-down) or, in other words, a given status entails all the other lower statuses (e.g. an entity which is in focus is necessarily also activated; an entity which is activated is necessarily familiar, etc.). As reflected in the hierarchy, English and Spanish demonstratives divide up between the activated and familiar statuses. On the one hand, demonstrative pronouns 'this' and 'that' (Spanish *esto*, *eso* and *aquello*) and proximal determiner 'this NP' (este NP) mark their referents as activated. On the other, the referents of English distal determiner 'that NP' and Spanish medial and distal *ese* NP/*aquel* NP are only familiar. This is actually surprising but the authors do not provide any reasons for this divide. Very likely, the separation between the two statuses is there to respect the traditional separation between distal and proximal demonstratives as proposed by Ariel and Fillmore and mentioned in section 2.

For Gundel et al., the different cognitive statuses stand for the memory or attention status that the intended referent is assumed to have in the mind of the addressee (2001: 39) and the role of the different referential expressions across languages is to signal a specific memory and/or attentional status. Most part of demonstrative expressions signals the status of their referents as activated. Crucial to the hypothesis presented in this paper is the distinction between in focus vs activated entities. Being activated means that there should be a representation of the referent in short-term memory (aka working memory). The referent of a zero pronoun or the English weak pronoun *it* must be cognitively *in focus*, meaning that the referent not only is in short-term memory but it is also at the current center of attention. At a given moment in discourse, in focus entities are the partially ordered subset of activated entities that are more likely to be the topic in subsequent discourse. Thus, in focus entities commonly include the topic of the previous clause as well as other still relevant topics. For Gundel et al., other factors like information structure or lexical information influence the cognitive status of the antecedents of pronominal anaphors. The following example[5] illustrates the distinction between in focus vs activated entities and the role of information structure on cognitive statuses.

(7) a. My neighbor's Bull Mastiff bit a girl on a bike.
b. *It's/That's* the same dog that bit Mary last summer.

(8) a. Sears delivered new siding to my neighbors with the Bull Mastiff.
b. *It's/That's* the same dog that bit Mary last summer.

The NP 'the Bull Mastiff' in (7a) can be re-mentioned with the weak pronoun 'it' in (7b) because the NP is in focus as it occupies a prominent position within sentence (7a) (e.g. subject and direct object positions are considered to be prominent in terms of information structure). The same entity can be referred to with a demonstrative pronoun because anything which is in focus is also rendered activated. Conversely, only the demonstrative pronoun 'that' can be used in (8b) to refer to the 'Bull Mastiff' because this NP occupies a more peripheral position within the sentence, that is, embedded within a prepositional phrase. Since peripheral syntactic positions do not commonly include the current topic or topics of discourse, the entity is rendered activated but not in focus. Therefore, reference with 'it' is not possible in (8b) as the hierarchy entailment only works in a top-down fashion. It is important to note that the status activated conferred to demonstrative pronouns in the GH it is so irrespective of the type of

[5] This example is from Gundel et al. (2001).

antecedent involved in the referential link. Thus, subordinate clauses, NPs, sentences or bigger chunks of discourse will all necessarily be activated when referred to via demonstrative pronouns.

In a subsequent paper, Gundel et al (2005) analyzed the behavior of referential pronouns without explicit antecedents. In that paper, pronouns without NP antecedents were classified as pleonastic (lacking a referent), possibly pleonastic, or referential. Referential pronouns were further classified by virtue of the type of referent (fact, proposition, activity, reason) that was introduced by a non-NP or as an inferrable. They observed that, something already found in Hegarty et al (2003), only around a 15% of pronominal reference to clausally introduced material in English was made using the pronoun 'it' as opposed to demonstrative pronouns 'this/that'. These were the results of an empirical study based on the Santa Barbara corpus of spoken American English. 330 third-person personal pronouns (16.1%) out of 2,046 were found to lack NP antecedents. In 110 out of these 330 cases, the pronoun 'it' was found to refer to some type of abstract object (fact, proposition, event, etc.)

	N	%
Fact	6	5.45
Proposition	10	9.09
Activity	27	24.55
Event	3	2.73
Situation	63	57.27
Reason	1	.91
Total	110	100.00

Table 2. Referential pronouns without NP antecedents

As Table 2 indicates, the number of eventualities (activities, events and situations) found in their corpus sample is comparatively much higher than that of propositional entities such as facts or propositions. They come to the conclusion, backed by Hegarty et al's suggestions, that the Givenness Hierarchy can explain the fact that most reference to abstract objects is made via demonstrative pronouns if it is assumed that material introduced in clauses or sequences of clauses is ACTIVATED as compared to material introduced in syntactically prominent noun phrases which is more likely to be IN FOCUS.

To a certain degree the status of demonstratives in GH resembles the intermediate position that demonstratives occupy in Ariel's SoA, but in my opinion this clearly goes against the more intuitive view of demonstratives as elements that bring entities into the current focus of attention. This is, in fact, the idea I will defend in this chapter, namely, that the main role of demonstratives (in deictic and anaphoric uses) is actually bringing entities into the current focus of attention of the participants in the conversation instead of being merely activated or medial accessibility markers. This hypothesis contravenes the status conferred to demonstratives in the GH and the accessibility of their referents in the SoA where the statuses activated and familiar and the intermediate position in the SoA are not enough to account for the pragmatic function of demonstratives in natural languages. Evidence from a corpus study that measures the degree of saliency of antecedents of Spanish demonstrative anaphors supports my hypothesis. But before we go on to present the methodology and results of the study in section 3 a few words are in order to introduce the notion of saliency into the current discussion.

2.3. Saliency

The task of giving an adequate and accurate definition of saliency is not at all trivial. This notion, deeply rooted in the cognitive sciences, was borrowed by linguists to account for the special status of certain discourse entities that were made more 'cognitively accessible' for the interlocutors under certain special conditions. When applied to discourse entities, notions like accessible and salient seem interchangeable. Simply by virtue of being salient an entity must be accessible for, otherwise, it would not be salient but instead concealed or inaccessible for an interpreter to a varying degree. In a similar fashion, a discourse entity, which is accessible for a hearer or interpreter, it is so by virtue of having been made salient by some linguistic or non-purely linguistic means. In any case, the distinction has been maintained between these terms in Linguistics and saliency is commonly used to refer to the (set of) most prominent entities in the speech situation. Saliency does not need to be a product of the speaker's strategy. A physical entity can be more salient than other competing entities in the same speech situation due to some special feature(s) that makes it to be more easily perceived by senses. Thus, for example, an entity that is closer to the discourse participants may be considered to be 'more salient' than other more distant entities although said entity may not be at the current focus of attention of the discourse participants. In this line, notions like foreground and background are intimately connected with saliency. Salient entities are commonly foregrounded whereas less prominent (perceptually speaking) entities are commonly in the background of the visual scene. Other factors that may contribute to making an entity salient are size, color, etc. Of course, an entity can be made salient by linguistic means as part of a speaker's communicative strategy and this is where demonstratives enter into the picture. In deictic uses, demonstratives are commonly accompanied by a deictic gesture such as a pointing finger or some other pointing device. This pointing gesture greatly contributes to single out an entity from a set of (possibly numerous) competing entities in the speech situation hence making it salient and focusing the addressee's attentional state on that particular object. The pragmatic contribution of deictic demonstratives to communication greatly derives from this ability to direct the hearer's focus of attention towards a particular element of the speech situation. This usage of demonstratives is clearly intentional unlike the non-calculated, non-communicative type of saliency mentioned before in this paragraph. Generally speaking, demonstratives serve to coordinate the interlocutor's *Joint Focus of Attention* (Diessel 2006). As this author points out (2006:465):

> "Joint attention is a complex phenomenon that involves three basic components: the actor, the addressee and an object of reference. In order to communicate, actor and addressee must share their attention on the same entity or situation. To this end, the actor directs the addressee's attention to a particular reference object in the surrounding situation; this may involve eye gaze, gesture, or the use of language. If the communicative act is successful, the communicative partners focus their attention on the same referent. In addition, they signal each other through eye gaze or other communicative means that they share the other person's focus of attention; that is, joint attention requires that the communicative partners recognize they are attending to the same thing."

3. The corpus study: methodology and results

In order to test the level of saliency of the antecedent of the demonstrative anaphor we segmented every example into its constituent clauses. We numbered each clause (CL_1, CL_2, CL_3 … CL_n) taking the clause containing the demonstrative anaphor (CL_0) as the reference point. Thus, clause CL_1 is the clause immediately preceding CL_0, CL_2 the second clause from CL_0 and so on. This way of annotating discourse would allow us to model the notion of distance in natural texts as proposed by Ariel and measure it in a controlled way. An example is shown in (9)[6]. Note that each segment is given in square brackets and the most likely antecedent in italics. The demonstrative anaphor *esto ocurrió* (this happened) is marked in small caps.

(9) P: ¿Hay muchos mitos en esta historia?
R: [Sí, los hay]$_{CL4}$; [como que Watson y Crick trabajaban en una barraca o en un cobertizo para bicicletas]$_{CL3}$. [No es verdad]$_{CL2}$. [Es cierto que *este grupo o cierta parte de este grupo ocupó la barraca que se convirtió en laboratorio*]$_{CL1}$, [pero *ESTO OCURRIO* cuatro años más tarde, en el 57]$_{CL0}$. Es como la historia de Newton y la manzana: hace falta la barraca y hace falta la manzana.

Q: Are there too many myths in this story?
A: [Yes, there are]$_{CL4}$; [like that one that says that Watson and Crick used to work together in a hut or a bicycle shed]$_{CL3}$. [That's not true]$_{CL2}$. [It is true that *this group, or a certain part of this group, occupied the hut that eventually became a lab*]$_{CL1}$, [but *THIS HAPPENED* four years later, in 1957]$_{CL0}$. It's like the story about Newton and the apple: we need the hut as much as we need the apple.

---

6 Source: CREA. *El País*, 23/04/2003. Spain.

We used the Spanish electronic corpus CREA[7] as the source of our examples. The corpus sample analyzed consisted of 193 examples: 82 cases for proximal demonstrative *esto*, 80 for medial *eso* and 31 for distal *aquello*. The disparity of the cases analyzed per demonstrative; in particular the low number (31) of cases for pronoun *aquello* is due to the actual frequency of use of demonstratives in modern Spanish. This is shown in Figures 1 and 2. Overall figures found in the corpus show that pronominal demonstrative *aquello* has a low frequency of use (6%) as compared to *esto* and *eso*. Even between these two pronouns the differences are quite relevant (*eso* 60%) and (*esto* 34%). This is a clear indication that pronominal demonstrative *eso* is preferred for speakers when it comes to referring to higher order entities in discourse like events, propositions or discourse topics.

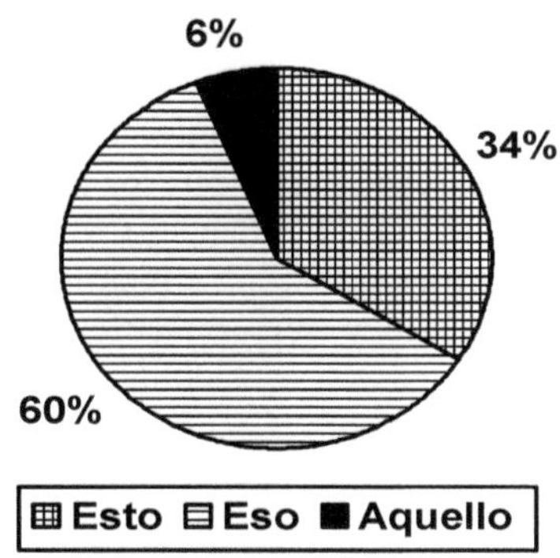

Figure 1. Overall frequency of use per demonstrative pronoun in modern Spanish

Nevertheless, overall figures change when the frequency of use of demonstrative adjectives is calculated. *Aquel* (NP) still shows a very low frequency of use (9%) when compared to *este* (NP) and *ese* (NP). But the total figures for these two demonstratives point in exactly the opposite direction as 30% of all corpus occurrences belong to demonstrative *ese* and a percentage as high as 61% to proximal *este*.

7 Corpus de Referencia del Español Actual accessible at http://corpus.rae.es/creanet.html.

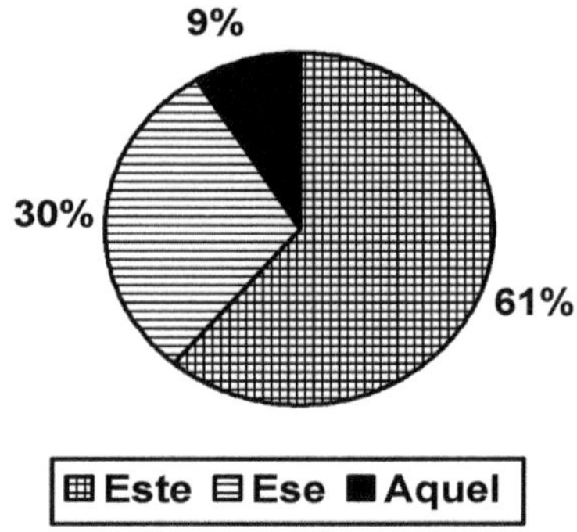

Figure 2. Overall frequency of use per demonstrative adjective in modern Spanish

For the purposes of our study, we restricted our corpus sample to events as type of referents of demonstrative anaphors. In order to restrict the referential potential of demonstratives, we searched the corpus for tokens of demonstrative plus typical predicates of events like *suceder* (happen), *ocurrir* (occur) or *pasar* (happen), e.g. *eso sucedió* ... (that happened ...), which force eventive readings. The principal advantages of this strategy were to restrict the high number of demonstratives found in the corpus as well as facilitating the annotation part of the study by narrowing down the type of referent to be scrutinized. The results per demonstrative pronoun and textual distance of their referents are given in table 3. The category N/A collects all those cases that could not be specified for whatever reason (e.g. antecedent could not be found due to lack of enough text retrieved from corpus, ambiguity due to two or more competing antecedents, not valid use of demonstrative anaphor, etc.). The category CAT stands for cases of cataphora, but the number of cases is trivial. Finally, category ≥5 stands for clause 5 or higher in the segment count.

	1CL	**2CL**	**3CL**	**4CL**	**≥5CL**	**N/A**	**CAT**	Total
ESTO	50	11	1	-	1	18	1	82
ESO	54	5	7	3	-	11	-	80
AQUELLO	19	4	-	1	1	6	-	31
Total	123	20	8	4	2	35	1	

Table 3. Cases of textual distance of referent per demonstrative

The graph in Figure 4 shows the overall frequency of demonstrative anaphors and referential distance as a percentage. N/A cases have been removed from this count thus reflecting valid cases only.

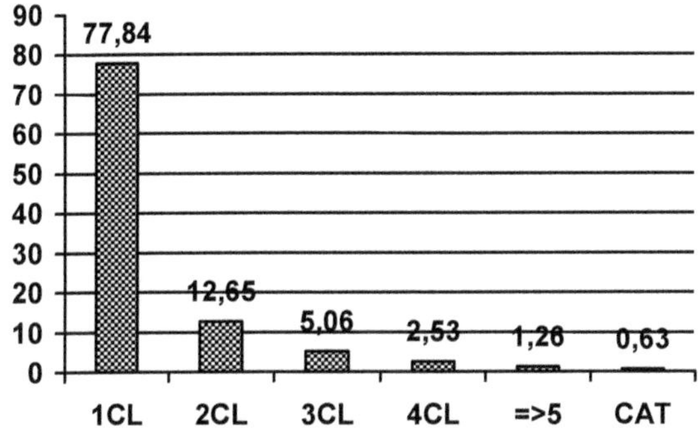

Figure 3. Textual distance of antecedent relative to anaphor location

As shown in Figure 3, Spanish demonstrative anaphors *esto*, *eso* and *aquello* show a strong preference for their antecedents to be found in the clause or sentence immediately preceding the clause hosting the anaphor. There are no major differences among demonstratives concerning textual referential distance. Overall, in 77% of the cases scrutinized the antecedent was found in CL_1. An observation already made for English demonstratives *this* and *that* (Gundel et al. 2001). Based on this figures, it is hard to see how and why entities that have been so recently mentioned in discourse relative to the utterance of the anaphor should not be in the current focus of attention of the discourse participants. In my opinion, the results presented here indicate that the cognitive status ACTIVATED for antecedents of Spanish demonstrative anaphors is not adequate. The reasons and an alternative solution to account for this puzzle will be discussed in the following section.

4. Conclusions

The examples and data on Spanish demonstrative anaphors presented in this paper question the viability of Ariel and Gundel et al.'s thesis on demonstrative elements. We saw that, according to the SoA, demonstrative referential expressions (in pronominal and adjectival form) are only medial accessibility markers. Let's remind that, as proposed by Ariel (1988, 1990), accessibility refers to the ease a hearer or addressee may encounter in accessing the referent of a particular referential expression (i.e. to be able to form a mental image of it, or mentally conceive the referent or retrieve from the memory storage). I have nothing to say regarding the appropriateness, applicability or relevance of the SoA as a theoretical construct. In my opinion, though, the primary pragmatic role of demonstratives in anaphoric use is not that of marking how accessible it is for an addressee to access its referent but rather to indicate the addressee that he/she should focus her attention on 'this/that' particular discourse referent. In this respect, Spanish demonstrative anaphors (and very likely most demonstrative anaphors across languages as well) should be better conceived as *pragmatic focus markers* that increase the level of saliency of their referents. Demonstratives thus contribute to communication by establishing a *joint attentional focus* between the participants in the conversation much in the way proposed by Diessel (2006). In this respect, demonstrative anaphors would not differ much from their deictic counterparts and the use by speakers of a pointing gesture to focus the attention of the addressee on a particular entity in a real-world discourse situation.

As the results of our corpus study clearly indicate, the antecedents of demonstrative anaphors in Spanish are most commonly found in the clause that immediately precedes the anaphor. In nearly 80% of the cases of demonstrative pronouns scrutinized the antecedent was found in clause category CL_1. This fact indicates that giving these antecedents (and semantic referents) a status other than in focus would be very difficult to reconcile with the fact that they have been but very recently processed in discourse. The recency of mention of antecedents to demonstrative anaphors does, intuitively at least, indicate that their referents should not be hard to access by the addressee in the sense given to this term in the Accessibility Theory. Much in the same line we can argue against the statuses ACTIVATED and FAMILIAR given to demonstrative expressions in the Givenness Hierarchy (Gundel et al., 1993). As proposed there, demonstratives signal their antecedents as being cognitively ACTIVATED (demonstrative pronouns *this/that* and proximal determiner *this*-NP) or FAMILIAR (distal determiner *that*-NP), a status lower in the hierarchy than the status IN FOCUS, which is the one assigned to null or weak pronouns like English *it*. The figures from our study indicate that, at the textual level, abstract antecedents should be more appropriately conceived of as IN FOCUS rather than being merely activated or familiar to the addressee. In my opinion, a characterization of demonstrative expressions as elements whose primary pragmatic role is that of signaling a certain cognitive status cannot be sustained in view of factors like referential distance. But even if we wish to deny the importance of referential distance to explain the saliency of certain discourse elements and are willing to accept syntactic prominence as a determining factor, we still would be forced to explain cases in which the (propositional) antecedent is found in subject position (the most likely discourse topic) and still referred to with a demonstrative anaphor as in example (6).

The ideas sketched in this paper are not intended to be conclusive at all. Other important factors should be explored that may contribute to a better understanding of the general discourse behavior of demonstrative anaphors. Thus, for example, it would be interesting to investigate to what extent the syntactic position of the antecedent within the clause may have an impact on the referential behavior of demonstratives. On the other hand, testing the differences between demonstratives and other pronominal elements may shed some light on the general referential capabilities of demonstrative anaphors. Other information structure related factors like the possible contribution of lexical information or referential types (e.g. do event-denoting antecedents behave on a par with, say, factual-denoting antecedents?); or the role of context in licensing demonstrative anaphors (e.g. may specific lexical items in the textual surroundings favor the use of demonstratives over other referential expressions?) may also contribute to a deeper knowledge of the distribution of referential expressions. The list is long but the challenge is compelling enough to be worth the effort.

References

Ariel, M. (1988): "Referring and accessibility," *Journal of Linguistics*, 24, 1, 65-87.

Ariel, M. (1990): "*Accessing Noun Phrase Antecedents*," London/New York, Routledge.

Asher, N. (1993): *Reference to Abstract Objects in Discourse*, Kluwer.

Davidson, D. (1980): *Essays on Actions and Events*, Oxford, Clarendon Press.

Diessel, H. (2006): "Demonstratives, joint attention and the emergence of grammar," *Cognitive Linguistics*, 17, 4, 463-489.

Fernández-Ramírez, S. (1951): *Gramática Española. 3.2: El pronombre*, Madrid, Arco Libros, 1986.

Fillmore, C. (1975): *Santa Cruz Lectures on Deixis*, Bloomington, Indiana University Linguistics Club.

Givon, T. (1983): "Topic continuity in discourse: an introduction," in T. Givon (ed.), *Topic Continuity in Discourse: A quantitative cross-language Study*, Amsterdam/Philadelphia, John Benjamins, 1-41.

Grosz, B., K. J. Aravind and S. Weinstein (1995): "Centering: a framework for modeling the local coherence of discourse," *Computational Linguistics*, 21, 2, 203-226.

Gundel, J. K., N. Hedberg and R. Zacharski (1993): "Cognitive status and the form of referring expressions in discourse," *Language*, 69, 274-307.

Gundel, J. K., M. Hegarty and K. Borthen (2001): "Information structure and pronominal reference to clausally introduced entities," in I. Kruijff-Korbay and M. Steedman (eds.), *Proceedings from the Workshop on Information Structure*, European Summer School on Logic, Language and Information (ESSLLI), Helsinki, 37-51.

Gundel, J. K., N. Hedberg and R. Zacharski (2005): "Pronouns without NP antecedents: how do we know when a pronoun is referential?" in A. Branco, T. McEnery and R. Mitkov (eds.), *Anaphora Processing: Linguistic, Cognitive and Computational Modelling*, John Benjamins, 351-364.

Hegarty, M., J. K. Gundel and K. Borthen (2003): "Cognitive status, information structure and pronominal reference to clausally introduced entities," *Journal of Logic, Language and Information*, 12, 3, 281-299.

Piwek, P. and A. Cremers (1996): "Dutch and English demonstratives: a comparison," *Language Sciences*, 18, 3-4, 835-851.

Reichenbach, H. (1947): *Elements of Symbolic Logic*, London, MacMillan.

Zulaica-Hernández, I. (2008): *Demonstrative Pronouns in Spanish: A Discourse-based Study*, PhD Dissertation, The Ohio State University.

PART THREE

Specific Applications

Working with English specialized corpora: *lexical bundles* in written scientific and technical English

Pedro A. Fuertes-Olivera
José Maria Rodrigues Rodrigues
Universidad de Valladolid

1. Introduction

Hunston provides one of the most comprehensive definitions of a specialized corpus:

> "A corpus of texts of a particular type, such as newspaper editorials, geography textbooks, academic articles in a particular subject, lectures, casual conversations, essays written by students, etc. It aims to be representative of a given type of text. It is used to investigate a particular type of language. Researchers often collect their own specialised corpora to reflect the kind of language they want to investigate. There is no limit to the degree of specialisation involved, but the parameters are set to limit the kind of texts included. For example, a corpus might be restricted to a time frame, consisting of texts from a particular century, or to a social setting, such as conversations taking place in a bookshop, or to a given topic such as newspaper articles dealing with the European Union" (Hunston 2002: 14).

According to the above definition, parameters such as written/spoken, diachronic/synchronic, historical/contemporary can be applied to both general and specialized corpora. Other parameters, however, emphasize a narrower approach to specialized corpora by indicating that specialized corpora usually refer to genre, register and topic-specific corpora designed to include only samples of language of a particular type, belonging to a particular genre, register, type of text, variety of English, etc.

Furthermore, specialized corpora are smaller than their general counterparts and can also be divided into sub-corpora. For example, the Michigan Corpus of Academic Spoken English (MICASE) can be split into specialized sub-corpora such as lectures, seminars, service encounters and tutorials (Powell and Simpson 2001). Flowerdew (2004: 21) summarizes the parameters by which corpus linguists tend to define specialized corpora, with examples that illustrate them (Table 1).

A review of the literature on corpus linguistics indicates the existence of two complementary research trends. First, researchers are compiling and working with *giga-corpora* (i.e., billion-word corpora using websites and newswire texts as data sources, such as the *English Gigaword Corpus* produced by the Linguistic Data Consortium (see http://www.ldc.upenn.edu/Catalog/CatalogEntry.jsp?

catalogId=LDC2003T05). Second, researchers are also compiling and working with small specialized corpora designed for studies of English for Specific Purposes (Thompson 2007).

Parameters	**Details / Examples**
Specific purpose for compilation:	To investigate particular grammatical, lexical, lexico-grammatical, discoursal or rhetorical features
Contextualization:	Setting (e.g. lecture hall) Participants (role of speaker / listener; writer / reader) Communicative purpose (e.g. promote, instruct)
Size: whole corpus subcorpus or small-scale corpus	 1-5 million words 20,000 – 250,000 words
Genre:	Promotional (grant proposals, sales letters)
Type of text / discourse:	Biology textbooks, casual conversations
Subject matter / topic:	Economics, the weather
Variety of English	Learner, non-standard (e.g. Indian, Singaporean)

Table 1. Parameters for defining corpora as specialized (Flowerdew 2004: 21)

In a recent paper, Fuertes-Olivera (2008) offers the stay of play in specialized corpus-based research differentiating between works carried out with *in-house localized specialized corpora* and *open-to-the-research community specialized corpora* (see Krishnamurthy and Kosem's (2007) review of existing EAP corpora). They are mainly differentiated in terms of size, focus, and participants. Fuertes-Olivera understands localized in-house corpora as corpora compiled by an individual or group of individuals, who work in the same institution, tend to be around 500,000 words, usually focused on a specific text type or genre (for example, 'research articles'), and aim mainly at drawing both pedagogical applications for the teaching and research activities carried out in the institution (see Hyland and Tse 2005; Flowerdew and Wan 2006). In broad terms, they are similar to "own purpose-built collections of texts/transcripts" (Thompson 2007: 285).

Fuertes-Olivera refers to open access corpora as "ready-made corpora" (Thompson 2007: 285), whose main characteristics are the following:

- they are larger corpora, sometimes in the millions of word range (e.g. *Wolverhampton Corpus of Written Business English*; *TOEFL 2000 Spoken and Written Academic Language Corpus* (T2K-SWAL));

- they are usually compiled by the joint effort of academic institutions and Publishing houses (e.g. *Cambridge and Nottingham Corpus of Business English* (CANBEC);

- they aim at covering different text types or genres of the same or different register(s) (T2K-SWAL);

- they can be freely accessed through the internet (e.g. *Michigan Corpus of Academic Spoken English* (MICASE); *British Academic Spoken English/ British Academic Written English* (BASE/BAWE)), or acquired from institutions such as ELRA (e.g. the *Wolverhampton Corpus of Written Business English*);

- they can be useful for replicating analyses and broadening the scope of research concerned with both drawing pedagogical applications and allowing the grammar of English for Specific Purposes (ESP) to emerge (see Biber et al., 2004; Simpson, 2004; Nesi & Gardner 2006; Swales 2006).

This paper is concerned with the *University of Valladolid Corpus of Written Scientific and Technical English* (*UVaSTECorpus*), an 'in-house' localized specialized corpus of written scientific and technical English (see Section 3, below). In particular, it analyzes the presence of some *lexical bundles* in order to meet two main research objectives. Firstly, is the presence of lexical bundles in written scientific and technical English quantitatively similar or different to Biber et al.'s (1999) findings concerning academic prose?

Secondly, if variation exists, is its extent deep enough to offer grounds to scholars who defend the existence of significant intra-variation within the same genre, register, domain, etc? For example, Hyland (2002: 389) claims that "the discourse of the academy does not form an undifferentiated, unitary mass but a variety of subject specific literacies."

In his introduction to the special issue of the *Journal of English for Academic Purposes* devoted to corpus-based EAP pedagogy, Thompson (2007:285) claims that corpora are "sources of evidence about language use, and permit a wide variety of analyses of how language is used in different registers, contexts and by different users." Considering that the two abovementioned objectives are interrelated, the paper fulfils another objective: corpus analyses are necessary for minimizing some of the critics regarding the use of corpus in classes: how teachers and learners are to gain access to corpora; the relative lack of relevant corpora; familiarity with corpus methodology, etc. (see Swales 2002; Gavioli 2005; Krishnamurthy and Kosem 2007).

2. Lexical bundles in specialized English

Corpus approaches to the behaviour of phraseology in specialized English have emphasized three interesting findings. First, phraseological units present difficulties for the novice writer. Charles (2006), for example, investigates the phraseological patterning that occurs in reporting clauses used to make references to other research. In her analysis, which involves texts from two disciplines – politics/international relations; material science – she concludes that it would be helpful for students to realize that one way of incorporating citation into texts is to use a *reporting verb* followed by a *that-clause* and that in this pattern a human subject is likely to be used. Second, genre constraints influence the type and patterns of phraseological units used (see Oakey 2002; Biber et al., 2004; Groom 2005; Hyland 2008). Biber et al. (2004), for example, have found that phraseological units are more frequent in classroom talks than in informal conversation and academic prose. Third, the analysis of phraseology in specialized discourse offers a lot of research opportunities, based on the key role these units play in natural occurring language. Nesi & Basturkmen (2006), for example, discuss some approaches to the categorisation of cohesive devices with reference to spoken academic discourse, multi-word units, and lexical bundles. They investigate the cohesive role of lexical bundles in a corpus of 160 university lectures (120 from the BASE corpus and 40 from MICASE), and found that the majority of phraseological units used showed discourse relations (i.e., they do not have a semantic value but a pragmatic one).

This paper adds to the abovementioned research scenario by analyzing some key aspects of *lexical bundles*, a special type of recurrent word combination or formulaic sequence. Biber et al. (1999: 990-1024) regard *lexical bundles* as sequences of word forms that commonly go together in natural discourse. They are identified empirically, as combinations of words that recur most commonly in a given register, genre and/or text-type. They add (1999: 992) that "[t]hree-word bundles can be considered as a kind of extended collocational association, and they are thus extremely common. On the other hand, four-word, five-word, and six-word bundles are more phrasal in nature and correspondingly less common."

To qualify as a lexical bundle, Biber et al. (1999: 992-3) add that the word combination must occur at least ten times per million words in a register, and these occurrences must be spread across at least five different texts in the register, and that only uninterrupted combinations of words must be treated as potential lexical bundles.

Our analysis follows current research by Biber and colleagues (Biber 2006; Biber et al. 1999; Biber and Barbieri 2007; Biber et al. 2004) who base their analysis on two corpora: the *Longman Spoken and Written English Corpus* (LSWE Corpus) and the *TOEFL 2000 Spoken and Written Academic Language* (T2K-SWAL) *Corpus*. Some of their findings emphasize that the cohesive function of lexical bundles is not obvious out of context, and that in some genres and registers, lexical bundles are widespread and perform a greater range of functions than in others. For example, classroom teaching not only has a greater frequency and variety of lexical bundles but the range of functions (e.g., marking stance, organizing discourse) performed by the lexical bundle was much greater than those functions found in textbooks or in conversation and academic prose.

More specifically, Biber et al. (1999: 994) claim that lexical bundles are widespread in academic prose. Firstly, three-word lexical bundles such as *in order to, one of the, part of the, the number of, the presence of, the use of, the fact that, there is a,* and *there is no* have over 200 occurrences per million words. Secondly, four-word lexical bundles such as *in the case of; on the other hand* have over 100 occurrences per million words. In addition, both groups agree on occurring in non-recurring expressions without syntactic and/or semantic value.

The above findings merit further investigation and will be explored in the *UVaSTECorpus*, thus gaining further knowledge on how some lexical bundles behave in written scientific and technical English, a key register of ESP, adequate for performing research leading either to specific pedagogical applications or to a better knowledge of ESP grammar.

The rationale for this research agrees with current corpus analyses that are interested in discovering generalizable findings that hold across texts (Ädel and Reppen 2008), as well as adding to our knowledge on (possible) variation within register. This analysis is innovative in, at least, two related ways. Firstly, the corpus analyzed has never been used for discovering the presence of lexical bundles in written scientific and technical English. Second, it offers a qualitative study of *in order to* and *the fact that* because they show similar but different trends to those discussed by Biber et al. (1999). One of them agrees quantitatively with Biber et al's (1999), whereas the other disagrees significantly by presenting smaller figures and showing different recurrent patterns and uses.

3. The University of Valladolid Corpus of written Scientific and Technical English (UVaSTECorpus)

The *University of Valladolid Corpus of Written Scientific and Technical English (UVaSTECorpus)* stands at our original target of 3,000,000 words of scientific and technical English. It was designed by Fuertes-Olivera and José María Rodrígues, collected at the University of Valladolid (April 2005, April 2006), and enriched with information of text type, genre, author(s), geographical variety, subject matter, year of production, purpose of the text, and origin of the documents (Fuertes-Olivera and José María Rodrígues 2007) (table 2).

Sub-corpus	*Genre*	*Number of words*	*% of sub-corpus*	*% of corpus*
Sub-corpus: 'Research'	Learned Informational:	2,137,171	100	**70.5**
	Research Articles	1,529,595	71.5	50.4
	Review Articles	607,576	28.5	20.1
	Sub-total	2,137,171	100	**70.5**
Sub-corpus: 'Official'	Informational (Reportage):	727,876	**81.3**	**24**
	Report	727,876	81.3	24
	Instructional:	167,078	**18.7**	**5.5**
	Sub-total	894,954	100	**29.5**
	TOTAL CORPUS	3,032,125		100

Table 2. Documents in the *UVaSTECorpus*

Assuming that a corpus should be compiled falling back on non-probability sampling techniques involving *judgment* and *convenience* (Meyer 2002: 44), the Corpus was randomly selected from English collections of written documents comprising scientific and technical informational and instructional genres, adequate for investigating particular grammatical, lexical, lexico-grammatical, discoursal or rhetorical features of written scientific and technical English.

The documents are the product of three types of users: native researchers; non-native researchers using English as a *lingua franca*; and official bodies in the UK and the USA producing different types of reports and/or instructional documents on 'science and technology'. Hence, the corpus is subdivided into two main sub-corpora of documents: informational learned 'research' texts (70.5% of the corpus) and informational reportage and instructional administrative documents (29.5% of the corpus).

The former comprise texts produced by researchers in different fields published in peer-reviewed international journals. This sub-corpus groups publications either as 'research' or as 'review,' depending on the purpose of the paper. If the paper presents new findings or methodologies they were classified as "research". If the paper summarizes the state of the art in a particular topic it was grouped as "review." Considering the amount of pages usually devoted in journals to the two categories, a 3:1 selection criterion was used for collecting them which resulted in 71.5% of the sub-corpus for 'research articles' and 28.5% for 'review articles' (including 'PhD summaries,' 'discussion notes,' 'letters,' etc.). All the texts were taken from leading journals indexed in the ISI Science Citation Index covering Science and Technology domains, and covering the most important domains dealing with science and technology. For example, in the genre 'research article' included in the sub-corpus 'research', the following domains and number of words per domain were compiled: (i) applied mathematics and statistics (237,911 words), (ii) physics, X-Rays and radiology (138, 615 words), (iii) chemistry and food processing (174,921 words), (iv) engineering (154,784 words), (v) materials, composites, and minerals (180,574 words), (vi) environment (206,437 words), (vii) computing (147,399 words), (viii) biotechnology (137,221 words), and (ix) information systems (151,382 words) (Figure 1).

The latter consist of official documents produced by government bodies and professional societies. These were grouped into two main categories: informational reports; instructional documents. Informational reports are the work of national and/or international committees. For example, the National Science and Technology Committee is an American public body that produces reports on national and/or international policies on science and technology (for example, *national priorities in science and technology policy*), or inform on research priorities and related issues (for example, *the science of climate change: adapt, mitigate or ignore?*).

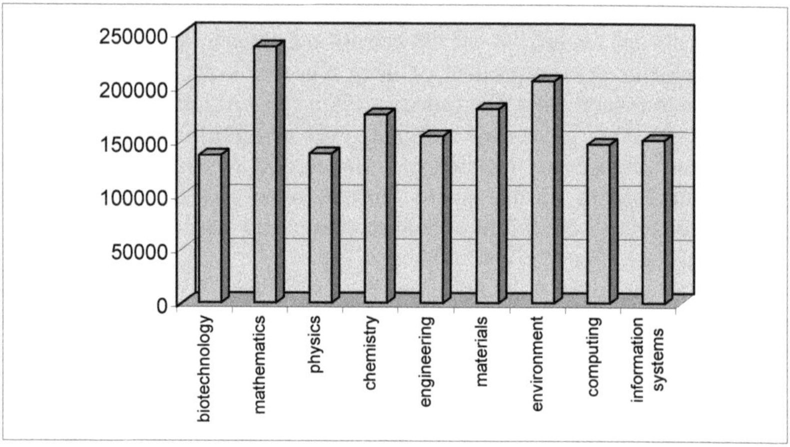

Figure 1. Number of words per domain of the research articles included in the sub-corpus 'Research'

Instructional documents are also produced by official bodies aiming at giving instructions on future course of actions regarding scientific and technical policies. For example, guidelines and bulletins to universities, professional societies and research bodies commenting on future allocation of funds for Science and Technology programs. Considering that *reports* are more widely disseminated (for example they are discussed in Parliaments), we selected them according to a 5:1 criterion: reports comprise around 81%of the sub-corpus and instructional documents amount to a figure just below 19% of the sub-corpus) (see Table 2, above).

4. Results and discussion

4.1. Quantitative discussion

Table 3 presents figures of the occurrences of lexical bundles in the UVaSTE-Corpus. They were extracted using WordSmith Tools (Scott 2004). For this analysis, we have chosen nine three-word lexical bundles that Biber et al. (1999: 994) claim that they occur over 200 times per one million words in academic prose. All the concordances of the nine lexical bundles studied were extracted and analyzed manually for deciding if they qualify as lexical bundles. The figures given in Table 3 represent the total number of occurrences of these expressions that meet the conditions for qualifying as lexical bundles (Biber et al. 1999: 992-3): all of them occur more than ten times per million words in a register; these occurrences are spread across more than five different texts in the register; all of them are uninterrupted combinations of words. Table 3 also shows the relative frequency of each lexical bundle per one million words. This allows us to compare our findings with other findings reported in the literature considering that the relative frequency figure is adequate for comparing the number of occurrences found in different corpora.

Lexical Bundles	Number of occurrences	Relative Frequency
The number of	471	155
In order to	436	144
The use of	359	118
One of the	336	110
There is a	288	95
Part of the	286	94
The presence of	132	43
The fact that	115	38
There is no	114	37

Table 3. Lexical bundles in the *UVaSTECorpus*:
Total occurrences and relative frequency per one million words

The results given in Table 3 indicate that Hyland's hypothesis that the discourse of the academy presents a lot of variation is confirmed. Firstly, Table 3 shows results very different, - particularly noticeable for *the use of, one of the, there is a, part of the, the presence of, the fact that,* and *there is no* – to those reported by Biber et al (1999), as none of the nine three-word lexical bundles occur over 200 times per one million words. Second, Table 3 also shows that there is a very significant variation among the nine lexical bundles, whose occurrence in the corpus goes from 471 occurrences (*the number of*) to only 114 (*there is no*). The variation is so significant that a proportion binomial test offers negligible results ($p<0.00000004$). This idea reinforces our interest for individual analyses of the above elements, a previous and necessary step to spot possible basic differences that will make necessary to accommodate our teaching materials to the new findings.

This variation may rest on either pragmatic constraints (for example, genre conventions in connection with the different types of genres present in the corpus), ethnographic information (for example, the texts' authors differ in terms of mother tongue, academic tradition; there are different academic traditions regarding the different subject-fields covered in the corpus), or grammatical preferences. Future research will focus on this and similar factors by producing a more fine-grained analysis breaking the general data into different categories based on authors' mother tongue, academic tradition, subject-field conventions, etc. Below, we will present a qualitative analysis of two of them based on grammatical preferences.

4.2. Qualitative analysis: 'in order to' and 'the fact that'

The qualitative analysis focuses on two lexical bundles: *in order to*, and *the fact that*. Their relative frequency in the corpus analyzed shows that they behave differently considering that the former partly agrees quantitatively with Biber et al.'s claim regarding overall frequency in Academic English, whereas the latter is very far from it.

In order to is formed by a subordinator (*in order*) + the infinitive marker *to*, introduces infinitival purpose clauses, is more formal than similar competing expressions (for example *so as to*), and is relatively common in academic prose where purpose clauses are frequently introduced with *in order to* in both initial and final position. *The fact that* comprises an English noun (*fact*) + *that* in two different constructions. One of them introduces a complement clause or a relative clause, occurs as subject of an extraposed *that*-clause that presents "the proposition in the *that*-clause as factual or generally accepted information" (Biber et al. 1999: 676), and is a good indicator of personal style. Biber et al. (1999: 679), for example, comment that "62% of all clauses beginning with *the fact that* found in academic prose are from four texts (13 out of 21 examples in a million-word sample), even though these texts comprise only c. 7% of all academic prose in the sample." The other one is a prepositional phrase ending in *the fact that* ('Type 3 marginal subordinator' in Quirk et al. 1985: 1002) expressing relationships of reason or concession. They are stylistically clumsy, as they can be substituted by a simple conjunction.

Our analysis of the 436 and 115 occurrences of *in order to* and *the fact that* in the *UVaSTECorpus* offers interesting findings. Regarding distribution, *in order to* prefers post predicative position in written scientific and technical English: 275 of the 436 occurrences with *in order to* are in final position (Table 4). This figure indicates that purpose clauses are almost two times more frequent in rhematic position than in thematic one, in accordance with English syntactic patterns which tend to give end-focus to predication adjuncts considering that the logical order of decoding opens with facts/methods before signaling what they are for (examples (1) and (2)).

Position	Number	%
Initial	275	63.07
Final	159	36.93
TOTAL	436	100

Table 4. Position of *in order to* in written Scientific and Technical English

(1) *In order to* in initial position

In order to achieve the full capability of BeamTool, the user is encouraged to explore the tool interactively. (*UVaSTECorpus*: Research: "BEAMTOOL: Interactive Beam Analysis for Today's Student and Tomorrow's Engineer").

(2) *In order to* in final position
In that framework, machine-learning techniques, such as association rule mining or clustering, are used to extract knowledge from Web documents *in order to* create new ontologies or improve existing ones.
(*UVaSTECorpus:* Research: "Web Mining: Machine learning for Web Applications")

There are eighteen clusters with *in order to* that account for 32.5% of the occurrences, thus giving support to the idea that corpus linguistics is very adequate for spotting recurrent facts (Table 5).

Cluster	Number of occurrences
In order to provide	20
In order to make	13
In order to achieve	11
In order to improve	10
In order to determine	9
In order to find	9
In order to get	9
In order to obtain	7
In order to satisfy	7
In order to show	6
In order to ensure	6
In order to test	5
In order to compute	5
In order to address	5
In order to avoid	5
In order to be	5
In order to develop	5
In order to maximize	5
TOTAL	142

Table 5. Clusters with *in order to* in written scientific and technical English

A detailed analysis of the sentences where the above clusters are found indicates that the purpose clause with *in order to* shows a preference for cognitively-oriented processes. For example, of the 20 occurrences of *in order to provide*, 10 of them refer to 'information' (example 3). Similarly, of the 13 occurrences of *in order to make,* 8 of them refer to mental acts such as 'making cuts in a system,' 'making progress in a research,' etc. (example 4).

(3) Many challenging downscaling and upscaling research issues remain to be addressed *in order to provide* the most useful information possible for decision support. (*UVaSTECorpus:* Official: "A Report by the Climate Change Science Program and the Subcommittee on Global Change Research").

(4) For scientific information to have an impact, it will have to rely on refined and extended research on the role, entry points, and types of water cycle knowledge required for water management and policy decisionmaking processes. *In order to make* rapid progress it will be necessary to integrate data from a broad range of sources and disciplines. (*UVaSTECorpus*: Research: "Preservation of Digital Object")

For indicating purpose, *in order to* is much more frequent than *so as to* in written scientific and technical English: there are only 30 occurrences of *so as to* in the corpus, compared with the 436 of *in order to*; i.e., there are almost 15 occurrences of *in order to* per one occurrence of *so as to* (example 5):

(5) To the extent possible, new or improved measurements will be integrated into existing networks *so as to* minimize redundant operations and costs. (*UVaSTECorpus:* Official: "A Report by the Climate Change Science Program and the Subcommittee on Global Change Research")

The fact that is more common in 'extraposed that-clauses' than in prepositional phrases functioning as 'marginal subordinator' (Quirk et al. 1985: 1001). There are only 20 occurrences of the latter, 8 of which are occurrences of *due to the fact that,* which agrees with the idea that using *due to the fact that* is stylistically clumsy and should therefore be avoided in academic prose (example 6).

(6) This is due to *the fact that* hard interference constraints are turned into soft constraints by the use of penalties. (*UVaSTECorpus:* Research: "Models and solution techniques for frequency assignment problems")

In 'extraposed that clauses', *the fact that* typically functions as subject reflecting the general preference for 'end-focus' in English, where 'light' subjects without semantic load are much more frequent than 'full subjects' in thematic positions (example 7).

(7) *The fact that* multiple signals may disturb communication quality is ignored in most models where only interference between pairs of connections or antennae is measured. (*UVaSTECorpus:* Research: "Models and solution techniques for frequency assignment problems")

As expected, the use of *the fact that* is highly conditioned by stylistic preference: only 57 of the 455 texts of the corpus (12.5%) shows instances of this use.

Although the general picture regarding the two lexical bundles analyzed agrees with the description made in corpus-based grammars and teaching materials, it also shows the presence of some recurrent patterns (see Table 5), and uses (*the fact that*) in extraposed '*that*-clauses') that shed light on the behaviour of the lexical bundles analyzed in written scientific and technical English

5. Conclusions

Every time we write or speak, we are faced with a myriad of choices in what we say and in how we say it. The vocabulary and grammar that we use to communicate are influenced by a number of factors, such as the reason for the communication, the context, the people with whom we are communicating, and whether we are speaking or writing. Taken together, these choices give rise to systematic patterns of use in English (Barnbrook et al. 2005; Biber 2006).

Traditionally, such patterns have not been subject to linguistic analyses, nor paid attention to in teaching activities. Most grammars, for example, have focused on the form and meaning of grammatical constructions rather than on how they are actually used in spoken and written discourse. In part, the restrictive emphasis of past descriptions has existed simply because grammar has been defined as the study of structures. But the disregard for paying attention to *use* has also been due to our lack of adequate information about the actual patterns of language features in real-world contexts (Hoey 2005).

Regarding our first research objective, we conclude that the existence of widespread variation in the discourse of the academy is confirmed in this paper: none of the nine three-word lexical bundles reported agree quantitatively with the results reported by Biber et al. referring to academic prose nor show a similar pattern among them. Put it differently, our findings show that intra-variation within genres and registers is deeper than previously reported.

Concerning the second research objective, this corpus-driven analysis (Tognini-Bonelli 2001) offers mixed results. On the one hand, the grammatical pattern of the two lexical bundles studied agrees with grammar descriptions. On the other hand, they show a marked preference for its presence in specific clusters and uses. Both findings must be highlighted in our teaching activities regarding written scientific and technical English, as they constitute defining features our students must know and take care of. For example, we can devise exercises comparing the use of *the fact that* as subject of an extraposed *that*-clause with a pre-predicate *that*-clause. Although they are alternative variants, it is important our students understand that the former is more adequate in academic prose whereas the second should be avoided in written scientific and technical English texts.

ACKNOWLEDGMENTS: Thanks are due to the *Ministerio de Ciencia e Innovación* for financial support (grant FFI2008.01703/FILO); also to the *Junta de Castilla y León* (grant VA-039A09). Thanks are also due to the organizers of CILC-09, especially to Dr. Aquilino Sánchez for his comments. For all remaining imperfections, only we are to blame.

References

Ädel, A. and R. Reppen, eds. (2008): *Corpora and discourse: The challenges of different settings*, Amsterdam/Philadelphia, John Benjamins.

Barnbrook, G., P. Danielsson and M. Mahlberg (eds.) (2005): *Meaningful texts: The extraction of semantic information from monolingual and multilingual corpora*, London/New York, Continuum.

Biber, D. (2006): *University language. A corpus-based study of spoken and written registers*, Amsterdam / Philadelphia, John Benjamins.

Biber, D. and F. Barbieri (2007): "Lexical bundles in university spoken and written registers," *English for Specific Purposes*, 26, 3, 263-286.

Biber, D., S. Johansson, G. Leech, S. Conrad, and E. Finegan (1999): *Longman Grammar of Spoken and Written English*, London, Longman.

Biber, D., S. Conrad, R. Reppen, P. Byrd, M. Helt, V. Clark, V. Cortes, E. Csomay and A. Urzua (2004): *Representing language use in the university. Analysis of the TOEFL 2000 spoken and written academic language corpus*, Princeton, NJ, ETS.

Charles, M. (2006): "Phraseological patterns in reporting clauses used in citation: a corpus-based study of two disciplines," *English for Specific Purposes*, 25, 310-331.

Cortes, V. (2004): "Lexical bundles in public and disciplinary writing: examples from history and biology," *English for Specific Purposes*, 23, 4, 397-423.

Cortes, V. (2006): "Teaching lexical bundles in the disciplines: an example from a writing intensive history class," *Linguistics and Education*, 17, 4, 391-406.

Flowerdew, L. (2004): "The argument for using English specialized corpora to understand academic and professional language," in U. Connor and T. A. Upton. (eds.): *Discourse in the professions. Perspectives from corpus linguistics*, Amsterdam/Philadelphia: John Benjamins, 11-33.

Flowerdew, J. and A. Wan (2006): "Genre analysis of tax computation letters: how and why tax accountants write the way they do," *English for Specific Purposes*, 25, 2, 133-153.

Fuertes-Olivera, P. A. (2008): "Pedagogical applications of specialized corpora in ESP teaching: The case of the UVaSTECorpus," *Scripta Manent. Journal of the Slovene Association of LSP Teachers*, 3, 2, 1-15.

Fuertes-Olivera, P. A. and J. M. Rodrigues Rodrigues (2007): "The University of Valladolid Corpus of Written Scientific and Technical English. Technical Report," Escuela Universitaria de Estudios Empresariales, University of Valladolid.

Gavioli, L. (2005): *Exploring corpora for ESP learning*, Amsterdam/Philadelphia, John Benjamins.

Groom, N. (2005): "Pattern and meaning across genres and disciplines: An exploratory study," *Journal of English for Academic Purposes*, 4, 3, 257-277.

Hanks, P. (ed.) (2008): "The lexicographical legacy of John Sinclair," Special Issue of *International Journal of Lexicography*, 21, 3, 219-229.

Hoey, M. (2005): *Lexical priming: A new theory of words and language*, London/New York, Routledge.

Huddleston, R. and G. K. Pullum (2002): *The Cambridge grammar of the English language*, Cambridge, Cambridge University Press.

Hunston, S. (2002): *Corpora in Applied Linguistics*, Cambridge, Cambridge University Press.

Hyland, K. (2002): "Specificity revisited: How far should we go?" *English for Specific Purposes*, 21, 4, 385-395.

Hyland, K. (2008): "As can be seen: lexical bundles and disciplinary variation," *English for Specific Purposes*, 27, 1, 4-21.

Hyland, K. and P. Tse (2005): "Hooking the reader: a corpus study of evaluative *that* in abstracts," *English for Specific Purposes*, 24, 2, 123-139.

Krishnamurthy, R. and I. Kosem (2007): "Issues in creating a corpus for EAP pedagogy and research," *Journal of English for Academic Purposes*, 6, 4, 356-373.

Meyer, C. F. (2002): *English corpus linguistics. An introduction*, Cambridge, Cambridge University Press.

Nesi, H. and H. Basturkmen (2006): "Lexical bundles and discourse signaling in academic lectures," *International Journal of Corpus Linguistics*, 11, 3, 283-304.

Nesi, H. and S. Gardner (2006): "Variation in disciplinary culture: university tutors' views on assessed writing tasks," in R. Kiely, G. Clibbon, P. Rea-Dickins and H. Woodfield (eds.), *Language, culture and identity in Applied Linguistics*, London, Equinox Publishing, 99-117.

Oakey, D. (2002): "Formulaic language in English academic writing: a corpus-based study of the formal and functional variation of a lexical phrase in different academic disciplines," in E. Reppen et al. (eds.), *Using corpora to explore linguistic variation*, Amsterdam/Philadelphia, John Benjamins, 111-129.

Powell, C. and R. Simpson (2001): "Collaboration between corpus linguistics and digital libraries for the MICASE web search interface," in R. Simpson and J. Swales (eds.), *Corpus linguistics in North America*, Ann Arbor, University of Michigan Press, 32-47.

Quirk, R., S. Greenbaum, G. Leech and J. Svartvik (1985): *A Comprehensive grammar of the English language*, London, Longman.

Reppen, R. (2004): "Academic language: an exploration of university classroom and textbook language," in U. Connor and T. A. Upton (eds.), *Discourse in the professions. Perspectives from corpus linguistics,* Amsterdam/ Philadelphia, John Benjamins, 65-86.

Scott, M. (2004): *Wordsmith Tools. Version 4*, Oxford, Oxford University Press.

Simpson, R. C. (2004): "Stylistic features of academic speech: the role of formulaic expressions," in U. Connor and T. A. Upton (eds.): *Discourse in the professions. Perspectives from corpus linguistics,* 37-64. Amsterdam/Philadelphia, John Benjamins.

Swales, J. M. (2002): "Integrated and fragmented worlds: EAP materials and corpus linguistics," in J. Flowerdew (ed.), *Academic discourse,* London, Longman, 150-164.

Swales, J. M. (2006): "Corpus linguistics and English for Academic Purposes," in E. A. Macià, A. S. Cervera and C. R. Ramos (eds.), *Information technology in Languages for Specific Purposes. Issues and prospects*, New York, Springer, 19-33.

Thompson, P. (ed.) (2007): "Editorial," Special issue on Corpus-based EAP pedagogy, *Journal of English for Academic Purposes*, 6, 4, 285-288.

Tognini-Bonelli, E. (2001): *Corpus linguistics at work.* Amsterdam/Philadelphia: John Benjamins.

In search of a new model for WSD: a multi-layered Lexical Constellation Model

Aquilino Sánchez
Pascual Cantos
LACELL[1], Universidad de Murcia

1. Polysemy, co-text and semantic ambiguity

All languages abound in words with many meanings. One may wonder why language, a system that looks for communicative effectiveness and accuracy, has developed a tool which assigns several meanings to the same form, apparently contributing to potential misunderstandings, and subsequent breakdown in communicative acts. Contrary to those expectations, however, native speakers rarely face problems rooted in the polysemy of words. In addition, semantic ambiguity plays a central role in some communicative situations, especially when puns and wit are involved. Puns in fact are an excellent exponent of polysemy in words. They are typically based on the use of words with two or more meanings, one of which is selected against the 'expectations' of the listener.

The 'expectations' of the listener regarding the message transmitted are not arbitrary. They are grounded on the co-text, as well as on the more general context and situation within which the message is embedded. First, the global communicative context guides and defines the broad semantic field the speaker has in mind or wants to transmit. Second, the words selected for the transmission of the message are decisive for gradually determining the potential meanings that accompanying polysemous items may offer or contain. The restrictive and selective semantic action of the lexical items around a specific item may exert its influence forwards and backwards, that is, forward linearity is not always the case. The degree of such a selective action by accompanying words is also variable, ranging from a maximum to a minimum.

In sentence (1),

> (1) 'We've lost the ability *to train* our own people within a separate military system', explained program co-director Dr. Brown.

the word *train* is marked with the verbal function by the preceding lexical item *to*. At the same time, the function of *to* as an infinitive marker is also conditioned by the previous word *ability*. *To* alone, however, is most often decisive

---

1 Grupo LACELL (*Lingüística Aplicada a la Computación, Enseñanza de Lenguas y Lexicografía*) is a Research Group (EO20-02) within the English Department at the University of Murcia (http://www.um.es/grupos/grupo-lacell/quees.php).

for fully fixing the verbal function of the following word (*train*). This is what speakers have already internalized. The *Lacell Corpus*[2] illustrates the case: out of 164 concordances of *to train*, only one instance was found with *to* followed by *train* functioning as a noun (and it is in the context of a newspaper headline: *55 killed as mob sets fire to train*).

In sentence (2),

> (2) *At the heart of Hinduism* is the monotheistic principle of Brahman, that all reality is a unity.

the figurative meaning of *heart* is signalled by the previous lexical chunk (*at the...*). Again, the Lacell Corpus contains 187 instances of *at the heart...*, and all of them illustrate the same figurative meaning. The semantic nature of the following word (*Hinduism*) may definitively confirm the non-physical character of *heart*, but this subsidiary contribution is not strictly necessary.

The following sentence (3) illustrates how a proper name which might apply to any man (*Isaiah*) is identified as the Isaiah mentioned in the Bible only when five words more have been elicited; the identification is further confirmed by other lexical items appearing later on in the sentence (*Word of God, proclaimed*):

> (3) *Isaiah* wrote that whenever the *Bible*, as the *Word* of God, was *proclaimed* it would never return void.

In this same sentence, the pattern *(Word) of God* is enough for disambiguating the meaning of *word*, which in the construct *Word of God* is to be taken as a synonym of *Bible*.

In sentence (4),

> (4) Charles *took* this quotation *to heart*.

took .... to is decisive for selecting the figurative meaning of *heart*. But *took* and *to* are separated by two items (*this quotation*), a fact that requires the reprocessing of *to* in relation to *took* only after our brain has processed *this quotation.* This back and forth processing and reprocessing is often necessary in the decoding of linguistic messages. Linguistic linearity of forms as they appear in discourse does not necessarily imply a strictly sequential and linear building of meaning, as if meaning resulted from the successive addition of 'isolated pieces' selected from inside each individual word. We will come back to this issue later on in this paper.

---

2 The *Lacell* corpus, compiled by the *Lacell* research group at the University of Murcia, is a 20 million word general corpus of English, representative of written and oral English in Great Britain, the USA, Australia, Canada, Ireland and New Zealand.

The physical distance of a key word regarding other items that may contribute to the shaping of its meaning is subject to restrictions, though. Distance restrictions are related to the capacity of our brain to process the incoming information. Swinney's (1979, in Anderson 2005: 403) experiments reveal that disambiguation of meanings by means of co-text is effective if words are presented within the time range of 700 ms. Disambiguation speed is higher among primed words (it takes only a time range of up to 400 ms). If this time threshold is surpassed, semantic disambiguation may turn difficult or impossible. Such a limitation has to do with the limited capacity of short-term memory, well documented in experimental psychology and neurolinguistics. Extensive research reveals that incoming information is temporarily held in transient sensory stores, and it will be lost unless attended to (Anderson 2005: 175ff). The situation apparently is that ambiguous words entering the system are presented at first with all the meanings known to the speaker. The selection of the appropriate meaning is triggered by context and co-text. Once the selection is done, the other meanings are deactivated. The linguistic input processing takes place very rapidly, probably through various neural channels working in parallel. So that when reading or listening to the sentence '***At the heart of Hinduism*** *is the monotheistic principle of Brahman, that all reality is a unity'* the various meanings of *heart* are momentarily present in memory, and the appropriate one is selected when *heart* is related back to *at the* and confirmed when related forward to *Hinduism*.

Linguists have paid attention to the disambiguation power of co-text and context rather recently (Halliday 1973, 1975; Hoey 2005; Sinclair 1991, 2004, among others). More recent research on cognitive processes of knowledge acquisition, psycholinguistics and neurolinguistics fully confirms the role of context and co-text in sense recognition and disambiguation (Anderson 2005; Frisch et al. 2002; Swinney 1979, among others). Regarding co-text, the disambiguating power of specific words is efficient but limited in time range and therefore extension, as mentioned above. Limitations on time range for keeping input in memory bring with similar limitations regarding the distance among elements with disambiguating potential. An average window span of +/- 5 words to the left and right of the key word is usually taken as an adequate distance for items considered relevant for disambiguation. Together with co-text, broader context contributes as well to disambiguation through the definition and selection of broader semantic fields which are permanently kept in or brought to short term memory.

The role of collocates in discourse and language in general is also well illustrated and supported by the theory of lexical priming (Hoey 2005), which assigns the lexicon a central role in the linguistic system. Lexis is the basic 'carrier' of meaning, but it is also deeply intertwined with and integrated within the phonological, morphological and syntactical components. The centrality of lexis in the linguistic system, in the selection of the relevant lexical features of the incoming words and in the final shaping of meaningful units is reinforced by recent studies on neurolinguistic and psycholinguistics, particularly if we analyse how lexical priming allows for a more rapid disambiguation process when polysemous words are present. Priming in fact is a kind of association between or among words which our brain stores and consolidates through practice and repetition. Associations however are not necessarily permanent: they may vary along the history of a language, depending on usage, which confirms or reinforces existing associations through frequency of occurrence, or deactivates and downgrades current associations if frequency of usage decreases. Priming therefore is not a permanent feature of words; specific priming may be reinforced, may weaken, disappear or even be created anew in the lifetime of a specific person or group of speakers.

2. A prototype for WSD at work

On the basis of what precedes there is a sound reason to take co-text or context as a disambiguating factor. Sánchez, Cantos and Almela have elaborated a WSD algorithm based on the discriminant factor analysis of co-text (see Sánchez, Cantos and Almela 2007 and 2008 for details on the structure and nature of the algorithm). The disambiguating power of our algorithm meets the average standards reported by other researchers in the field (Agirre and Edmonds 2006) and in some instances it reaches outstanding marks (Sánchez et al. 2007). Taken as a whole, the results were the ones shown in *Figure 1* (based on a manually supervised sample test of 100 to 150 concordances for each item).

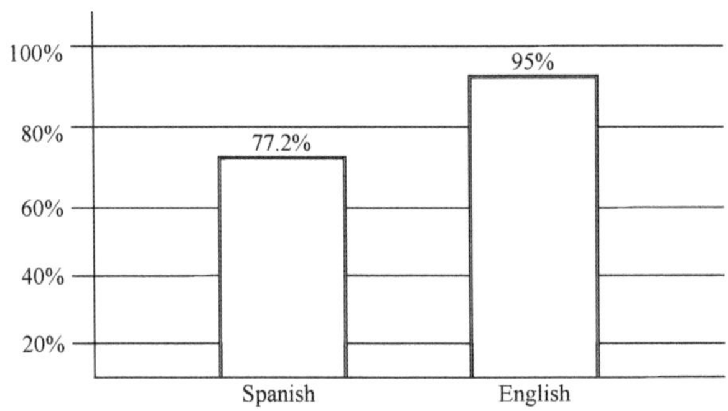

Figure 1. Percentage of success in the automatic disambiguation of words related to parts of the human body and family

On the other hand, the algorithm failed to fully disambiguate meanings in words with high semantic granularity. The success rate in disambiguating highly polysemous words was lower than expected, particularly if compared to the success rate in words with poor semantic granularity. The results are not surprising *per se*, since it is to be expected that words with many senses, as compared to words with only two or three senses, for example, will require the identification of more refined contrasting contextual features to differentiate meanings. Still, the decisive disambiguating power of context applies in all circumstances and instances and failure in disambiguating senses implies failure in context identification. Our challenge is to discover the flaws leading to failure in our prototype. The analysis of the results of two items (*heart* and *hand*) disambiguated by our algorithm will illustrate the case. The meanings of *heart* were grouped in 7 senses, as follows:

1. The hollow, muscular organ in a vertebrate animal that receives blood from the veins and pumps it through the arteries by alternate dilation and contraction
2. The human heart considered as the central part or core of something.
3. The human heart considered as the centre or source of emotions, personality attributes, etc.,
4. Any of the various humane feelings, like compassion, love, devotion, enthusiasm, etc
5. Something like a heart in shape; conventionalized design or representation of a heart, shaped like this.
6. A red figure of a heart stamped on a playing card, or a playing card marked with a conventionalized figure of a heart.

Structuring the meaning of *heart* in six senses is somehow a subjective decision. But options are rather limited. Linguists do not agree on what a sense is exactly and dictionaries do not coincide in the amount of the meanings they offer for each entry. The *Merriam-Webster Dictionary* (MWD, 2000) specifies 6 main meanings for *heart*, plus many sub-meanings within almost each one of them. The meaning of *heart* as *thoughts/emotions/feelings* counts with six sub-meanings. Moreover, some meanings further include more sub-meanings. The *New Oxford Dictionary of English* (NODE, 1998) specifies only 4 main meanings for this word. The distribution of meanings and sub-meanings across the semantic field covered is different, both in quantity and content. The sub-meanings for 'courage, enthusiasm' and 'centre of thoughts and emotions' are included within the basic meaning 1, referred to the 'muscular organ,' while the meaning 'the central or innermost part of anything' –clearly derived from and dependent on meaning 1–, is located at the same level or hierarchy as meaning 1. The same hierarchy is awarded to meaning 3 ('shape of a heart'). One of the sub-meanings refers to the 'vital part or essence' and the other one to 'the close compact head of a cabbage or lettuce.' We can therefore conclude that the selection taken for our prototype is balanced and reasonable.

We took a sample of 126 concordances of *heart* from the Lacell Corpus and disambiguated them with the algorithm. Meaning 1 was correctly disambiguated in 80% of the instances, while disambiguation of meaning 2 was successful in 39.3% of the sentences, meaning 3 in 49% of the instances, and disambiguation of meaning 4 failed in the two occurrences, as shown in *Table 1*:

	Total number of samples and %	Success (number of samples and %)	Failure (number of samples and %)
Meaning 1	50 (39.6%)	40 (80%)	10 (20%)
Meaning 2	33 (26.1%)	13 (39.3%)	20 (60.7%)
Meaning 3	41 (32.5%)	20 (48.8%)	21 (51%)
Meaning 4	2 (1.5%)	0	2 (100%)

Table 1. Disambiguation data for *heart*

The percentage of success is fairly high, as a whole. The analysis of errors reveals however that the context taken as a discriminating factor may fail in apparently unexpected instances. The sentence *In this plan he conceived of the Kings Domain as the new cultural HEART of the city where the Shrine would be located attended by the city's major arts institutions,* was wrongly assigned meaning 1 and meaning 3, having received both the same (rather low) coefficient (0.0766), while meaning 2, the right one in this case, has not even been selected. Should we assume that the context taken by the algorithm (*Domain as the new cultural HEART of the city where the)* has not discriminated adequately? A human user of the language would probably have gathered enough discriminating information from the word *cultural* and from the group of words *of the city*, just taking information from the knowledge of the world humans already have. In fact, the meaning of *heart* as a 'physical organ' does not match with *cultural* or *the city*. Our algorithm does not have this kind of world knowledge information and is not even able to include the whole phrase *of the city* –a three word phrase- as a discriminating unit because it processes words individually, unless explicitly told otherwise (as we do for idiomatic expressions). As for *cultural* the contextual information provided to the system has not been ample and rich enough to include this lexical item. The conclusion is that our algorithm fails because it is unable to identify the discriminating information available in the window span considered. The inclusion of *cultural* would ask for enlarging the corpus on which the data base has been built. The failure in the identification of *(heart) of the city* reveals the inadequacy of the algorithm to identify relevant patterns beyond the word level.

A similar procedure was applied to a sample of 126 concordances of *hand*. The sample was taken from the *Lacell* corpus. Our automatic disambiguator obtained the following results (*Table 2*):

	Total number of samples and %	Success (number of samples and %)	Failure (number of samples and %)
Meaning 1	110 (87.3%	92 (83.6%)	18 (16.3%)
Meaning 2	7 (0%)	0 (0%)	7 (5.5%)
Meaning 3	1 (0.8%)	0 (0%)	1 (0.8%)
Meaning 4	3 (2.4)	0 (0%)	3 (2.4)
Meaning 5	1 (0.8%)	0 (0%)	1 (0.8%)
Meaning 6	3 (2.4)	0 (0%)	3 (2.4)
Meaning 7	1 (0.8%)	0 (0%)	1 (0.8%)

Table 2. Disambiguation data for *hand*

The meanings of *hand* detected in the sample did not include all the meanings recorded in dictionaries. Only seven of them were detected (idioms have been excluded from the sample):

1. The part of the human body attached to the end of the forearm, including the wrist, palm, fingers, and thumb
2. A side, direction, or position indicated by one hand or the other [at one's right hand]
3. The hand as an instrument for making or producing
4. [pl.] Possession [the documents now in his hands]
5. Control; power; authority [to strengthen one's hand]
6. Assistance; aid; help [to lend a hand]
7. A person (or, sometimes, thing) from or through which something comes; source [essays by several hands]: often used with an ordinal number [to get a story at second hand]

The form *hand* is also a highly polysemous word, as shown in standard dictionaries. As a noun, the NODE includes 6 main meanings and 14 sub-meanings. The MWD defines 20 main meanings, or 33 meanings and sub-meanings. In addition to that, other more fine-grained senses are recorded within some of the sub-meanings. The main meaning of *hand* refers to *the part of the human body attached to the end of the forearm, including the wrist, palm, fingers, and thumb* (meaning 1 in Table 2). Other meanings connected to the functions of this 'part of the human body' are: *power, control or possession; direction; making or producing something; help or assistance*, etc.). Sánchez (2005) analysed the distribution of the meanings of *hand* in a large sample of the BNC (ca. 2,000 concordances) and concluded that 80% of the uses refer to meaning 1. The sample disambiguated here adjusts fairly well to such a distribution, since meaning 1 covers 87% of the meanings registered.

From the point of view of disambiguating potential, our WSD algorithm failed to detect 18 meanings, out of 110. The success rate, 83.6%, is quite satisfactory from a global perspective. A more detailed analysis however suggests that the success rate must be interpreted with some caveats. The 18 errors refer all of them to meanings other than the basic one (*hand* as 'a part of the human body'). That is, success is high in detecting the main or basic meaning of *hand* but it fully fails when detecting more fine-grained meanings.

The analysis of errors in disambiguating the right meaning reveals that the numerical coefficients worked out by our algorithm for discriminating among senses are often too distant from each other, particularly if we compare the one corresponding to the right sense against the others. This is clearly the case in the sentence *His widowed mother Jane had a strong HAND in all this and being a pious Christian until the end she died aged 102 in 1841.* The right meaning of *hand* in this sentence (*control, power, and influence*) obtains a probability coefficient of only 0.09362363404390361, while the wrong meaning assigned reaches a rather high figure, 0.796. The distance is too large and it means that the context taken as decisive (the window +/-5 words) is ineffective and favours the selection of the wrong meaning. In this particular case, the words *mother Jane had a strong --- in all this and being* would need further help from other contextual features, or from other instances missing in the restricted window span taken by our algorithm.

Enlarging the discriminating window span is very expensive in terms of computational resources and will not fully solve the problem when capturing information at different hierarchical levels is needed. On the other hand, human beings in similar circumstances face similar disambiguation problems and succeed. When we process linguistic input, if the near-by context is not capable of disambiguating a specific lexical item, or a phrase, the central processing device resorts to other complementary elements present at the level of the sentence, the paragraph and discourse in general or the shared knowledge on the world we live in. The challenge is therefore (i) to identify all the contextual and co-textual information needed for building specific meanings, and (ii) to design an algorithm able to manage the amount of information necessary to automatically 'reconstruct' the meaning present in natural language.

3. In search of new linguistic models valid for computational purposes

Some researchers have suggested that 'the traditional WSD research task, so effective at driving research, has reached a plateau' and 'is not likely to lead to fundamentally new research' (Agirre and Edmonds 2006: 7). They conclude that we need 'to look for new research directions in the field.' The complexity of language, particularly at the level of relationships and correspondences between form and meaning and among word meanings, is extremely high and a new feeling is emerging about the need for new models and new computational tools. It seems that the computational tools currently available fail to adequately capture and interpret the necessary and relevant context, particularly beyond the word level. The question is if linguists themselves provide the adequate information on how the context intervenes in sense discrimination and which elements must be taken into consideration in which specific circumstances. While computational experts are responsible for the implementation of linguistic models to be processed by computers, linguists should provide reliable models on how meaning is built along speech or in discourse. Traditional linguistic theories are unable to offer any decisive help to break through in WSD. We are in need of models transferable to computational applications, yet flexible and comprehensive to deal with the complexity and variety of semantic realizations as found in natural language. Connectionist models in cognitive science (Jeffrey el al. 1996; McClelland et al. 1986; Pinker et al. 1988; Marcus et al. 2001; Rumelhart et al. 1986) may be useful for understanding complexity keeping at the same time flexibility and variety. After all, the reconstruction of cognitive processes in language production would conveniently lead to the development of computational tools capable of reproducing those processes. This would equal the quest for the Holy Grail in WSD.

Connectionist theory aims at describing mental phenomena departing from simple units (neurons and neural networks) densely interconnected among themselves, following the biological structure of our brain, with neurons as basic elements and synapses as neural connective centres. Biological systems in fact must capture, organize and interpret the flow of incoming information and the bits received must be processed first by the receptive units, which later will transfer the results to other processing modules, most probably working in parallel and following implicit and explicit instructions, detecting patterns in the information received and processed and finally taking decisions to be carried out by other biological units. From a linguistic perspective, the function of neurons may find a parallel in words, and synapses may be represented by larger and more complex linguistic structures, at various levels.

Most of the reported results on WSD reached a high and reasonable success rate in disambiguation tasks, especially when referred to coarse-grained meanings (Agirre and Edmonds 2006). The lexical constellation model advanced by Sánchez and Cantos (2001) and the algorithm for WSD connected to it (Sánchez et al. 2007, 2008; forthcoming) met also comfortably well the standards in the field. This model further suggests that the disambiguation process may take place at different levels and advocates for cyclical or iterative applications of the algorithm departing from previous stages on which meanings assignment has already been decided.

Sheer linear processing, similar to the so called 'von Neumann architecture,'[3] as applied to computers and based on sequential processing and execution of explicit instructions, cannot fully capture meaning in discourse, because (i) the building of meaning is not only linear and one-way, and (ii) the linear model does not adequately account for more than one dimension in sense division. If we look at the structure of meanings in *heart* (see *Figure 1* above) it can be appreciated that transition from one sense to another takes place through the activation of specific features at each one of the levels, within a multidimensional framework, following hierarchical and 'conditional' procedures. The identification of the meaning of *heart* in the sentence

(5) They are questions that lie at the *heart* of the art of politics.

needs first the identification of a specific semantic path in previous levels (*heart* as 'muscular central organ'; *heart* as 'central part [of something]'), and the exclusion of other possible paths (as 'muscular central organ' > 'thoughts / emotions / feelings,' for example). The identification of a specific disambiguation path depends on the input received from contextual elements, very much in the way the connectionist theory refers to 'activation.'

The real biological model is based on a network in which all units (neurons and synapses) are candidates for activation at any time. Activations have the potential to trigger an action, or to initiate a process in which many other neurons and modules may be implicated and participating (spreading activation). This may be an inspiring model for the disambiguation process of senses through contextual semantic features. Specific semantic features of co-occurring words may signal the activation path for the selection of specific meanings within the chain of lexical elements present in the sentence. Reports in cognitive psychology (Anderson 2005: 401ff) refer to experiments in which participants display a higher neural activity when facing ambiguous sentences or words in the input they must process. The 'extra' neural work displayed is related to the additional processing of meanings required by ambiguous lexical items (Frisch et al. 2002).

When a word enters our cognitive system it is probably taken by the receiver with all the meanings (s)he knows. The selection of the intended meaning will result from the additional and complementary information of contextual words, especially primed words. Contextual words, however, may have been previously elicited by the speaker; in that case its presence in the working memory is necessary, and this fact implies that our processing system goes forth and backtracks in the reinterpretation and readjustment of the semantic features of the words captured and still operative in the working memory (which is limited to a

[3] The 'von Neumann architecture' is defined in Wikipedia as: 'A design model for a stored-program digital computer that uses a processing unit and a single separate storage structure to hold both instructions and data.'

time range of ca. 400-700 ms). The final decision on the meaning of a sentence is taken when all the information on the words implied has been adequately processed. In some cases the control of all those elements may result in a highly complex construct. When complexity is high, WSD most often fails. We are therefore in need of a model able to cope with the complexity of meaning distribution in natural language.

4. The Lexical Constellation Model

As a kind of 'side effect' in the analysis of lexical attraction and the hierarchical domains which may define their organization and structure, Cantos and Sánchez (2001) conceived the model of Lexical Constellations. The authors conclude that:

> "Constellations represent lexical relations among collocates in a structured hierarchical way *versus* the standard plain representation of most collocational analyses. It is precisely the plain vision of standard collocational work that misses two main things of collocational behaviour:
>
> - Their non-linear dependency: not all collocates are necessarily attracted by the same node word and, furthermore.
> - Those that co-occur within a determined unit (phrase, sentence, etc.) form a kind of complex lexical hierarchy.
>
> Interesting is also the fact that by means of constellational analysis we might also get rid of the optimum span dilemma, as this analysis always takes the sentence unit: what matters is not the span, but the lexical hierarchy collocates form within this linguistic unit. The lexical hierarchies are neither predetermined nor assumed (as happens in most semantic networks or word sense hierarchies), they result from the co-occurrence probabilities and the attraction calculations, which might, sometimes, inevitably lead to divergences depending on the corpus or language samples analyzed." (Sánchez and Cantos 2001: 223).

It is particularly relevant here the statement about the 'non-linear dependency' of collocates, and the importance of the lexical hierarchy, which may prevail over the physical distance in the span considered. Those two points however increase the degree of complexity and difficulty in current applications for WSD.

The lexical constellation model allows for a more adequate description of meanings in hierarchies and it can also be hypothesized that a disambiguation algorithm could be applied in cycles and iteratively, adjusting to the different hierarchies detected. Coming back, once more, to the cognitive model in the processing of language, we can also point out that lexical disambiguation takes place, when needed, with information extracted from the various levels of language use, be it a the phrase level, at the sentence level, or bringing to the working memory the global and basic meaning of a paragraph, a chapter or the whole situation that defines a particular communicative act. From that perspective, it seems that algorithms based on restricted and contextual span windows are likely to fail whenever the proper hierarchical constellation is not taken into account because it is out of the range of the window span under analysis.

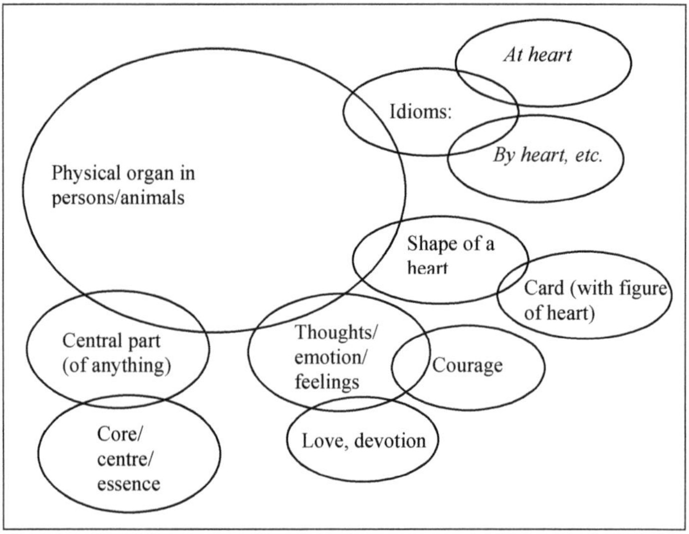

Figure 2. Constellation of meanings for *heart*

A lexical constellation illustrates the three-dimensional activation paths that may connect words and word meanings and the hierarchical dependency they are governed by. Lexical constellations may also result a useful tool to understand the degree of semantic granularity of each one of the meanings and sub-meanings that constitute a semantic unit. The model is adequate as well to capture different and sequential levels of sense differentiation in a word. Coarse meanings correspond to higher levels in the hierarchy, while more fine-grained meanings are found in the correlations between contexts and senses at lower levels, in more specific domains.

The constellation of the meanings of *heart* can be visualized in a three dimensional representation, as in *Figure 2* above. We are, however, more used to analyse the constellation of meanings in a two-dimensional matrix, as follows (*Table 3*, illustrated with examples):

HEART: 1. **Physical organ** (in persons/animals) (*That in turn reduces the risk of heart disease*)	1. **Central part** (of sth) (*Falls Creek is in the heart of the Village area.)*	1. **Centre** (of anything) *(They are questions that lie at the heart of the art of politics.)* 2. **Core/essence** (of something) *(The film doesn't take the viewer into the heart of a battle. The move to cut the heart out of America's defences by cutting defence spending.)*
	2. (Source of) **thoughts/emotions/ feelings** *(Young at heart. They draw near to me with their lips, but their hearts are far from me.)*	1. **Love, devotion** *(If you can't mentally connect with someone they are not likely to win your heart.)* 2. **Courage** (*Things are not as bad as they seem, so don't lose heart.)*
	3. **Shape** (of a heart) *(Female* figure *standing, concave* heart-*shaped face)*	1. **Card with such a figure** *(You used my cards yesterday and now the three of hearts is missing.)*
	4. **Idioms**	1. **To heart** (*They both took to heart the words of Paul.)* 2. **By heart** (*She knew the statistics off by heart.)*

Table 3. Matrix of meanings for *heart*

The two dimensional representation may be misleading, since it suggests a strict linearity which, as explained above, does not correspond to the real structure of meanings and the processing that takes place in our brain. Still, it perfectly illustrates the hierarchical character of the meanings, as shown below (Figure 3):

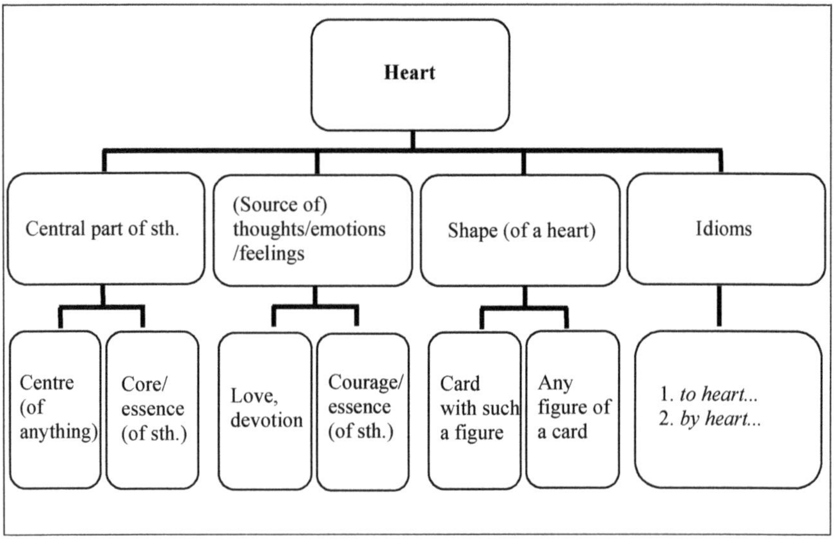

Figure 3. Hierarchical character of meanings (*heart*)

The options in the grouping of meanings carry with some practical implications:

1. We may organise all the meanings linearly, without considering the level they belong to, in which case hierarchy is not taken into account. In that case we have 11 meanings for *heart* (plus an indefinite number of idioms) and we may list them as they appear in most dictionaries.
2. We may take into consideration the hyperonimic hierarchy of each meaning, and classify them according to the level they belong to. The result is that *heart* counts with one basic meaning in level 1, four main sets of meanings (level 2), plus 4 subsets of meanings with subsequent submeanings (level 3).
3. Or we may take the constellation model. The advantage of this model over 1 and 2 lies in its three-dimensionality. Dependency and hierarchy are enriched by the possibility for each meaning to connect with other meanings and/or lexical units in many directions. This feature is particularly important in understanding the semantic web. Meanings in fact are not only connected to other lexical units in a linear way; this allows for a meaning or a semantic feature to be simultaneously connected to several other constellations, within or outside the same lexical unit, as illustrated in *Figure 4*, where meaning *H* is shared by three semantic nuclei or lexical units.

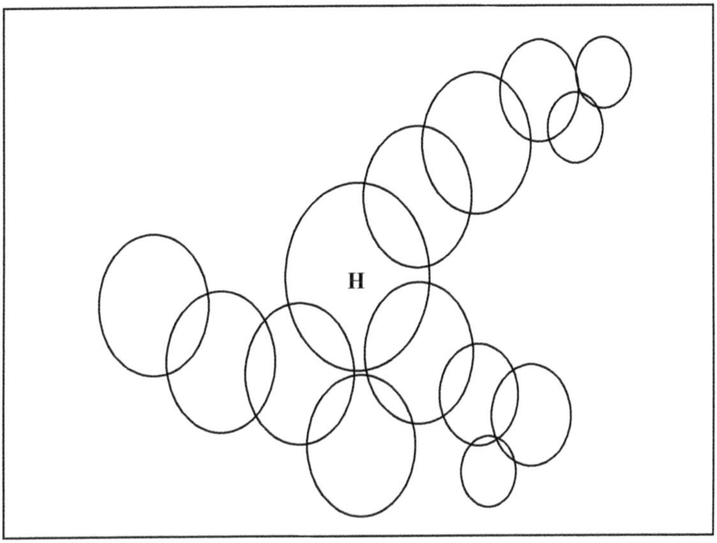

Figure 4. A lexical constellation with shared semantic features

5. The Lexical Constellation Model and WSD

Sharing semantic features with other words is a property of lexical units that pervades the linguistic system. The multiple connections among words may find a similar prototype in the neural system of our brain, where each neuron is connected to other neurons through dozens of connecting points. A problem added to the semantic web is that those connecting points are established by reasons of various kinds. Some connections are fully arbitrary and depend on sheer chance consolidated by frequency of usage; other connections are rooted on the nature of the things represented by the words (they belong to the same semantic field, with different degree of dependency). The traditional thesauri and the most modern ontologies are excellent exponents of the efforts and studies conducted in order to explain the semantic relationships among words. From that point of view, traditional dictionaries do not help much, since they use to describe words in isolation, as if they were fully autonomous items.

Coming back to the lexical constellation model, it can be stated that it opens the possibility to approach the problem from a broader perspective, and it offers a more comprehensive understanding of semantic interconnectivity. The elaboration of a dictionary of words in which lemmas are defined following the lexical constellation model would be the foundation of a more ambitious project, in which each constellation should appear with information on the connections that every single word or lexical unit shares with other lexical units. Such a task is difficult to foresee at present, due to the magnitude of the work implied, but coordinated research and analysis and the help of computational tools may contribute the construction of useful databases of this kind in the midterm.

The elaboration of such a lexicon would offer relevant information for determining why and how disambiguation of word senses takes place. The selection of specific semantic features in polysemous lexical units seems to proceed according to a pathway determined by the potential of the lexical unit itself and the possibilities or constraints derived from contextual items or discourse as a whole. In this view, the semantic contour of each lexical unit is defined by other accompanying lexical units, and the lexical constellation should offer a faithful visualization of the underlying threads building the semantic web. The identification of the pathway driving to and triggering the selection of the adequate semantic features is complex, but nonetheless it would pave the way to discover the 'idiosyncratic' connections among words within the sentence or discourse.

An additional problem comes into play when those idiosyncratic features do not depend on words alone but on groups of words capable of delimiting the meaning of a sentence or any other larger piece of discourse. The sentence

> (6) His widowed mother Jane had a strong *hand* in all this and being a pious Christian until the end she died aged 102 in 1841.

illustrates the case in focus here. The figurative meaning of *hand* in the sentence cannot be detected taking into account the words preceding *hand* (*His widowed mother Jane had a strong* ***hand***). In fact, if the sentence ended here, the word *hand* would most probably be assigned the meaning of 'a physical organ…'. But just with the addition of *in,* the selection of the figurative meaning of *hand* is practically definitive, even though what follows confirms (… *all this*) and reconfirms (… *and being a pious Christian….*) the adequacy of the feature selected. A search of the phrase *had a strong* ***hand*** *in* Google confirms the hypothesis: out of 2,000 hits matching this linguistic structure, the meaning of *hand* was found to be always the same (*control, power*) in more than 100 concordances selected by chance. A similar query with the *WebCorp*[4] extracted 92 instances of this same phrase. All of them had the same figurative meaning. It is therefore the pattern (*had) a strong* ***hand*** *in* –and not any of those words separately– what defines and decides the pathway for disambiguating the meaning of *hand* in the sentence.

6. Attempting to model WSD by means of Lexical Constellations

In what follows we shall intuitively attempt to present a potential WSD-model based on lexical constellations. Suppose we have a fictitious word *w* and have created its word map or lexical constellation, built up by means of related collocates (*a–q*). Each collocate is hierarchically structured and organized form-

---

4 http://www.webcorp.org.uk

ing clusters. In turn, each cluster configures a possible distinctive meaning for *w* (Figure 5).

Note that collocates are organized and structured according to their collocational behaviour: co-occurrence, relevance and hierarchical dependency. For instance, collocates *i, j, k* and *l*, are all grouped together because whenever the word *w* collocates with *i*, *i* collocates with *j*, *j* collocates with *k* and *k* collocates with *l*. It does not follow from this that collocability has to be necessarily immediate. There might be instances where *i* collocates with *k*, however, *j* collocates more strongly with *k*; and this determines that *k* is assigned a collocate of *j* and not of *i*. This also explains that if we find an instance where the word *w* collocates with *i*, *j* and *k*; *w* is responsible for its co-occurrence with *i*, but not necessarily for its co-occurrence with *j* and *w*. This would be a case of indirect collocability[5]. The dominant element is *w* attracting *i*; *i* attracting *j*; *j k*; and *k l*. This does not mean that *w* does not attract *j*; it does, in fact. However, there is evidence that this attraction is not direct, but by means of an intermediate item or lexical structure formed by *i*.

Furthermore, the lexical constellation model is a method for extracting and representing the contextual-usage meaning of words by statistical computations applied to a large corpus of text. The underlying idea is that the contexts in which a given word appears provide a set of constraints that largely determine the similarity of meaning of words and sets of words to each other. Consequently, in principle, any lexical constellation model of a word also implicitly represents the potential meanings of that word.

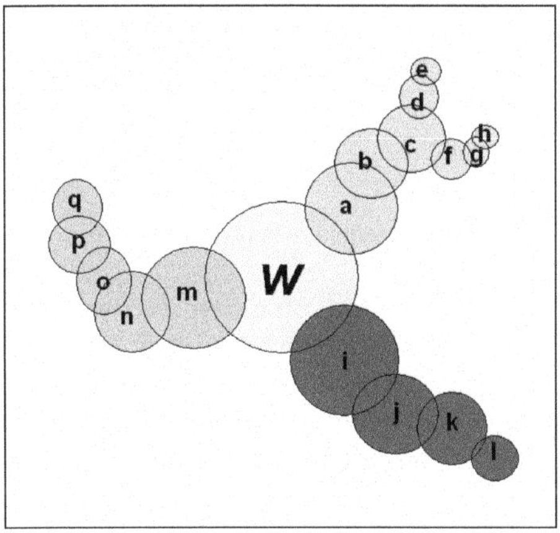

Figure 5. Lexical constellation for the word *w*

[5] For a more detailed account see Cantos and Sánchez (2001: 218-221).

We consider all significant collocates to be attracted somehow by the node word as they do actually co-occur within the same unit: the sentence. On this assumption, each sentence unit is formed by minor units and these in their turn are formed by other minor units and so on, which indicates that each unit is a structure formed by other sub-structures, and each sub-structure by sub-sub-structures, etc. There seems to be a hierarchical structure where each constituent (structure) is either directly or indirectly dependent on other constituents. Consequently, we do not just get simple lists of collocates but structured hierarchical collocational data, revealing the lexical dependencies and relationships between collocates that co-occur within the same sentence domain. Consequently, the lexical constellation model is also a practical method for the characterization of word meaning (Figure 6).

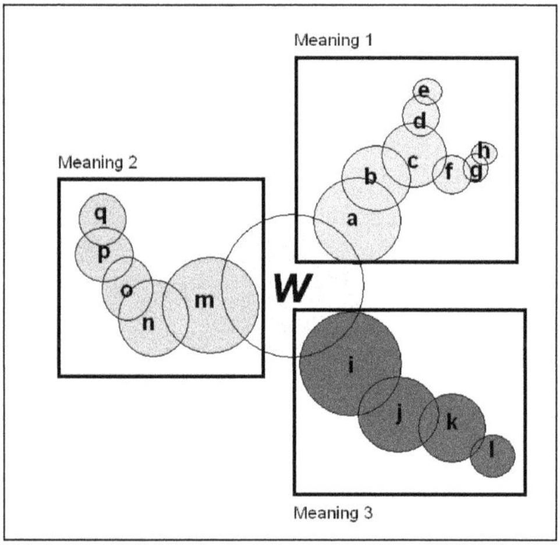

Figure 6. Potential meaning for the word *w*

The lexical constellation approach produces relation models that resemble several human cognitive phenomena involving association or semantic similarity. There seems to be a close resemblance between what lexical constellation approach extracts and the way peoples' representations of meaning reflect what they have read and heard, as well as the way human representation of meaning is reflected in the word choice of writers. As one practical consequence of this correspondence, the lexical constellation model allows us to closely approximate human judgments of meaning similarity between words and to objectively predict the consequences of overall word-based similarity between sentences.

Another way to think of this is that the lexical constellation model represents the meaning of a word as a kind of average of the meaning of all the sentences in which it appears, and the meaning of a sentence as a kind of average of the meaning of all the words it contains.

To avoid any biasing, let us start assuming the following concordance lines of the fictional word *w*. In addition, and for practical reasons, we shall substitute the co-occurrences with senseless letters that should stand for words. Our main focus here is on the structuring of the co-textual information around the node word, not on the optimal span. This explains why the concordance lines have been truncated to a span -5 +5. And this is what we get:

		-5	**-4**	**-3**	**-2**	**-1**	**0**	**+1**	**+2**	**+3**	**+4**	**+5**
SENTENCE	**1**	A	B	C	D	E	*W*	F	G	H	I	J
	2	Z	A	B	C	E	*W*	K	L	M	N	O
	3	Y	A	B	C	R	*W*	P	O	X	V	Z
	4	L	K	J	H	G	*W*	F	E	C	D	A
	5	K	L	J	H	G	*W*	T	H	F	W	C

Table 4. Co-occurrence data of five fictional sentences with the word w

The headline of Table 4 indicates the position of the co-occurrence relative to the node word: negative figures show that the co-occurrence comes before the node word and positive figures indicate post nodal positioning. The first column refers to the various concordance lines.

A preliminary analysis shows that the most "influential" co-occurrence is *c* appearing 5 times within the context of *w*.

Type	**Frequency**
C	5
A	4
H	4
B	3
E	3
F	3
G	3
J	3
K	3
L	3
D	2
O	2

Type	**Frequency**
Z	2
I	1
M	1
N	1
P	1
R	1
T	1
V	1
W	1
X	1
Y	1

Table 5. Frequency data

A more detailed analysis of word *c* reveals however that *c* occurs more frequently before the node word *w*, mostly in position -2 but also in -3. Interesting are in this respect concordances 2 and 3 forming an apparent pre-nodal semantic structure "*a b c*" ranging from positions -4 to -2, allowing an "intruder" in position -1. This takes us to think that the meaning of *w* in concordances 2 and 3 is very likely to be the same one. But what happens with *c* in concordances 4 and 5? In these two concordance lines *c* is post-nodal and probably less semantically influenced by the node word *w*?

The notion of gravity (Mason 1997, 1999) states that the influence of the node word on the co-occurring items fades away with distance. That is, words close to the node word exert a greater influence on the meaning of the node words, whereas more apart words are less influential on the node word. If we assume this analogy: the closer the more influential.

We can move further, weighting the co-occurrences above according to its relative distance to the node word. In addition, the "influence" on the node word can be combined, considering also the frequency on the belief that not only distance but also the number of occurrences is determined; that is,

$$Influence = Weight * Frequency$$

If a word appears very often next or close to another word, then we might assume that this co-distribution is not due to mere random but due to some "effect," or some attraction exerted by any or both words on one another to some degree. So, combining both notions: distance and frequency, we get the following weighting for the co-occurrences[6]:

Distance	-5	-4	-3	-2	-1	0	+1	+2	+3	+4	+5
Weight	1	2	3	4	5	0	5	4	3	2	1

Table 6. Weighting

Note that the further apart, less weighting, showing a reverse relationship between distance and weight. In addition, and in order to distinguish whether the co-occurrence is pre- or post-nodal, we need to add a plus or minus sign to the weights. This results into:

Distance	-5	-4	-3	-2	-1	0	+1	+2	+3	+4	+5
Weight	-1	-2	-3	-4	-5	0	+5	+4	+3	+2	+1

Table 7. Weighting considering positioning

6 Note that we deliberately skip here talking about collocations. We prefer to use the vaguer term co-occurrence.

This distribution of weighting is pretty naïve though effective for our purposes. However, by considering the position relative to the node word, we shall consider separately the counts of the pre- and post-nodal co-occurrences. For instance, *a* occurs overall 4 times, yet it only appears 3 times pre-nodal as in the first concordance line. So the resulting influence measures for concordance line 1 are:

Distance	**-5**	**-4**	**-3**	**-2**	**-1**	**0**	**+1**	**+2**	**+3**	**+4**	**+5**
Concordance	**A**	**B**	**C**	**D**	**E**	**W**	**F**	**G**	**H**	**I**	**J**
Weight (W)	-1	-2	-3	-4	-5	0	+5	+4	+3	+2	+1
Freq. (F)	3	3	3	1	2	0	2	1	2	1	1
Influence (W * F)	-3	-6	-9	-4	-10	0	+10	+4	+6	+2	+1

Table 8. Influence measures of the co-occurrence data in sentence 1

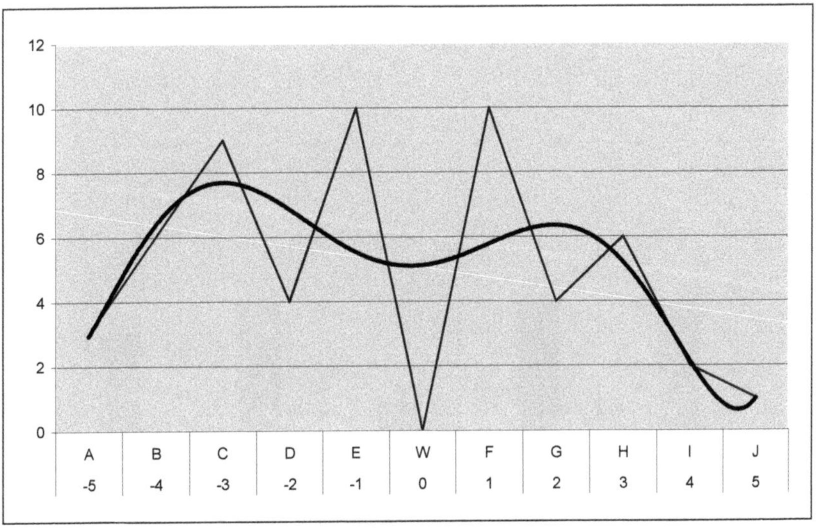

Figure 7. Influence of co-occurrences on node word in sentence 1

A visual display (Figure 7) shows how the most prominent influence on the node word is exerted by the co-occurrences *e* and *f*. In addition, the trend line points that the pre-nodal influence is overall greater than its counterpart. More solid evidence to this is the total sum of the pre and post-nodal influences. We just need to maximize both sums, that is, we ignore the minus sign and concentrate on the number with the highest cardinality:

Pre-nodal: max[(-3) + (-6) + (-9) + (-4) + (-10)] = 32
Post-nodal: max[15 + 4 + 6 + 2 + 1] = 28

The pre- and post-nodal influence of all concordance lines are:

Sentence	Pre-nodal	Post-nodal
1	32	28
2	38	28
3	33	19
4	30	28
5	30	25
Total	163	128

Table 6. Pre- and post-nodal influences

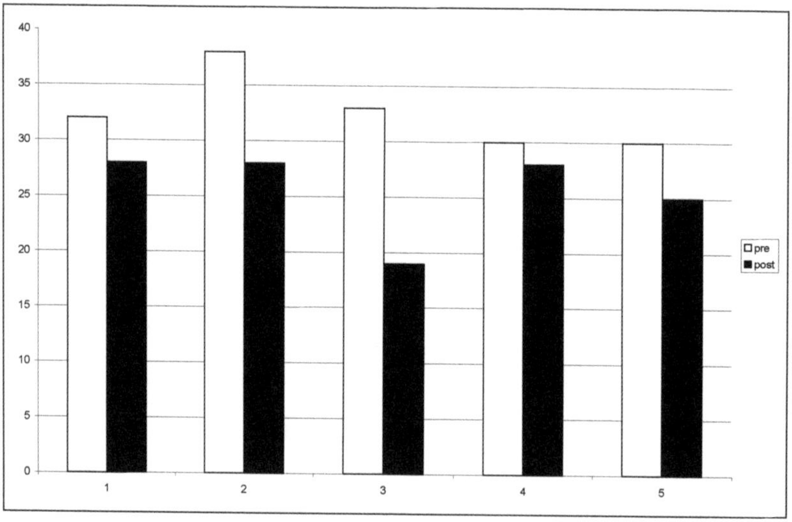

Figure 8. Pre and post-nodal influence relative to positions (± 1 to ± 5)

Clearly, the pre-nodal influence (163) is greater than the post-nodal one (128). This again speaks in favour of separating both influences when analysing the semantic structure of words. Consequently, if we assume that the pre-nodal influence is more determined, we could now proceed in grouping the concordances according to their pre-nodal co-occurrences.

A possible method for grouping objects of similar kind (sentences/concordances) into respective categories (meanings/senses) is cluster analysis. A general question facing researchers in many areas of inquiry is how to *organize* observed data into meaningful structures, that is, to develop taxonomies. In other words cluster analysis is an exploratory data analysis tool which aims at sorting different objects into groups in a way that the degree of association between two objects is maximal if they belong to the same group and minimal otherwise. Given the above, cluster analysis can be used to discover structures in data without providing an explanation/interpretation. In other words, cluster analysis simply discovers structures in data without explaining why they exist.

A cluster analysis of the pre-nodal data reveals that (i) on the one hand, sentences 2 and 3, and (ii) on the other hand, sentences 4 and 5 are very much similar. Furthermore, as all sentences are extracted using the same node word, we can determine that the word *w* might have two main behaviours, probably related to two different meanings, too (see *Figure 9*):

- Meaning 1: expressed by sentences 2 and 3
- Meaning 2: sentences 4 and 5

Interesting is also the fact that the potential meaning of sentence 1 is closer related to the meaning of sentences 2 and 3, and not to meaning 2 (sentences 4 and 5). This might take us to, possibly consider, two main meanings:

- Meaning 1: expressed by either sentence 1 or sentences 2 and 3
- Meaning 2: sentences 4 and 5

And a sub-meaning of sentence 1, expressed by sentences 2 and 3, or viceversa, getting this final meaning structure:

- Meaning 1: sentence 1 or sentences 2 and 3
- Meaning 1.1.: sentence 1 or sentences 2 and 3
- Meaning 2: sentences 4 and 5

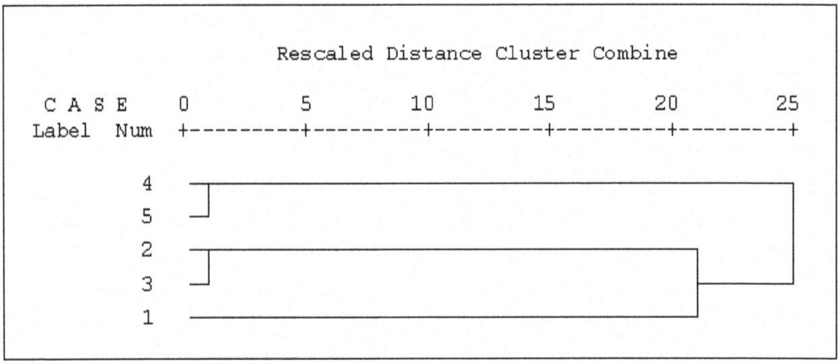

Figure 9. Cluster analysis using pre-nodal data

Exploring now only the post-nodal occurrences:

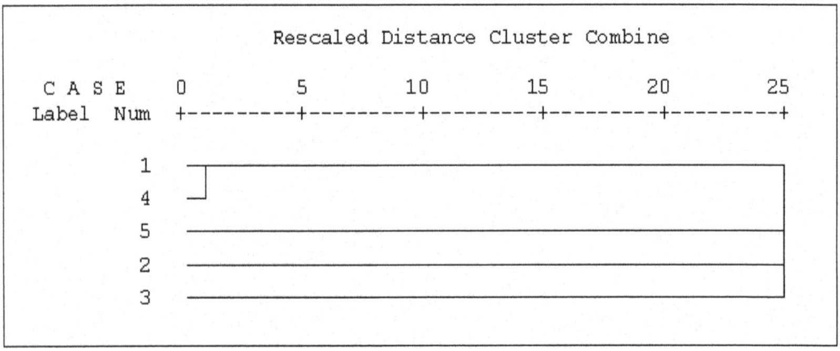

Figure 10. Cluster analysis using post-nodal data

We find only similarities between sentences 1 and 4. This might be a hint that the pre-nodal structure of the node word *w* is semantically more determined in order to elucidate possible meanings of *w*.

Finally, considering the whole co-occurrence information (pre- and post-nodal data), we get:

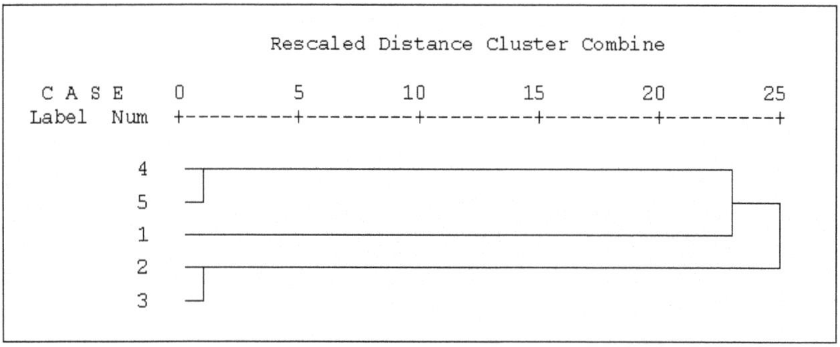

Figure 11. Cluster analysis using pre- and post-nodal data

In principle, the pre- and post-nodal clustering is quite similar to the pre-nodal clustering, except for sentence 1, which is grouped to concordances 4 and 5.

Interesting, however, is the fact that the pre-nodal influence has a greater influence in the sense grouping than the post-nodal one. This points towards important implications: (i) the need to separate pre- and post-nodal data when considering the meaning or semantic clustering of a words or idioms and (ii) the semantic structures that the pre- and post-nodal co-occurrences form have different weight or influence on the meaning of a word, strengthening the notion that a different form necessarily implies a different meaning.

These preliminary results, though not conclusive, reinforce the idea that sense-discrimination, moreover WSD, can positively benefit from lexical constellations. We are confident that this new view within WSD can be a positive contribution. The approach presented is transparent in nature and empirically testable, producing a good description of the storehouse of vocabulary items. That is, how words are connected through their associations and how lexical knowledge is schematic and associative.

7. Final remarks

WSD has reached a critical stage: much has been done in the late twenty years or so, and at present we are fully aware of the bottleneck lying ahead of us. Traditional linguistic theories are of little use to solve the problem and computational tools lack a semantic model they might take as a basis for designing automatic disambiguating procedures. The lexical constellation model predicts that WSD does not only depend on the constellation of meanings of isolated words, but on larger constellations including two or more words, or larger linguistic structures. The challenge is then to identify disambiguating factors within lexical units and beyond the word level (latent level). Reaching this goal poses a tremendous pressure on linguists, but it will be difficult to increase the success rate in automatic disambiguation unless the tools used with this purpose are able to manage higher complexity rooted in real and broad, not limited, context.

References

Agirre, E. and P. Edmonds (2006): "Introduction," in E. Agirre and P. Edmonds (eds.), 1-28.

Agirre, E. and P. Edmonds (eds.) (2006): *Word Sense Disambiguation. Algorithms and Applications*, Berlin, Springer Verlag.

Almela, M. (2006): *From Words to Lexical Units: A Corpus-Driven Account of Collocation and Idiomatic Patterning in English and English Spanish*, Frankfurt, Peter Lang.

Almela, M., A. Sánchez and P. Cantos (2004): "Lexico-Semantic Mapping of Meanings in English and Spanish. A Model of Analysis," in J. M. Bravo (ed.), 11-41.

Anderson, J. R. (1983): *The Architecture of Cognition*, Cambridge, MA, Harvard University Press.

Anderson, J. R. (2005): *Cognitive Psychology and its Implications*, New York, Worth Publishers.

Bravo, J. M. (ed.) (2004): *A New Spectrum of Translation Studies*, Valladolid, Universidad de Valladolid.

Bravo, J. M. (ed.) (2006): *Aspects of Translation*, Valladolid, Universidad de Valladolid.

Cantos, P. and A. Sánchez (2001): "Lexical constellations: what collocates fail to tell," *International Journal of Corpus Linguistics*, 62, 2001, 199-228.

Cantos, P. (1996): *Lexical Ambiguity, Dictionaries, Corpora*, Murcia, Servicio de Publicaciones de la Universidad de Murcia

Cruse, A. (2004): *Meaning in Language: An Introduction to Semantics and Pragmatics*, Oxford, Oxford University Press.

Frisch, S., M. Schlewsevsky, D. Saddy, and D. Alpermann (2002): "The P600 as an indicator of syntactic ambiguity," *Cognition*, 85, B83-B92.

Gelbukh, A. (ed.) (2007): *Computational Linguistics and Intelligent Text Processing. Proceedings of the 8th International Conference, CICLing 2007,* (Mexico City, Mexico, February 2007), Berlin-Heidelberg, Springer.

Halliday, M. A. K. (1973): *Explorations in the Functions of Language*, London, Edward Arnold.

Halliday, M.A.K. (1975): *Learning how to mean*, London, Edward Arnold.

Hoey, M. (2005): *Lexical Priming. A new theory of words and language*, London, Routledge.

Ide, N. and J. Véronis (1998): "Word sense disambiguation: the state of the art," *Computational Linguistics*, 241, 1-40.

Ide, N. and Y. Wilks (2006): "Making sense about sense," in Agirre, E. and P. Edmonds (eds.), pp. 47-73.

Jeffrey L. E., E. A. Bates, M. H. Johnson, A. Karmiloff-Smith, D. Parisi and K. Plunkett (1996): *Rethinking Innateness: A connectionist perspective on development*, Cambridge, MA, MIT Press.

Kilgarriff, A. (1993): "Dictionary word sense distinctions: an enquiry into their nature," *Computers and the Humanities*, 26, 365-387.

Kilgarriff, A. (1997): " 'I don't believe in word senses' ," *Computers and the Humanities*, 312, 91-113.

Kilgarriff, A. (2006): "Word Senses," in: E. Agirre and P. Edmonds (eds.), 29-46.

Klein, D. and G. Murphy (2001): "The representation of polysemous words," *Journal of Memory and Language*, 45, 259-282.

Klein, D. and G. Murphy (2002): "Paper has been my ruin: conceptual relations of polysemous senses," *Journal of Memory and Language*, 47, 548-570.

Landauer, T. K. and S. T. Dumais (1997): "A solution to Plato's problem: the Latent Semanctic Analysis theory of the acquisition, induction, and representation of knowledge," *Psychological Review*, 104, 211-140.

Landauer, T. K., P. W. Foltz, D. Laham (1998): "Introduction to Latent Semantic Analysis," *Discourse Processes,* 25, 259-284.

Lyons, J. (1980): *Language, Meaning and Context*, Cambridge, Cambridge University Press.

Lyons, J. (1995): *Linguistic Semantics: An introduction*, Cambridge, Cambridge University Press.

Marcus, G. F. (2001): *The Algebraic Mind: Integrating Connectionism and Cognitive Science Learning, Development, and Conceptual Change*, Cambridge, MA: MIT Press

Màrquez, L., G. Escudero, D. Martínez and G. Rigau (2006): "Supervised corpus-based methods for WSD," in E. Agirre and P. Edmonds (eds.), 167-216.

McClelland, J.L., D.E. Rumelhart and the PDP Research Group (1986): *Parallel Distributed Processing: Explorations in the Microstructure of Cognition. Volume 2: Psychological and Biological Models*, Cambridge, MA, MIT Press.

Pérez, D. et al. (2005): "About the effects of combining Latent Semantic Analysis with natural language processing techniques for free-text assessment," *Revista Signos*, 3859, 325-343.

Pinker, S. and J. Mehler (1988): *Connections and Symbols*, Cambridge, MA, MIT Press.

Pustejovsky, J. (2001): *The Generative Lexicon*, Cambridge, MA, MIT Press.

Ravin, Y. and C. Leacock (eds.) (2000): *Polysemy. Theoretical and Computational Approaches*, Oxford, Oxford University Press.

Rumelhart, D.E., J.L. McClelland and the PDP Research Group (1986): *Parallel Distributed Processing: Explorations in the Microstructure of Cognition. Volume 1: Foundations*, Cambridge, MA, MIT Press.

Sánchez A. and P. Cantos (1997): "Predictability of word forms types and lemmas in linguistic corpora," *International Journal of Corpus Linguistics*, 22, 251-272.

Sánchez, A. and M. Almela (2004): "Polysemy and sense discrimination in lexicography," in J. M. Bravo (ed.), 141-174.

Sánchez, A. (2005): "Estructuración semántica y redes léxicas de *hand* y *mano*," in F. Garrudo, and J. Comesaña (eds.), *Estudios de Filología Inglesa en honor de Antonio Garnica*, Sevilla, Universidad de Sevilla, 391-430.

Sánchez, A., (ed.) (2001): *Gran Diccionario de uso del español actual* basado en el Corpus *Cumbre*, Madrid, SGEL.

Sánchez, A., P. Cantos and M. Almela (2007): "Lexical constellations and the structure of meaning: a prototype application to WSD," in A. Gelbukh (ed.), 275-287.

Sánchez, A., P. Cantos and M. Almela (2008): "Desambiguación automática de significados mediante el contexto en términos polivalentes: prototipo aplicado al inglés y al español," forthcoming.

Sánchez, A., R. Sarmiento, P. Cantos and J. Simón (1995): *CUMBRE. Corpus lingüístico del español contemporáneo. Fundamentos, metodología y aplicaciones*, Madrid, SGEL.

Sinclair, J. (1991) : *Corpus, concordance, collocation*, Oxford, Oxford University Press.

Sinclair, J. (2004): *Trust the Text: Language Corpus and Discourse*, London, Routledge.

Sinclair, J. (1991): *Corpus, concordance, collocation.* Oxford: Oxford University Press.

Turing, A. M. (1950): "Computing machinery and intelligence," *Mind*, 59, 433-460.

Turney, P. (2001): "Mining the Web for synonyms: PMI-IR versus LSA on TOEFL," *Proceedings of the 12th European Conference on Machine Learning*, Freiburg, Germany, 491-502.

Yarowsky, D. (2000): "Word sense disambiguation," in Dale et al. (ed.), *Handbook of Natural Language Processing*, New York, Marcel Dekker, 629-624.

Zipf, G.K. (1949): *Human Behaviour and the Principle of Least Effort*, Cambridge, MA, Addison-Wesley.

PART FOUR

Broadening the Scope

Analysing linguistic decline in early-stage Alzheimer's disease: a corpus-based approach

Pascual Cantos Gómez
Grupo LACELL[1]
Universidad de Murcia

1. Alzheimer's disease

Alzheimer's disease (AD) is a neurological disorder of the brain named after Alois Alzheimer, who first described it in 1906 (Alzheimer 1907). This most well-known and common form of dementia is progressive and irreversible (Ghosh 2008: 338; Weiner and Lipton 2009: 333), worsening over time and eventually interfering with many aspects of brain function (Mader 2008: 340; Weimer and Lipton 2009: 12). One of the earliest symptoms is memory loss, along with a gradual decline of other cognitive functions and changes in personality or behaviour (Stones 1997: 8; James 2008: 6).

AD advances progressively from mild deficits in cognitive and functional status to widespread loss of mental abilities (Lawrence et al. 2004: 372). Advanced AD-affected people become completely dependent on others for every aspect of their care. The time course of the disease varies by individual, ranging from 5 to 20 years (Schellenberg 1995: 8552).

A significant progress in finding and understanding the possible causes of AD is being made; however many questions still remain. Recent research points towards a complex interaction among different inherited and environmental factors (Guttmacher and Collins 2002: 1519; Weimer and Lipton 2009: 430). Two confirmed AD-risk factors are age and family history (Agronin 2007: 91; Agronin and Maletta 2006: 135). Some environmental factors have also been proven as risk factor for AD, such as occupational exposures, head trauma, smoking, alcohol and aluminium (Weimer and Lipton 2009: 237).

AD research is not only centred in finding what might trigger this disease in some people, but also in identifying the progressive loss of cognitive function and brain changes associated with it, including the characteristic brain lesions in

---

1 Grupo LACELL (*Lingüística Aplicada a la Computación, Enseñanza de Lenguas y Lexicografía*) is a Research Group (EO20-02) within the English Department at the University of Murcia (http://www.um.es/grupos/grupo-lacell/quees.php).

plaques[2] and *tangles*[3] around and inside nerve cells (Deutsch 1995: 207; Sherwood 2008: 163).

As the disease process progresses, the brain continues to degenerate: nerve cells shrink and die, and the brain reduces in size and the wrinkles along its surface become smoother (Agronin 2007: 93: Weiner and Lipton 2009: 460).

1.1. Early-stage AD

AD-affected people evidence a progressive and irreversible decline in some cognitive abilities with early onset sporadic memory disorders (Galton et al. 2000). One of the most typical early symptoms is memory loss with minor forgetfulness, becoming steadily more acute with the progression of the disease (Weimer and Lipton 2009: 197).

AD is hardly or not noticeable at all at the preclinical stage. There are nearly "no reliable and valid symptoms and signs which would allow a very early diagnosis before the manifestation of irreversible deficits. For a clinical diagnosis of dementia, cognitive impairment has to be severe enough to compromise the activities of daily living" (Förstl and Kurz 1999: 288). AD diagnosis is usually confirmed with tests of cognitive and functional assessments, often followed by a brain scan if available (Agronin 2007: 18; Weimer and Lipton 2009: 243).

The early-stage signs and symptoms of AD are complex and behavioural symptoms vary widely according to each person (Graham and Ritchie 2005: 35). This makes that a person's diagnosis might become particularly difficult in the early stages (Agronin 2007: 82). To characterize AD, some health professionals use a few simple tests to assess any change in cognitive functions. One of these basic measures is the widely used Mini-Mental State Examination (MMSE) (Harrison and Owen 2002: 256; Graber and Wilbur 2008: 705; Weimer and Lipton 2009: 65). However, the MMSE is just an initial examination and fairly inaccurate at early stage AD detection (Spaan et al. 2005; Duchek and Balota 2005). The definitive diagnosis of AD can only be made after death with an autopsy (Becker and Giacobino 1990: 297; Emilien et al. 2004: 5; Weimer and Lipton 2009: 164). "Verification of the diagnosis requires the demonstration of amyloid plagues and neurofibrillary tangles within the substance of the brain" (Garrard 2009: 252).

The possibility to identify and measure the very earliest stage of AD could provide important insights into *cognitive reserve* (Garrard 2009: 253). According to Stern (2002; 2006), cognitive reserve suggests that the brain actively attempts to cope with brain damage by using pre-existing cognitive processing approaches or by enlisting compensatory approaches. The brain of individuals with more cognitive reserve would use more alternative networks to compensate

---

2 A localized abnormal patch on a body part or surface.

3 Twisted fibres that build up inside the nerve cells.

for the damages caused than the brain of other indivuals with less cognitive reserve (Chung 2008). Consequently, the same brain damage can have different effects on different people:

> "The concept of cognitive reserve provides a ready explanation for why many studies have demonstrated that higher levels of intelligence and of educational and occupational attainment are good predictors of which individuals can sustain greater brain damage before demonstrating functional deficit. Rather than positing that these individuals' brains are grossly anatomically different than those with less reserve [...], the cognitive reserve hypothesis posits that they process tasks in a more efficient manner" (Stern 2006: 451).

1.2. Pre-diagnostic detection of AD

According to Bertrand (2003) early diagnosis is quite critical. However, more and more researchers are focusing their attention on the early stages of AD, when there is a greater chance of enabling patients to lead normal lives for a longer period of time. Positive results may improve diagnostic techniques and drugs (e.g. cholinergic drugs) that can diminish the degeneration of the brain in its embryonic phases (Marieb and Hoehn 2007: 469; Nelson and Gilbert 2005: 44).

The challenge and importance of pre-diagnostic AD detection is very much related to mild cognitive impairment (MCI), as patients, at this phase, may be aware of their degenerative process and may be able to report on their symptoms (Ready et al. 2006: 245). Some studies have already demonstrated that the use of patients' language samples dating back years before the clinical confirmation of AD might be a useful source for detecting MCI (Snowdon 2003; Garrard et al. 2005; Garrard 2009; Lancashire and Hirst 2009).

1.3. Language and AD

The famous and prestigious British writer Dame Iris Murdoch died from AD in 1999; diagnosed at autopsy. Garrard and his colleagues (Garrard et al. 2005) found that her later novel reveals early signs of AD. They analysed the text of her last novel and found that although no structural and grammatical changes were found, her language revealed some effects of the disease. Her last book *Jackson's Dilemma* (1995), evidenced shorter sentences and higher repetition rates for more common words (Garrard et al. 2005: 255-8).

This evidences that language is very vulnerable to MCI at the earliest stages of AD. Language decline is probably one of the fastest and most predominant changes in primary progressive aphasia present at the earliest stages of AD, and associated with global cognitive deficits: decreased speech output, reduced conversational initiation, *echolalia*[4] and changes in the pragmatics of conversation (Lubinski 1995: 98; Johnson 2007: 119; Weiner and Lipton 2009: 221).

---

4 The repetition of vocalizations made by another person.

Various authors have examined and compared the language in normal aged people with AD affected ones. Major changes were found in vocabulary richness (Maxim and Bryan 1994): in normal aging, the mental lexicon continues expanding indefinitely; however, lexical retrieval becomes slower. In contrast, AD affected people have more serious problems in lexical retrieval and the mental lexicon becomes eventually inaccessible.

Maxim and Bryan (1994:46) also found differences in the use of indefinite words (i.e. thing, matter, something, someone, etc.); a modest increase is found in healthy normal aging, while patients with AD show a dramatic overuse of indefinite words (Nicholas et al. 1985).

Word repetition and phrase repetition have also been found different between normal aging and AD; healthy people evidence some increase; however, AD patients show greater increase in repeating words and phrases (Nicholas et al. 1985).

Regarding syntax, Bates et al. (1995) discovered significant differences in normal aging compared to AD; where normal aging has no effect on the range and variability of syntactic structures used, AD patients underused passives and embedded sentences (Ellis 1996).

Discourse also exhibits differences between normal aging and AD. Data obtained from AD patients reveal incoherence, sentence shortening and uncontrollable repetition of a particular response, such as a word, phrase, or gesture, despite the absence or cessation of a stimulus (Harnish and Neils-Strunjas 2008).

However, despite these studies, the evolution of language disturbance in AD patients has rarely been examined systematically, especially in order to detect and analyse MCI at the earliest stages of AD, except for Garrard's (2009) recently published article *Cognitive Archaeology: Uses, Methods and Results*. Garrard analyses the vocabulary trends in transcripts[5] of former British Prime Minister Harold Wilson's performance in the spontaneous speech throughout his two terms of office (1964-70 and 1974-76). The analysis is based on quantification techniques using the 30 most frequent words and the 30 most frequent content words and comparing them intra-speaker: Harold Wilson 1965-66, 1969-70 and 1975-76; and inter-speakers Harold Wilson (1965-66, 1969-70 and 1975-76) versus the rest of the Members of Parliament (1965-66, 1969-70 and 1975-76). The findings showed that the content of Wilson's speeches was identifiably different from those of other members of the House throughout his career as Prime Minister. However, the difference was smaller during the months leading up to his resignation –a sign that he was losing his distinctive voice. Garrard (2009) concludes that this could be a symptom of the earliest stages of AD.

---

5 Obtained from the Hansard: the printed transcripts of parliamentary debates in the Westminster system of government.

Garrard's conclusions shed new light in pre-diagnostic AD detection; however, his research also evidences some imprecision and flaws: (i) minor errors in some calculations, such as mean word frequency (41.4 instead of 42.2, as stated) (Garrard 2009: 260); (ii) lack of precision in some statements: "... a set of mid-frequency words to be compared," (Garrard 2009: 262) which makes it very hard for any researcher to falsify his study; and (iii) probably more sophisticated techniques would have resulted more adequate, reliable and revealing (i.e. multivariate statistical techniques) than the use of just Wilcoxson's Signed Rank Test and Friedman's Test. In addition, Garrards's methodology is very difficult to apply as it requires not just the linguistic data of the potential AD patient but also data of other fellow subjects.

2. Featuring linguistic variables for pre-clinical AD detection

Apart from the many difficulties in falsifying Garrard's findings (2009), his research does not reveal anything on the potential linguistic variables interacting in MCI at the earliest stages of AD or more precisely at the pre-clinical stages of AD.

Our aim here is to try to identify linguistic variables likely to be altered due to AD affection at embryonic stages.

As Garrard (2009), we shall perform the analysis on the same case study: Former British Prime Minister Harold Wilson, a would-be affected AD patient at the time of resignation in 1976.

2.1. Methodology

As noted, this research is based on a case study, involving the study of a single person: Harold Wilson. A case study may show a correlation between two or more variables/factors, and whether or not a causal relationship can also be proven. This research method is ideal when a holistic, in-depth investigation is needed (Feagin et al. 1991), and it is particularly useful in depicting a holistic portrayal of a person's behaviour, in our case: the linguistic output of a single individual.

Furthermore, our case study method involves an in-depth examination of a single case, contrasting two periods: 1964 and 1976. 1964 is Harold Wilson's first year of office (not affected by AD) and 1976, the year of Harold Wilson's resignation (potentially affected by AD and showing some signs of MCI). The two comparison years might be understood as the pre- and post AD affected periods respectively.

2.2. Data

Data will only be collected from Harold Wilson's oral outcomes –not his fellow MPs–, and extracted from the Hansard.

The Hansard contains the printed transcripts of the parliamentary debates in the two Houses of Parliament. Although it does not always report exactly every single word uttered by the MPs, departures from verbatim are rare, except for some deletions of repeated words and eventually some grammatical corrections (Garrard 2009: 258).

As noted above, two comparison periods were chosen: 1964 and 1976. More precisely: (i) from 16 October 1964 to 31 December 1964; and (ii) from 1 January 1976 to 4 April 1976.

To focus our analysis on spontaneous speech, we proceeded like Garrard (2009: 259) and deleted statements, as these are normally read from texts that may not even have been written by the speaker. So we limited the data to spontaneous speech, containing verbal exchanges (responses, follow-up questions and subsequent exchanges).

Table 1 summarizes the data collected for the two comparison periods (1964 and 1976).

	Harold Wilson 1964	**Harold Wilson 1976**
Tokens	29,863	34,129
Types	2,972	3,211
Sentences	1,321	1,569

Table 1. Language source data: Harold Wilson 1964 versus 1976

2.3. Variables

Regarding the variables for the analysis, we shall define AD as the dependent variable. This is the central variable on which the other variables intervene in case a relationship exists. In fact, this variable is the observed one in order to determine if there is any effect, caused by the action of other variables.

In addition, we shall need to select the intervening variables in order to determine their relationship or effect on the dependent variable (AD). This is a most difficult task as we have not found in the literature any studies related to linguistic variables for pre-clinical AD detection, so we shall *a priori* select as independent variables all those variables used in previous or similar studies related to language decline in AD patients. Furthermore, we shall also take into account studies on genre and text classification. Automatic text classification methods verify which variables have a greater influence on determining the belonging of a particular text to a category or genre and whether these variables work better in isolation or in combination. We are confident that these techniques can fruitfully contribute to our research and shed some light on which independent variables are most prominent or representative to diagnose AD at a pre-clinical stage. This might help us to find out which variables or groups of variables discriminate more reliably between the non-affected AD stage and the affected one, applied to our case study: Harold Wilson.

Independent variable		Source	Type of research
Typology	**Variable**		
Punctuation variables	Periods, commas, semicolons, colons, hyphens, parenthesis, exclamations, questions	Cantos and Martínez (in press)	Genre and text classification
Lexical distribution measures	Words/period, character/period, standard. Type-token ratio, mean word length, long word counts, hapax legomena, hapax dislegomena, Automated readability index, Coleman-Liau Index		
Frequency of occurrence of the 30 most frequent words	The, of, and, a, in, to, it, is, was, I, for, you, he, be, with, on, that, by, at, are, not, this, but, 's (genitive), they, his, from, had, she, which		
Frequency of occurrence of the 30 most frequent content words	Hon., friend, gentleman, house, question, government, member, made, matter, Sir, time, opposition, members, minister, secretary, statement, answer, matters, questions, country, united, party, clear, defence, make, aware, leader, put, agree, policy	Garrard (2009)	AD
Deictic markers	Person deixis (subject/object personal pronouns, possessive determiners/pronouns), place deixis (demonstrative determiners/pronouns, place adverbs)	March et al. (2006, 2009)	AD
Use of nouns	Nouns		
Use of nouns versus pronouns	Nouns and pronouns		
Part-of-speech distribution	Types and hapax legomena	Garrard et al. (2005)	AD
Syntactic complexity	Conjunctions		
Repetition of words/phrases	Hapax legomena, n-grams (2-12 words)		
Use of indefinite words	Any-/some(body, one, thing, etc.), thing(s)	Nicholas et al (1985); Maxim and Bryan (1995)	AD

Table 2. Independent variables analysed

Table 2 displays all the independent variables selected, the sources these variables have been taken from, and whether these variables have already been applied to AD research or other studies.

Once the data is analysed, we shall be in disposition to decide *a posteriori* whether and to what degree the selected intervening variables are related to the dependent variable (AD).

2.4. Results

In what follows, we shall focus only on those variables that have output significant differences between the two comparison periods (1964 and 1976).

2.4.1. Punctuation variables[6]

Significant differences are found in the use of semi-colons, colons and question marks. There are important underuses of these punctuation variables in 1976, compared to 1964 (Table 3).

	HW64[7]	**HW76**	**Diff. %**	***p***[8]
Semi-colon	0.0144[9]	0.0070	-105.1545	0.041
Colon	0.0061	0.0013	-361.5385	0.031
Question	0.0273	0.0083	-231.7073	0.000

Table 3. Punctuation variables

A more detailed analysis of these punctuation variables reveal that with respect to the use of semi-colon, underuse in HW76 is particularly noticeable compared to HW64, when used to join closely related independent clauses not conjoined with a coordinating conjunction (-250%).

The use of colon to introduce quotations –a very common practice in HW64– is not used at all in HW76.

Regarding interrogatives, HW64 offers a more extensive variety of question types, compared to HW76 (Table 4).

Alternative interrogatives (e.g. ... *will he say whether it was deliberate or because he did not know any better?*), and question tags are not used at all in HW76. Other significant changes are related to the underuse of *yes/no questions* (-166.66%) and *wh-questions* (-260%).

---

6 Note that punctuation marks are placed in the oral transcripts by professional transcribers at the House of Commons.

7 HW64 and HW76 stand for *Harold Wilson's speech in 1964* and *1976* respectively.

8 Fisher Exact Test.

9 All figures are normalized for direct comparison and expressed as a percentage of the total number of sentences, tokens, etc., used in each period.

	Yes/No questions	Alternative Interrogatives	WH questions	Tags	Other
HW64	15	3	13	2	3
HW76	9	0	3	0	1

Table 4. Typology of interrogatives

2.4.2. Lexical distribution measures

No significant lexical distribution differences are found between HW64 and HW76, except for hapax dislegoma. Furthermore, the *standardized type-token ratio*[10] is surprisingly higher in HW76 (37.8764) than in HW64 (36.4034), which suggests that vocabulary size is superior in HW76. This is a striking finding and contradicts *a priori* other findings on AD (Garrard et al. 2005; Lancashire and Hirst 2009). For a more in-depth analysis of this finding, we shall divide both corpora into 5,000 word chunks. This will allow us to observe how types grow along the corpus.

	Types	
Tokens	HW64	HW76
5,000	1,035	1,119
10,000	1,611	1,692
15,000	2,106	2,134
20,000	2,445	2,456
25,000	2,724	2,716
30,000		2,969

Table 5. Type-growth in HW64 versus HW76

If we look at the data (Table 5), we realise that type-growth is superior in HW76 from 5,000 to 20,000 tokens. Nevertheless, things change from 25,000 tokens onwards, where type-growth is greater in HW64. Unfortunately, the HW64 corpus is smaller than the HW76 one, and it becomes impossible to continue the comparison. It seems that in HW76 the appearance rate of new types is greater at the beginning, compared to HW64, but from a point onwards, type growth seems less steep; whereas in HW64 type-growth starts less steep and is more constant throughout, and from 25,000 tokens onwards, eventually superior to HW76.

Another finding, related to hapax legomena and hapax dislegomena, reveals that hapax legomena are more frequent in HW76 (47.72%) than in HW64 (44.71%). Curiously, hapax dislegoma and types with a frequency range of 3 to 10 are more common in HW64 than in HW76.

10 The number shown is a percentage of new types for every 1,000 tokens.

2.4.3. Frequency of occurrence of the 30 most frequent words
Apparently, a quick examination of the graph (Figure 1) shows a similar usage-pattern of the 30 most frequent words in HW64 versus HW76 (Wilcoxon's Signed Rank Test: p = 0,082). Significant changes involve HW64 overuses of: *a, to, it, is, was be, that, this* and *but*; and overuses in HW76 regarding: *the, I, by* and *at.*

A more in-depth analysis reveals, however, a very significant overuse of singular subject personal pronoun *you* in HW76 (Table 6). It is used on average nearly three times more (0.010 in HW64 versus 0.0291 in HW76).

2.4.4. Frequency of occurrence of the 30 most frequent content words
Overall, no significant differences were found (Wilcoxon's Signed Rank Test: p = 0,139). Nevertheless, important individual differences can be depicted if we compare the data on the 30 most frequent content words used (Table 7): HW76 overuses *friend, member, Sir, matter(s), country, party* and *aware.*

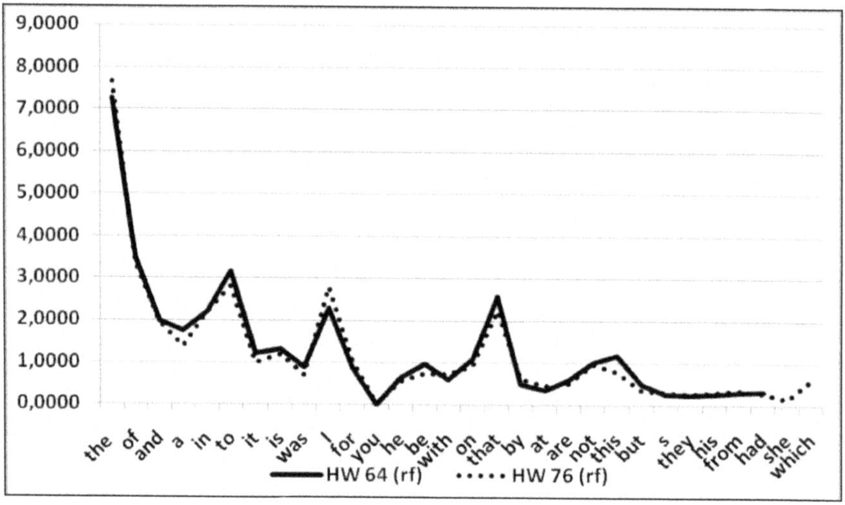

Figure 1. Use of the 30 most frequent words

2.4.5. Deictic markers
According to Jaszczolt (2002: 191) "deixis is the phenomenon of encoding contextual information by means of lexical items or grammatical distinctions that provide this information only when paired with this context." Therefore, the interpretation or understanding of such an expression is relative to the extra-linguistic context of the utterance, as opposed to anaphora which includes only references to preceding utterances, that is, linguistic co(n)text.

In this case study, we shall examine the use of person and place deixis, (March at al. 2006; 2009).

Type	HW64	HW76	% Diff. (HW76-64)
the	7.2705	7.6657	5.4346
of	3.4852	3.3352	-4.3044
and	1.9911	1.9441	-2.3604
a	1.7609	1.3882	-21.1670
in	2.2178	2.2089	-0.4035
to	3.1617	2.8055	-11.2655
it	1.2106	0.9837	-18.7480
is	1.3140	1.1961	-8.9732
was	0.8938	0.6985	-21.8552
I	2.2979	2.7910	21.4572
for	0.8971	1.0535	17.4303

Table 6a. Use of the 30 most frequent words

Type	HW64	HW76	% Diff. (HW76-64)
you	0.0100	0.0291	190.8724
he	0.6470	0.5471	-15.4371
be	0.9638	0.7421	-23.0044
with	0.5903	0.7247	22.7580
on	1.0973	0.9313	-15.1254
that	2.5847	2.2438	-13.1887
by	0.4869	0.6141	26.1111
at	0.3569	0.4511	26.4072
are	0.5970	0.5238	-12.2508
not	1.0139	0.9604	-5.2751
this	1.1773	0.7945	-32.5143
but	0.4903	0.3463	-29.3596
s' (*genitive*)	0.2612	0.3135	20.0326
they	0.2501	0.2648	5.8776
his	0.2635	0.2998	13.7716
from	0.3168	0.3405	7.4697
had	0.3368	0.2823	-16.1942
she[11]		0.1542	
which	0.7771	0.6228	-19.8540

Table 6b. Use of the 30 most frequent words

11 Note that the pronoun *she* did not occur at all in HW64. This is because Harold Wilson did not imply any female MP in his verbal exchanges during his first year at office. Things changed in 1976 with Margaret Thatcher as Leader of the Opposition.

Type	HW64	HW76	% Diff. (HW76-64)
Hon	1.3830	1.8606	34.5345
friend	0.2846	0.7179	152.2069
gentleman	0.6664	0.3750	-43.7184
House	0.4018	0.4600	14.4796
question	0.3784	0.4395	16.1509
government	0.3382	0.3370	-0.3709
member	0.1574	0.3252	106.6498
made	0.2578	0.2256	-12.4996
matter	0.1574	0.2784	76.8624
Sir	0.1105	0.2959	167.8042
time	0.1641	0.2315	41.0720
opposition	0.1942	0.1875	-3.4479
members	0.2043	0.1465	-28.2784
minister	0.2076	0.1260	-39.3143

Table 7a. Use of the 30 most frequent content words

Type	HW64	HW76	% Diff. (HW76-64)
secretary	0.1239	0.1641	32.4330
statement	0.2076	0.0908	-56.2498
answer	0.1105	0.1612	45.8339
matters	0.0469	0.2080	343.7519
questions	0.1239	0.1289	4.0545
country	0.0703	0.1699	141.6677
United	0.1842	0.0674	-63.4089
party	0.0737	0.1612	118.7509
clear	0.0871	0.1377	58.1737
defence	0.1741	0.0586	-66.3460
make	0.1306	0.0967	-25.9612
aware	0.0737	0.1436	94.8872
leader	0.1440	0.0820	-43.0230
put	0.1072	0.1113	3.9067
agree	0.1005	0.1143	13.7505
policy	0.1072	0.1084	1.1723

Table 7b. Use of the 30 most frequent content words

Person deixis is reflected directly in the grammatical categories of person. The basic person deictics are expressions which necessarily refer to the speaker(s) or the addressee(s) of the utterance in which they occur (Levinson 1983: 68). In English, this is generally accomplished with pronouns (personal pronouns and possessive pronouns/determiners). Our findings reveal significant differences in person deixis ($\chi 2 = 217.943$; $p = 0.000$). Individual analyses of (i) personal subject pronouns (PS), (ii) personal object pronouns (PO) and (iii) possessives (Pos) also shows statistically significant differences (PS: $\chi 2 = 82.779$; $p = 0.000$; PO: $\chi 2 = 5.114$; $p = 0.000$; Pos: $\chi 2 = 109.903$; $p = 0.000$).

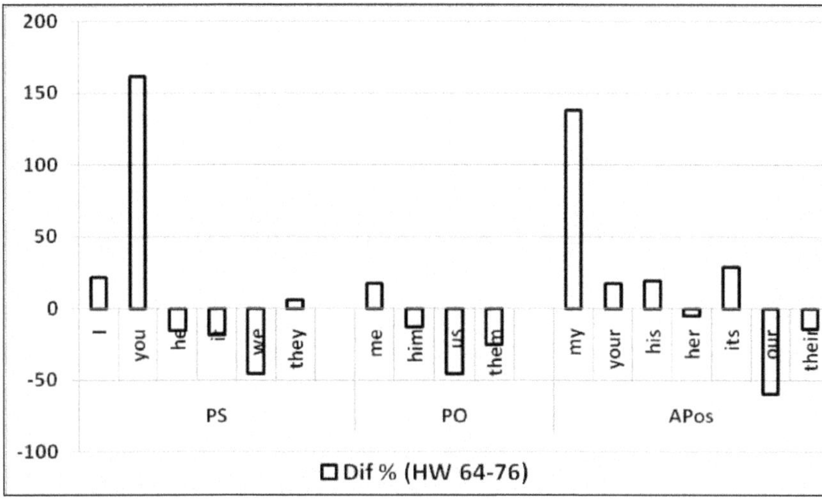

Figure 2. Person deixis[12]

The most striking differences are found in: (i) HW76's overuse of deictic *you* and *my*; and (ii) HW76's underuse of *we, us* and *our.*

Place deixis, also known as space deixis, "concerns the specification of locations relative to anchorage points in the speech event" (Levinson 1983: 79). The most salient English examples are the adverbs "here" and "there" and the demonstratives "this" and "that", though they are far from the only deictic words. In our analysis we consider (i) demonstrative pronouns/determiners (Dem) and (ii) place adverbs (PAdv). The comparison between HW64 and HW76 outputs statistically significant differences regarding place deixis ($\chi 2 = 49.924$; $p = 0.000$); more precisely, differences are also encountered in individual comparisons: demonstrative pronouns/determiners (Dem: $\chi 2 = 8.204$; $p = 0.042$) and place adverbs (PAdv: $\chi 2 = 37.574$; $p = 0.000$).

A graphical display of the results (Figure 3) is very revealing; whereas singular demonstratives are underused in HW76, especially *this*, all place adverbs are overused, except for *opposite.*

12 Note that only pronouns and determiners actually present in the corpora are considered (e.g. *yours* does not appear in the graph because it does not occur in Wilson's speeches).

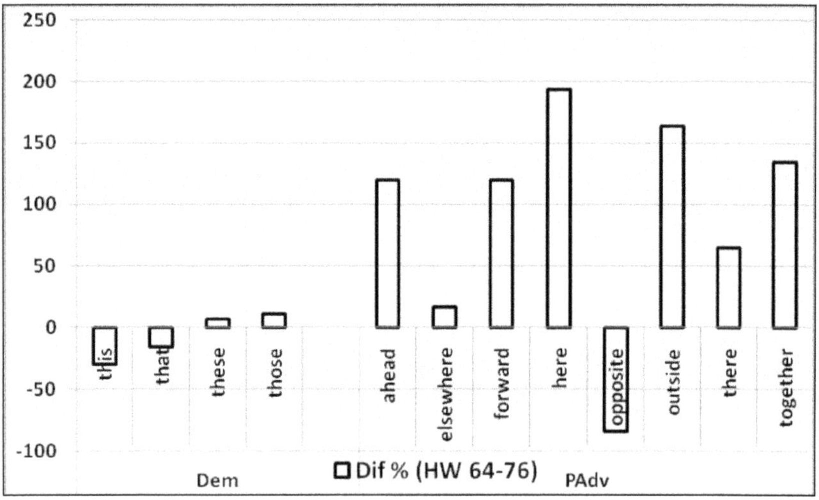

Figure 3. Place deixis

2.4.6. Use of nouns

The use of total nouns (tokens) is statistically more prominent in HW76 compared to HW64 (Wilcoxon's Signed Rank Test: $p = 0.005$), whereas the amount of different nouns (types) is not significant (Wilcoxon's Signed Rank Test: $p = 0.445$). This means that on average HW64 and HW76 use a similar number of nouns; however HW76 repeats nouns at a higher rate.

A more thorough analysis of noun-use shows (Table 8) that repetition is particularly outstanding in HW76 regarding *singular nouns of direction* (e.g. north, southeast) and *common nouns* which are neutral for number (e.g. sheep, cod, headquarters).

2.4.7. Syntactic complexity

Syntactic complexity is measured just by means of connectors or conjunctions. Statistically significant differences are found in the use of conjunctions ($\chi 2 = 48.336$; $p = 0.001$). Individual differences are also evidenced regarding coordinated conjunctions ($\chi 2 = 8.931$; $p = 0.030$) and subordinated ones ($\chi 2 = 39.313$; $p = 0.003$).

HW76 exhibits significant overuses in a number of conjunctions (Table 9): *nor, although, as though, so that, than* and *while.*[13] Most notably is the absence in HW76 of the conjunction *whether,* a very common connector in HW64 (with a raw frequency of 30 and a usage rate of 1.5798%).

13 Only items that occur in both HW64 and HW76 (with a joint-frequency ≥ 3) are considered for analysis.

	HW64	HW76	% Diff. (HW76-HW64)
	Mean repetition	Mean repetition	
singular noun of direction	3.3333	6.8333	105.0000
common noun, neutral for number	4.2857	8.5000	98.3333
singular common noun	4.8662	5.5444	13.9373
plural common noun	3.5714	3.5248	-1.3069
preceding noun of title	10.0000	10.8000	8.0000
temporal noun, singular	7.7333	11.1579	44.2831
temporal noun, plural	10.0000	10.3333	3.3333
singular proper noun	3.2657	2.9439	-9.8541
singular weekday noun	2.4000	2.8000	16.6667
singular month noun	4.3000	5.7273	33.1924

Table 8. Noun use

	HW64	HW76	% Diff. (HW76-HW64)
and	31.1216	33.2497	6.8380
but	7.7409	5.8676	-24.2002
nor	0.1053	0.3511	233.3250
or	5.4239	5.3159	-1.9904
after	0.2106	0.3511	66.6625
although	0.6319	1.2036	90.4714
as	6.5298	7.9238	21.3487
as far as	0.1580	0.2006	26.9809
as though	0.0527	0.3009	471.4142
because	2.3170	1.3541	-41.5599
before	0.7372	0.4012	-45.5796
except	0.2106	0.1505	-28.5732
if	5.3712	4.6640	-13.1674
since	0.8952	1.1535	28.8483
so that	0.0527	0.3511	566.6499
than	0.9479	2.4072	153.9619
that	30.4371	28.7864	-5.4234
though	0.5266	0.4514	-14.2879
unless	0.1053	0.1003	-4.7643
until	0.1580	0.1505	-4.7643
when	2.9489	3.4102	15.6434
where	0.4213	0.7021	66.6625
while	0.2633	0.5015	90.4714

Table 9. Use of conjunctions

	HW64	HW76	% Diff. (HW76-HW64)
2-gram	2.6756	2.7630	3.2701
3-gram	1.0012	1.1310	12.9603
4-gram	0.3181	0.5245	64.8691
5-gram	0.1373	0.2344	70.7324
6-gram	0.0335	0.1465	337.5018
7-gram	0.0167	0.0908	442.5023
8-gram	0.0067	0.0645	862.5040
9-gram	0.0000	0.0469	
10-gram	0.0000	0.0264	
11-gram	0.0000	0.0147	
12-gram	0.0000	0.0088	

Table 10. N-gram repetitions

2.4.8. Repetition of words/phrases

Regarding word (type) repetition, no significant difference is found between the mean-word-repetition in HW64 (10.05; *sd* = 60.638) compared to HW76 (10.63; *sd* = 67.291; Independent one-sample *t*-test; $p = 0.722$).

In contrast, the comparison of phrase-repetition HW64 versus HW76 is very revealing (Table 10). Statistical testing shows significance among 2-8 gram phrases ($\chi^2 = 58.898$; $p = 0.000$). Very high differences are found in the use of 6 to 8-gram structures in HW76 compared to HW64.

	HW64	HW76	% Diff. (HW76-HW64)
2-gram	2.6756	2.7630	3.2701
3-gram	1.0012	1.1310	12.9603
4-gram	0.3181	0.5245	64.8691
5-gram	0.1373	0.2344	70.7324
6-gram	0.0335	0.1465	337.5018
7-gram	0.0167	0.0908	442.5023
8-gram	0.0067	0.0645	862.5040
9-gram	0.0000	0.0469	
10-gram	0.0000	0.0264	
11-gram	0.0000	0.0147	
12-gram	0.0000	0.0088	

Table 10. N-gram repetitions

Another enlightening finding is the absence of n-gram with 9 and more words in HW64, whereas HW76 shows some preference for the use of these "prefabricated" chunks. Note also that 7-gram and 8-gram usage in HW64 is similar to 11-gram and 12-gram usage in HW76 respectively.

3. Conclusions

In this research, we have assumed, as Garrard (2009), (i) that HW76 is a period previous to AD-symptom onset and (ii) that spontaneous language can reveal early signs of AD: potential pre-clinical markers of cognitive dysfunction.

These two assumptions have led us to analyse the spontaneous speech of former British Prime Minister Harold Wilson, by contrasting two periods: 1964 (not affected by AD) and 1976 (potentially affected by AD and showing some signs of MCI), in order to identify linguistic variables likely to be altered due to AD affection at embryonic stages.

The result findings have revealed significant changes in a number of linguistic variables that might point towards the presence of some degenerative neuropathology in HW76:

(1) Possible changes in the organization and structuring of the mental lexicon: (i) type-growth is constant all through HW64, whereas in HW76 it is steeper at the beginning but starts declining from 20,000 tokens onwards (a potential indicator of lexical closure); (ii) higher rate of hapax legomena; however, hapax dislegomena and types with a frequency range of 3-10 are less used in HW76; (iii) average word-repetition rate is higher in HW76; (iv) higher usage rate of fixed structures (2-8 grams); first-time occurrences of structures with more than nine words (and up to twelve words); (v) very significant usage increase of some types: *you* and some hypernym-like nouns (*friend, member, matter(s), Sir* and *country*).

It seems as if some kind of lexical bi-polarization is going on in Wilson's mental lexicon: (i) rare and little used words get used even less; this explains the increase in hapax legomena; in contrast, (ii) more common and frequent words, particularly hypernyms become overused (see increase in type repetition rate).

Surprisingly, vocabulary size measures such as (standardized) type-token ratio are not reliable indicators as potential pre-clinical markers of cognitive dysfunction in AD: HW76 exhibits a higher vocabulary size than HW64. This is basically due to the different type-growths (see above), and because the type-token ratio is not a distribution indicator.

(2) Potential changes of personality: significant overuses of first person singular (possessive determiner *my*) and second person singular (personal subject pronoun *you*); this runs parallel with an important underuse of first person plural (*we, us* and *our*); nevertheless, no significant changes are found in the usage of third person (singular/plural) and/or second person (plural).

It seems as if the participant roles become limited just to the speaker (first person singular) and addressee (second person singular).

(3) Latent signs of spatial disorientation: significant overuse of place adverbs and singular nouns of direction.

Spatial disorientation in AD is related to the degeneration of the same pathways linking the hippocampus with the superior parietal and posterior cingulate cortex in the right hemisphere (Giannakopoulos et al. 2000: 189).

(4) Likely symptoms of less lexical and grammatical complexity: (i) less lexical precision, as evidenced by the overuse of hypernyms –a possible indicator of problems in accessing more precise and less frequent words in the mental lexicon; (ii) resort to more common and frequent words (higher type repetition rate); (iii) construction of shorter sentences: average number of words (tokens) per sentence is 22.6063 in HW64 compared to 21.7520 in HW75, and average types per sentence is 2.2498 and 2.0465 in HW64 and HW75 respectively –this also results into less informative sentences; (iv) overuse of some conjunctions and syntactic structures: co-ordinated clauses with *nor*, and subordinated clauses with *although, as though, so that* and *while*; and (v) complete suppression of the subordinator *whether,* a most common connector in HW64 (with a usage rate of 1.5798%).

(5) In the early stages, very commonly recognised symptoms are memory loss and impairment of concurrent manipulation of information in working memory. This is evidenced by a number of signs: (i) shorter less-informative sentences; (ii) less usage of related independent clauses not conjoined with a coordinating conjunction; (iii) absence of literal quotes –a very common practice in HW64; (iv) underuse of interrogatives compared to HW64 (*yes/no questions* and *wh-questions*); furthermore, HW64 offers a more extensive variety of question types, compared to HW76; additionally, alternative interrogative and question tags are not used at all in HW76.

Analysis of the data also points towards the hypothesis that Harold Wilson might have been aware of his MCI, and might have started using various surrogate measures of his cognitive reserve as an attempt to cope with his cognitive dysfunctions. These substitute measures might have included the use of pre-existing cognitive processing approaches or enlist compensatory approaches such as (i) accessing more generic and frequent words; and (ii) using repetitively "prefabricated" chunk of words. We are confident that Wilson had more cognitive reserve and was "more successful" than other AD affected people at coping with the same amount of brain damage. This might also explain why his fellow MP's at the House, press, etc., did not realise anything about his onset of AD.

4. A further issue

The above conclusions have been derived from a thorough data analysis and it seems evident that some independent variables interact with one another and are at the same time responsible for different "dimensions" featuring AD. For instance, the overuse of more common/frequent words is related to changes in the mental lexicon, symptoms of less lexical complexity and a possible surrogate measure of cognitive reserve. This suggests that the early stage of AD involves observation and analysis of more than one statistical variable at a time.

Thus, we might think of using more sophisticated technique to perform studies across multiple dimensions while taking into account all statistically significant variables found on spontaneous speech production for preclinical AD detection. This takes us inevitably to multivariate data analysis.

Multivariate statistics looks at the pattern of relationships between several variables simultaneously. It provides the possibility of analysing complex sets of data. They allow analysis where there are many independent variables and possible dependent variables which correlate with each other to varying degrees. Consequently, multivariate statistics might help us to summarize data and reduce the number of variables needed to describe and identify pre-clinical AD. Among other applications, multivariate statistics can be employed in classifying data or to develop a system of classification for the data.

In what follows, we shall aim at building a statistical model that might assign HW64 and HW76 to either the AD affected group or the AD non-affected group. A positive classification model might suggest that there is indeed some correlation among various independent variables and the dependent variable at pre-clinical AD as well as that pre-clinical AD detection might be feasible.

One multivariate technique that allows classification is discriminant function analysis (DFA, hereafter). DFA is concerned with the problem of assigning individuals, for whom several variables have been measured, to certain groups that have already been identified in the sample. It is used to determine these variables that discriminate between two or more naturally occurring groups. The main purpose of this is to search for that structure in the data which enables clusters of individuals such as subjects, variables, etc. to be identified.

We shall apply DFA with those independent variables that have shown statistical significant differences between HW64 and HW76:[14]

- Punctuation variables: Semi colon, colon and questions.
- Lexical distribution measures: Hapax dislegomena.
- Frequency of occurrence of the 30 most frequent words: *A, at, be, but, by, I, is, it, that, the, this, to, was* and *you.*

[14] Data analysis was conducted using SPSS V. 15.0 (SPSS Inc., 2006, PC version).

- Frequency of occurrence of the 30 most frequent content words: *aware, country, friend, matters, member, party* and *Sir.*
- Deictic markers: (1) Person deixis: *you, we, us, my* and *our*; (ii) place deixis: *this, ahead, forward, here, outside* and *together.*
- Use of nouns: *singular nouns of direction* and *common nouns neutral for number.*
- Syntactic complexity: *nor, although, as though, so that, than* and *while.*
- Repetition of words/phrases: *4-8 grams*.

This results into 49 variables for our DFA model. Our aim now is twofold:

- Predict the categorical dependent variable (AD), to *a priori* defined groups (HW64 and HW76), for the 49 independent variables, and check if the discriminant model as a whole is significant; and
- If the model shows significance, then to assess the individual independent variables, selecting those variables with a greater discriminant capacity and to generate a predictive discriminant model to classify new cases.

The data relative to our model reveals that it explains 100% of the variance. That is, the function contributes significantly to determining group differences (AD affected versus AD non-affected).

Once the DFA has turned out to be positive, we can try a stepwise procedure. This will allow us to assess each individual independent variable in order to select the best predictor or set of predictors. SPSS now optimises and simplifies the model and outputs a new model with similar predictive power, using just the two best predictors:

- Deictic markers: person deixis: *our*
- Syntactic complexity: *so that*

	Alzheimer	
	No	Yes
Person deixis: *our*	184,386.9	-21,866.9
Syntact. complexity: *so that*	-81,044.5	321,699.9
(Constant)	-41,230.5	-54,350.2

Table 11. Fisher Function Coefficients

A further use of DFA is that, once those variables with a greater discriminant capacity have been selected, it is possible to generate a predictive discriminant model to classify new cases by means of the *Fisher Function Coefficients* (Table 11).

For new classifications, we just need to measure the values for the predicting variables *person deixis (our),* and *syntactic complexity (so that)*, instantiate them in the two discriminant functions and maximise[15] the values. For instance, suppose we have a speech sample of Harold Wilson with the following measures 0.503 and 0.065, relative to *person deixis (our),* and *syntactic complexity (so that)* respectively; we get:

No = 0.503*184,386.9 + 0.065*(-81,044.5) + (-41,230.5) = 46,248.2182
Yes = 0.503*(-21,866.9) + 0.065*(321,699.9) + (-54,350.2) = 4,476.2428

So maximising the two coefficients, we find that this hypothetical speech sample of Harold Wilson is most likely to correspond to a non-affected AD period, as *No* is the highest resulting coefficient (46,248.2182), compared to *Yes* (4,476.2428).

From the results above it seems that pre-clinical AD prediction is feasible, at least for our case study. Using DFA might help us to summarize data and reduce the number of variables needed to describe and identify pre-clinical AD.

Of course it does not follow automatically from this that the data obtained from our case study can be freely extrapolated to other potentially affected AD patients in order to predict whether (s)he is affected by AD; this is an empirical question that remains to be resolved. It also remains to be seen whether same linguistic variables are equally prominent and valid for other languages than English in order to detect pre-clinical AD.

5. Final remarks

Early AD identification and intervention can take us to more positive social outcomes, such as slowing down disease progression and improved life quality for the AD patients' families and caregivers (Weimer and Sager 2009: 215). "Early detection empowers people with the disease to participate in decisions about their treatment and future care, as well as consider clinical trial opportunities. Being diagnosed early is vital to receiving the best help and care possible" (Sager 2009).

In Addition, "patients with AD and other dementias are heavy users of long-term care services, especially nursing home care, with estimated annual costs upward of tens of billions of dollars" in the US just (Sakai 2009). These costs could be greatly reduced by earlier diagnosis and treatment.

"The future of AD is to intervene decades before someone becomes symptomatic" (Sager 2009).

---

15 To take the maximum value obtained.

References

Agronin, M. (2007): *Alzheimer Disease and other Dementias: A Practical Guide*, Philadelphia, Lippincott Williams & Williams.

Agronin, M. and G. Maletta (2006): *Principles and Practice of Geriatric Psychiatry*, Philadelphia, Lippincott Williams & Williams.

Alzheimer, A. (1907): "Über eine eigenartige Erkrankung der Hirnrinde," *Allgemeine Zeitschrife Psychiatrie*, 64, 146–148.

Bates, E., C. Harris, V. Marchman, B. Wulfeck and M. Kritchevsky (1995): "Production of complex syntax in normal aging and Alzheimer's disease," *Language and Cognitive Processes*, 10, 487–539.

Becker, R. and E. Giacobini (1990): *Alzheimer Disease: Current Research in Early Diagnosis*, London, Taylor & Francis Ltd.

Bertrand, P. (2003): "Keeping Alzheimer's at Bay," *AARP Bulletin* (http://www-static-w4-md.aarp.org/health/conditions/articles/ alzheimers_ bay.html)

Cantos, P. and N. Martínez (forthcoming): "Proposal of a *budget* text-classification technique for English genres," *Corpus Linguistics and Linguistic Theory*.

Chung, J. (2008): "Leisure activity participation and cognitive reserve," *Web-Based Resource Centre for Dementia Care,* 9 (http://www.ginkgogroup.org/eng/?action-viewnews-itemid-43).

Curell, N., O. Bruna and M. Puyuelo (2006): "Intervención neuropsicológica y del lenguaje en la enfermedad de Alzheimer: descripción de un caso clínico," *Revista de Logopedia, Foniatría y Audiología,* 26, 4, 231-238.

Deutsch, M. (1995): *Neuropsychological Assessment*, Oxford, Oxford University Press.

Duchek, J. M. and D. A. Balota (2005): "Failure to control prepotent pathways in early stage dementia of the Alzheimer's type: evidence from dichotic listening," *Neuropsychology,* 19, 5, 687-695.

Ellis, D. G. (1996): "Coherence patterns in Alzheimer's discourse," *Communication Research,* 23, 472–495.

Emilien, G., C. Durlach, K. Minaker, B. Winblad, S. Gauthier and J. M. Maloteaux (2004): *Alzheimer Disease: Neuropsychology and Pharmacology*, Basel, Birkhäuser Verlag.

Feagin, J., A. Orum, and G. Sjoberg. (eds.) (1991): *A Case for Case Study*, Chapel Hill, NC, University of North Carolina Press.

Förstl, H. and A. Kurz (1999): "Clinical features of Alzheimer's disease," *European Archives of Psychiatry and Clinical Neuroscience*, 249, 288-290.

Galton, C. J., K. Patterson, J. H. Xuereb and J. R. Hodges (2000): "Atypical and typical presentations of Alzheimer's disease: a clinical, neuropsychological, neuroimaging and pathological study of 13 cases," *Brain,* 123, 3, 484-498.

Garrard, P. (2008): "Changing language in Harold Wilson's Commons speeches indicates cognitive deterioration during his final Term of Office, new research suggests" (http://www.sciencedaily.com/releases/2008/11/081110091553.htm)

Garrard, P. (2009): "Cognitive archaeology: uses, methods and results," *Journal of Neurolinguistics*, 22, 3, 250-265.

Garrard, P., L. M. Maloney, J. R. Hodges and K. Patterson (2005): "The effects of very early Alzheimer's Disease on the characteristics of writing by a renowned author," *Brain*, 128, 250–260.

Gatz, M., C. A. Prescott and N. L. Pedersen (2006): "Lifestyle risk and delaying factors," *Alzheimer Disease & Associated Disorders,* 20, 84-88.

Ghosh, A. (2008): *Mayo Clinic Internal Medicine Review: Eighth Edition*, Rochester, MN, Mayo Clinic Scientific Press.

Giannakopoulos, P. G. Gold, M. Duc, J. P. Michel, P. Hof and C. Bouras (2000): "Neural substrates of spatial and temporal disorientation in Alzheimer's disease," *Acta Neuropathologica*, Heidelberg, Springer, 189-195.

Graber, M. and J. Wilbur (2008): *Family Practice Examination and Board Review*, New Yok, McGraw-Hill.

Graham, J. and K. Ritchie (2005): "Mild cognitive impairment: ethical considerations for nosological flexibility in human kinds," *Philosophy, Psychiatry, & Psychology*, 13, 1, 31-43.

Grant, D. M., G. H. Goodfellow, K. S. Sugamori and K. Durette (2000): "Pharmacogenetics of the human arylamine N-acetyltransferases," *Pharmacology,* 6, 3, 204-11.

Guttmacher, A. and F. Collins (2002): "Genomic medicine – A primer," *The New England Journal of Medicine*, 347, 1512-1520.

Harnish, S. M. and J. Neils-Strunjas (2008): "In search of meaning: reading and writing in Alzheimer's disease," *Seminars in Speech and Language,* 29, 44–59.

Harrison, J. and A. Owen (2002): *Cognitive Deficits in Brain Disorders*, London, Martin Dunitz Ltd.

James, V. (2009): *The Alzheimer's Advisor: A Caregiver's Guide to Dealing with Tough Legal and Practical Issues*, New York, AMACOM.

Jaszczolt, K. M. (2002): *Semantics and Pragmatics*, London, Longman.

Johnson, A. (2007): *Medical Speech-Language Pathology: A Practitioner's Guide*, New York, Thieme Medical Publishers.

Kempler, S. (1989): "Life-span changes to adults' language: effect of memory and genre," *Applied Psycholinguistics,* 10, 49-66.

Lancashire, I. and G. Hirst (2009): "Vocabulary changes in Agatha Christie's mysteries as an indication of dementia: a case study," (Poster, 19th An-

nual Rotman Research Institute Conference, *Cognitive Aging: Research and Practice*, 8-10 March 2009, Toronto)
Lawrence, J., I. Deary, C. Appleton and J. Starr (2004): "Cognitive reserve and the neurobiology of cognitive ageing," *Ageing Research Reviews,* 3, 4, 369-382.
Levinson, S. (1983): *Pragmatics*, Cambridge, Cambridge University Press.
Lubinski, R. (1995): *Dementia and Communication*, Florence, KY, Cengage Delmar Learning.
Mader, S. (2008): *Inquiry into Life*, New Yok, McGraw-Hill.
March, E. G., R. Wales and P. Pattison (2006): "The uses of nouns and deixis in discourse production in Alzheimer's disease," *Journal of Neurolinguistics,* 19, 311-340.
March, E.G., P. Pattison and R. Wales (2009): "The role of cognitive-dependent language use: evidence from Alzheimer's disease," *Journal of Neurolinguistics,* 22, 18-36.
Marieb, E. and K. Hoehn (2007): *Human Anatomy and Psychology*, San Francisco, Pearson-Benjamin Cummings.
Maxim, J. and K. Bryan (1994): *Language of the Elderly: A Clinical Perspective*, London, Whurr.
Nelson, A. and S. Gilbert (2005): *Achieving Optimal Memory*, New York, McGraw-Hill.
Nicholas, M., Obler, L. K., Albert, M. L. and N. Helm-Estabrooks (1985): "Empty speech in Alzheimer's disease and fluent aphasia," *Journal of Speech and Hearing Research*, 28, 405–410.
Ready, R., B. Ott and J. Grace (2006): "Insight and cognitive impairment," *American Journal of Alzheimer Disease and Other Dementias,* 21, 4, 242-248.
Rodriguéz-Ferreiro, J., R. Davies, M. González-Nosti, A. Barbón and F. Cuetos (2009): "Name agreement, frequency and age of acquisition but not grammatical class, affect object and action naming in Spanish speaking participants with Alzheimer's disease," *Journal of Neurolinguistics,* 22, 37-54.
Sager, M. (2009): "Early Alzheimer's diagnosis offers large social, fiscal benefits," (http://www.eurekalert.org/pub_releases/2009-05/uowead051209)
Schellenberg, G. (1995): "Genetic dissection of Alzheimer disease, a heterogeneous disorder," *Proceedings of the National Academy of Sciences*, 92, 8552-8559.
Sherwood, L. (2008): *Human Physiology. From Cells to Systems*, Belmont, CA, Brooks/Cole.
Snowdon, D.A. (2003): "Healthy aging and dementia: findings from the Nun Study," *Annals of Internal Medicine,* 139, 450-454.

Spaan, P., J. G. W. Raaijmakers and C. Jonker (2005): "Early assessment of dementia: the contribution of different memory components," *Neuropsychology,* 19, 5, 629-640.

Stern, Y. (2003): "The concept of cognitive reserve: a catalyst for research," *Journal of Clinical and Experimental Neuropsychology,* 25, 5, 589-593.

Stern, Y. (2006): "Cognitive reserve and Alzheimer disease," *Alzheimer Disease & Associated Disorders,* 20, 2, 112-117.

Stones, M. (1997): *Alzheimer Disease and Aggression: A Guide for Caregivers,* North York, Captus Press.

Warner, T. T. and A. H. Shapira (2003): "Genetic and environmental factors in the aetiology of Parkinson's disease," *Annals of Neurology,* 53, 16-25.

Weiner, M. and A. Lipton (2009): *The American Psychiatric Publishing Textbook of Alzheimer and other Dementias*, Arlington, VA, American Psychiatric Publishing.

PART FIVE

Variation and Change

Enlarging noun phrases little by little: on structural complexity and modification in the history of English[1]

Javier Pérez Guerra
Ana E. Martínez Insua
Universidade de Vigo

1. Introduction

This paper is part of a larger diachronic project, the main goal of which is the characterisation of written-to-be-read (henceforth, simply 'written') and written-to-be-spoken ('speech-based' onwards) texts by using linguistic tools and variables. The assumption which underlies this investigation reflects Aristotle's observation that "[t]he style of written prose is not that of spoken oratory" (in Poole and Field 1976: 305). We aim here at exploring variation in a corpus of historical texts, looking particularly at the connection between written/speech-based text types (registers or genres) and structural complexity. The null hypothesis will be that 'no (synchronic and/or diachronic) variation among registers exists,' variation being measured by applying structural and syntactic metrics to a textual corpus. The variable used as a potential determinant of this type of microvariation in the language will be the structure and the distribution of modifying material in the noun phrase. More specifically, we will investigate the modification strategies which affect noun phrases functioning as either subjects (external arguments) or objects (internal arguments) from 1350 onwards.

The paper is organised as follows. In section 2 we describe the corpus. Section 3 discusses the concept of expansion as well as the typology of expansion strategies which will be used in this investigation. In section 4 we analyse the data by examining variables such as the connection between expansion strategies and (i) the syntactic role of the noun phrase, (ii) the differences between pre- and post-head expansion, (iii) the text types in the corpus, (iv) the historical period, and (v) the length of the modifier. Finally, section 5 is summarises findings and suggests avenues of further research.

2. The data

It is assumed here that the current word order of clausal constituents was fixed or syntacticised in the language during the Late Middle English period, and for

---

1 The research reported has been funded by the Spanish Ministry of Education and Science (grant number FFI2009-11274/FILO) and Xunta de Galicia (INCITE08-PXIB204016 PR), which is hereby gratefully acknowledged.

this reason we will restrict ourselves to exploring periods which share such ordering of the constituents either completely or partially. Thus, the periods analysed will be Late Middle, Early Modern, Late Modern and Present-Day English. Empirical data have been drawn from The Helsinki Corpus of English Texts (for the periods Middle English III and IV, and Early Modern English II; see Kytö 1996 for a description of the corpus) and from the British component of ARCHER (A Representative Corpus of Historical English Registers; for the Late Modern and Contemporary English periods; see Biber et al. 1994).

In an attempt to focus on formal (written-to-be-read) and informal ('(possibly) speech-based') textual material, two registers prototypically representative of the aforementioned dimensions have been considered: news and handbooks, as representative of formal language written to be published, and letters, which typically contain a more informal kind of language that exists somewhere close to the boundaries between writing and speech, and between private and public communication. With respect to the opposition of formal versus informal language, letters permit the inclusion of informal speech since they do not normally require any kind of literary expertise. As Hopper (1997: 3) notes, letters are examples of vernacular written narrative, where "'vernacular' is meant to suggest that it is the kind of narrative that does not usually find its way into print, and is not held up as a model of prose to be imitated." As far as the opposition between the binomial written versus oral language is concerned, letters occupy an intermediate position between prototypical written text types and speech-based linguistic discourses. In fact, in a corpus of fifteenth- and seventeenth-century letters, Markus (2001) explores characteristics such as lack of agreement, dangling constructions with unclear referents, omissions and marked word order, all of which are typical of oral language. Biber and Finegan (1997) investigate the linguistic evolution of letters, as well as other genres, from 1650 to 1990 and corroborate the existence of a "general historical trend towards more 'involved production' (...) and more 'situated reference'" (p. 75), that is, a drift toward orality. In this respect, Biber (2001: 212), dealing with the functional interpretation of his multidimensional analysis in its application to eighteenth-century letters, claims that "written registers were generally more sharply distinguished from spoken registers in the eighteenth century than they are at present." Finally, as regards the public versus private dichotomy, Markus (2001: 182) claims that "[t]he language of letters is and, as can be assumed, was as close to the linguistic usage of individuals as can be, perhaps with the exception of diaries."

The texts analysed here belong to 1350-1500, 1570-1640 and the second halves of the eighteenth, the nineteenth and the twentieth centuries, and the number of words analysed amounts to 179,092, distributed as shown in Table 1 below.

register/ period	1350-1500	1570-1640	1750-1799	1850-1899	1950-1990	Total
handbooks	23,191	12,623				35,814
news			26,138	23,213	24,235	73,586
letters	21,909	13,283	12,006	10,800	11,694	69,692
Total	45,100	25,906	38,144	34,013	35,929	179,092

Table 1. Corpus

3. Modification and complementation

Since text types are here understood as codifications of linguistic features (Taavitsainen 2001: 141), one can characterize a given text type or register by exploring its linguistic characteristics. This paper, then, investigates complexity in different textual variants by quantifying the strategies of pre- and post-modification in core noun phrases (henceforth, NPs), a factor which in the literature is seen as a determinant of structural complexity (see below). The final picture consists of the connection between diachronic textual variation and structural complexity as evinced by NP modification. The description of text types in terms of the degree of structural complexity which they exhibit is not free of controversy. Whereas a number of scholars support the view that written texts are structurally more complex (O'Donnell 1974; Akinnaso 1982; Rijkhoff 2002; specifically on NPs, Biber 2003: 172-74 on newspaper and academic prose), others contend that speech is structurally more complex (Poole and Field 1976; Halliday 1985: 63 when he says that "the complexity of written language is lexical, while that of spoken language is grammatical").

Our analysis of structural modification or expansion at the NP level follows the trend established by scholars such as Haan (1989), who investigates exclusively clausal postmodification, Ni (2003) on modification in Present-day English media texts, and especially Biber and Clark (2002), who, on data retrieved also from ARCHER (drama, fiction, newspapers and medical prose in the seventeenth, eighteenth, nineteenth and twentieth centuries), conduct a study similar to the one which we undertake here.

We have already pointed out that this analysis focuses on core nominal arguments, where 'core' stands for unmarked subject and object NPs. Our database thus contains all the preverbal nominal subjects (unmarked external arguments) and postverbal nominal objects (unmarked internal arguments) of the declarative sentences in the corpus described above. Compliance with this notion of core unmarked NPs has led to the exclusion of a large number of non-nominal and pronominal arguments and constituents:

(i) postverbal subjects, which are marked as far as word order is concerned (*Mr. Finch, of Grace-church-street, London* is placed after the predicate in the example of subject-verb inversion in (1)):

(1) Gloucester, Jan. 3. Last week was married, at St. Nicholas church, *Mr. Finch, of Grace-church-street, London*, to Miss Cowcher, daughter of Mr. Alderman Cowcher, of this city (1785GEN2.N3)

(ii) preverbal objects, which are marked as far as word order is concerned (*this tretis, divided in 5 parties* is promoted to sentence-initial position in the example of object topicalisation in (2)):

(2) *This tretis, divided in 5 parties*, wol I shewe the under full light reules and naked wordes in Englissh; for Latyn ne canst thou yit but small, my litel sone (CMASTRO.H1)

(iii) pronominal subjects and objects. No pronominal constituents have been considered in this study since the distribution of the very few examples of expanded NPs with pronominal heads (see example (3)) do not allow for statistically testing.

(3) Alsoe *he +tat tolde me this* seid that it were better for yow to come upp then to be fotte out of your house with streingth (CMPRIV.X1)

(iv) prepositional phrases functioning as subjects or objects (the prepositional phrase *between 15,000 and 17,000 Vietnamese* is the subject of *will land* in (4)):

(4) United Nations High Commission for Refugees officials in Malaysia estimate that *between 15,000 and 17,000 Vietnamese* will land on Malaysian shores each month for the next six months (1979STM2.N9)

(v) coordinated constructions (or conjunction phrases):

(5) True, true; but by the world she has *wit too, as well as beauty* (1766GAR.D3)

(vi) clausal constituents (the Complementiser Phrase *whether Tito, who attended in 1960 when Khrushchev held the stage, will come* is the subject of *is* in example (6)):

(6) but *whether Tito, who attended in 1960 when Khrushchev held the stage, will come* is still uncertain (1967STM2.N9)

(vii) ellipsis (the NP *the cat's* in the (unattested) example (7) has not merited attention since the complement of such a possessive phrase (covert *dishes*) is ellipsed and thus the NP is not complete):

(7) [The dog's dishes are here] and the cat's __ are over there.

In the category of elliptical NPs we include examples like *the poor*, which lack a nominal head. These examples are treated by de Mönnink (2000: 20), among others, as NPs with adjective heads (*poor*).

Table 2 sets out the distribution (raw numbers and normalised frequency per 1,000 words) of the 8,017 nominal constituents in the six periods and the two text types.

register\ period		1350-1500	1570-1640	1750-1799	1850-1899	1950-1990	Total
news/ hand-books	subjects	351 nf= 15.13	206 nf= 16.31	830 nf= 37.75	968 nf= 41.86	1,078 nf= 44.48	3,433
	objects	240 nf= 10.34	245 nf= 19.4	301 nf= 11.51	649 nf= 27.95	735 nf= 30.32	2,170
letters	subjects	236 nf= 10.77	227 nf= 17.08	231 nf= 19.24	192 nf= 17.77	190 nf= 16.24	1,076
	objects	211 nf= 9.63	259 nf= 19.49	375 nf= 31.23	228 nf= 21.11	265 nf= 22.66	1,338
Total		1,038	937	1,737	2,037	2,268	8,017

Table 2. Distribution of NP subjects and objects
(nf = normalized frequency per 1,000 words)

The main focus of this study is the presence/absence of expansion in the NPs under analysis. Determiners are not considered examples of strategies of expansion[2] and thus the label 'expansion' refers exclusively to pre- and/or postmodifiers or complements of nouns in such NPs. Since our approach is not of a generativist nature and hence is not subject to proposals such as the DP hypothesis (Bernstein 2001), in what follows we shall assume, first, that the noun is the head of the NP and, second, that all the constituents other than the determiners that surround the noun within the NP illustrate strategies of expansion, that is, complementation or modification/subordination. Because we make no distinction here between modifiers (in principle, optional and not subcategorised) and complements (subcategorised and required), we prefer to use the neutral label of expansion rather than modification, even though the qualifier 'modifier' will be used extensively in what follows as an umbrella term to cover both modifiers proper and complements.

2 De Mönnink's (2000: 19) 'limiters' are not included in the present study. De Mönnick includes in this category adverbs such as *only* in examples like *only these people*, which we analyse as modifiers of determiners and thus do not investigate here, and adverbs like *particularly* in examples like *particularly my father*, which in our view premodify the whole NP. Since de Mönnink's limiters cannot be taken as examples of (exclusively) noun modification, they are not examined here.

A wide variety of expansion strategies were attested;[3] on a par with NPs which are not expanded at all, we have found instances of NPs containing pre-head expansion, post-head, and both pre- and post-head expansion (the latter in (8)).[4] The typology of pre-head constituents ranges from nouns and NPs (in (9)) to coordinative constructions or conjunction phrases (in (10)), including adjective phrases (in (11)), possessive phrases (in (12)) and adverb phrases (in (13)):

(8) Among alle Englysch men I fynd *many Northffolk men the qwyche haue this maner off laughing* (CMMETHAM.H1)
(9) And I sent them to dyner a galon whyne and thay sent me a *heronsew* roste (CMPRIV.X1)
(10) and although *nice and curious* Hus-wiues will haue a third howre betwixt them (CEHAND2B.H0)
(11) but these wil giue their *vsuall* measure euen the night before they calue; and therefore are said to be Kine deep of milke (CEHAND2B.H0)
(12) I seyd I sopposyd *his lordys evydens* were seche (CMPRIV.X1)
(13) but I hope, that, except in the Night, we shall have *almost entirely your Company* (1773HUME.X3)

The variety of post-head constituents is wider and includes not only phrasal (in (14) to (20)) but also clausal constituents (in (21) to (25)), the latter being either finite (e.g. relative clauses) or non-finite (mainly *-ing* and *-ed* clauses):

(14) *my brodyr Rychard may vndyrstond that of my Lorde* (CMPRIV.X1) [postmodifying NP]
(15) *The Diuell himselfe hath not such a name* (CEPLAY2A.D0) [postmodifying pronoun]
(16) *Understond wel that these houres inequales ben clepid houres of planetes* (CMASTRO.H1) [postmodifying adjective phrase]
(17) *The payling of the nwe parke is made an end of.* (CEPRIV2.X0) [postmodifying *of*-prepositional phrase]
(18) *that I hawe resseywyd an letter ffrom yow beryng date at London the xiij day of Octobyr in hast / wheche Y do whell vndyrstond* (CMPRIV.X1) [postmodifying prepositional phrase]

---

3 Our inventory of examples of modification includes all the categories identified by de Mönnink (2000: 21-22) as well as her 'appositions' (2000: 24).

4 Since this study does not adopt a transformational framework which accepts the existence of movement in noun phrases (see de Mönnink 2000: Chapter 5 for mobility in NPs), we analyse NPs such as de Mönnink's (2000: 66-67) *a different sort of person from her aunt* as constituents which comprise pre-modifiers (*different*) and post-modifiers (*from her aunt*). Examples like this are normally treated as illustrations of structural discontinuity; in other words, in *a different sort of person from her aunt* the adjective phrase *different from her aunt* would be discontinuous in such a way that the adjective *different* precedes the head noun *person* and the prepositional phrase *from her aunt*, acting as the complement of the adjective, follows the head noun.

(19) *Of whiche longe strikes the space bitwene contenith a myle wey* (CMASTRO.H1) [postmodifying adverb phrase]

(20) *and therefore are first to take barrels very close and wel made, and after they haue salted it well, they fill their barrels therewith* (CEHAND2B.H0) [postmodifying conjunction phrase]

(21) *That persone that ys born the fyrste day off the mone schuld be dysposyd to be wyse and dyscrete and longe lyffyd* (CMMETHAM.H1) [postmodifying relative clause]

(22) but yt shall hawe that lysens that yt shall passe wythhowght howlde woll, appon yt selffe (CMPRIV.X1) [post-head finite clause]

(23) *Thyn Astralabie hath a ring to putten on the thombe of thi right hond in taking the height of thinges* (CMASTRO.H1) [post-head infinitive clause]

(24) *And understond also that alle the sterres sitting within the zodiak of thin Astrelabie ben clepid sterres of the north* (CMASTRO.H1) [postmodifying *-ing* clause]

(25) *while the Squadron fitted out at Cadiz doth the same on the other* (1762PUBL.N3) [postmodifying *-ed* clause]

4. Analysis of the data

4.1. Lack of expansion

By 'unexpanded' NPs we understand noun phrases without modifiers or complements. For the sake of precision, we recall that we have assumed that the occurrence of determiners or determinatives in the NP does not have consequences for the classification of such an NP as expanded. Figure 1 shows the distribution of the NPs in our database which do not contain any modifiers, the filter being the syntactic role of the NP in the sentence. Figure 2 offers the same information according to period and text type.

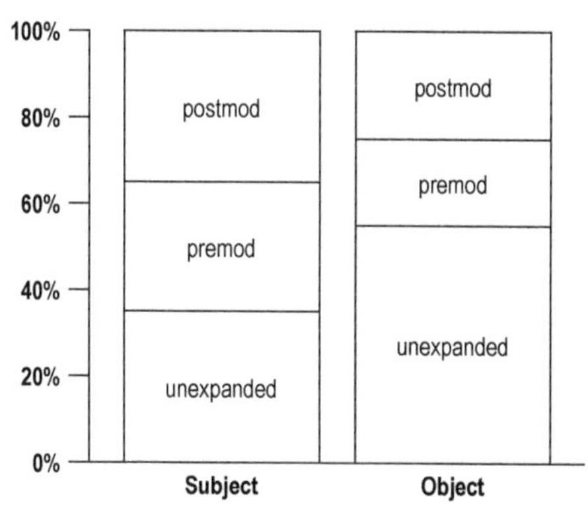

Figure 1. Unexpanded NPs (syntactic distribution)

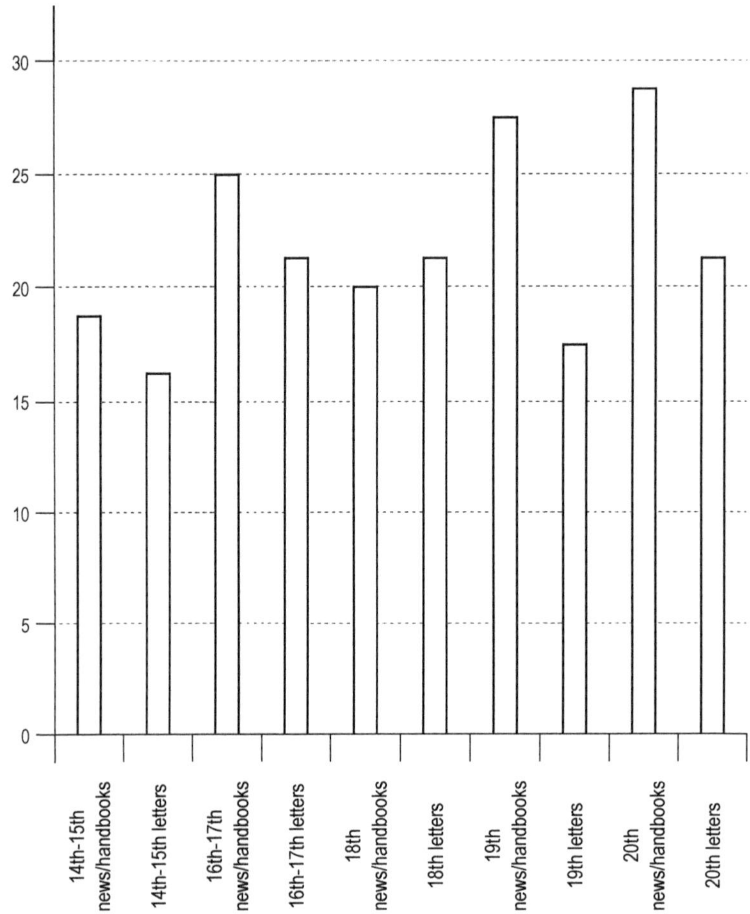

Figure 2. Unexpanded NPs (temporal and textual distribution)

The proportion of bare or unexpanded NPs in Figure 1 is larger for objects than subjects. Even though at first sight this does not seem to be in keeping with the principle of end-weight (Quirk et al. 1985: 1362), we will argue below that end-weight is actually in operation here since the (fewer) postmodifiers in the object NPs are longer than in the subject NPs. This is to say that there are fewer expanded objects but the average length of those which contain (post-)modifiers is considerably larger than that of NP subjects.

As regards the distribution of the unexpanded NPs across time, Figure 2 shows that the frequencies of this type of NPs are similar in both text types (letter and news/handbooks) in the fourteenth and fifteenth centuries (normalised frequencies or n.f.: 15.5–18.5). From the sixteenth to the eighteenth centuries, the proportions of bare NPs in both text types are higher, the differences between the registers under investigations not being statistically significant (around n.f.=20 in both text types). The nineteenth century constitutes a crucial period as far as the connection between lack of expansion and degree of textual formality is concerned. In this period the news/handbooks material exhibits a significant increase of unexpanded NPs (n.f.: 27.2 and 28 in, respectively, the nineteenth and the twentieth centuries). By contrast, the proportions of unexpanded NPs in the letters in our database do not undergo variation other than the general increase from Middle to Early Modern English, the statistical differences in the remaining periods (around n.f.=20) not being significant for this text type.

4.2. Expansion per text type and period

Table 3 lays out the relative proportions of the major pre-head expansion strategies per text type, and Table 4 shows the distribution of the most frequent post-head expansion strategies per text type.

	news/ handbooks	letters
A/AP	62.1%	65.8%
N/NP	30.6%	26.8%
PossP	5.2%	5.1%
ConjP	1.3%	0.5%
Adv/AdvP	0.8%	1.8%

Table 3. Pre-head expansion strategies

	news/ handbooks	letters
PP	64.1%	52.6%
N/NP	7.5%	10.7%
relative_cl	10.7%	15.4%
other	17.7%	21.3%

Table 4. Post-head expansion strategies

In the light of these findings, the following conclusions can be drawn. First, as far as pre-head expansion is concerned: (i) the adjectives are the prototypical dependents in the news/handbooks and the letters, the differences between the ratio of adjectives in the letters and the proportion of adjectives in the news/ handbooks not being statistically significant (Yates chi-square value: 0.52, p=0.4708); (ii) the frequencies for noun modifiers are also comparable in the news/handbooks and the letters (chi square: 1.62, p=0.2031); and (iii) the proportions of possessive phrases in the news/handbooks and the letters are statistically equivalent (chi square: 0.01, p=0.9203). News/handbooks and letters, then, do not diverge with respect to the selection of grammatical categories which function as premodifiers in NPs.

Second, as regards post-head expansion, (i) prepositional phrases, relative clauses and appositive nouns constitute the prototypical dependents occupying the slot of post-modification in the NPs investigated, which is in keeping with Biber and Clark (2002: 57); and (ii) the statistical differences between the news/handbooks and the letters in terms of the productivity of postmodifying prepositional phrases, nouns and relative clauses are scarcely significant (p=0.0035, 0.0146 and 0.0032, respectively).

Tables 5 and 6 display the evolution of, respectively, pre- and post-head expansion in the periods and text types analysed.

	A/AP	N/NP	PossP	ConjP	Adv/ AdvP
14th-15th news/handbooks	67.7%	29.7%	1.3%	0.4%	0.9%
14th-15th letters	62.0%	35.3%	2.3%	0.5%	0.0%
16th-17th news/handbooks	63.3%	31.0%	2.7%	1.3%	1.8%
16th-17th letters	56.9%	37.8%	3.4%	0.8%	1.1%
18th news/handbooks	64.8%	31.8%	2.1%	0.8%	0.5%
18th letters	63.2%	31.1%	3.8%	0.6%	1.3%
19th news/handbooks	61.2%	32.7%	4.0%	1.6%	0.4%
19th letters	61.2%	33.5%	3.8%	0.4%	1.1%
20th news/handbooks	53.7%	38.6%	6.7%	0.9%	0.1%
20th letters	62.8%	32.0%	4.0%	0.4%	0.8%

Table 5. Evolution of pre-head expansion strategies

	PP	N/NP	relative_cl	other
14th-15th news/handbooks	48.4%	10.6%	16.9%	24.1%
14th-15th letters	39.7%	12.8%	17.8%	29.7%
16th-17th news/handbooks	37.3%	12.7%	21.6%	28.4%
16th-17th letters	38.8%	15.2%	19.7%	26.2%
18th news/handbooks	51.5%	12.8%	14.4%	21.3%
18th letters	47.1%	10.8%	18.8%	23.3%
19th news/handbooks	56.4%	8.7%	13.5%	21.5%
19th letters	42.6%	12.9%	18.8%	25.7%
20th news/handbooks	56.7%	9.3%	13.1%	20.9%
20th letters	44.1%	13.3%	18.0%	24.5%

Table 6. Evolution of post-head expansion strategies

First, regarding pre-head expansion in the news/handbooks (Table 5), (i) a slight decrease in the prevalence of adjectives is seen in the news/handbook data (from

67.67 to 53.65% of the NPs investigated contain premodifying adjectives), which squarely contradicts Biber and Clark's (2002: 51) findings; (ii) the number of premodifying nouns increases reasonably across time only in the news/handbooks (from 29.74 to 38.59%), which is in keeping with Biber and Clark (2002: 62); and (iii) even though statistically less relevant, the proportion of possessive phrases is gradually larger in the periods examined here in both text types. Second, the situation for the letters is as follows: (i) the proportions of adjectives are similar across time, which favours Biber and Clark's (2002) findings; and (ii) a slight decrease of premodifying nouns is observed in the periods investigated (from 37.78 in the sixteenth and seventeenth centuries to 32.01% in the twentieth century).

With reference to post-head expansion strategies (Table 6), we can state the following. First, the texts in the news/handbooks attest: (i) an increase of post-modifying prepositional phrases (from 48.39 to 56.71% of the NPs with post-modifiers contain post-head prepositional phrases), as in Biber and Clark (2002: 60), even though the increase in our ata is not as dramatic as in their research; (ii) a slight decrease in the frequency of nouns (from 10–12 to 9.28% in the contemporary period); and (iii) progressively lower proportions of relative clauses (from 21.57% in the sixteenth and seventeenth centuries to 13.14% in the twentieth century). Second, findings for the letters lead to the following remarks: (i) there is a slight increase of post-nominal prepositional phrases, although not as drastic as in Biber and Clark (2002: 60); (ii) a very slight diachronic increase in nouns is observed; and (iii) there is no statistical variation in the proportion of relative clauses (17-19% in the periods under examination).

4.3. Length of the modifiers

The size or length of the constituents has been used as a metric for measuring structural complexity in a number of studies. Thus, Wasow (1997: 81) contends that grammatical weight implies "size of complexity," Yaruss (1999: 330) claims that any "attempts to separate length and complexity are somewhat artificial" and Arnold et al. (2000: 35), among others, maintain that the degree of structural complexity exhibited by a constituent can be "measured as the relative length of the (...) constituents, in terms of the number of words."[5]

Table 7 collates the normalised frequencies of pre- and postmodifiers (columns) containing 1 to 15 words (rows).

---

[5] Akinnaso (1982) measures the length of a constituent by looking at the length of each of the words in the constituent, an approach which has not been adopted elsewhere in the literature and, hence, is not followed here.

		Normalised frequencies	
		pre-head	post-head
Number of words	1	11.168	0.917
	2	1.579	2.990
	3	0.509	2.917
	4	0.202	1.659
	5	0.047	1.336
	6	0.008	0.929
	7	0.008	0.804
	8	0.012	0.704
	9	0.004	0.489
	10	--	0.300
	11	--	0.351
	12	--	0.266
	13	--	0.210
	14	--	0.138
	15	--	0.125

Table 7. Pre- and post-head length (up to 15 words)

This table shows that the postmodifiers tend to be considerably longer than the premodifiers. For a normalised frequency higher than 1 the vast majority of the premodifiers comprise up to 9 words and most are 1- or 2-words long. On the one hand, there are few examples of 1-word constituents in the postmodifying slot of the NPs (n.f.: 1.08). On the other hand, normalised frequencies higher than 1 are attested in NPs with postmodifiers comprising from 1 to 8 words. As noted above, this leads us to accept that the principle of end-weight is at work in the NPs examined.

Tables 8 and 9 focus on the length of the premodifiers in, respectively, the news/handbooks and the letters.

		Normalised frequencies				
		1350-1500 news/handb	1570-1640 news/handb	18thc news	19thc news	20thc news
Number of words	1	2.932	4.357	11.860	19.946	29.998
	2	0.086	0.475	1.263	2.628	2.847
	3	0.000	0.238	0.727	1.335	0.908
	4	0.000	0.000	0.115	0.560	0.454
	5	0.000	0.000	0.000	0.215	0.165
	6	0.000	0.000	0.000	0.000	0.000
	7	0.000	0.000	0.000	0.000	0.000
	8	0.000	0.000	0.038	0.000	0.083
	9	0.000	0.000	0.000	0.000	0.041

Table 8. Length of premodifiers in news/handbooks

		Normalised frequencies				
		1350-1500 letters	1570-1640 letters	18thc letters	19thc letters	20thc letters
Number of words	1	2.100	6.700	14.826	9.722	9.236
	2	0.593	0.301	2.166	2.870	2.565
	3	0.046	0.376	1.000	0.370	0.086
	4	0.046	0.151	0.333	0.278	0.086
	5	0.000	0.000	0.000	0.093	0.000
	6	0.000	0.000	0.083	0.000	0.000
	7	0.000	0.000	0.083	0.000	0.000
	8	0.000	0.000	0.000	0.000	0.000
	9	0.000	0.000	0.000	0.000	0.000

Figure 9. Length of premodifiers in letters

With respect to the size of the premodifying material in the noun phrases under analysis, the following can be noted. First, the length of the premodifiers in the news/handbooks undergoes a dramatic increase from Middle to contemporary English, especially in the case of 1-word constituents; the number of 1-word premodifiers in the fourteenth century is in fact similar to the ratio of 2-word premodifiers in the twentieth-century news. The eighteenth century is the period in which the strategy of premodification is fixed in terms of length; from the eighteenth century onwards the vast majority of the premodified NPs in the news/handbooks comprise only 1 word. Moreover, the data show a progressive increase in the proportion of one-word premodifiers in the news/handbooks until the present. Second, the picture as far as the letters are concerned is considerably different since a decrease of the length of the premodifiers from the eighteenth to the nineteenth centuries can be seen; in fact, there are no examples comprising more than 4 words in the nineteenth and the twentieth centuries. Such a tendency towards the reduction of the length of the premodifiers is particularly dramatic in the 1-word constituents (n.f.: 14.8 in the eighteenth century and 9.2 in the twentieth century). As already discussed with relation to premodification in the news/handbooks, the eighteenth-century data are relevant to the distribution of the lexical material in the NP because until this century the proportions of 1-word premodifiers were similar in the news/handbooks and in the letters. From the eighteenth century onwards, however, the frequency for 1-word premodifiers increases considerably in the news/handbooks and decreases progressively in the letters.

The length of the postmodifying material is sketched in Tables 10 and 11, which focus on the news/handbooks and the letters, respectively.

		Normalised frequencies				
		1350-1500 news/handb	1570-1640 news/handb	18thc news	19thc news	20thc news
Number of words	1	0.431	0.396	1.492	1.680	0.578
	2	1.164	1.030	4.668	5.213	4.952
	3	2.846	0.475	3.290	5.471	5.282
	4	0.561	0.238	1.913	3.662	3.260
	5	0.388	0.634	1.492	2.283	2.434
	6	0.431	0.475	0.995	1.465	1.857
	7	0.561	0.238	1.224	1.766	1.651
	8	0.043	0.158	0.956	1.465	1.651
	9	0.086	0.079	0.574	1.680	1.155
	10	0.086	0.000	0.421	0.689	0.784
	11	0.129	0.079	0.421	0.560	0.660
	12	0.086	0.079	0.421	0.431	0.536
	13	0.000	0.079	0.268	0.517	0.536
	14	0.043	0.000	0.230	0.345	0.371
	15	0.043	0.000	0.153	0.172	0.371

Table 10. Length of postmodifiers in news/handbooks

		Normalised frequencies				
		1350-1500 letters	1570-1640 letters	18thc letters	19thc letters	20thc letters
Number of words	1	0.365	1.506	0.916	1.204	0.599
	2	0.913	1.957	4.165	2.593	3.250
	3	0.867	1.430	3.915	2.685	2.907
	4	0.502	1.054	1.832	1.944	1.625
	5	0.274	0.753	2.249	1.481	1.368
	6	0.137	0.226	1.832	1.019	0.855
	7	0.091	0.000	1.000	0.741	0.770
	8	0.183	0.226	0.916	1.019	0.428
	9	0.137	0.226	0.416	0.278	0.257
	10	0.091	0.000	0.583	0.093	0.257
	11	0.046	0.151	0.666	0.370	0.428
	12	0.000	0.075	0.500	0.278	0.257
	13	0.091	0.000	0.333	0.278	0.000
	14	0.046	0.000	0.083	0.093	0.171
	15	0.000	0.075	0.250	0.185	0.000

Table 11. Length of postmodifiers in letters

Tables 10 and 11 show the evident division between 1-word and longer post-modifiers. Whereas the normalised frequency for 1-word postmodifiers is lower than 2 in the two text types, the normalised values for 2-word postmodifiers are, for example, 4–5 for both text types in the eighteenth century. This century proves to be the determinant point for the fixation of the length of post-head modifiers since it is now that the longest postmodifiers can be seen. As far as postmodification in the news/handbooks is concerned, Table 10 shows a gradual increase in the length of the postmodifiers from the eighteenth century onwards, which underlines the effectiveness of the principle of end-weight in this text type. By contrast, Table 11 shows that the postmodifiers included in the database of letters are shorter in the nineteenth and twentieth centuries. In the following section we will make some concluding remarks on the structural characterisation of noun phrases in informal versus formal language.

5. Summary and concluding remarks

With respect to NPs without either pre- or postmodifiers, our database includes more unexpanded objects than subjects, which seems to contradict the principle of end-weight, according to which initial elements tend to be shorter than constituents which occupy later positions in the clause. The diachronic investigation on the proportion of unexpanded NPs leads to the conclusion that around the nineteenth century the news/handbooks contain more NPs of this sort than the letters, whose ratio of occurrence is similar to the frequencies for unexpanded NPs from the sixteenth to the eighteenth centuries. A further remark is in order here: before the eighteenth century a rise in the proportion of NPs without modifiers is found in both of the text types under investigation. This must be connected to similar findings for the strategies of pre- and postmodification in the same period.

Concerning premodification, the adjectival categories have proved to be prototypical both in the news/handbooks and in the letters. Even though the text types investigated here do not diverge in terms of the selection of grammatical categories, a slight decrease of premodifying adjectives is attested in the news/handbooks, accompanied by an increase of pre-head nouns. The picture for NPs in the letters is considerably different: whereas the ratio of premodifying adjectives is similar across time, a slight decrease of premodifying nouns is evinced by the NPs registered in the letters. Thus, the modern and contemporary periods are revealing as regards the categorial characterisation of the strategies of premodification in the noun phrase: a significant number of pre-head nouns is attested in the more formal texts, whereas fewer premodifying nouns are found in the NPs included in the more informal texts.

This paper has looked at the strategy of postmodification. The prototypical category which fulfils the syntactic role of postmodifier is the prepositional phrase and, as was the case with premodification in the earlier periods, the news/handbooks and letters do not diverge in this respect. From a historical perspective, an increase of postmodifying prepositional phrases is evinced by the data both in the news/handbooks and in the letters, whereas the number of post-head nouns becomes larger in the letters than in the more formal texts.

The length of the modifiers in our database of NPs has also been considered here. In general, postmodifiers are longer than premodifiers, which underlines the adequacy of end-weight. In fact, we have observed that there are few examples of 1-word constituents functioning as postmodifiers. On diachronic grounds, a dramatic increase in the proportion of premodifiers, especially of 1-word constituents, is seen from Middle to contemporary English, with the eighteenth century a pivotal period here since in this century the vast majority of the premodified NPs in the news/handbooks comprise only 1 word, with this tendency continuing in the ensuing periods. In the letters we see the decrease of premodifiers from the eighteenth century onwards. Again, this century is significant, since previously the proportions of 1-word premodifiers were similar in the news/handbooks and in the letters and it is from the eighteenth century onwards that the frequency for 1-word premodifiers increases considerably in the news/handbooks and decreases progressively in the letters. As far as postmodification is concerned, the number of 1-word postmodifiers is strikingly low, most modifiers comprising 2 or 3 words. From a historical point of view, the eighteenth century is a determinant time in the fixation of the length of post-head modifiers, the longest postmodifiers belonging to this period. In fact, the news/handbooks data attest a gradual increase in the length of the postmodifiers from the eighteenth century onwards whereas in the letters the postmodifiers become shorter in the nineteenth and twentieth centuries.

This paper has shown that the modern period, in particular Late Modern English, has an important role in the fixation of statistical tendencies in the structure of noun phrases. First, in the eighteenth-century data we saw a significant increase in the number of unexpanded constituents, especially in the news/handbooks. Analysis of the informative content conveyed by such NPs without modifiers in the formal texts – which is left for further research – may lead to the conclusion that principles such as end-focus prevail over structural axioms such as end-weight. This might explain not only the high frequency of unexpanded NPs in the news/handbooks, as compared to the letters, but also the preference for unexpanded objects in general, and thus would compensate for the lack of compliance with end-weight which the raw data indicate. Second, the eighteenth-century data have also attested an increase of premodifying nouns in the formal texts and an opposite tendency as regards the letters. This trend is accompanied by the increase in the number of postmodifying nouns in the more informal texts. Such a preference for (more) nominal premodifiers – in principle, informatively heavier and syntactically more complex than other predicative categories such as the adjectival ones – in the formal texts and more nominal postmodifiers in the informal texts might suggest that end-focus and end-weight operate more easily in informal than in formal texts. This would also explain the, in principle, strikingly higher number of unexpanded NPs in the handbooks. Finally, from the eighteenth century onwards most premodifiers comprise 1 word in the formal texts and more words in the informal textual material. This observation, which is not in keeping with the well-known correlation between formal style and structural complexity, might be explained if we assume that, on the one hand, elaborate text types are not strongly subject to this tendency and, on the other hand, informal texts comply with such a principle in a more natural way.

The aim of the present investigation has been to give support to the view that register variation can be definable in terms of structural complexity. The study of microvariables of structural complexity can shed light on the characterisation of text types in the recent history of English. As Biber and Clark (2002: 64) point out in a study couched in a methodology similar to the one used here, "we appear [in contemporary English] to be in the midst of a dramatic period of change for the preferred patterns of noun modification." We thus reject those views which deny the connection between text-type variation and linguistic complexity – among these, Beaman (1984: 46), who contends that "spoken language is just as complex as written, if not on some measures"; Halliday (1985: 62), who claims that "each [sublanguage] is complex on its own way. Written language displays one kind of complexity, spoken language another"; and Biber et al. (1999: Chs. 8-10), who maintain that modification is prevalent in both spoken and written registers.

Further lines of research include: (i) the comparison of our data with material from other text types; (ii) the consequences of left- versus right-branching expansion for structural complexity – it is assumed that left-branching involves more (syntactic) complexity than right-branching (Yngve 1960; Frazier 1985; Hawkins 1994; Liiv and Tuldava 1996; Esser 2006); (iii) the differences between complementation and modification (Anderson 1997; Fries 1999; Keizer 2004); and (iv) the differences between phrasal versus non-phrasal modification (Biber and Clark 2002: 44; Rijkhoff 2002).

References

Aitchinson, J. and D. M. Lewis (eds.) (2003): *New Media Language*, London, Routledge.

Akinnaso, F. N. (1982): "On the difference between spoken and written language," *Language and Speech*, 25, 2, 97-125.

Anderson, J. M. (1997): *A Notional Theory of Syntactic Categories*, Cambridge, Cambridge University Press.

Arnold, J. E., Th. Wasow, A. Losongco and R. Ginstrom (2000): "Heaviness: the effects of structural complexity and discourse status on constituent ordering," *Language*, 76, 1, 28-55.

Baltin, M. and Ch. Collins (eds.) (2001): *The Handbook of Contemporary Syntactic Theory*, Oxford, Blackwell.

Beaman, K. (1984): "Coordination and subordination revisited: syntactic complexity in spoken and written narrative discourse," in D. Tannen (ed.), 45-80.

Bernstein, J. B. (2001): "The DP Hypothesis: identifying clausal properties in the nominal domain," in M. Baltin and Ch. Collins (eds.), 536-561.

Biber, D. (2001): "Dimensions of variation among eighteenth-century speech-based and written registers," in S. Conrad and D. Biber (eds.), 200-214.

Biber, D. (2003): "Compressed noun-phrase structures in newspaper discourse," in J. Aitchinson and D. M. Lewis (eds.), 169-181.

Biber, D. and V. Clark (2002): "Historical shifts in modification patterns with complex noun phrase structures," in T. Fanego et al. (eds.), 43-66.

Biber, D. and E. Finegan (1997): "Diachronic relations among speech-based and written registers in English," in T. Nevalainen and L. Kahlas-Tarkka (eds.), 253-276 [Reprinted in S. Conrad and D. Biber (eds.), 66-83]

Biber, D., E. Finegan and D. Atkinson (1994): "ARCHER and its challenges: compiling and exploring a representative corpus of historical English registers," in U. Fries et al. (eds.), 1-14.

Biber, D., S. Johansson, G. Leech, S. Conrad and E. Finegan (1999): *Longman Grammar of Spoken and Written English*, Harlow, Pearson.

Collins, P. and D. Lee (eds.) (1999): *The Clause in English. In Honour of Rodney Huddleston*, Amsterdam, John Benjamins.

Conrad, S. and D. Biber (eds.) (2001): *Variation in English: Multi-dimensional Studies*, Harlow, Longman.

de Mönnink, I. (2000): *On the Move. The Mobility of Constituents in the English Noun Phrase: A Multi-method Approach*, Amsterdam, Rodopi.

Dowty, D. R., L. Karttunen and A. M. Zwicky (eds.) (1985): *Natural Language Parsing. Psychological, Computational, and Theoretical Perspectives*, Cambridge, Cambridge University Press.

Esser, J. (2006): "Stylistic change across generations? Conflicting evidence from psycholinguistic and corpus linguistic data," in Ch. Mair et al. (eds.), 79-97.

Fanego, T. M., J. López-Couso and J. Pérez-Guerra (eds.) (2002): *English Historical Syntax and Morphology. Selected Papers from 11 ICEHL, Santiago de Compostela, 7-11 September 2000*, Amsterdam, John Benjamins.

Frazier, L. (1985): "Syntactic complexity," in D. R. Dowty et al. (eds.), 129-189.

Fries, P. H. (1999): "Post-nominal modifiers in the English noun phrase," in P. Collins and D. Lee (eds.), 93-110.

Fries, U., G. Tottie and P. Schneider (eds) (1994): *Creating and Using English Language Corpora*, Amsterdam, Rodopi.

Haan, P. de (1989): *Postmodifying Clauses in the English Noun Phrase. A Corpus-based Study*, Amsterdam, Rodopi.

Halliday, M. A. K. (1985 [1989]): *Speech and Written Language*, Oxford, Oxford University Press.

Hawkins, J. A. (1994): *A Performance Theory of Order and Constituency*, Cambridge, Cambridge University Press.

Hopper, P. J. (1997): "Dispersed verbal predicates in vernacular written narrative," in A. Kamio (ed.), 1-18.

Kamio, A. (ed.) (1997): *Directions in Functional Linguistics*, Amsterdam, John Benjamins.

Keizer, E. (2004): "Postnominal PP complements and modifiers: a cognitive distinction," *English Language and Linguistics*, 8, 2, 323-350.

Kytö, M. (1996): *Manual to the Diachronic Part of the Helsinki Corpus of English Texts: Coding Conventions and Lists of Source Texts*, Helsinki, Department of English, University of Helsinki.

Liiv, H. and J. Tuldava (1996): "Syntactical structures of a text and its readability," in K. Sajavaara and C. Fairweather (eds.), 179-186.

Mair, Ch., R. Heuberger and J. Wallmansberger (eds.) (2006): *Corpora and the History of English. Papers Dedicated to Manfred Markus on the Occasion of his Sixty-fifth Birthday*, Heidelberg, Universitätsverlag Winter.

Markus, M. (2001): "The development of prose in early Modern English in view of the gender question: using grammatical idiosyncracies of 15th and 17th century letters," *EJES*, 5, 181-196.

Nevalainen, T. and L. Kahlas-Tarkka (eds.) (1997): *To Explain the Present. Studies in the Changing English Language in Honour of Matti Rissanen*, Helsinki, Société Néophilologique.

Ni, Y. (2003): "Noun phrases in media texts," in J. Aitchison and D. M. Lewis (eds.), 159-181.

O'Donnell, R. C. (1974): "Syntactic differences between speech and writing," *American Speech*, 49, 102-110.

Poole, M. E. and T. W. Field (1976): "A comparison of oral and written code elaboration," *Language and Speech*, 19, 4, 305-312.

Quirk, R., S. Greenbaum, G. Leech and J. Svartvik (1985): *A Comprehensive Grammar of the English Language*, London, Longman.

Rijkhoff, J. (2002): *The Noun Phrase*, Oxford, Oxford University Press.

Sajavaara, K. and C. Fairweather (eds.) (1996): *Approaches to Second Language Acquisition*, Jyväskyla, University of Jyväskyla.

Taavitsainen, I. (2001): "Changing conventions of writing: the dynamics of genres, text types, and text traditions," *EJES*, 5, 2, 139-150.

Tannen, D. (ed.) (1984): *Coherence in Spoken and Written Discourse*, Norwood, NK, Ablex.

Wasow, Th. (1997): "Remarks on grammatical weight," *Language Variation and Change*, 9, 1, 81-105.

Yaruss, J. S. (1999): "Utterance length, syntactic complexity, and childhood stuttering," *Journal of Speech, Language, and Hearing Research*, 42, 2, 329-344.

Yngve, V. H. A. (1960): "A model and an hypothesis for language structure," *Proceedings of the American Philosophical Society*, 105, 444-466.

Looking at suffixation in Early Modern northern English: a preliminary approach in the light of The Salamanca Corpus

Javier Ruano-García
Universidad de Salamanca

1. Introduction

The study of regional dialects in Early Modern English (henceforth EModE) still presents remarkable *lacunae* that need to be filled, in order to give a full and non-biased overview of the English linguistic setting during the sixteenth and seventeenth centuries.[1] It has traditionally been contended that the lack of reliable data hampers to a very great extent a scientific and philological approach to provincial 'Englishes' at this time. In fact, derogatory comments cast by orthoepists or contemporary grammarians on 'uneducated' forms of expression are far from comprehensive, and regional word-lists do not provide an in-depth account of dialectalisms that might lend aid to sketching the lexical geography of England in thorough detail. Still, recent research has shown in a persuasive way that other textual sources, both of a literary and non-literary kind, yield trustworthy information on EModE regional varieties. On the one hand, relevant studies such as those presented by Wakelin (1980, 1988), García-Bermejo (1999a, 1999b, 2002, 2008a, 2008c) or Shorrocks (2000, 2004) clearly demonstrate that literary recreations of dialect are useful guidances to sixteenth- and seventeenth-century provincial speech. On the other, non-literary texts, i.e. probate inventories, depositions, diaries and the like, have proved to be fruitful witnesses to the language of common people in the past (Weiner 1997, Britton 2000, Fox 2000: 83-89, Kytö, Grund and Walker 2007, Ruano-García 2010a). They all add to our understanding of EModE regional varieties, for they all complete the scattered records of provincialisms in grammars or glossaries.

Amongst all these sources, literary artefacts have received a particularly more detailed linguistic attention, since dialect data are more profusely attested in dramatic or popular dialogues, at the time that a greater amount of printed

1 It is a commonplace that canonical histories of the English language have been too much concentrated on the standard variety. In this vein, Fox (2000: 51-52) sensibly claims that "In early modern England there was far greater linguistic diversity than today. (...) it is scarcely possible to speak of a national language or native tongue. There was instead a multiplicity of different dialects, (...) which divided up the country in a complex configuration of overlapping 'speech communities'." See also Görlach (1999) or Milroy (2007: 33).

specimens have come down to us. Indeed, Eckhardt (1910), Blake (1981: 55-107) or Blank (1996: 69-168, 2006) testify to this fact. Unfortunately, their valuable accounts of EModE regional traits do not obviously represent thorough linguistic analysis that may provide us with dialect nuances other than salient, and often, archetypal northern or southern markers. To my knowledge, Wales (2006) is the first and foremost piece of research that has successfully endeavoured to tell the full story of a regional variety. Her groundbreaking study gives a diachronic insight into northern English from a linguistic, cultural and social perspective. She relies both on literary and non-literary supports, although the former somehow predominate. It is a fact that all these reference works present phonetic or lexical regionalisms that do actually supply information of utmost value on the distribution of certain words or the realisation of Middle English phonemes in specific areas. Yet, our knowledge of other relevant linguistic issues such as the word-formation processes in EModE provincial speech is inadequate, if not nonexistent. Dossena (1998) or Markus (2008) are some of the very few instances that have addressed particular morphological questions in varieties of British English other than the southern standard. Their studies are not concerned with EModE, though. Also, Macafee and Anderson (1997) have considered aspects related to word-formation patterns in Scots, although their survey is not restricted to EModE only.

Given these circumstances, this paper seeks to bridge some of the gaps that have traditionally distinguished the evaluation of EModE regional speech. It attempts to present a descriptive analysis of suffixation in sixteenth- and seventeenth-century northern English by means of a selection of examples extracted from The Salamanca Corpus. In particular, our approach is based on a group of literary documents that contain EModE northern linguistic features. In this way we hope to contribute to previous research on northern speech, with a view to shedding light upon some aspects of its suffixation patterns and the chronology of certain derivatives.

2. The Salamanca Corpus: scope, contents and EModE data

Owing to the widely-held belief that has commonly overlooked the study of post-medieval regional varieties of English due to an apparent dearth of direct textual evidence, a research team at the University of Salamanca headed by Dr. María F. García-Bermejo and Dr. Pilar Sánchez has compiled a corpus of dialect literary texts that defies these widespread assumptions. In particular, The Salamanca Corpus (henceforth SC) covers a time span that ranges from the sixteenth up to the beginnings of the twentieth century. It comprises specimens of literary dialect and dialect literature that supplement well-known catalogues such as Joseph Wright's Bibliography to his celebrated *English Dialect Dictionary* (1898-1905) (henceforth *EDD*). This compilation, not yet in public distribution, focuses therefore on literary samples that witness to regional 'Englishes' since the first sixteenth-century recreations of popular speech were made with a literary intent. Different genres have been considered, so that instances of drama, verse and prose have been included. In sum, more than four hundred texts have been hitherto compiled, which will allow the research community to handle an overwhelming amount of diachronic data that have remained in oblivion to date. It is worth noting that the SC is not only a promising repository of dialect spellings, regional vocabulary, morphosyntactical or pragmatic markers that add to our understanding of provincial language, but also represents a remarkable contribution to the history of English literature. As García-Bermejo (2008b) has clearly explained, it aims to be one of the first structured and systematic accounts of literary dialects and dialect literature in England, this being a somehow untrodden field of investigation in literary studies.

As far as the EModE period is concerned, the SC counts with literary artefacts that have been chosen according to several criteria (see Kytö and Rissanen 1993: 7). In terms of chronology, these texts were written from 1500 to 1700. Needless to say, these temporal limits correspond to the traditional dates of the EModE linguistic stage (Görlach 1991; Barber 1997; Nevalainen 2006). Diatopically, these samples include regional traits natural to the North. Among them, deviant spellings suggestive of phonetic features, provincial words or morphological markers that testify to northern speech. From a typological perspective, they are all literary texts that cover different genres: drama, prose and verse (see Table 1 below). This section of the SC comprises examples of dialect literature and literary dialects for two main reasons. Firstly, it is a fact that specimens of literary dialects were for the most part written by writers who were themselves users of the standard variety of the time. In this vein, it is thus possible to gain access to the writers' attitudes towards provincialisms, for they may be taken as instances of perceptual dialectology. Actually, these traits might have been recognised as salient at the time they were written. Weiner (1997: 235) argues that "it [literary dialect] enables us to discover contemporary attitudes to regional dialect from one side of the borderline." Secondly, dialect literature mirrors the specifics of regional language beyond stylistic literary constraints, therefore offering transcriptions of dialect speech from the inside that corroborate the validity and complete the data attested in literary dialects. Significantly, this part of the SC contains instances of EModE popular ballads that, to my knowledge, have been for the first time considered in a diachronic corpus.

Our research is thus grounded on one hundred and thirty-four texts (over 1.4 million words) that have been found thanks to the information supplied by some of the above-mentioned works, and individual time-consuming searches in electronic databases such as *Early English Books Online*, *Literature Online*, *Bodleian Broadside Ballad Project* or *The Restoration Comedy Project*. Further, this corpus benefits from hitherto unpublished pieces held at Leeds University Library and The Folger Shakespeare Library. Suffice it to say that they have been tagged, so that their analysis may be conducted in an easier, quicker and more precise way. For the electronic formatting of our compilation, *Corpus Presenter* (Hickey 2003) has been used.

	Literary dialect		**Dialect literature**	
	N of texts	**Running words**	**N of texts**	**Running words**
Drama	34	765,309	0	
Prose	4	128,848	0	
Verse	93	558,792	3	1,898
Ballads	77	50,421	2	1,335
Chapbooks	1	3,099	0	
Others	15	505,272	1	563
SUBTOTAL	131	1,452,847	3	1,898
TOTAL	**134 texts (1,454,949 running words)**			

Table 1. EModE contents of the SC

It is worth mentioning that only three EModE texts included in the SC might be counted as proper instances of dialect literature. In particular, the anonymous *A Yorkshire Dialogue between an Awd Wife, a Lass, and a Butcher* (1673), localised to the county of Yorkshire, 'A Lancashire tale' (c.1690-1730) and 'Robin an's Gonny...' (c.1690-1730), whose traits belong to the area of Lancashire.[2] Obviously, the regional information they provide reflects a more reliable transcription of genuine speech than that yielded by the one hundred and thirty-one cases of literary dialect recorded. As expected, most of these offer somehow more schematic linguistic depictions of the North, for, I insist, they were often composed by non-northern speakers. It is a widespread feature among these recreations that writers seldom discriminated between properly northern English and Scottish traits. Actually, there are numerous specimens that testify to this linguistic vagueness, thereby lending non-localised and some times sketchy representations.[3] To name but a few, Richard Brathwait's 'An Egloge between Billie and Jockie' (1615) or Thomas Shadwell's *The Squire of Alsatia* (1688). Even those pieces that apparently mirror Scotticisms do also make room for

2 For a detailed linguistic evaluation of the 1673 Yorkshire dialogue and the anonymous 'A Lancashire tale' (c.1690-1730) see Ruano-García (2008, 2010c).

3 This indistinct and blur perception of northern features that was common among literary writers points obliquely to widespread cultural ideas of the North which were settled in the general subconscious. The linguistic borders were rather unsettled in the popular imagination, which might be explained due to the historical and linguistic closeness of the territories at each side of the border. Indeed, broadside 'border ballads' testify clearly to this fact. See Wales (2002, 2004).

other traits used both North and South of the border: John Tatham's *The Scots Figgaries* (1652), George Stuart's *A Joco-Serious Discourse in Two Dialogues between a Northumberland Gentleman and his Tenant a Scotchman* (1686) or John Lacy's *Sauny the Scot* (1698). But for a very few examples, it is therefore not possible to undertake a thorough county-orientated investigation of northern English if we rely on this kind of sources. As a matter of fact, diachronic corpora do unfortunately provide "a limited and biased picture of the reality of the language" (Rissanen 1991: 202). Nonetheless, a cautious assessment of data might further our understanding of what was spoken North of the Humber, especially before an age of audio recording.

3. Suffixation in Early Modern northern English

3.1. Methodology and data for analysis

In order to carry out the analysis of suffixation in Early Modern northern English, a careful reading of every text has been mandatory and each of them has been given an abbreviation.[4] Regional markers have conveniently been extracted from dramatic dialogues, poems, etc. and subsequently arranged into individual databases devised for phonetic, lexical and morphological traits where information of different kinds has been included (Table 2). Once this classification has been made, our attention has been focused on the lexical section. A thorough scrutiny has been undertaken, with a view to differentiating first between authentic regional words and those items of a widespread distribution that were also used in literary recreations of dialect. By way of illustration, terms such as *lisk* 'the loin or flank' and *mell* 'a heavy hammer' are used in the 1673 Yorkshire dialogue. Still, they cannot be treated equally as provincial words, since the former apparently had a wider usage.[5] Distinctions of this kind having been established, we have looked closely at the regional vocabulary gathered, in order to select those dialect items which show suffixation patterns. Since the EModE section of the SC is neither lemmatised nor tagged, this has been done by searching for all the regional words which consist of a base plus a suffix. In this sense, all kinds of suffix have been considered, so that instances of different word classes and meanings may be evaluated following Nevalainen's (1999) model of analysis. For instance, nouns such as *clamper* 'heavy, thick shoes' (*EDD*) or *waedeum* 'woefulness', adjectives like *gobby* 'talkative, loquacious' or verbs such as *gobbl* 'to swallow in large mouthfuls.' Different spelling variants of the suffixes have been collected from the *OED* and the corpus itself;

---

4 For a list of the abbreviations of the literary works cited, see appendix. Conventional abbreviations for Old English (OE), Middle English (ME), etc. are also used.

5 Unless otherwise indicated, definitions are taken from the *Oxford English Dictionary* (henceforth *OED*). Needless to say, an attentive and thorough contrastive study is needed so as to distinguish the lexical status of words like *lisk* or *mell*; see further Ruano-García (2010b).

afterwards, examples in which they occur have been collected aided by the *Corpus Presenter* suite. However, our final selection of items has been made manually, so as to comply with our purposes. Hence, only derivatives attested from 1500 onwards have been considered, although some cases whose first citations are dated to the last decades of the 1400s have also been taken for analysis. To put it clearly, a northern suffixal derivative like *sykernesse* 'certainty with regard to fact' has been weeded out, since it dates back to 1300. On the contrary, *weanell* 'an animal newly weaned,' for example, has been examined, for its first occurrence is recorded in 1488.

In sum, seventeen different suffixes have been gathered. Not only will this enable us to look at the affixes which were seemingly used in northern English at this time, but also to analyse the chronology of these derivatives.

Lemma	ME	PdE	Freq.	%	Texts	Freq.	%	Date
baith	/ a: /	both	15	0,0	CKG	3	0.24	1660
					JSD	11	0.06	1686
					TGAM	1	0.07	n.d.
beath	/ a: /	both	9	0,0	AE	1	0.0	1586
					SW	2	0.32	1672-96
					CL	1	0.15	1674-79
					SS	1	0	1698
					...	...	...	...

Table 2. Sample of database: phonetic and spelling traits for words descending from ME / a: / (< OE /A:/)

3.2. *Survey of data*

Traditional research on EModE derivational morphology has been mainly concerned with listing different affixes which proved to be productive at this time. Needless to say, the literature on this topic – Görlach (1991: 136-181) or Barber (1997: 219-241) – has clearly shown that the EModE word-stock increased considerably on account of foreign borrowings. Besides, new affixes entered the language which, together with the native elements, multiplied the possibilities of forming new words. In fact, Barber (1997: 232) points out that "most of the new words in eModE were not loans, but were produced by various methods of word-formation." Nevalainen (2006: 61-62) estimates that there were more than one hundred and twenty different affixes in Shakespeare's time. Yet, the amount of suffixal means of derivation clearly outnumbered that of prefixes. A summary look at our data does also evince similar conclusions as far as the North is concerned: only three prefixes have been attested, namely *be-* (*bedirten* 'fouled with dirt'), *mis-* (*mislear'd* 'ill-bread') and *un-* (*unsonsy* 'unlucky'), all of a native origin.[6]

As suffixation involves a change in the word class, thus modifying the grammatical potential of the lexeme, our survey groups suffixes on account of the word class they form and the one they combine with. In the ensuing discussion, Nevalainen's (1999: 392-407) classification is followed, so as to present clearly the word class of our items alongside the word class they were attached to.

3.2.1. Noun suffixes

3.2.1.1. Denominal nouns: concrete

Amongst the words surveyed, the suffixes that form concrete nouns by being added to a noun are as follows:[7]

(1) *-by*:
- "His cote was checked with patches rede and blewe; / Of *Kyrkeby* Kendall was his shorte demye", TBC (1510), 358-359.

(2) *-ing*:
- "Bred, Ise ge ye sick a Rattle wy a Rom ore tha *Riggins* sall mack your Ribs reore sirs", TSF (1652), I.
- "Come to the house some other day, I'll pay the *Lawing*, gang your way", JSD (1686), 63.
- "The Butter-Box got many Knocks, / The *Riggans* pav'd for a' then", BKC (n.d.), 11-12.

(3) *-le*:
- "A Lambe or a Kidde, or a *weanell* wast: / With that to the wood would he speede him fast", TShC (1579), Aegl. IX, 198-199.

(4) *-ock*:
- "This end was just twa inches o're / And that was sax, and *bittock* more", JSD (1686), 60.

(5) *-y*:
- "My son shall have a gude blew Bonnit / (...) / Bubblet Breches, & a *Pladdy*", BC43 (1679-1682), 13-15.
- "And I can hoop a Kin-a-Kin / and I can hoop a *Cogie*", DC (1683), 25-26.

---

6 The *OED* dates the first documentations of these three words to 1550, 1692 and 1560, respectively. It is noteworthy that our corpus antedates the first occurrence of *mislear'd* to 1686, as it is attested in JSD. The *Dictionary of the Older Scottish Tongue* (henceforth *DOST*) records it for the first time in 1560. There are other examples which show that these prefixes were used in northern speech: *miskenn* 'to refuse to recognize', *unbirs'd* 'unbruised', etc.

7 As illustrated below, suffixes are ordered alphabetically and examples in which words affected by them occur are presented in chronological order. Suffixal derivatives are italicised. Phonetically assimilated forms (*-in* or *-an* for *-ing*, *-le* for *-el*, etc.) are subsumed under the relevant suffix. Original capitals, punctuation, etc., have been respected in our transcriptions.

With the exception of *-by* (< ON *bœ-r, bý-r*), these suffixes represent native elements that were apparently used in the North by the time our works were written. In fact, *bittock* 'a little bit,' *cogie* 'a small cogue,' *lawing* 'a reckoning at a tavern bill,' *rigging* 'the back' and *pladdy* 'a small plaid' are documented for the first time in EModE. Significantly, the *OED* dates the first citations of *bittock, cogie* and *pladdy* to 1802, 1750 and 1719, respectively, whilst our evidence reveals that they were used earlier in time. Others like *weanell* 'an animal newly weaned' are recorded in the fifteenth century, at the time that *kyrkeby* 'above 20 small towns' (Coles 1676 s.v. *kirkby*) has not hitherto been lemmatised in the *OED* or the *DOST*.

In semantic terms, our examples disclose, on the one hand, that *-le, -ock* and *-y* have a diminutive sense. On the evidence of our corpus citations, it is worth noting that the usage of *-y* is not identical. The denotation of smallness evident in *cogie* is enriched by virtue of the morphosemantic connotation of endearment that is inherent in *pladdy*.[8] It is also noteworthy that *weanell* suggests that *-le* (< OE *-el*), with a diminutive force, was still productive in northern speech at a time that this affix was seemingly no longer operative in the standard.[9] The *OED* informs that *weanell* is formed on a verb-stem plus *-el* (< OF *-el*) which was used to create diminutives. Yet, the etymological data provided by the dictionary are apparently erroneous, for, according to the *OED* itself, the originally French suffix used to create diminutives from nouns and adjectives. Remarkably, the dictionary records the first example of *wean* (n.) in 1692, which would make it unlikely that, in the light of its data, *weanell* descended from a noun. However, the SC quotes *wean* a century earlier in TSH (1590-1591), which backs our assumption that *weanell* might represent a denominal noun. Furthermore, it seems plausible that *weanell* was effectively formed due to the OE affix *-el* that produced diminutives when added to nouns (*OED* s.v. *-el, suffix*[1]). As far as *-ock* is concerned, *bittock* shows that this affix was used in the North once its productivity had diminished in the standard (cf. *bullock, hillock*, etc.).

On the other hand, *-ing* conveys the meaning of 'of the kind of' or 'one possessed of the quality of' (*OED* s.v. *-ing*[3]). Our quotations suggest that this suffix created concrete nouns in the North, although Quirk *et al.* (1985: 1548) or Nevalainen (1999: 394-395, 2006: 62) do not account for this. Indeed, *lawing*

[8] The *OED* (s.v. *plaidie*) remarks that *pladdy* is a "sentimental, or poetic name for a plaid." The example provided by the SC shows a child-centred speech situation; endearment is not only achieved by applying diminutives to the addressee (*laddy*), but also to other elements that are described as belonging to the context: *daddy* or *pladdy*. See further Dossena (1998: 34-35 n.6). She refers to Robinson (1997: 55-57) where it is argued that *pladdie* is not a diminutive as it owes its ending to ON *-ey* 'isle' (Dossena 1998: 24).

[9] Standard diminutives formed on this pattern were mainly created in OE and ME; that is the case of *bramble*, for example (*OED* s.v. *-le, suffix*).

and *rigging* refer to concrete items which are not distinguished by the degree of abstraction natural to standard terms such as *farming* or *carpeting*.

It follows, therefore, that some denominal nouns were used and created in northern English by means of certain suffixes that were not so much productive in the standard. Others were apparently natural to the North, at the same time as those whose productivity was effectively spread in southern English apparently show some differences with our examples.

3.2.1.2. Denominal nouns: abstract

(6) *-dom*:
- "But then twa days after, again they fell to it; / Their *waedeum* seem'd vanish't", JSD (1686), 2.

In keeping with standard English, the native *-dom* was used to create abstract denominal nouns in northern speech. The only example collected, *waedeum* 'woefulness,' reveals that it has an identical semantic potential, as it refers to 'status' or 'condition' (Nevalainen 1999: 394). Remarkably, this appears to be the only occurrence of this noun so far documented. The *OED* does not index *waedeum*, whilst the *DOST* (s.v. *waedom*) dignifies it with a lexical status in view of the usage exemplified in our text.[10]

3.2.1.3. Deverbal nouns: concrete

(7) *-els*:
- "he took his Flayle, / An' hang't by th' *Swypple* on a nayle", AYD (1673), 37-38.
(8) *-er*:
- "I weare na shooen but wodden *clampers*", TVS (1637), II.

Of a native ascendancy, both *-els* and *-er* create regional nouns with an instrumental and agentive meaning, respectively. In fact, *swypple* 'the part of the flail that strikes the grain in thrashing' refers to an implement, and *clamper* 'heavy thick shoes, pattens' (*EDD* s.v. 2) names an object with an agentive function. Whilst *-er* showed a high rate of productivity in southern English at this time (Nevalainen 1999: 399), *-els* had apparently ceased being a productive formative already in ME. In fact, a careful survey of the *-els*-formations recorded in the *OED* reveals that these are mostly quoted for the first time in OE: *hidels*, *wriels*, etc. *Swypple* is seemingly one case which proves that this affix was still operative by the second half of the fifteenth century (*OED* s.v. *swipple*, 2). Our examples suggest, thus, that these suffixes were used in northern dialects to create nouns on verb-stems in EModE or immediately previous decades.

10 Our example is documented in the *OED*, although it is subsumed under *woefulness*.

It is worth pointing out that *clamper* has been first documented in 1876 both in the *OED* and the *EDD*. The *DOST* does not attest its usage in pre-1700 Scots, whilst the *Scottish National Dictionary* (henceforth *SND*) records this derivative in the nineteenth century.

3.2.1.4. Deverbal nouns: abstract

(9) *-ing*:
- "The Lawiers eate the carnels, ause muche reising of rentes, and *gressomyng* of men, causyng greate dearth, much pouertie", FP (1573), 10.
- "Sawl Masses, Diriges, Monethmayndes and Buryinges, Alsowin-days, *Kirkings*, Baneasking and weddings", CC (1581), III, iv.
- "I reck no friend, nor ay reck no foe, als ene to me, git the *ganging* and trouble not my whayet", TSH (1590-1591), I, i.

These examples show that this OE suffix produced nouns which indicate an activity or state related to the verb-form from which they derive: *ganging* 'the action of the verb *gang*', *gressomyng*,[11] *kirking* 'first attendance at church after marriage.' As is true of the standard variety where *-ing* proved to be fully productive in EModE, the reveal that this was also used in regional speech. It must be acknowledged that items such as *kirking* could be regarded as concrete nouns, for they indicate the result of the action or activity indicated by the verb (Nevalainen 1999: 397).

3.2.2. Adjective suffixes
3.2.2.1. Denominal adjectives

(10) *-less*:
- "Perigot is well pleased with the doome / Ne can Willye wite the *witelesse* herdgroome", TShC (1579), Aegl. VIII, 135-136.

(11) *-y*:
- "But ah! alack, and weel-a-day! / The *Canny* Duke", SB (1679), 125-126.
- "Yere sire was as neat as ony / an stealing a[u] [C]ow hee was *Cony*", BC43 (1679-1682), 19-20.
- "But *cony* Meggy as yu art / Neane ere could leave ye better" BC34 (?168-) 14-15.
- "What's said before, to's Charge was layd, / And other *Clarty* tricks he play'd", JSD (1686), 47.

[11] *Gressomyng* has not been recorded by any of the dictionaries consulted for this paper. Conversely, the verb *gersum* 'to subject to a fine, impose a fine upon', from which our sample derives, has been recorded as early as 1483 by the *OED*. Needless to say, *gressomyng* shows a clear semantic connexion with this verb. It could be thus defined as 'the action of the verb *gersum*'. The *EDD*, *DOST* or *SND* do not record the verb-form either.

- "I'll tell ye whay a Trick he play'd me / And fain wou'd *Gobby* here deceiv'd me", JSD (1686), 59.

Of OE origin, *-less* and *-y* disclose in these examples the semantic potential with which they are used in the southern standard. As such, the former creates adjectives on noun-stems with a privative sense – *witeless* 'blameless' –, whereas the latter derives adjectives that express the qualities of the noun they are attached to meaning 'full of, covered with', etc: *canny* 'sagacious; seemly, comely; artful, crafty', *clarty* 'dirty, sticky', *gobby* 'talkative, loquacious'. As exemplified, these affixes were apparently used in the North during the sixteenth and the seventeenth century. By way of illustration, *witeless* is first attested in 1560; *clarty* in 1586 (*OED*). It is worth stressing that *gobby* has not been recorded by the *OED* or the *DOST*; the *EDD* records its first attestation in 1869. In parallel, the *OED* quotes the first occurrence of *canny* 'sagacious' in 1637, whilst those recorded for the meanings 'artful' and 'seemly' date from 1768 and 1875, respectively.

In sum, *-less* and *-y* appear to have the same semantic and grammatical potential as they do in the standard variety. Their usage in EModE to create northern adjectives is likely to have been widespread, especially those formed by means of *-y*.

3.2.2.2. Deverbal adjectives

(12) *-ing*:
- "And freed me fra that *fleetching* Knave", JSD (1686), 64.

(13) *-y*:
- "Sae *Greathy* was the place where I was driven / That I me sicker thought I was in Heaven", EBJ (1615), 37-38.

Both of OE origin, these affixes show their ability to form adjectives on verb-stems. Firstly, *-ing* suggests that northern English created participial adjectives that express qualities or characteristics related to the verb they are attached to: *fleetching* 'coaxing, wheedling.' It goes without saying that northern dialects retained the original ending under the form *-and(e)*.[12] Yet, examples such as the above-indicated show that *-ing* was also used as a means of suffixation in the North during EModE, as *fleetching*, for example, is first recorded in 1513 (*OED* s.v *fleeching*, *ppl.a*). Secondly, *-y* is, according to Nevalainen (1999: 405), "The only native suffix to produce deverbal adjectives" in EModE with the sense

[12] Our corpus shows that *-and* was effectively spread in northern English as a suffixal means of derivation. For instance, *farrant* 'fashioned, seeming' (*EDD* s.v. *farrand*, 1) testifies to this fact. Unfortunately, no item that witnesses to the productivity of this affix in EModE has been found; *farrant* is attested for the first time in the fourteenth century (*OED* s.v. *farrand*, *a.*).

'having the tendency to.' As far as *greathy* 'well-stored, well-provisioned' (*EDD* s.v. *graith*, 1.v. (3)) is concerned, this widespread standard meaning is not so clear. Indeed, our example appears to indicate a positive result or characteristic closely linked to the action expressed by the verb; in this case, related to *graith* 'to equip, furnish; to array (...) to bedeck' (*OED graith* v, 3). It is worth noticing that this is the only occurrence of *greathy* that has hitherto been collected. The *EDD* refers to this example too.

3.2.2.3. Deadjectival adjectives

(14) *-ly*:
- "and after Ay mun cut off the Lugs and Naes on en, and Ay wot, he'll be a pratty *swatley* Fellee, bawt Lugs and Naes", ChS (1677), III, i.
- "He lookt like a *grethly* onnist mon's Son", ALT (c.1690-1730), 45.

Descendant of OE *-lic*, this suffix, also called *-ly*[1], appears to be productive during the seventeenth century in the formation of adjectives on adjectival stems. Although it has been argued that this means of suffixation ceased to be operative after OE times (*OED*), recent research has demonstrated that *-ly*-adjectives were certainly created in ME, especially when attached to nouns (Chao-Castro 2006). Besides, it has been found out that "those adjectives apparently derived from this pattern [adjective + *-ly* = adjective] from ME onwards would be the result of conversion from the corresponding adverbs in *-ly*." (Chao-Castro 2006: 2). Still, a closer examination of our items does not seem to corroborate this view which is applicable to standard *-ly*-adjectives. Firstly, it is rather complex to regard the hitherto unrecorded *swatley* 'quiet, still' as a converted form of the adverb *squatly* 'in a squat manner,' for this occurs for the first time in 1894 (*OED*).[13] Also, it is difficult to ascertain whether *swatley* may result from *-ly* being added to a noun-stem, since there is no connected sense that might relate *squat* to our sample (see *OED* s.vv. *squat* n^1, n^2, n^3, n^4). Secondly, *grethly* 'decent, respectable' does not seem to be produced after a conversion process, for the meanings of *gradely* – 'promptly, readily' and 'carefully, exactly; properly; quite, really, well' (*OED* s.v. *gradely*, *adv.* 1, 2)[14] – are not linked to the sense expressed by our item. Moreover, *grethly* does not appear to be formed on a nominal base, since there is no semantic connexion between *graith* and our derivative (see *OED* s.v. *graith n.*).

It follows, as a result, that *-ly*[1] could have been used in northern speech as a means of creating adjectives on adjectival bases by the second half of the seven-

13 It is worth mentioning that *swat* is a dialect orthographic variant of *squat* that the *OED* dates to the nineteenth century. As a matter of fact, the dictionary gathers this form in various northern regional glossaries from 1841 onwards (*OED* s.v. *squat*, *a.* 2.).

14 According to the *EDD*, *gradely* is an alteration of *graithly* due to folk etymology.

teenth century. Significantly, both *swatley* and *grethly* have been attested in specimens of Lancashire speech, at the same time as the *OED* and the *EDD* quote the first occurrences of the latter in eighteenth-century dialect texts localised to this area. Yet, it would be rather adventurous to assert that this process of suffixation was natural to Lancashire English, for the lexical pool we rely on is extremely restricted.

3.2.3. Adverb suffixes

(15) *-lin(g)s*:
- "Hee'l come belive, or *aebles* tittar", AYD (1673), 35.

(16) *-ly*:
- "Tho Roben hood, liell Iohn, Frier Tucke, and Marian *deftly* play", AE (1586), V, 121.
- "Peyson'd! be me saw I kan dew that *brawly*", DS (1652), IV.
- "Then I embrac't this lovely Lass, / and stroak't her Wem so *bonnily*", TLC (1674), 75.

Of OE origin, *-lin(g)s* was originally attached to nouns to create adverbs of direction like *headling(s)* or *sideling(s)*. Also, it was used to produce adverbs of condition or situation from adjectives: *blindlings*, *firstlings*, etc. Apparently, *aebles* 'possibly, perhaps' does not reflect the latter process, since, with the exception of *-s*, there is no clear evidence that might account for the presence of this affix. Nevertheless, it is especially noteworthy that the *OED* and the *EDD* collect the adverbs *ablins* and *ablings* as properly northern forms with the same meaning since 1597. Furthermore, the *SND* records *aiblins* in Scotland since the eighteenth century onwards. It appears therefore plausible that *aebles* represents a phonetically reduced variant of *-lin(g)s*. Remarkably, AYD (1673) offers the only textual occurrence we have found that might shed light upon this process in seventeenth-century northern English. In fact, Rydland (1992: 28) refers to *ables* 'perhaps' as an undocumented adverb that testifies to the valuable data compiled in the *Orton Corpus* related to twentieth-century Northumbrian dialects. The evidence attested in the SC appears to corroborate its northern usage three centuries earlier.

As regards *-ly*, the productivity of this native affix in EModE northern dialects appears to run parallel to that of *-ly*-adverbs in the standard. As our examples clearly show, this suffix also created regional adverbs of manner, degree, etc.: *bonnily* 'beautifully, finely', *brawly* 'finely, excellently', *deftly* 'softly, gently.' It is noteworthy that our corpus antedates the northern usage of *brawly* and *deftly* to the seventeenth century, as the *OED* records them in 1794 and 1787, respectively.[15]

---

[15] The *DOST* quotes the first occurrence of *brawly* in 1595; *deftly* is not recorded.

3.2.4. Verb suffixes

(17) *-er*:
- "They girn'd and *glowerd* all at anes", CKG (1663), 145.

As illustrated, *glower* 'to stare with wide-open eyes; to gaze intently' testifies to the northern formation of frequentative verbs by means of the native *-er*. In parallel with the standard variety, this also exhibits a reiterative sense.

3.3. Brief etymological and chronological notes

As indicated and Fig. 1 shows, a high percentage of the suffixes collected (sixteen out of seventeen) are of native origin, whilst only *-by* shows a Scandinavian ascendancy. On the other hand, as illustrated in Figure 2, our formations were created on already existing words among which those of OE and ON ascendancy predominate. Finally, a careful assessment of the first attestations of our case studies also yields significant information. As Fig. 3 exemplifies, a high proportion of EModE formations are documented – *aebles*, *bonnily*, *canny*, *clarty*, *glower*, *lawing*, *rigging*, or *witeless* –, among which a remarkable amount of neologisms – *bittock*, *brawly*, *cogie*, *clamper*, *deftly*, *grethly*, *gobby*, *pladdy* –, and *hapax legomena* – *greathy*, *gressomyng*, *kyrkeby*, *swatley*, *waedeum* – are attested.

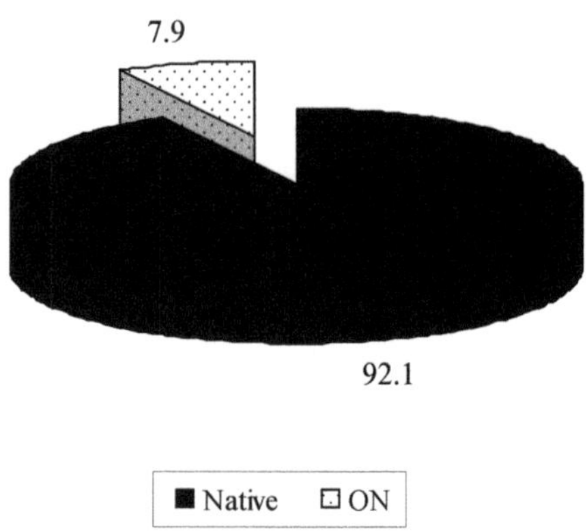

Figure 1. Origin of the suffixes collected

Origin	N	%
OE	16	92.1
ON	1	7.9
Total	17	100

Table 3. Origin of the suffixes collected

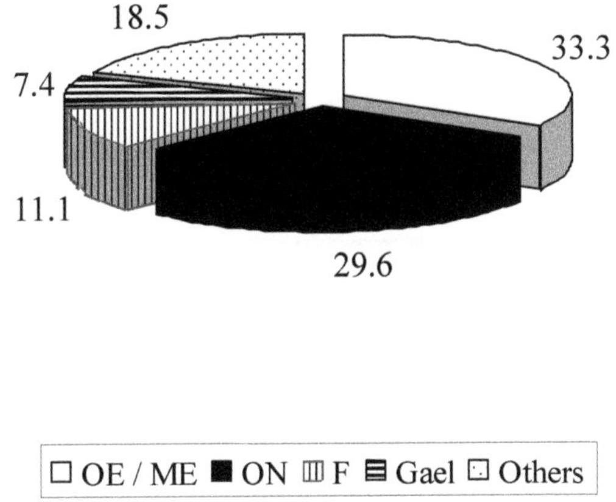

Figure 2. Etymology of the bases

Origin	N	%
OE / ME	9	33.3
ON	8	29.6
F	3	11.1
Gael.	2	7.4
Others	5	18.5
Total	29	99.9

Table 4. Etymology of the bases

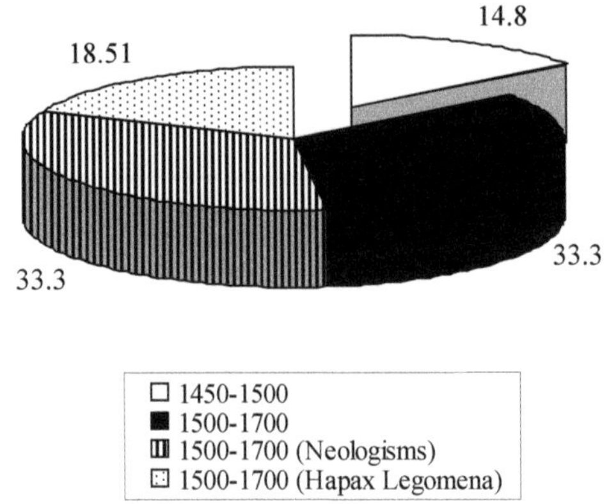

Figure 3. Chronology of the suffixal derivatives collected

Time span	N	%
1450-1500	4	14.8
1500-1700	25	85.1
Neolog.	10	33.3
Hapax	5	18.51
Others	10	33.3
Total	29	99.9

Table 5. Chronology of the suffixal derivatives collected

4. Concluding remarks

On the evidence of this analysis, it is clear that this represents a limited insight into some suffixation patterns in sixteenth- and seventeenth-century northern English (in its broadest geographical and linguistic sense). As illustrated, most of the suffixal derivatives collected were produced by means of affixes that also created new words in the southern standard. In this vein, it is worth pointing out that the regional restriction that could be attributed to these derivatives is mostly dependant on the provincial status that distinguished the nouns, adjectives, etc. to which they were attached: *bonnily*, for example. But for *-ock* (*bittock*) or *-el* (*weanell*), the rest of the affixes were also used in southern English at this time. Still, the survey we have undertaken brings to our attention some differences with the South, especially those suggested by denominal concrete *-ing*-nouns (*lawing* or *rigging*), or by cases such as *swatley* that hint at the possibility of *-ly*[1] being operative to produce adjectives on adjectival stems. In parallel, it has been shown that the North is somehow more conservative, since its suffixation processes rely almost exclusively on native affixes that stray from the widespread southern tendency that looked beyond English geographical boundaries for a great deal of foreign formatives which were incorporated into its vocabulary resources.[16] This northern conservatism does not mean, however, that its EModE lexicon should be regarded as an unchangeable and archaic testimony to the OE or ME past. As illustrated, over an 80% of the items collected were EModE products – *clarty*, *fleetching*, *glower*, etc. – and neologisms – *bittock*, *clamper*, *deftly*, etc. – created on existing words that characterise the northern vocabulary as morphologically active.

In spite of the literary bias of the sample and the inaccurate conclusions which might stem from a limited lexical pool such as the one presented, this has attempted to be a descriptive approach to a relatively untrodden field of research in regional dialect studies. Parallel data will provide us with more examples that will no doubt improve these preliminary assumptions. In fact, comparison with other text types could possibly tell us if affixation shows preference for specific fields of discourse. The evidence recorded in the SC suggests that suffixation in the North had a wide scatter, with words from different fields of the general vocabulary. All in all, there is great expectation that further investigation on regional dialects will help us get a glimpse into the intricacies of provincial language. Indeed, the SC offers the invaluable opportunity to evaluate regional data that have been disregarded. This will obviously aid us to put a remedy to this great deficit in historical and diachronic linguistics.

Appendix: abbreviations of the literary works

AE – *Albions England* (1586), W. Warner
ALT – 'A Lancashire tale' (c.1690-1730), anon.
AYD – 'A Yorkshire dialogue between an awd wife, a lass and a butcher' (1673), anon.
BC34 – 'As I went downe yond burne so clear…' (?168-), anon.
BC43 – 'How now Sawny what's the matter' (1679-1682), H. Fairfax
BKC – 'The memorable battle fought at Killy Crankie' (n.d.), anon.
CC – *The Conflict of Conscience* (1581), N. Woodes
ChS – *The Cheats of Scapin* (1677), Th. Otway
CKG – 'Christs Kirk on the green' (1663), anon.

16 Nevalainen (2006: 70) reminds us, however, that "lexical statistics show that native affixes produced more new words than the numerous latinate affixes" in the southern standard. Indeed, foreign formatives "continued to be applied to borrowed rather than native vocabulary in the Early Modern period." (70). Barber (1997: 233-234) also comments that native affixes such as *-ness* and *-y* produced most of the nouns in this period, at the same time as *-ed* and *-y* created a great amount of adjectives. Likewise, Görlach (1991: 171) remarks that "etymological restrictions made it quite unusual to combine foreign affixes with a native base."

DS – *The Distracted State* (1651), J. Tatham
EBJ – 'An Eglogue between Billie and Jockie' (1615), R. Brathwait
JSD – *A Joco-Serious Discourse in Two Dialogues between a Northumberland Gentleman and his Tenant a Scotchman* (1686), G. Stuart
FP – *A Dialogue against the Fever Pestilence* (1573 [1564]), W. Bullein
SB – 'A new Scotch ballad called Bothwell-Bridge' (1679), anon.
TBC – *The Bowge of Courte* (1510), J. Skelton
TLC – 'The lass of Cumberland' (1674), anon.
TSF – *The Scots Figgaries* (1652), J. Tatham
TSH – *The Scottish History of James IV* (1590-1591), R. Greene
TShC – *The Shepherds Calender* (1579), E. Spenser
TVS – *The Valiant Scot* (1637), J. Webster

References

Primary sources

anon. 1663. 'Christs Kirk on the green'. <http://eebo.chadwyck.com>.

anon. 1673. *A Yorkshire Dialogue between an Awd, Wife, a Lass, and a Butcher*. In Skeat, Rev. Walter W., ed. *Nine Specimens of English Dialects*. 1896. London: published by the English Dialect Society. 111-116.

anon. 1674. 'The lass of Cumberland'. London: printed for F. Coles, T. Vere, J. Wright and J. Clark. <http://www.bodley.ox.ac.uk/ballads/>.

anon. 1679. 'A new Scotch ballad called Bothwell-Bridge'. London: printed for T.B. <http:// eebo.chadwyck.com>.

anon. ?168-. 'As I went downe yond burne so clear…'. The Brotherton Library. BC MS Lt 34: fols. 9r-9v.

anon. c.1690-1730. 'A Lancashire tale'. The Folger Shakespeare Library. MS V.a. 308: fols. 53v-55v.

anon. n.d. 'The memorable battle fought at Killy Crankie'. <http://www.bodley.ox.ac.uk/ballads/>.

Brathwait, R. 1615. 'An Egloge between Billie and Jockie'. In Brathwait, R. *A Strappado for the Divell*. London: printed by I.B. for R. Redmar. 129-135. <http://eebo.chadwyck.com>.

Bullein, W. 1573 (1564). *A Dialogue against the Fever Pestilence*. London: printed by I. Kingston. <http://eebo.chadwyck.com>.

Fairfax, H. 1679-1682. 'How now Sawny what's the matter'. The Brotherton Library. BC MS Lt 43: fols. 38v-41r.

Greene, R. 1590-1591. *The Scottish History of James IV*. London: printed by Th. Creede. <http://eebo.chadwyck.com>.

Otway, Th. 1677. *The Cheats of Scapin*. London: printed for R. Tonson. <http://eebo.chadwyck.com>.

Skelton, J. 1510. *The Bowge of Courte*. <http://eebo.chadwyck.com>.

Spenser, E. 1579. *The Shepherds Calender*. London: printed by H. Singleton. <http://eebo.chadwyck.com>.

Stuart, G. 1686. *A Joco-Serious Discourse in Two Dialogues between a Northumberland Gentleman and his Tenant a Scotchman*. London: printed for B. Tooke. <http://eebo.chadwyck.com>.

Tatham, J. (1651): *The Distracted State*, London, printed by W.H. for I. Tey. <http://eebo.chadwyck.com>.

Tatham, J. (1652): *The Scots Figgaries*, London, printed by W.H. for I. Tey. <http://eebo.chadwyck.com>.

Warner, W. (1586): *Albions England*, London, printed by G. Robinson for Th. Cadman. <http://eebo.chadwyck.com>.

Webster, J. (1637): *The Valiant Scot*, London, printed by Th. Harper for I. Waterson. <http://eebo.chadwyck.com>.

Woodes, N. (1581): *The Conflict of Conscience*, London, printed by R. Bradocke. <http://eebo.chadwyck.com>.

Secondary sources

Barber, Ch. (1997 (1976)): *Early Modern English*. Edinburgh: Edinburgh UP.

Blake, N.F. (1980): *Non-standard Language in English Literature*, London, André Deutsch.

Blank, P. (1996): *Broken English: Dialects and the Politics of Language in Renaissance Writings*, London, Routledge.

Blank, P. (2006): "The babel of Renaissance English," in L. Mugglestone (ed.), *The Oxford History of English*, Oxford, Oxford University Press, 212-239.

Britton, D. (2000): "Henry Machyn, Axel Wijk and the case of the wrong riding: the south-western Yorkshire character of the language of Machyn's diary," *Neuphilologische Mitteilungen*, 4 (CI), 571-596.

Chao Castro, M. (2006): "Adjectives in -*ly* and their homomorphic adverbs: measuring the productivity of adjectival -*ly*[1]," in M. Losada et al. (eds.), *Proceedings of the 30th International AEDEAN Conference*. Huelva: Universidad de Huelva Publicaciones. [CD-ROM]

Coles, E. (1676): *An English Dictionary*, London, printed by S. Crouch, <http: //eebo.chadwyck.com>.

Craigie, Sir W. A., et al. (eds.) (1931-2002): *Dictionary of the Older Scottish Tongue*, 12 vols., London / Milford, Oxford University Press.

Dossena, M. (1998): "Diminutives in Scottish standard English," *Scottish Language*, 17, 22-39.

Eckhardt, E. (1910): *Die Dialekt-und-Ausländertypen des älteren Englischen Dramas. Teil I: Die Dielekttypen*, Leipzig, A. Uystprust.

Fox, A. (2000): *Oral and Literate Culture in England 1500-1700*, Oxford, Clarendon Press.

García-Bermejo, M. F. (1999a): "Methods for the linguistic analysis of Early Modern literary dialects," in P. Alonso et al. (eds.), *Teaching and Research in English Language and Literature*, León, Celarayn, 249-266.
García-Bermejo, M. F. (1999b): "The Northern/Scottish dialect in Nathaniel Woodes' *A Conflict of Conscience* (1581)," *Sederi*, 9, 9-21.
García-Bermejo, M. F. (2001): "Regional dialects in sixteenth-century jestbooks," *Sederi*, 12, 113-136.
García-Bermejo, M. F. (2008a): "Early sixteenth-century evidence for [Iə] < OE ā in the North?" in M. F. García-Bermejo, P. Sánchez et al. (eds.), *Multidisciplinary Studies in Language and Literature: English, American and Canadian*, Salamanca, Ediciones Universidad de Salamanca, 59-65.
García-Bermejo, M. F. 2008b. Towards a history of literary dialects and dialect literature in the 18th and 19th centuries: The Salamanca Corpus. Paper presented at the *Thirteenth International Conference on Methods in Dialectology*. Leeds, 04-08 August 2008.
García-Bermejo, M. F. (2008c): "The southern dialect in Thomas Churchard's *The Contention bettwixte Churchyearde and Camell* (1552)" (Paper presented at the *Fifteenth International Conference on English Historical Linguistics*, Munich, 24-30 August 2008).
García-Bermejo, M. F and P. Sánchez (eds.) (forthcoming): *The Salamanca Corpus*.
Görlach, M. (1991): *An Introduction to Early Modern English*, Cambridge, Cambridge University Press.
Görlach, M. (1999): "Regional and social variation," in R. Lass (ed.), *The Cambridge History of the English Language III 1476-1776*, Cambridge, Cambridge University Press, 459-538.
Grant, W. et al. (eds.) (1931-1976) : *The Scottish National Dictionary*, Edinburgh, The Scottish National Dictionary Association.
Hickey, R. (2003): *Corpus Presenter: Processing Software for Language Analysis with a Manual and A Corpus of Irish English as Sample Data*, Amsterdam, Benjamins.
Kytö, M. and M. Rissanen (1993): "General introduction," in M. Rissanen et al. (eds.), *Early English in the Computer Age: Explorations through the Helsinki Corpus*, Berlin, Mouton de Gruyter, 1-17.
Kytö, M., P. Grund and T. Walker (2007): Regional variation and the language of English witness depositions 1560-1760: constructing a 'linguistic' edition in electronic form," in P. Pahta et al. (eds.), *Studies in Variation, Contact and Change in English 2: Towards Multimedia in Corpus Studies*, Helsinki, VARIENG, <http://www.helsinki.fi/varieng/journal/Volumes/02/kyto_et_ al/>.
Markus, M. (2008): "Diminutives in English standard and dialects (based on Wright's *English Dialect Dictionary*)" (Paper presented at the *Fifteenth*

International Conference on English Historical Linguistics, Munich, 14-30 August 2008).
Macafee, C. and A. Anderson (1997): "A random sample of Older Scots lexis," *Transactions of the Philological Society*, 95, 2, 247-278.
Milroy, J. (2007): "The history of English," in D. Britain (ed.), *Language in the British Isles*, Cambridge, Cambridge University Press, 9-33.
Nevalainen, T. (1999): "Early Modern English lexis and semantics," in R. Lass (ed.), *The Cambridge History of the English Language III 1476-1776*, Cambridge, Cambridge University Press, 332-458.
Nevalainen, T. (2006): *An Introduction to Early Modern English*, Oxford, Oxford University Press.
Quirk, R. et al. (1985): *A Comprehensive Grammar of the English Language*, London, Longman.
Rissanen, M. (1991): "The diachronic corpus as a window to the history of English," in J. Svartvik (ed.), *Directions in Corpus Linguistics. Proceedings of Nobel Symposium 82. Stockholm, 4-8 August 1991*, Berlin, Mouton de Gruyter, 185-205.
Rydland, K. (1992): "The Orton Corpus. A collection of dialect material from the North-East of England," *Zeitschrift für Englische Philologie*, 110, 1-35.
Ruano-García, J. (2008): "North-East Yorkshire speech in the late seventeenth century: a phonological and orthographical evaluation of an anonymous printed broadside," *Sederi*, 18, 97-119.
Ruano-García, J. (2010a): " 'The Account Book of William Wray': an evaluation of Yorkshire lexis in two inventories (1599-1600)," in C. Prado-Alonso et al. (eds.), *New Trends and Methodologies in Applied English Language Research: Diachronic, Diatopic and Contrastive Studies*, Linguistic Insights 103, Bern, Peter Lang, 101-128.
Ruano-García, J. (2010b) (forthcoming), *Early Modern Northern English Lexis: A Literary Corpus-Based Study*, Linguistic Insights 105, Bern, Peter Lang.
Ruano-García, J. (2010c) (forthcoming), "*I'll tell o how Gilbert Scott sowd is mere Berry*: 'A Lancashire Tale' as a source for Lancashire speech in the late seventeenth and early eighteenth century," in B. Heselwood and C. Upton (eds.), *Papers from Methods XIII: Proceedings of the Thirteenth International Conference on Methods in Dialectology*, Frankfurt am Main, Peter Lang.
Shorrocks, G. (2000): "The dialects of Early Modern English and their study" (Paper presented at the *Eleventh Sederi Conference*, Universidad de Huelva).

Shorrocks, G. (2004): "The Rev. William Hutton's *A Bran New Wark*: the Westmorland dialect in the late Early-Modern period," *Sederi*, 14, 117-135.

Simpson, J. and E. Weiner (eds.) (2004-2005 (1989)): *Oxford English Dictionary*, Second edition, Version 3.1 in CD-ROM, Oxford, Oxford University Press.

Wakelin, M. (1980): "Evidence for spoken regional English in the sixteenth century," *Revista Canaria de Estudios Ingleses*, 1: 1-25.

Wakelin, M. (1988): "The phonology of south-western English 1500-1700," in J. Fisiak (ed.), *Historical Dialectology: Regional and Social*, Berlin, Mouton de Gruyter, 609-644.

Wales, K. (2002): " 'North of Watford Gap': a cultural history of northen English (from 1700)," in R. Watts and P. Trudgill (eds.), *Alternative Histories of English*, London, Routledge, 45-66.

Wales, K. (2004): "North of the Trent: images of northern-ness and northern English in the eighteenth century," in H. Berry and J. Gregory (eds.), *Creating and Consuming Culture in North-East England, 1660-1830*, Ashgate, Aldershot, 24-36.

Wales, K. (2006): *Northern English: A Social and Cultural History*, Cambridge, Cambridge University Press.

Weiner, E. (1997): "The use of non-literary manuscripts for the study of dialect lexis," in E. W. Schneider (ed.), *Englishes Around the World Vol. 1. Studies in Honor of Manfred Görlach*, Amsterdam, John Benjamins, 235-253.

Wright, J. (1981 (1898-1905)): *The English Dialect Dictionary*, Oxford, Oxford University Press.

Electronic databases

Bodleian Library Broadside Ballads Project (2000), M. Heaney et al. (eds.), Bodleian Library, Oxford University (<http://www.bodley.ox.ac.uk/ ballads/>).

Early English Books Online: *English Prose-Drama Full Text Database* (2003-2009), Chadwyck-Healey (ed.), Cambridge (<http://eebo.chadwyck.com>).

Literature Online (1996-2009): Chadwyck-Healey (ed.), <htpp://lion.chadwyck.co.uk>.

The Restoration Comedy Project (1995-2009), J. A. Prieto-Pablos et al. (eds.), Universidad de Sevilla (<http://alojamientos.us.es/restoration/>).

Modal verbs in Early Modern English recipes*

Francisco Alonso-Almeida
Universidad de Las Palmas de Gran Canaria

Nila Vázquez
Universidad de Murcia

1. Introduction

Recipes from the medieval period have been the focus of several studies from a genre and register perspective. Modern English recipes have not received an equal treatment from scholars. However these recipes represent excellent material for the study of linguistic innovation in this period. Apart from this, recipes are also source for research dealing with social, historical and cultural aspects in general. Our corpus of texts contains books in toto, including introductions and prefaces, since these provide suitable context for interpretation. The analyses, however, are performed on the recipe genre, only. Our paper deals with authorial stance and the use of modal verbs in a time span of two centuries (1500-1700) in order to retrieve the different meanings in usage according to contextual premises.

Our revision of the literature includes Biber, Johansson, Leech, Conrad and Finegan (1999) –henceforward Biber et al. (1999), Biber (2004), Hyland (2000 and 2001). The historical study of stance expressions is restricted to few studies, such as Biber, Conrad and Reppen (1998), Taavitsainen (2001), Biber (2004), and Alonso-Almeida (2009). Taavitsainen (2001) concentrates on mood and modality in the medical register, among other aspects. Biber (2004) studies stance in a multi-register corpus from a historical perspective to conclude that stance marking varies across registers. Stance strategies sharing a similar function may be different from one register to another, this includes variation in frequency of occurrence.

Our paper is organized as follows: Section 1 offers a description of our corpus of study. Section 2 includes the main tenets in the study of stance and the terminology frequently associated to this concept. The following section is the analysis of findings in the corpus, and their pragmatic interpretation. Finally, the conclusions are given in section 4.

---

* Dr. Francisco Alonso is part of the Research Project "Evidencialidad en un corpus multidisciplinar de artículos científico-técnicos en lengua inglesa," grant FFI2009-10801 (FEDER, Spanish Ministry for Science and Innovation), and Dr. Nila Vázquez is part of the Research Project "Variation, Linguistic Change and Grammaticalization," grant HUM2007-60706 (Spanish Ministry for Science and Innovation). Both grants are hereby gratefully acknowledged.

2. Data

The data for the present paper have been extracted from *The Corpus of Early English Recipes* (henceforth CoER), a project currently underway in the University of Las Palmas de Gran Canaria. This Corpus is genre restricted and only recipes are collected for analysis. We aim at compiling no less than three million words from texts in manuscripts and printed sources, which have been typed directly into machine. The time span is 1375 to 1850 so that contrastive analyses can be performed. The books are transcribed *in toto* for practical purposes with the addition of XML labels to indicate the beginning and end of genres other than recipes.

Stages	**Functions**	**Language structures**
Title	To indicate what the recipe is good for. To show the beginning of the recipe.	Infinitive of purpose Purpose NP Relative clauses Indexicals (*Here is...*) Anaphoric referential devices
Ingredients	To list the ingredients needed.	Use of the imperative Use of formulaic *Take* Relative clauses Numbers Weight references
Preparation	To instruct the reader how to combine the ingredients	Use of the imperative Parataxis Personal pronouns: object type (*it*) Numerals to indicate measure Weight references
Application	To show how to administer the finished product to the patient.	Coercive verbs Possessive pronouns and adjectives Numerals to indicate duration Use of paratactic expressions
Storage	To offer instructions on how the product must be stored for future use.	Imperative Infinitive of purpose
Evaluation	To describe the expected remedy results	Modals Certainty adverbs

Table 1. Functional labelling of recipes

The project working definition of genre follows Martin (1984: 25), and it is defined as "a staged, goal-oriented, purposeful activity in which speakers engage as a member of our culture." In this line, the recipes included in this compilation have been previously analyzed following functional-systemic linguistics, as in Halliday (1985a, 1985b), and Halliday and Matthiesen (2004). The very nature of the recipe is then formulaic in that it is made up of sections with a highly standardized use of language which can, to some extent, be predicted by the members of a particular culture. The recipe stages are TT-title, I-ingredients, P-preparation, A-application, S-storage, and E-evaluation. The functions of these stages and the language associated to each one are summarised in Table 1.

For the analyses we have randomly selected ca. 350,000 words from eleven different books (only recipes are enquired in data retrieval). These books are listed below, together with a short name for further reference in this paper. The titles are transcribed *literatim* from the originals without editorial intervention.

Year	Volume	Reference
1572	*A booke of the arte and maner, howe to plant and graffe all sortes of trees howe to set stones, and sowe pepines to make wylde trees to graffe on, as also remedies and medicines.*	plant
1573	*The Treasurie of commodious Conceits, & hidden Secrets. and may be called, The Dutwiues Closet, of healthfull prouision.*	treasurie
1579	*A booke of soueraigne approued medicines and remedies as well for sundry diseases within the body as also for all sores, woundes.*	soueraigne
1579	*A thousand notable things, of sundry sortes Wherof some are wonderfull, some straunge, some pleasant, diuers necessary, a great sort profitable and many very precious.*	thousand
1584	*A briefe and pleasaunt treatise, entituled, Naturall and Artificiall conclusions.*	naturall
1621	*A delight daily exercise for ladies and gentlewomen.*	daily
1631	*The vviddovves treasure Plentifully furnished with sundry precious and approued secrets in physicke and chirurgery, for the health and pleasure of man-kinde.*	widowes
1650	*A Book of COOKERY, And the order of Meates to be served to the Table, both for Flesh and Fish dayes.*	cookery
1653	*A choice manuall, or rare and select secrets in physick and chyrurgery collected, and practised by the Right Honorable, the Countesse of Kent, late deceased.*	choice
1658	*ARCHIMAGIRUS ANGLO-GALLICUS: OR,Excellent & Approved Receipts and Experiments in COOKERY*	archimagirus
1673	*The vvhole Body of COOKERY DISSECTED*	body

Table 2. Corpus description

The syntactic nature of modals in our corpus is as in Present day English. With the exception of *ought to* and *have to*, all modals are followed by the infinitive without *to*. Adverbs embedded in the verb phrase precede the infinitive, including *not*. The negative of *can* is *can not* in all contexts.

3. Stance

Stance is related to the expression of the speakers or writers' "personal feelings, attitudes, value judgements, or assessments." The study of discourse stance has been carried out under different terms, such as evaluation (Hunston, 1994; Hunston and Thompson, 2000), evidentiality (Chafe 1986), and affect (Ochs, 1989). Hyland (1998: 5) studies the term hedge and, under this label, he includes "the means by which writers can present a proposition as an opinion rather than a fact: items are only hedges in their epistemic sense, and only then when they mark uncertainty."

The concept metadiscourse is also related to the above concepts. Metadiscourse is "a fuzzy term, often characterized as simply 'discourse about discourse' or 'talk about talk'." Hyland points out that the interpersonal concepts of stance, evaluation, and engagement overlap with metadiscourse: "Metadiscourse is the cover term for the self-reflective expressions used to negotiate interactional meanings in a text, assisting the writer (or speaker) to express a viewpoint and engage with readers as members of a particular community" (Hyland 2005: 37-38). This definition of metadiscourse pursues the similar function than the definition of stance by Biber et al. (1999, §12). Both seek to unravel information other than propositional in the text. Biber et al. (1999, §12) classify stance from a semantic perspective into (a) epistemic stance ("comments on the status of information in a proposition"), (b) attitudinal stance (these markers "report personal attitudes or feelings"), and (c) style of speaking stance ("comments on the communication itself"). The marking of stance can be done in several ways: (a) lexical marking, (b) grammatical marking, and (c) person marking.

Lexical stance markers rely on the evaluative lexical items: nouns, adjectives, and verbs. Grammatical stance markers are categorized into the following devices: (a) stance adverbials, (b) stance complement clauses, (c) modals and semimodals, (d) stance noun + propositional phrase, and (e) premodifying stance adverb (stance adverb + adjective or noun phrase). In this study, we intend to describe the modal verbs in the eModE part of CoER, with the exception of shall and will that are left for future research.

Finally, person marking is defined thus: person marking refers to first, second or third person marking of a verb or predicative adjective. Person marking identifies "grammaticalization of a subject's attitudes and opinions" (Palmer 1986).

4. Analysis of data

Modals affect the meaning of the complete proposition they hedge. They show two types of meaning, namely epistemic and deontic. Epistemic is "concerned with matters of knowledge or believe on which basis speakers express their judgements about state of affairs, events or actions" (Hoye 1997: 42). Deontic modals refer to the "necessity of acts in terms of which the speaker gives permission or lays and obligation for the performance of actions at some time in the future" (Hoye 1997: 43). This distinction coincides with Biber et al.'s (1999: 485) intrinsic and extrinsic modality:

> "Each modal can have two different types of meaning, which can be labeled intrinsic and extrinsic (also referred to as 'deontic' and 'epistemic' meanings). Intrinsic modality refers to actions and events that humans (or other agents) directly control: meanings relating to permission, obligation, and volition (or intention). Extrinsic modality refers to the logical status of events or states, usually relating to assessments of likelihood: possibility, necessity, or prediction."

The corpus contains the distribution of modal verbs shown in the table below:

Item	**Frequency**
will	34.58
may	22.10
shall	18.14
must	13.85
can	5.30
would	2.39
should	2.00
ought	1.55
could	0.07
might	0.02

Table 3. Frequency of modal verbs in corpus (percentage)

	obligation	necessity	permission	probability	possibility	ability	volition	prediction	conditional
may			5	1167		12			
ought to	69	14							
should	30	2			74				
have to	3	1							
could					2	2			
might					1				
would					9		5	86	28
can					281	3			
must	734	4						4	

Table 4. The meaning of modal verbs in eModE CoER, except *shall* and *will* (number of cases)

These modal verbs, with the exception of *shall* and *will*, are used as shown in the following table. In the next sections, we describe them grouped into intrinsic (or deontic) and extrinsic (or epistemic) modality.

4.1. Intrinsic modality

As already explained, this type coincides with Hoyes's deontic modality and refers to events that humans directly control. In Figure 1, the frequency of intrinsic modality is given, together with the forms used to show this meaning. As seen there, *must* appears as the most frequent modal verb with the meaning of obligation. The following instances illustrate all this (spelling as in the originals):

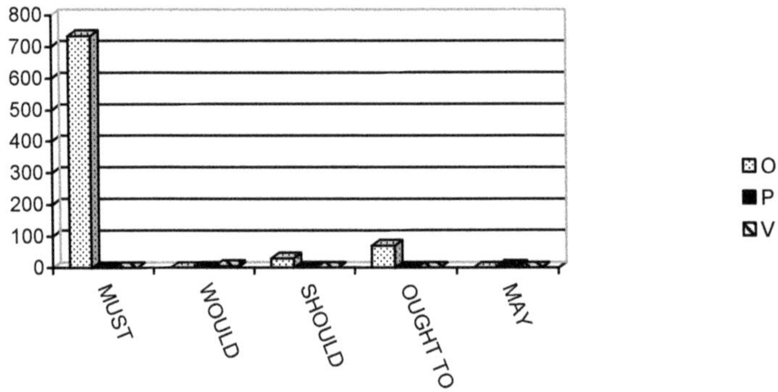

Figure 1. Intrinsic modality in eModE *CoER*[1]

(1) *For the bloody Flixe. Seeth mylke, and in the seething put in a peece of Roche Allam, whiche will cause a curd, which curd being cleane taken from the whay, you must drynke the sayd whay as hot as is possible: also yf your stomacke can possible beare it, you must eate the curd, and with Gods help you shal recouer* (soueraigne).

(2) *You must boyl and blanch your Calves feet, and when they are cold, mince them with half the quantity of beef suet, with a handful of good sweet herbs, Parslee and Spinnage minced, put to them a good quantity of Currans, some Cloves, Mace, Cinamon, Ginger, Nutmeg, Sugar and Salt, with a little Rose water* (body).

In these examples, we can infer obligation. In both (1) and (2) *must* indicates required actions either to cure the sick person in the case of the second instance, or to be able to perform the next instruction in the recipe, i.e. *mince them*. The case of the *must* forms in (1) is specially relevant in the context of the following proposition in the text: *and with Gods help you shall recover.*

1 O = obligation; P = permission; V = volition.

The author conditions the truth of this proposition to the fulfilment of *drinking the whey and of eating the curd*. However, a further condition is added in the string *with Gods help*. This is why *shall* is used in *you shall recouer* that may indicate either prediction or tentative possibility. The former is assumed if we consider that the help of God is beyond human choice, and so the meaning is deontic. The latter is epistemic in the sense that the action is likely to happen in normal circumstances after the fulfilment of the conditions. The help of God is received if the patient merits its grace. One similar example in the corpus is *and by the grace of God he shall sleepe within one quarter of an houre* (*soueraigne*).

Would implies volition. The example in (3) below, illustrate this meaning. Here, the author relies on the voluntary performance of the action by the doer, and so *would* evidences this.

(3) *To make a Trifle.Take a pint of thicke Creame, and season it with Suger, Ginger and Rose-water, and stirre it as you would, then hew it and make it luke warme in a dish upon a Chafingdish of coles* (cookery).

Ought to exclusively shows obligation in our selection of texts. Examples are:

(4) *With what dung ye ought to dung your trees* (plant).
(5) *This medicine following, is proued by experience, and as a certayne diuine thing, doth cure euerie plurisie, and doth relieue the sicke from death: which ought not to be applied vnto the sicke partie, vntyll the fowrth daye be past. Take of Dealtha two ounces, (which is to be had at the Apothecaries:) the oyle of sweete Almondes halfe an ounce, myxe them together: with which oyntment (being warme,) let the grieued place be annointed* (thousand).

The use of *ought to* in the first instance indicates lack of volition on the part of the doer, and so the instruction must be followed as indicated. As also happens with other intrinsic modulation of propositions indicating obligation, we may perceive the author's authoritative voice. A similar function is fulfilled in the second case. The doer (practitioner or lay folk) is compelled by the author not to apply the product on the patient until four days of preparation have gone by. This utterance with *ought to* stands as a premise for the successful outcome of the disease. The writer exhibits his expertise and command on the topic and so, from an interpersonal perspective, the author places himself higher in the rank.

Should and *have to* also appear in the corpus showing obligation, but their frequencies of occurrence are only 3.5% and 0.3% of the modals with this meaning, respectively. In the instances below, the author expresses obligation with these two modals. In the specific case of (6), *should* may be interpreted as a recommendation rather than an obligation. Considering the instructive nature of the recipe, and the large number of equal contexts in which *must* is used instead, we think it is safe to consider *should* as a marker of obligation here, if the correct result wants to be achieved. Similarly, in the case of (7), the writer shows the obligatory step of performing the action "to slice the Coller" before proceeding forward in the recipe. This obligation is captured in the form *have to*.

(6) *In the baking thereof you should put some Wine or strong broth, being thickened up with a yolk or two of an egg, will serve for a leare to put over it, so garnish it* (body).

(7) *To fry Coller'd Pork. You may see how to Coller it, as before; all that you have to do is to slice the Coller, and your Pan being very hot, fry it with clarified stuff: you may eat it with Mustard as you do Sowse; this may serve when you have occasion to add a dish to your common dyet* (body).

The last form showing intrinsic meaning is *may*. This verb is used to indicate permission, as in the example in (8). In this case, the author indicates the reader that there is no restriction for the intake of the medicine, once it cools down. However, we could also infer an extrinsic meaning in this context. Then, the author would imply possibility rather than permission. Our first option is permission since, frequently at this point, the recipe information on restrictions regarding application and dosage is given.

(8) *A Medicine for any Wound old or new. Take a pint of Sallade oyle, and four ounces of Bees Wax, and two ounces of Stone-pitch, and two ounces of Rosin, and two ounces of Venice Turpentine, and one pennyworth of Frankincense, and a handfull of Rosemary tops, and a handfull of Tutson leaves, and a handfull of Plantain leaves; these Hearbs must be stamped, and the juyce of them put to the things aforesaid, and let them boyle altogether about a quarter of an hour, or thereabouts, this being done, put it into an earthen pot, and when it is cold you may use it as you have occasion, and keep it two year a most excellent Medicine* (choice).

4.2. Extrinsic modality

Extrinsic modality in the corpus is shown in Figure 2, below. As seen all the modals in the corpus are indexed for at least for one of the extrinsic categories. *May* is the most frequent means to register possibility or tentative possibility, followed by *must* and *ought to*. In the case of prediction this is mainly marked by *must* and *would*. Finally, necessity is expressed by means of *ought to*, *should*, *have to*, and *must*. This last meaning of modals is very sporadic. It is noteworthy the combination of *must* and needs to show this meaning: *Note also, that divers persons do onely make use of the single pepper instead of other spices, although it must needs be granted that the composed spices all together, must needs be more pleasing and Aromatick than the pepper alone* (*archimagirus*). The adverb *needs* here indicates a step that cannot be avoided. It could be argued that *must* indicates obligation, but, in our view, the presence of *needs* mitigates this meaning, and so necessity is inferred in this context.

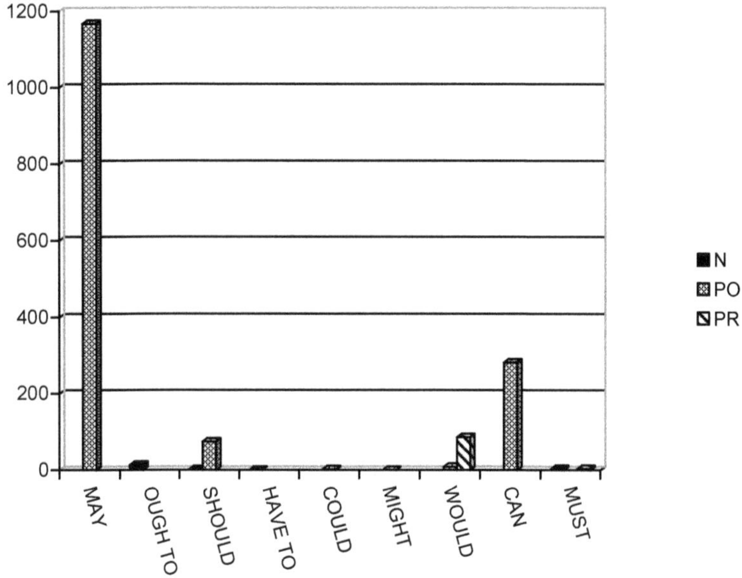

Figure 2. Extrinsic modality in CoER

As already stated above, the most frequent forms to show possibility are *may* and *must*, in this order. In (9) below, *may* is used to show tentative possibility. This modal verb hedges the proposition in such a way that it qualifies its truth. The writer cannot fully account for the exact timing required to boil the product. This idea of vagueness is also reinforced by the lexical item *suppose* that indicates an assumption rather than a fact.

(9) *To pickle Quinces. Take your fair Quinces, and core them with your boring irons or scoop; take the worst of your Quinces, and cut them to pieces, and boyl your core or pieces in your pan of liquor, so that you make the liquor strong, then boyl your Quinces prepared to pickle, till they may be supposed a quarter boyled, then strain out your liquor your hair-sieve, or strained, and put a small quantity of salt, add there to some strong beer, and put up your Quinces whole in your Vessel or Pot, and pour in some of the same liquor, and stop them close up* (body).

The following examples imply prediction with *must*. In (10) the author expects the syrup to show certain degree of thickness and this knowledge is obtained through experience. The author also manifests some hesitation in the use of the modal, and so it could also indicate some kind of imprecision. This vagueness is reinforced by the use of *somewhat* that hedges the adjective *thick*. In (11) *would* provides the proposition with this same meaning of prediction. The author shows his attitude towards what is said by presupposing the truth of the future action.

(10) *and let them boyle softly till you think they be enough, and the sirrop must be somewhat thick; then let your Orenges stand all night upon the fire* (cookery).

(11) *WHo so would haue a very whyte & delycate skyn. Let them boyle or heate Lytarge of Syluer invinegar distylled: and wash therwith theyr skynne which they desyre to haue fayre, trym and whyte. This I tooke out of Mizaldus* (thousand).

The same meaning of prediction with *would* is present in the following instance:

(12) *Parsley with crums of bread applyed in stead of a plaster, doth heale the Shingles, but the decoction of the same drunke doth breake the Stone. Florenci. Mints put into Milke, it neither suffereth the same to curd, nor to become thicke, in so much that laid in curded milke, it would dissolue the same againe, so that by the same vertue and property, he saith toresist and abate the generation as well in man as woman* (widowes).

5. Conclusion

This study has shown the various meanings of modal verbs during the eModE period in a corpus of recipes in a time-span of two centuries. One main conclusion is that modals are not systematically used, and so one function may be fulfilled by more than one form. Still, data show the tendency to standardization of functions, and so *may* for instance is the preferred form to mark possibility. Our interpretation of modals in relation to the authors's intention requires a thorough analysis of the linguistic context in order to determine their meaning category in the intrinsic/extrinsic distinction put forward by Biber et al. (1999). Much work remains to be done in order to complete the picture of modals in these specialized texts of the Modern English period. One such task is to consider the professional and social contexts in the interpretation of modulation.

References

Alonso-Almeida, F. (2009): “Stance marking and register in Middle English charms,” *Studia Anglica Posnaniensia*, 45, 13-29.

Biber, D. (2004): “Historical patterns for the grammatical marking of stance: a cross-register comparison,” *Journal of Historical Pragmatics*, 5, 107-136.

Biber, D., S. Johansson, G. Leech, S. Conrad and E. Finegan (1999): *Longman Grammar of Spoken and Written English*, New York, Longman.

Chafe, W. L. (1986): "Evidentiality in English conversation and academic writing," in L. Wallace, Chafe, J. Nichols (eds.), *The Linguistic Coding of Epistemology*, Norwood, NJ, Ablex, 261-272.

Fitzmaurice, S. (2003): "The grammar of stance in early eighteenth-century English epistolary language," in C. Meyer and P. Leistyna (eds.), *Corpus Analysis*, Amsterdam, Rodopi, 107-131.

Halliday, M. A. K. (1985a): *Spoken and Written Language*. Geelong, Vic., Deakin University Press.

Halliday, M. A. K. (1985b): *Introduction to Functional Grammar*, Edward Arnold, London.

Hoye, L. (1997): *Adverbs and Modality in English*, Essex, Longman.

Hunston, S. (1994): "Evaluation and organization in a sample of written academic discourse;" in M. Coulthard (ed.), *Advances in Written Text Analysis*, London, Routledge, 191-218.

Hunston, S. and G. Thompson (eds.) (2000): *Evaluation in Text*, Oxford, Oxford University Press.

Hyland, K. (1998): *Hedging in scientific research articles*, Amsterdam/ Philadelphia, Benjamins, 207-226.

Hyland, K. (2000): *Disciplinary Discourses: Social Interaction in Academic Genres*, London/New York, Longman.

Hyland, K. (2001): "Humble servants of the discipline? Self-mention in research articles," *English for Specific Purposes*, 20.3.

Hyland, K. (2005): *Metadiscourse: Exploring Interaction in Writing*, London, Continuum.

Martin, J. R. (1984): "Language, genre and register," in F. Christie (ed.), *Children Writing: Reader*, Geelong, Vic., Deakin University Press, 21-29.

Ochs, E. (ed.) (1989): "The pragmatics of affect," Special issue of *Text*, 9, 1.

Palmer, F. R. (1986): *Mood and Modality*, Cambridge, Cambridge University Press.

Precht, K. (2000): *Patterns of Stance in English* (Unpublished doctoral dissertation. Northern Arizona University. Retrieved from UMI Microform 9982897).

Taavitsainen, I. (2001): "Evidentiality and scientific thought-styles: English medical writing in Late Middle English and Early Modern English," in M. Gotti and M. Dossena (eds.), *Modality in Specialized Texts: Selected Papers of the 1st Cerlus Conference*, Bonn, 21-52

PART SIX

Annotating and Quantifying

A web corpus of Spanish automatically annotated with semantic roles

M. Pilar Valverde Ibáñez
Universidade de Santiago de Compostela

Eckhard Bick
Institute of Language and Communication
University of Southern Denmark

1. Semantic roles

A semantic role is the actual role a participant plays in a situation, irrespectively of its linguistic encoding. Therefore, assigning semantic roles to the arguments of a verb is a way of adding deep semantic information to the analysis of a sentence. With this type of information, we can answer questions like who, when, where or what happened, which is useful in systems that require the comprehension of sentences, like dialogue systems, information retrieval, information extraction or automatic translation.

The idea of semantic roles has a long linguistic tradition, originated in the concept of case roles (Fillmore 1968), later termed thematic or theta roles in Government & Binding theory (Jackendoff 1972).

While there is a certain agreement in the linguistic community about the inventory of syntactic categories and functions and their definition, this is not the case at the semantic level, where there is more skepticism about the very definition of semantic role, at least in the more traditional sense.

As the level of analysis scales, so does the abstraction of the description and the gradual nature of language becomes more evident. In the corpus annotation task, this fact results in a low level of agreement among the different projects that deal with role annotation and also in a lower level of inter-annotator agreement or consistency in each annotation. With regard to the available resources for Spanish that contain manually extracted information about semantic roles, the ADESSE database (García-Miguel and Albertuz 2005) uses a set of 143 roles, the AnCora corpus (Taulé et al. 2008) 20 roles and the Sensem corpus (Alonso et al. 2007) 24 roles. In addition, among the three projects, only the AnCora corpus assigns a semantic role to all the complements of the clause, while the rest only treat valency-bound complements.

In our corpus, we use a set of 52 semantic roles, as shown in table 1, following the set of roles used by Bick (2007) for the annotation of Portuguese texts. Those cover the major categories of the tectogrammatical annotation layer of the Prague Dependency Treebank (Hajicova et al. 2000), as well as those of the

Spanish AnCora project. In contrast to the latter, the arguments selected by the verb are not incrementally numbered (ARG0, ARG1, ARG2, ARG-M) according to their degree of proximity in relation to the verb, mainly because the combination of syntactic function and semantic role tags allows the later addition of ARG- attributes on demand, without loss of information. Only ARG-0 and ARG-1 are used internally in the grammar to treat diathesis alternation, as explained in section 2.1.2.

Role	**Definition**	**Example**
§AG	agent	*alguien* come algo
§AGcau	causative agent	*alguien* lo hizo caer
§COG	cognizer	*alguien* se acuerda de algo
§SP	speaker	*alguien* dice algo
§PAT	patient	alguien come *algo*, *algo* se cae
§DON	donor	*alguien* da algo a alguien
§REC	recipient	dar algo a *alguien*
§BEN	benefactive	ayudar a *alguien*
§EXP	experiencer	*alguien* teme algo
§TH	theme	ver *algo*, alguien piensa en *algo*
§TP	topic domain	hablar sobre *algo*
§STI	stimulus	sentir *algo*, *algo* gusta a alguien
§RES	result	producir *algo*
§MES	message	decir *algo*
§SOA	state of affairs, fact	comprobar *algo*, exagerar *algo*
§ROLE	role	trabajar como *guía*
§COM	co-argument	coincidir con *alguien*
§ATR	static attribute	alguien es *alto*
§ATR-RES	resulting attribute	alguien se pone *nervioso*
§MAT	source material	hecho de *hierro*
§POS	possessor	alguien tiene *algo*
§CONT	content	algo contiene *azúcar*
§ID	identity	él se llama *Pedro*
§LOC	location	vivir en la *ciudad*
§ORI	origin, source	venir del *campo*
§DES	destination	ir a la *playa*
§PATH	path	pasear a lo largo del *río*
§LOC-TMP	temporal location	*em 2007, hace un año*
§ORI-TMP	temporal origin	desde *enero*
§DES-TMP	temporal destination	hasta el *domingo*
§EXT-TMP	temporal extension	durante dos *semanas*
§FREQ	frequency	*de vez en cuando, 10 veces*

Table 1a. Semantic roles

Role	Definition	Example
§EXT	extension, amount	pesar 70 *kilos*
§CAU	cause	porque ..., a causa de...
§COMP	comparation	mejor que nunca
§CONC	concession	aunque ...
§COND	condition	si..., siempre que...
§EFF	effect, consequence	fueron tantos que....
§FIN	purpose, intention	para..., destinado a...
§INS	instrument	cortar con un *cuchillo*
§MNR	manner	de esta manera, lentamente
§COM-ADV	accompanier	junto con..., com algo en la mano
§META	meta adverbial	según..., tal vez, *obviamente*
§ADV	dummy adverbial	many gerund clauses: *admitiendo ...*
§MED	pronominal/unaccus.	*se* acuerda de algo, *se* ha caído
§VOC	vocative	tranquilo, *Juan*!
§FOC	focalizer	*sólo, también*
§NEG	negation	no, sin...
§EV	event, act, process	*algo* termina/comienza
§PRED	(top) predicator	(main verb)
§DENOM	denomination	(lists, headlines)
§INC	verb incorporated	darse *cuenta* de

Table 1b. Semantic roles

The principles followed in the development of the role grammar (and therefore in the annotation of the corpus) are the following:

a) All clause-level complements (valency governed or not)[1], are systematically assigned a semantic role, including relative pronouns as well as subordinate clauses and coordinate clauses that fulfil an adverbial role. A phrase-level complement can receive a role only when a given rule can be applied to clause-level as well as phrase-level complements safely. For example, the noun *sala*, in the noun phrase *la reunión de los profesores en la sala de estudio,* receives the role §LOC, because it is a noun that refers to a place and it is preceded by the preposition *en*, and this type of structure is usually §LOC irrespectively of its syntactic function.

1 In the HISPAL parser, the main clause-level syntactic functions are the following: subject (@SUBJ), accusative object (@ACC), dative object (@DAT), prepositional object (@PIV), adverbial complement (@ADVL), subject adverbial complement (@SA), object adverbial complement (@0A), subject complement (@SC), object complement (@OC), passive agent complement (@PASS), adjunct predicative (@PRED), vocative (@VOK), top node noun phrase (@NPHR) and main verb. For more details about the symbol set, see http://beta.visl.sdu.dk/visl/es/info/symbolsopen.es.html and http://beta.visl.sdu.dk/visl /pt/info/portsymbol.html.

b) As exemplified in the example of appendix A, the role tags (at the end of line, and preceded by §) are assigned to the semantic head of the implicit semantic dependency relation, i.e. to the noun in a noun phrase, or to the dependent of a preposition. The notational convention is that semantic role tags are assigned to tokens, Constraint Grammar-style, alongside syntactic and dependency tags.

The semantic head is not necessarily equivalent to the syntactic head, and therefore the constituent's syntactic function and role function may be on different tokens. That happens mainly in the following cases:

- Prepositional phrases, where the syntactic head is the preposition, but the semantic head is the dependent.
- The semantic head of a (sub)clause (or any clause-level function) is the verb. If there is a verbal chain, the syntactic head is the first verb, while the semantic head is the last one. In addition, in clauses introduced by *el hecho de que* (like in *El hecho de que te haya llamado no significa que quiera venir a la fiesta*) the syntactic head is the noun *hecho*, while the semantic head is the verb of the subordinate clause.

c) Only one role is allowed for each token, and thus ambiguity is not allowed. Only the main verb can receive two role tags. The main verb always receives and "internal" role, as the semantic head of the clause (§PRED), and can also receive an "external" one, when the clause as a whole plays a role (§TP, §CAU, §EFF, etc.), as in the example of appendix A.

d) The rules of the grammar use syntactico-semantic information available in the input (lemma, semantic prototype of the head, type of preposition, etc.) as well as information extracted from corpus-based resources. One of our main sources to obtain semantic information about verbs has been the ADESSE database (García-Miguel and Albertuz 2005). As for the syntactic information, we have used the Spanish CorpusEye corpora (http://corp.hum.sdu.dk).

2. The grammar

We have developed a role grammar made up by 568 Constraint Grammar handwritten rules that exploit syntactic and semantic information to assign role tags to the clause-level complements. The input to the semantic role grammar is provided by the HISPAL parser (Bick, 2006a).

2.1. The linguistic approach

Linguistically, the three main difficulties in the assignment of semantic roles are the following. First, the relative lack of lexico-semantic information, which is essential for the correct assignment of semantic roles (section 2.1.1). Second, the fact that there is no clear correspondence between syntactic functions and semantic roles, for which some systematic diathesis alternations have been established (section 2.1.2). And third, the behaviour of the particle *se* (section 2.1.3), which can receive in Spanish several syntactic and therefore semantic interpretations.

2.1.1. Semantic information

The ADESSE database, that contains syntactico-semantic information about the clauses and verbs of a Spanish corpus of 1.5 million words, allows us to study the relationship between the syntactic function and semantic role in valency-governed clause-level complements.

All in all, 96 sets of verb lexemes that typically allow a given role with a given syntactic function have been defined, moving part of the lexical information into grammar. For example, the following LIST of verbs (V-SP-SUBJ) contains verbs whose subject is usually a speaker.

(a) LIST V-SP-SUBJ = "contar" "decir" "explicar" "hablar" "preguntar";

With the list in (a) and the following MAP rule, the grammar assigns the role "speaker" (§ SP) to any subject (or agent complement in the passive voice) (§ARG0&) whose dependency-parent (p) is one of the verbs of the list.

(b) MAP (§ SP) TARGET §ARG0& (p V-SP-SUBJ);

In addition to that, the semantic features of the head (whether this is an animate entity, a human, a place, a tool, etc.) can also determine the role played by the complement. In certain occasions, the semantic prototype information that is available in the HISPAL lexicon in an experimental way (Bick 2006b), has also been used: for example, rule (c) assigns the role "destination" (§DES) to a dependent of preposition (@P<) if its semantic prototype is in the set N-LOC (that contains the semantic prototypes related with a locative meaning) and its parent is in the set of prepositions PRP-DES (that contains prepositions that typically introduce this role, like *hasta, en dirección a*, etc.).

(c) MAP (§DES) TARGET @P< (0 N-LOC LINK p PRP-DES);

2.1.2. Diathesis alternation

Secondary tags (§ARG0&, §ARG1&) are used internally in the grammar to systematize the most frequent diathesis alternation constructions, allowing a more straightforward mapping between syntactic functions and semantic roles.

The tags §ARG0& and §ARG1& are assigned respectively to two types of arguments: the argument semantically closest to the predicate (0) (that corresponds to the subject in active voice) and the second closest one (1) (that corresponds to the accusative object of transitive verbs in active voice). Specifically, §ARG1& is assigned to:

- the subject of passive clauses (with participle or with *se*)
- the subject of unaccusative verbs (inherently unaccusative or with *se*)
- the accusative object of the rest of verbs (including impersonal constructions with *se*).

The tag §ARG0& is assigned to the rest of subjects and to the passive agent of the passive voice.

The grammar takes the active voice as a reference, and the roles that would be assigned to the subject in the active voice are instead assigned to §ARG0&, and the roles that would be assigned to the accusative object in the active voice, are assigned to §ARG1&.

In the following examples, the complements with the head *manifestantes*, which depend on the same verbal lemma in the three cases, receive the tag §ARG1& (and therefore the same semantic role, §BEN), by means of only one rule, despite displaying different "surface" syntactic functions (accusative object, subject and accusative object, respectively) in different syntactic constructions:

El presidente ha multado a los *manifestantes*
Los *manifestantes* han sido multados por el presidente.
Se ha multado a los *manifestantes*

2.1.3. The particle se

The particle *se* constitutes one of the main sources of ambiguity in the automatic syntactic analysis of Spanish, and at the same time its interpretation is crucial for the correct assignment of roles. In addition, the particle itself can receive several roles:

- Pronominal (§MED), with intrinsically pronominal verbs.
- "Subject" roles. The *se* in passive, impersonal or unaccusative constructions receives the role that the subject would receive in the active version of the same constructions.
- In reflexive and reciprocal constructions the *se* functions as accusative or dative object and therefore receives the corresponding role, in the same fashion as a full phrase. It should be noted that in reflexive sentences with a subject and accusative object, both functions refer to the same entity, despite receiving different roles (§AG and §PAT, respectively, for example, like in *ella se asea*).
- *se* as a form of *le* (in *se lo, se la*, etc.) functions as dative object, and therefore receives the corresponding role, in the same fashion as a full phrase.

2.2. CG3

Our Constraint Grammar uses the new CG3 compiler, that was developed by the Danish company GrammarSoft in an open source framework, in cooperation with the VISL project at the University of Southern Denmark (for documentation, see http://beta.visl.sdu.dk/constraint_grammar.html). In fact, the semantic role annotation project served as a kind of test bed for a number of CG3 features, allowing the authors to influence compiler development according to their needs.

Like previous incarnations of the Constraint Grammar paradigm (Karlsson 1995), CG3 is basically a disambiguation and information mapping methodology designed to operate on token-based grammatical tags that can be added, removed or changed in an incremental and context-sensitive fashion. Unlike previous editions of the formalism, however, CG3 explicitly moves beyond shallow syntax, by allowing the direct creation and use of dependency and other binary relations. Together with the use of arbitrary window sizes –rather than a strict sentence window– the new structural links also support anaphora and discourse markup. In terms of parsing strategy, CG3 provides for the hybridisation with other major parsing paradigms, by integrating corpus-derived statistical information and feature-attribute unification. Finally the new formalism allows the use of regular expressions, increasing rule and tag set economy and permitting the on-the-fly reference to lexical information by reference to e.g. grammatical morphemes and affixes.

In a CG rule, a context condition (in parenthesis) contains an obligatory position marker, consisting of a number indicating relative distance in tokens. The default (positive number) is a right context, while a negative number indicates a left context. For example, rule (d) maps the role §META to constituents like *en su opinión, en nuestra opinión*, etc, using distance between tokens. Specifically, the rule maps the role §META to a dependent of preposition (@P<) if the dependent itself (0) corresponds to the lemma "opinión," immediately preceded (-1) by a possessive pronoun, immediately preceded by preposition *en*.

(d) MAP (§META) TARGET @P< (0 ("opinión") LINK -1 (<poss.*>r) LINK -1 PRP-EN);

In CG3's direct use of dependency links, as we have seen in rule (c), topological position markers are replaced with p (parent), c (child) or s (sibling) relations. Thus, the context "p PRP LINK p V LINK c @SUBJ LINK 0 §AG" could be used to establish a preposition-link independent of the actual distance between the preposition and its argument, and to check for the agent-hood of the clause's subject (through its verb).

To understand the workings of a CG system, it is important to note that it is not a one-pass method. First, different layers of analysis are treated progressively, allowing higher levels (such as semantic role annotation) to use already established "safe" information from previous levels (e.g. part of speech disambiguation or syntactic function). Second, rules –though in sequential and/or heuristic order–, can be rerun in a second or third pass in a kind of bootstrapping iteration, first providing new context for later rules, then themselves profiting from the tagging or disambiguation performed by these same later rules. In a wider sense, we exploit a similar bootstrapping effect by tagging a corpus with an immature Constraint Grammar in order to extract, for instance, verb complementation patterns or preposition statistics, which can then be fed into the system as lexical valency information or word sets in the grammar.

3. The web corpus

An Internet corpus of 11.2 million words has been automatically annotated at the dependency-syntactic level with the HISPAL parser, and at the semantic role level with our role grammar. The evaluation of the results is described in section 4.1, and the relationship between semantic roles, syntax and lexical categories found after the annotation is commented in section 4.2.

The corpus has been compiled from the Internet, using a method described in Sharoff (2006) and also used for the Leeds Internet corpora (http://corpus.leeds.ac.uk/internet.html). The method is designed to ensure a uniform source and domain spread, as well as good general lexical coverage of the harvested data. First, from a corpus-based frequency list, we manually chose the top 500 words that were specific to Spanish (i.e. not at the same time Portuguese, English, etc.) and seeded an URL collection with Google lookups of fifty thousand random 3-tuples and five thousand 4-tuples from this word list. All in all we ended up with 127,500 unique URLs. Of these only 31% where classical .htm(l) addresses. About 12% were marked as pdf or WORD documents which were discarded for the current corpus project for technical reasons, but on the other hand might offer a source of more coherent or more carefully added text in the future.

Even after source selection, the downloaded data still contained considerable amounts of binary data and other non-textual data, such as unmarked (and hence undetected) pdf data and xml meta data that had to be filtered out. Other post-processing steps involved encoding normalisation (to ISO-latin-1) and sentence splitting. As the most sophisticated filter we wrote a program (*hisponly*) designed to separate Spanish text from text in other languages, in particular English text on Spanish web sites. The program computes language probabilities for each line, using specific character combinations and frequent trigger words, and discards lines with more foreign language than Spanish triggers. As a default, neutral lines without triggers (especially: short lines) inherit their language attribute from the preceding line. Since this heuristic method worked reasonably well, we did not resort to the safer, but much slower, method of looking all words up in a monolingual Spanish dictionary. Note that a certain language tolerance threshold is actually desirable, because Spanish sentences often contain minor amounts of foreign material, such as names, loan words, quotes and –nowadays– English technical terms, not least from the internet domain.

After cleaning, our data was distributed across encoding types as shown in table 2 (counting only function-carrying words, not punctuation tokens, etc.):

iso-8859-1	13.072.056 words	36,6 %
utf-8	7.374.397 words	20,7 %
Windows	2.182.745 words	6,1 %
unknown	13.079.055 words	36,6 %
all	35.708.253 words	100,0 %

Table 2. Encoding types

Since character recognition is crucial to the HISPAL parsers lexical lookup, and since its native mode is ISO-latin, a higher error percentage can be assumed even for utf-8 and windows-1252, since not all characters can be successfully filtered into iso-8859-1 (e.g. dashes and certain quotes). This is especially true for the data with unknown encoding, which for this reason was kept apart in the corpus search interface. For our semantic role annotation, the safe (known-encoding) part was further cleansed by excluding lines starting in '*' (lists) or '<', or containing "words" with double CamelCase (e.g. aBcD, typical of binary data), underscores or internal colon (URLs), resulting in a subcorpus of 11.16 million words.[2]

We decided to make the annotated corpus accessible at VISL's Corpuseye site (http://corp.hum.sdu.dk). The interface is based on the CQP engine and allows us to do normal and regular expression text searches as well as "refined" menu-based searches, where it is possible to look for any combination and sequence of lemma, word category, syntactic function or semantic role. Results can be evaluated in terms of frequency statistics and cooccurrence strengths. To accommodate for the semantic role categories, the search engine as such had to be changed since no other corpora at the site previously offered this type of information.

2 Though in principle relevant in a web corpus, we did not so far –apart from ensuring URL-uniqueness– try to treat text duplication. The phenomenon is by no means infrequent, due to extensive copying or repetition between related web sites (as well as possible "plagiarism" between unrelated websites), but it is not a trivial task to remove duplicates while at the same time provide for natural repetition of shorter text strings such as individual sentences and sub-sentence segments.

4. Results

In section 4.1 we provide some preliminary evaluation measures for the automatic annotation with semantic roles, and in 4.2 we examine the relation between semantic roles, syntax and lexical categories in the resulting annotation.

4.1. Evaluation

A soft evaluation has been carried out by manually revising the role labels in a fragment of 5,000 running words. The standard evaluation measures recall, precision and F_1 are provided. Overall, the automatic role annotation achieves a 89.0% recall, 75.4% precision and 81.6% F_1 (tp=1062, fp=347, fn=131).[3]

As expected, the results of an automatic role labelling system depend to a large extent on the precision of the previous syntactic analysis (Gildea and Palmer, 2002). If we only take into account the errors that can be attributed to the role grammar itself, ignoring the errors due to wrong input, a promising 91.4% recall, 88.6% precision and 90.0% F_1 are achieved (tp=1249, fp=160, fn=117).

In addition, this first preliminary evaluation allows us to detect some source of errors in the role grammar that can be fixed in a second developmental phase. For example, 20 of the false negatives (fn) are due to the fact that, by mistake, one of the rules of the role grammar only includes the passive clitic *se* as a target when this is placed to the right of the verb, and not when it is place to the left as well.

Among false positives (fp) that receive a wrong role tag, more linguistic issues arise. The revision shows that (manually) annotating a corpus with semantic roles (or other type of semantic information) is a difficult task, given the inherent gradual nature of semantic concepts. In some cases, it is not clear which semantic role a given complement should receive because there is no clear-cut division between them. For example, 32 errors correspond to the role §BEN and 12 to §DES, that conflict with §REC. Those three functions constitute an important source of error not only in the automatic annotation but also in the manual annotation of Spanish corpus with semantic roles (cf. Vaamonde 2008). Therefore, an accurate definition of the most conflictive roles, or systematic criteria for unclear cases needs to be established to reach a higher level of consistency.

On the other hand, 15 errors correspond to relative pronouns (*el que, el cual,* etc), for which we need to have information about the antecedent to improve the precision of its annotation.

The new annotated corpus has shown that there is still room for improvement in our grammar, which at the same time will be facilitated by the great amount of data now available. In addition, we need to carry out a more precise

---

3 tp = number of correctly detected cases; fp = number of incorrectly detected cases; fn = number of non-detected cases. Recall = tp / (tp+fn) ; Precision = tp / (tp+fp) ; F1 = (2* precision *recall) / (precision+recall)

evaluation in order to be able to compare our results more reliably with other role labelling systems for Spanish that are based on machine learning (Márquez et al. 2007, Morante et al. 2007, Surdeanu et al. 2008), which achieve an F_1 of around 86%.

4.2. The relation between semantic roles, syntax and lexical categories

With the information available in the corpus, and keeping in mind that we base our observations on non-revised, automatically annotated data, that necessarily implies a certain error margin, we can study some tendencies about the relationship between syntactic information and semantic roles. In table 3, typical correspondencies are listed for some major roles in the order of corpus frequency, covering (a) syntactic function, (b) part of speech and (c) semantic prototype (nouns only). Arrows in the function column indicate dependency attachment direction (i.e. @<ACC has its verb to the left).

As expected, we find that every role can be fulfilled by multiple syntactic functions. The less ambiguous roles in this respect are the §AG, §SP and §COG roles, that correspond always to the subject (in the active voice) or the agent complement (in the passive voice). The §TH, which is the most frequent role, corresponds always to the subject or to the accusative object. However, while the roles §SP and §COG are primarily determined by the head verb, the roles §AG and §TH cover a wide range of verbs and semantic features. In fact, they are the default roles for the functions §ARG0& and §ARG1&, respectively. In addition, since the functions of accusative object and subject are the most frequent (clause-level and valency-governed) functions in Spanish, they are also the most ambiguous in the semantic role level. They can potentially play many roles[4], especially when they are a phrase or pronoun (i.e. not a clause): both can correspond to around 20 different roles out of the 52 roles in our list, depending on the target's semantic features, the governing verb, etc.

However, certain tendencies can be observed, which might be of interest to descriptive linguistics, and could also be exploited in parser design. Thus, §AG has the highest and §BEN and §TP the lowest subject/object ratio[5], as table 4 shows.

Our data also permit to judge the markedness of pre- or postverbal position. Thus, typically human roles (§AG, §PAT, §BEN, §REC) typically occur left of the verb, while non-human roles (§TH, §LOC, §TP) are more frequent to the right. Interestingly, the rightward tendency is less marked in temporal (§LOC-TMP) than in spatial (§LOC) constituents. The roles §PRED, §DENOM, §MED

---

4 Cf. appendices A and B for corpus example sentences for every role of the subject and accusative object, respectively.

5 The ratio is here defined as subject frequency divided by the sum of subject and object frequency.

and §VOK are dummy roles, since they always correspond to the same and unique syntactic tags.

Role	Syntactic function[6]	Part of speech[7]	Semantic prototype class[8]
§TH (14.6.%)	@<ACC (51%), @SUBJ>, @<SUBJ	N (57%), PERS, INF, VFIN	<sem-c> (10%), <f>, <f-psych>
§AG (6.6%) (~§SP, §COG)	@SUBJ> (77%), @<SUBJ, @<PASS	N (45%), PROP, INDP, PERS	<Hprof> (7%), <sem-c>, <HH>, <H>
§ATR (6%)	@<SC (65%), @PRED>, @<PRED	N, ADJ, PCP	<act> (7%), <sem-c>, <H>
§BEN (5%)	@ACC> (37%), @<DAT, @DAT>	INDP (35%), PERS, PRP-N, N	<HH> (13%), <H>, <Hprof>
§LOC-TMP (4%)	@<ADVL (37%), @ADVL>, @N<	ADV (34%), PRP-N, N, VFIN, PRP-INF	<per> (31%), <temp>, <dur>
§EV (3.7%)	@<ACC (54%), @SUBJ>, @<SUBJ	N (85%), INF, VFIN	<act> (33%), <act-s>, <act-d>
§LOC (3%)	@<ADVL (39%), @N<, @ADVL>, @<SA	PRP-N (55%), PRP-PROP, ADV, VFIN	<L> (10%), <Lh>, <Lcountry>
§REC (1.6%)	@<DAT (40%), @DAT>, @<ADVL	PERS (41%), PRP-N, PRP-PROP	<H> (9%), <act>, <Hprof>, <HH>
§TP (1.5%)	@FS-<ACC (34%), @<ACC, @<ADVL, @<PIV	VFIN (33%), N, PRP-N	<sem-c> (14%), <f>, <act>, <sem-s>, <ac>
§PAT (0.4%)	@SUBJ> (65%), @<ACC, @<SUBJ	N (55%), INDP, PROP	<sem-c> (7%), <f>, <H>, <HH>

Table 3. Relation between semantic roles, syntax and lexical categories

6 SUBJ=subject, ACC=direct object, PASS=passive agent, DAT=dative, ADVL=adverbial, PIV=prepositional object, N<=postnominal, FS-ACC=finite subclause (que/interrogative clause).

7 N=noun, PROP=proper noun, PERS=personal pronoun, INDP=independent pronoun, VFIN=finite verb, INF=infinitive, PRP-N=prepositional phrase (pp) with noun, PRP-PROP=pp with proper noun.

8 <H>=human, <Hprof>=professional, <HH>=human group/organisation, <sem-c>= cognitive semantic product, <f>=feature, <f-psych>=psychological feature/emotion, <act>= action, <act-s>=speech act, <act-d>="do"-act, <L>=location, <Lh>=human/functional place, <Lcountry>=country, <per>=period, <temp>=point in time, <dur>=duration, <ac>=abstract countable. Due to unresolved polysemy or subspecifications, more than one tag may occur with each noun.

Role	Frequency	Subject/object ratio	L/R ratio (Left or right of verb)
§TH	14.6 %	25.4 %	31.0 %
§AG	6.6 %	97.2 %	78.4 %
§ATR	6.0 %	-	21.7 %
§BEN	5.0 %	3.2 %	59.2 %
§LOC-TMP	4.0 %	23.7 %	42.6 %
§EV	3.7 %	43.4 %	30.0 %
§LOC	3.0 %	0.0 %	23.0 %
§REC	1.6 %	87.8 %	44.7 %
§TP	1.5 %	4.0 %	7.5 %
§PAT	0.4 %	80.0 %	68.5 %

Table 4. Frequency, subject/object ratio and left to right ratio

Finally, with regard to the relationship between semantic roles and syntactic categories, the following tendencies stand out: the roles §EFF and §COND are always played by a clause, while the roles §DES, §ORI, §ID, §COM-ADV, §COM, §ROLE and §MAT are always introduced by a preposition.

For annotation examples, we refer to the grammatical search interface we established for our Internet corpus, (http://corp.hum.sdu.dk/cqp.es.html), with both concordances and statistics.

5. Conclusions and future work

Automatically assigning role tags to clause-level complements is a difficult task. First, it relies on a previous syntactic analysis, that in the case of automatic analysis systems imply a certain error margin. Second, the mapping between syntactic functions and semantic roles needs a kind of linguistic information that is not widely available from current corpora, or is difficult to use because of the disagreement on the inventory of roles in the different resources. And third, semantic annotation (of roles or other type of semantic information), automatically or manually driven, is a difficult task because of the inherent gradual nature of semantic concepts, that conflicts with the discrete categories used in corpus annotation.

However, as our system is rule-based, we expect a positive bootstrapping effect from the construction of corpora automatically annotated with semantic roles, such as our Spanish web corpus. As opposed to manually annotated data, there are no volume constraints, and the sheer size of such corpora will allow the statistical identification of patterns and structures that in turn can be used to improve the valency and semantic class lexica underlying both the syntactic and role parsers, improving the scope and performance of the rules at each new iteration of the bootstrapping process described. Future work will also have to explore the possibility of integrating our semantic role annotator in an applicative context such as Question Answering or Information Extraction.

Appendix A. Tagging sample

"<Los>"
"el" <fr:83> <f:1835430> <artd> <exdem> DET M P @>N #1->2
"<fabricantes>"
"fabricante" <cjt-head> <fr:0> <f:17> <'producer'> <HHorg> N M/F P @SUBJ> §ARG0& **§AG** #2->7
"<y>"
"y" <fr:100> <f:1904300> <Rare> <co-subj> KC @CO #3->2
"<productores>"
"productor" <cjt> <fr:98> <f:9998> <'producer'> <HHorg> N M P @SUBJ> §ARG0& **§AG** #4->2
"<tienen>"
"tener" <fr:100> <f:68529> <se:12> <vq> <x+PCP> <xque> <vdb> <vr> <vt> <'have'> <mv?> <aux> <mv> V PR 3P IND VFIN @FS-STA #5->0
"<que>"
"que" <clb> <fr:38> <f:1720876> <komp> <corr> KS @PRT-AUX< #6->5
"<probar>"
"probar" <fr:100> <f:1881> <se:45> <a^xp> <vdb> <vr> <vq> <vt> <'prove'> <mv?> <mv> V INF @ICL-AUX< **§PRED** #7->5
"<que>"
"que" <clb> <clb-fs> <fr:38> <f:1720876> <komp> <corr> KS @SUB #8->11
"<sus>"
"su" <fr:100> <f:335709> <poss 3S/P> <si> DET M/F P @>N #9->10
"<productos>"
"producto" <fr:84> <f:39275> <'product'> <ac-cat> N M P @SUBJ> §ARG0& **§TH** #10->11
"<son>"
"ser" <fr:97> <f:260305> <x+PCP> <vK> <vk+ADJ> <vk+N> <'be'> <mv?> <mv> V PR 3P IND VFIN @FS-<ACC **§PRED §TP** #11->7
"<seguros>"
"seguro" <fr:100> <f:6442> <'sure'> ADJ M P @<SC **§ATR** #12->11
"<$.>"
"$." #13->0

```
"<$¶>"
	"$¶" #1->0
</s>
```

Appendix B. Semantic roles of the subject (in alphabetical order)
§AG: Con ellos el **usuario** puede buscar y visualizar fragmentos encontrados y descargarlos o enviarlos por e-mail usando el navegador web habitual y sin necesidad de estar en casa o en la oficina.

§AGCau: Y la **evolución** hace aflorar eso que está implícito en las entrañas de las cosas.

§BEN: Si el PP se refunda **UPN** se va a llevar una gran sorpresa.

§COG: El **presidente** de EA de Gipuzkoa Iñaki Galdós consideró ayer que el pacto con el PNV y Ezker_Batua-Aralar resulta <<insuficiente para avanzar en un proceso de normalización política e incluso para un escenario de gobernabilidad y se mostró partidario de implicar al PSE.

§COMP: Madeleine Slade quien estuvo durante 23 años al lado de el Mahatma indiao hasta que éste murió asesinado en 1948 está caracterizada en el cine por la nueva estrella Geraldine James que es mucho más guapa que **yo** según reconoció la interesada cuando le fueron presentadas las primeras fotografías poco antes de su muerte.

§CONT: Estos **criterios** sobre apertura se contenían también en el informe Cashman que aprobamos con amplia mayoría hace dos semanas en Estrasburgo.

§DON: En 1963 la **CIA** le envió de regalo un traje de buzo impregnado con bacilo de tuberculosis, intentó plantar un caracol explosivo en un arrecife donde Castro hacía pesca submarina y hasta probó con un bolígrafo envenenado.

§EV: Las **investigaciones** de el Hubble de enero de 1997 han mostrado interacciones interesantes entre las jóvenes estrellas de el cúmulo de el Trapecio con los discos protoplanetarios.

§EXP: A su juicio los doce **consejeros** de el Ejecutivo foral de UPN-CDN se han sentido también atacados en su propia dignidad cuando han visto que al presidente de su comunidad se le insultaba de manera personal y se ponía en duda su dignidad personal como la dignidad del cargo.

§EXT-TMP: Ya sólo quedan 13 días de Bush y **13 días** pasan rápido, afirmó Sebastián en unas declaraciones.

§INC: La misma **pregunta** se podría hacer en otro aspecto si, dice John Edwards o „Tubby Banerjee", dos brillantes jóvenes ejecutivos con buenos grados, y que conocen bien el negocio, hubieran sido promovidos al tablero.

§MES: Asimismo habilitará un sistema eficaz para recibir y responder las **consultas,** los **reclamos** y las **denuncias** de los beneficiarios de las instituciones educativas y de las empresas de transporte.

§NEG: El presidente del Ejecutivo foral hizo hincapié en que su formación no quiere romper el pacto con el PP pero advirtió de que tampoco quiere que **nadie** pueda coartar nuestra libertad para adoptar nuestras propias decisiones.

§PAT: **Cinco** de nuestros compañeros fueron detenidos en la 26 comisaria de Pudahuel luego de constatar lesiones fueron vejados maltratados y torturados.

§POS: **Fidel** tiene un raro olfato primero para conocer a las personas y segundo para presentir las emboscadas.

§REC: Aparentemente todos estos descubrimientos se perdieron por algún tiempo de modo que fue Christian_Huygens **quien** recibió principalmente el crédito de su redescubrimiento independiente en 1656 por ejemplo por Charles Messier cuando la agregó a su catálogo el 4 de marzo de 1679.

§RES: El ex espía cree que aquella **cápsula** de veneno fue fabricada por la CIA como parte de un plan tramado en 1960 con la mafia de Chicago que fue expuesto la semana pasada cuando la agencia desclasificó más de 700 páginas de antiguos documentos.

§SOA: Abundan problemas como la basura, la **destrucción** de los manglares y la contaminación por agroquímicos.

§SP: En concreto la **coalición** de izquierdas ha señalado que no formará parte del futuro ejecutivo de la Diputación si no se paraliza la construcción de la futura incineradora de residuos sólidos urbanos.

§STI: **James Dean** gustó mucho entonces y sigue haciéndolo en la actualidad en todo el mundo.

§TH: Precisamente la **bandera** de la defensa de estos proyectos constituye un elemento clave en la negociación de un programa de gobierno foral.

§TP: No hay financiaciones indiscriminadas, sino que se comprueba la **calidad** de las acciones, se insiste en ella y las propias acciones deben ser objeto de un control y seguimiento y sus resultados han de hacerse públicos.

Appendix C. Semantic roles of the accusative object

§BEN: La posibilidad de una negociación entre EA y el PSE en Gipuzkoa podría abrir un debate en el primer partido entre quienes defienden la autonomía de la ejecutiva que preside Galdós para trazar su política de alianzas y quienes consideran que afecta a la dirección nacional porque temen que un pacto de esta naturaleza desestabilice el **Gobierno Vasco**.

§CONT: Un hombre devuelve un bolso extraviado que contenía un **cheque** de 30.000 euros.

§DES: Las Asambleas Continentales de Europa, África y América nos han señalado **caminos** nuevos, senderos inexplorados, temas apenas balbuceados, incertidumbres e interrogantes propios de nuestro tiempo.

§EV: El candidato de la unidad regional exhortó a los partidos nacionales que eviten las **imposiciones** y **maniobras** desde Caracas que tanto daño le han causado a la unidad en las regiones.

§EXP: La que más **me** fascina es precisamente aquella de la que menos sé.

§EXT-TMP: Tras nuestra negativa de retirar la instrumentaria mientras ellos los pacos no explicaran la razón de la parcial suspensión de la actividad a los vecinos que esperaban dicho acto los pacos procedieron a llamar refuerzos que demoraron **menos** de 5 minutos en presentarse en el lugar.

§EXT: La encuestadora Zogby le otorga un 50 por **ciento** contra un 43 por ciento de su rival republicano.

§INC: Señor presidente, la comunicación de la Comisión constituye, creo, un verdadero hito en la historia de la política social, porque pone fin a un período en el que la **mención** a la tercera edad se hacía desde la consideración de estas personas como la generación de los retirados.

§LOC-TMP: La idea lleva ya un **tiempo** en su cabeza.

§NEG: Habló durante 4,51 minutos hasta que el presidente del tribunal le cortó porque lo que estaba diciendo **nada** tenía que ver con el juicio.

§ORI-TMP: Vinieron amigos que habían estado con él hace cinco **años**, otro que estaba en Asturias.

§PAT: El programa puede eliminar todos los **rastros** de aplicaciones monitorizadas o borrar igualmente aplicaciones no monitorizadas.

§PATH: Miembros del aparato militar cruzaron hace tres semanas la **frontera** para entregar los explosivos al comando.

§REC: Para apoyar la creatividad y el avance de los conocimientos hace falta identificar las nuevas generaciones de investigadores dotándo**las** de los medios de independencia necesarios para que desarrollen sus propias ideas, estima Bertil Anderson, director ejecutivo de la Fundación Europea para la ciencia FEC y miembro del Comité Nobel.

§RES: Galdós subrayó en una conferencia de prensa en San Sebastián las claves políticas que entiende que se derivan de las últimas elecciones una vez que en Gipuzkoa el socialista Buen ha mostrado su preferencia por formar un **gobierno** de coalición entre el PSE y EA en la Diputación foral.

§SOA: Pero también sé, porque a mi me suele ocurrir, que a un presidente que tiene la cabeza en una cuestión que reclama toda la **atención** social y mediática de el país no le vayas con un tema regional.

§STI: El engorde con melamina podría ser frecuente en otros sectores, lo que ha hecho a las autoridades ordenar el análisis de los piensos para animales pero no habría causado entre la población fallos renales masivos como los provocados en bebés y mascotas estadounidenses gracias a que los adultos gozan una **dieta** más variada.

§TH: Galdós consideró que para avanzar en un proceso de normalización política en Euskal Herria hay que tener en cuenta al Partido Socialista y citó como referencia a tener en cuenta el **diálogo** entre el PSN y Nafarroa Bai.

§TP: Amigos soy Adulfo Pistarino el Moderador del Blog en el cual sus eminencias Pablo Fattini y Martin Von Pazzz discutirán variados **temas** sin tal vez llegar a una conclusión ya que estos prohombres tienen cada uno una manera de ver la vida [...].

References

Alonso, L., J. Capilla, I. Castellón, A. Fernández, and G. Vázquez, G. (2007): "The Sensem Project: syntactico-semantic annotation of sentences in Spanish," in *Recent Advances in Natural Language Processing IV. Selected papers from RANLP 2005. Current Issues in Linguistic Theory,* John Benjamins, 89-98.

Bick, E. (2006a): "A constraint grammar-based parser for Spanish," in *Proceedings of TIL 2006 - 4th Workshop on Information and Human Language Technology.*

Bick, E. (2006b): "Noun sense tagging: semantic prototype annotation of a Portuguese treebank," in J. Hajic and J. Nivre (eds.), *Proceedings of TLT 2006*, 127-138.

Bick, E. (2007).: "Automatic semantic role annotation for Portuguese," in *Proceedings of TIL 2007 - 5th Workshop on Information and Human Language Technology / Anais do XXVII Congresso da SBC*, 1713-1716.

Fillmore, C. (1968): "The case for case," in E. Bach and R. Harms (eds.), *Universals in linguistic theory*, Holt, Reinehart and Winston, New York.

García-Miguel, J. and F. Albertuz (2005): "Verbs, semantic classes and semantic roles in the ADESSE project," in K. Erk, A. Melinger and S. Schulte im Walde (eds.), *Proceedings of the Interdisciplinary Workshop on the Identification and Representation of Verb Features and Verb Classes.*

Gildea, D. and M. Palmer (2002): "The necessity of parsing for predicate argument recognition," in *ACL 2002.*

Hajicova, E., J. Panenova and P. Sgall (2000): *A Manual for Tectogrammatic Tagging of the Prague Dependency Treebank*, Technical report, UFAL/CKL Technical Report TR-2000-09, Charles University, Chzech Republic.

Jackendoff, R. (1972): *Semantic interpretation in Generative Grammar*, Cambridge, MIT Press.

Karlsson et al. (1995): *Constraint Grammar - A Language-Independent System for Parsing Unrestricted Text*, Natural Language Processing, No 4., Berlin / New York, Mouton de Gruyter.

Morante, R. and A. V. den Bosch (2007): "Memory-based semantic role labelling," in *Proceedings of the International Conference on Recent Advances in Natural Language Processing (RANLP-2007*), 388-394.

Màrquez, L., L. Villarejo and M. Martí (2007): "Semeval-2007 Task 09: Multilevel semantic annotation of Catalan and Spanish," in *SemEval 2007. Proceddings of the 4th International Workshop on Semantic Evaluations*, 42-47.

Sharoff, S. (2006): "Open-source corpora: using the net to fish for linguistic data," in *International Journal of Corpus Linguistics* 11, 4, 435-462.

Surdeanu, M., R. Morante and L. Màrquez (2008): "Analysis of joint inference strategies for the semantic role labelling of Spanish and Catalan," in *Lecture Notes in Computer Science*, 4919, 206-218.

Taulé, M., M. Martí and M. Recasens (2008): "AnCora: multilevel annotated corpora for Catalan and Spanish," in *Proceedings of LREC 2008.*

Vaamonde, G. (2008): "Algunos problemas concretos en la anotación de papeles semánticos. Breve estudio comparativo a partir de los datos de AnCora, SenSem y ADESSE.," *Procesamiento del lenguaje natural*, 41, 233-240.

Useful statistics for corpus linguistics

Stefan Th. Gries
University of California, Santa Barbara

1. Introduction

By its very nature, corpus linguistics is a distributional discipline. In fact, it has been argued that corpora as such contain nothing but distributional frequency data, more specifically distributional data of two or three types, depending on how one wants to look at it:

a) frequencies of occurrence of linguistic elements, which can be studied from two different perspectives:
   - how frequent are morphemes or words or patterns/constructions in (parts of) a corpus? This information can be provided in various different forms of frequency lists;
   - how evenly are morphemes or words or patterns/constructions distributed across (parts of) a corpus? This information can be provided in the form of various dispersion statistics;

b) frequencies of co-occurrence: how often do linguistic elements such as morphemes, words, patterns/construction co-occur with another linguistic element from this set or a position in a text.

In other words, in the first instance and from a purist's perspective, all a corpus returns is whole numbers greater than or equal to 0, namely frequencies of how often something occurred in a corpus. Everything else that (corpus) linguists are actually interested in must then be operationalized on the basis of some kind of frequencies.

While the degree of commitment to this a bit more radical view may be subject to debate, it is nevertheless probably fair to say that, for these reasons, branches of linguistics that have been using corpora or text databases have always been among the most quantitatively oriented subdisciplines of the field. While this would typically lead to the expectation that corpus linguists are very much statistically-minded – after all, statistics is the scientific discipline that teaches us how to deal with quantitative distributions – it is unfortunately also fair to say that not all corpus-based studies utilize the available statistical methods to their fullest extent. In fact, it is only in the last few years or so that corpus linguists have begun to use more, more sophisticated, and more comprehensive tools, both for handling of corpus data as well as for the statistical analysis of the resulting data. However, this trend is new enough for the discipline to not have evolved to a state where such resources are widely used and taught, and so far there is only one dedicated introduction to statistics for corpus linguists (Oakes 1998), which in spite of its merits at the time of publication is beginning to be a bit dated, plus one introduction to corpus linguistics with a detailed overview chapter on statistical methods (Gries 2009a).

In this chapter, I provide a brief survey of several statistical concepts and methods that are relevant to two stages of corpus-linguistic applications. Sections 2 discusses basic concepts regarding the kinds of distributional data mentioned above as well as very simple descriptive methods to use such data: absolute and relative frequencies of occurrence (Section 2.1), the distribution of linguistic elements across a corpus (Section 2.2), and statistical measures for frequencies of co-occurrence (Section 2.3). More specifically, I discuss several widely-used measures or methods, but then also point to additional less widely used methods which I think the field as a whole should consider more often.

Section 3 deals with statistical methods whose purpose is to evaluate the data obtained from the methods in Section 2 and which often involve significance levels and *p*-values. Once frequencies of (co-)occurrence have been obtained, the corpus linguist typically wants to explore and describe the interrelation(s) between what may be causes and effects in a monofactorial or a multifactorial way (Sections 3.1 and 3.2 respectively) or detect structure in large and often messy corpus data (Section 3.3).

Limitations of space require two comments before we begin. First, I cannot discuss the very foundations of statistical thinking, the notions of (null and alternative) hypotheses, (independent and dependent) variables, Occam's razor, etc., but must assume the reader is already familiar with these (or reads up on them in, say, Gries 2009a: Ch. 5). Second, most of the time I cannot exemplify the relevant methods in detail. The number of collocational statistics (25+), the number of dispersion measures and adjusted frequencies (20+), the technicalities of logistic regression or cluster analysis make it impossible to, for example, provide practical examples with the statistical code to analyze that example, which is why I will provide references for further reading in each (sub)section.

2. Distributional data from corpora

2.1. Frequencies of occurrence

The most basic corpus-based statistic is of course the *observed absolute frequency* of some phenomenon. For example, looking for the word forms *give* and *bring* in the British Component of the International Corpus of English returns 441 and 197 matches respectively. A similarly simple example involves the observed frequencies within a part of the corpus: *give* occurs 297 and 144 times in the spoken part and the written part respectively whereas *bring* occurs 128 and 69 times in the spoken part and the written part respectively. Obviously, there are more occurrences of *give* in this corpus than *bring*; obviously there are more occurrences of *give* and *bring* in the spoken component of the corpus than in the written component of the corpus

2.1.1. Normalization, comparison, and logged frequencies

While this is so basic as to hardly merit discussion, it is a point of entry for some other concepts. First, it is necessary to point out that a higher frequency occurrence of some element in some corpus (part) does not automatically that the element observed more often is more frequent because the observed frequencies are of course dependent on the sizes of the corpus parts that are compared. In this case, it is possible to directly compare the observed absolute frequencies of *give* and *bring* in the ICE-GB, but it is not possible to directly compare the observed absolute frequencies of *give* and *bring* across the spoken and written components because these two components are not equally large. Instead, what is needed are the *observed relative frequencies*, which are typically normalized and reported as frequencies per 1,000 or 1,000,000 words.

In this particular case, the ICE-GB contains 1,061,263 words, which means that the observed relative frequencies of *give* and *bring* in the whole corpus become those in (1), and for the above reason the ratio of these two relative frequencies is identical to those of the absolute frequencies:

(1) a. *give* (whole corpus): $\frac{441 \cdot 1000000}{1061263} \approx 415.54$

b. *bring* (whole corpus): $\frac{197 \cdot 1000000}{1061263} \approx 185.63$

However, the situation changes for the spoken and the written data. The spoken and the written components contain 637,682 and 423,581 words respectively. Thus, the relative frequencies for *give* and *bring* in the spoken and written data become those shown in (2), and it is obvious that just because the observed absolute frequency of *give* in speaking is about two times as high as that in writing does not mean that this is the actual ratio between *give*'s frequencies in speaking and in writing, which is approximately 1.37:

(2) a. *give* spoken: $\frac{297 \cdot 1000000}{637682} \approx 465.75$, and written: $\frac{144 \cdot 1000000}{423581} \approx 339.96$

b. *bring* spoken: $\frac{128 \cdot 1000000}{637682} \approx 200.73$, and written: $\frac{69 \cdot 1000000}{423581} \approx 162.9$

It is therefore important to bear in mind that one can only compare corpus frequencies or use them to make statements about what is more frequent when the frequencies have been normalized.

Second, relative frequencies can be used to compare different corpora with each other just by computing the *relative frequency ratio*, the quotient of the relative frequencies of a word in both corpora (Damerau 1993). For example, consider the Wikipedia entries on the two multi-purpose programming languages Perl and Python, which at some point of time contained 6,065 and 5,596 words respectively. Table 1 shows the 10 largest and smallest relative frequency ratios for words occurring in both entries (with their frequencies of occurrence). A statistically more elaborate way to compare corpus frequencies, which often yields similar results, has been popularized as the method of key words (cf. Scott 1997).

Words characteristic for Perl			**Words characteristic for Python**		
Word	**Frequencies**	**RelFreqRatio**	**Word**	**Frequencies**	**RelFreqRatio**
perl	249 : 8	28.72	*python*	3 : 208	0.01
source	14 : 1	12.92	*classes*	1 : 12	0.08
interpreter	27 : 2	12.46	*set*	1 : 11	0.08
statement	13 : 1	11.99	*objects*	1 : 9	0.09
regular	24 : 2	11.07	*within*	1 : 8	0.1
returns	11 : 1	10.15	*function*	2 : 14	0.12
structures	10 : 1	9.23	*numbers*	1 : 7	0.13
write	9 : 1	8.3	*well*	1 : 7	0.13
tasks	9 : 1	8.3	*style*	2 : 13	0.13
community	9 : 1	8.3	*dictionary*	1 : 6	0.14

Table 1. Highest and lowest relative frequency ratios for the Wikipedia entries for *Perl* and *Python*

Third, it is also worth mentioning that there are also a variety of contexts in which one does not use the observed absolute or relative frequencies of linguistic elements but the logarithms of their observed absolute frequencies. This is especially useful when corpus frequencies are correlated with other data such as data from psycholinguistic experiments (e.g. reaction times). The log transformation – usually to the base of 2, sometimes to the bases of *e* (2.71828) or 10 – has the effect that the otherwise very skewed distribution of word frequencies is linearized and allows us to use simpler linear correlation measures to compare the corpus frequencies with other data.

2.1.2. Further hints: useful but underutilized statistics

One very useful statistic is *entropy* H or *relative entropy* H_{rel}. Entropy is the average amount of uncertainty of a random variable: the larger H or H_{rel}, the more random a distribution is and, at the same time, the more difficult it is to predict an element's occurrence. The entropy and the relative entropy of a distribution with n observations are defined as in (3):

(3) a. $$H = \sum_{i=1}^{n} (p(x) \cdot \log_2 p(x)) \text{ with } 0 \cdot \log_2 0 = 0$$

b. $$H_{rel} = {}^{H}\!/_{H_{\max}} = {}^{H}\!/_{\log_2 n}$$

Since H is correlated with n, H_{rel} allows to compare entropies of distributions of different *n*s. For example, the frequencies of the inflectional forms of the two verbs *give* and *sing* in the ICE-GB are as follows:

give: 441	*gives*: 105	*giving*: 132	*gave*: 175	*given*: 376
sing: 38	*sings*: 2	*singing*: 45	*sang*: 3	*sung*: 2

Table 2. Observed frequencies of *give*'s and *sing*'s inflectional forms in the ICE-GB

If one knew the above frequencies of *give* and was asked to predict what the next form of the lemma *give* in a corpus would be, one would guess *give*, because that form is the most frequent form. However, there would be a relatively large amount of uncertainty because *given* is also fairly frequent, and even the other verb forms are not at all infrequent. With the lemma *sing*, the situation is different: one would guess *singing*, but in general the uncertainty is lower: while *sing* is also relatively frequent, the other three forms are very infrequent. The entropy values capture that and show that the average uncertainty for the lemma *give* is larger: H for the lemma *give* is 2.1 (H_{rel}=0.91) while H for the lemma *sing* is only 1.4 (H_{rel}=0.62). Entropies are an interesting and revealing way to summarize the randomness of distributions that has many applications (one of which will be discussed below).

One problem that arises often especially when one uses smaller corpora is that of observed frequencies of zero, i.e. when a particular linguistic expression is not observed at all. While the non-occurrence of an expression may in some cases be meaningful, in fact even expected, in other cases it is not meaningful and/or can be problematic for statistical estimation purposes. A rather ingenuous method to estimate the probability of unseen items, and accordingly adjust the probability of all attested items, is called Good-Turing estimation. While the underlying mathematics are somewhat complicated, Gale and Sampson (1995) provide an accessible introduction to this approach (as well as R code for its implementation).

Another final, more frequent and potentially much more threatening problem is based on the fact that, strictly speaking, observed frequencies and all statistics based on them can in fact be very misleading. This threat is the topic of the next section.

2.2. Dispersion and adjusted frequencies

For what follows, it is useful to briefly realize what an observed relative frequency is. Imagine a corpus consisting of three parts of seven elements each that is shown in (4), where the corpus parts are delimited by "|":

(4) q w w e e e r | q r r t t t t | q y y y y y y

The observed absolute frequency of *y* in this corpus is 6, the observed relative frequency is $^6/_{21}$=28.57%. A moment's thought will reveal that this relative frequency is in fact a mean, namely the mean one of the distribution when every *y* is changed to 1 and every other character to 0:

(5) 0 0 0 0 0 0 0 | 0 0 0 0 0 0 0 | 0 1 1 1 1 1 1

As one learns in every introduction to statistics, "never provide a mean without also providing an index of dispersion." This rule applies here, too. The overall mean does not reveal that the distribution of *y* across the three is extremely uneven: While *y*'s overall relative frequency is 28.57%, its relative frequencies across the corpus varies between 0 and 85.71%, and neither of these frequencies is summarized well by the overall mean. Note how *q*, on the other hand, has a perfectly regular distribution: its overall relative frequency is 14.29%, as is its relative frequency in each corpus part.

Situations like these can not only be rather frequent but can also potentially undermine any statistic based on frequencies. If an overall corpus frequency is high, then this will be reflected in whatever other statistic is based on that frequency, but if the high frequency is completely unrepresentative of most of the corpus, the results will be of dubitable value only.

In order to cope with this kind of problem, two different but related solutions have been proposed: on the one hand, one can quantify the degree of *dispersion* of the counted linguistic expression in the corpus so that one knows how well the corpus frequency reflects the expressions overall distribution. On the other hand, one can downgrade the observed frequency to a so-called *adjusted frequency* in proportion to the degree that the expression in point is unevenly distributed in the corpus.

There is too large a number of dispersion measures and adjusted frequencies here to discuss them all, and unfortunately there is also as yet little work, let alone agreement, on which measure is best (cf. Gries 2008, 2009c), which is why I will just mention the most recently proposed dispersion measure, DP_{norm} (for normalized deviation of proportions). This measure ranges from 0 to 1, where values around zero mean that the relative frequencies of occurence of the linguistic expression in the corpus are directly proportional to the sizes of the corpus parts whereas large values close to 1 mean the linguistic expression is distributed very unevenly among the corpus parts. For *y* and *q*, DP_{norm} amounts to 1 and 0 respectively: *y*'s maximally uneven distribution is clearly reflected.

The importance of (under)dispersion cannot be overestimated. If, as mentioned above, every corpus statistic ultimately relies on frequencies, then frequencies based on uneven distributions can undermine all subsequent analytical steps, which is why measures of dispersion should be provided for virtually all corpus frequencies.

2.3. *Frequencies of co-occurrence*

The second most basic corpus statistic involves frequency of co-occurrence of linguistic expressions. Unfortunately, the existing terminology is not used consistently by different researchers; the following are kinds of co-occurrence that are distinguished:

- co-occurrence of words (*collocation*);
- co-occurrence of words and constructions/patterns (*collostruction* or one sense of *colligation*);
- co-occurrence of constructions/patterns (another sense of *colligation*);
- words and textual positions (another sense of *colligation*).

The most basic way of providing co-occurrence information is again just providing the observed absolute frequency. For example, in the ICE-GB *give* and *bring* (words) occur as a ditransitive verb (the pattern) 232 and 2 times respectively. However, since we already know that *give* and *bring* are differently frequent in this corpus (cf. above), the absolute observed frequencies are not the meaningful statistic to report, and the next section will explore more suitable alternatives.

2.3.1. Expected frequencies and association measures

Since the absolute frequencies cannot be directly compared, what is needed is a measure that takes the overall frequencies of *give* and *bring* into consideration. The most frequent strategy is to instead report a statistical *association measure* between the words and the construction. More than 20 such measures have been proposed in the literature (cf. Evert 2004 and Wiechmann 2008), but nearly all of them are based on 2×2 co-occurrence tables of the kind exemplified in Table 2 for *give*. For such a table, one needs the frequency of *give* (441), the frequency of *give* as a ditransitive verb (232), the frequency of ditransitive verbs (1,803), and the frequency of all verbs (138510), which are italicized in Table 3, from which the missing frequencies can be computed by subtraction.

	Construction *ditransitive*	Not construction *ditransitive*	Totals
Word *give*	*232*	209	*441*
Not word *give*	1571	136498	138069
Totals	*1803*	136707	*138510*

Table 3. Observed co-occurrence frequencies of *give* and the ditransitive in the ICE-GB

The most frequent measure more useful than the observed frequency of 232 include *pointwise Mutual Information*, the *t*-score, and maybe $-\log_{10} p_{Fisher\text{-}Yates\ exact\ test}$. They all require to first compute the frequencies one would expect if give and the ditransitive occurred together only randomly, which are computed as shown in Table 4.

	Construction *ditransitive*	Not construction *ditransitive*	Totals
Word *give*	$\frac{441 \cdot 1803}{138510} \approx 5.7$	$\frac{441 \cdot 136707}{138510} \approx 435.3$	441
Not word *give*	$\frac{138069 \cdot 1803}{138510} \approx 1797.3$	$\frac{138069 \cdot 136707}{138510} \approx 136271.7$	138069
Totals	1803	136707	138510

Table 4. Expected co-occurrence frequencies of *give* and the ditransitive in the ICE-GB

On the basis of these frequencies, the three association measures are:[1]

(5) pointwise *MI*: $\log_2 \frac{\text{observed frequency}}{\text{expected frequency}} = \log_2 \frac{232}{5.7} \approx 5.3$

(6) *t*: $\log_2 \frac{\text{observed frequency - expected frequency}}{\sqrt{\text{expected frequency}}} = \log_2 \frac{232 - 5.7}{\sqrt{5.7}} \approx 94.8$

(7) $-\log_{10} p_{Fisher\text{-}Yates\ exact\ test}$: $-\log_{10}(8.7 \cdot 10^{-315}) \approx 314.1$

If pointwise *MI* and *t* are positive, then the observed frequency of co-occurrence is larger than the expected by chance, and the larger all association measures, the stronger this effect is. Without much experience, these values are hard to interpret, but these are all rather high values which point to a very strong posi-

1 The formula for the Fisher-Yates exact test involves summing multiple *p*-values derived from the hypergeometric distribution and is too complex to be provided here; cf. the above references.

tive association between *give* on the one hand and ditransitives on the other hand; this is probably easiest to see from the very large difference between the observed frequency of 232 and the very small frequency expected by chance of 5.7. Usually, however, analogous computations are performed for (many) different verbs, and the values for *give* are set into perspective by comparing them to those for *bring*:

(8) pointwise *MI*: $\log_2 \frac{\text{observed frequency}}{\text{expected frequency}} \approx -0.4$

(9) *t*: $\log_2 \frac{\text{observed frequency - expected frequency}}{\sqrt{\text{expected frequency}}} \approx -0.4$

(10) $-\log_{10} p_{\textit{Fisher-Yates exact test}}$: $-\log_{10}(0.53) \approx 0.28$

The negative values for pointwise *MI* and *t* in (8) to (10) show that *bring* occurs less often in the ditransitive (2) than would be expected by chance (2.6), but all measures show that this dispreference of *bring* to occur in the ditransitive is not strong.

The most frequent application of such co-occurrence measures is in fact not in the domain of collostructions/colligations, but in the domain of collocations, i.e., the association between words. The overall logic is the same: the co-occurrence frequency becomes the co-occurrence frequency of the two words, the overall frequencies of the word and the construction become the overall frequencies of the two words, and the frequency of all verbs becomes the corpus size in words; the association measure is then interpreted the same way.

2.3.2. Further hints: properties of association measures

Just like with the dispersion measures, a large number of association measures has been proposed. Unlike with dispersion measures, however, the properties of association measures are better known. In general, it is probably fair to say that association measures often behave similarly, but unfortunately they can still output very different results and it is therefore necessary to bear a few things in mind when choosing a measure.

First, it is important to recognize that association measures are in general sensitive when it comes to very low frequencies. In such cases, association measures will often overestimate the association between elements even though the small frequencies of the elements would not support a high degree of confidence into a strong association.

Second, some association measures are asymptotic in nature and, thus, presuppose a particular distribution of the data (at least when they are used for significance testing), but, for example, corpus data are usually not normally distributed. One must therefore be careful to properly justify the choice of a measure or, maybe safer, choose measures that do not make such distributional assumption (such as the Fisher-Yates exact test or the *binomial test*).

Third, given the different mathematical properties of the association measures, it is important to know that they are differently sensitive to low frequencies and will also rank-order collocations differently depending on the words' frequencies. For example, pointwise *MI* is known to return very high association scores to low-frequency words as well as technical terms or other expressions that exhibit very little or no variation. On the other hand, the *t*-score returns high association scores to word pairs with high co-occurrence frequencies and provides a better measure of the non-randomness of the co-occurrence (cf. Evert 2009b for more discussion).

2.3.2. Further hints: some desiderata and underutilized approaches
Let us complete this section with a few desiderata.

First, nearly all of the association measures are based on token frequencies only. That is, the frequencies entered into Table 2 do not reveal anything about the number of different verbs that make up the 1571 non-*give* ditransitives. On the one hand, this makes the association measures much easier to compute, but on the other hand, they lose information. Obviously when *give* occurs in the ditransitive 232 times and the remaining 1751 ditransitives are made up of 300 other verbs, then this speaks more in favor of a strong association of *give* to the ditransitive than when the remaining 1751 ditransitives are made up of 3 other verbs. Unfortunately, I know of only one association measure that incorporates such information – Daudaravičius and Marcinkevičienė's (2004) gravity counts – and in spite of its uniqueness and promise, this measure has so far hardly been explored (but cf. Mukherjee and Gries 2009).

Second, while the study of collostructions, colligations, or collocational frameworks (i.e., patterns such as *a ___ of*) involves the co-occurrence of a word with a construction in a precisely defined syntactic slot, many approaches to collocation rather adopt a window-based approach in which all words in a window of, often, four or five words around the relevant node word are considered. Again, this is computationally easy, but again it loses information. A better but also underutilized approach is Mason's (1997, 1999) lexical gravity. (Daudaravičius and Marcinkevičienė's (2004) gravity counts are based on this work by Mason). Mason proposes to explore a much larger window of slots around a node word by computing, for each slot around a word, the entropies of the collocates in that slot to determine which positions around a node word of interest exhibit how much variation. This approach is an interesting way to determine the relevant contextual slots of words in a bottom-up fashion and readily allows to consider asymmetrical windows around node words.

Another interesting set of problems arises when the notion of collocation is applied to collocations of more than two words. (When *n* words in question form a chain, they are often referred to as *n*-grams). One problem is that many of the statistical measures that have been proposed for the collocation of two words cannot straightforwardly be applied to collocations of more than two words or *n*-grams with $n>2$. For instance, one problem involves the question of how to compute the expected frequencies: should the expected frequency of *in spite of* be based on independent probabilities of *in*, *spite*, and *of*, or on the independent probabilities of *in spite* and *of*, or on the independent probabilities of *in* and *spite of*? Commercially available software usually computes expected frequencies in the first of these three ways, but it is not clear (yet) whether this is really the appropriate way.

Another often underestimated problem is even more fundamental, namely the question of which *n* to assume for *n*-grams. For example, it is obvious that it would rarely be useful to treat *in spite* as a 2-gram – the relevant *n*-gram is the 3-gram *in spite of*. For example, it may be less useful to treat *the one hand* as a 3-gram, because the 'real' *n*-gram may well be *on the one hand*, etc. Most studies using *n*-grams have so far defined an *n* a priori but it may often be more prudent to let the corpus data decide in a bottom-up, *n*-gram specific fashion what the best statistically best *n*-gram sequences are.

A final corpus-linguistically completely understudied problem related to the previous one involves discontinuous *n*-grams, the identification of which is not only statistically difficult in the above way, but also computionally extremely demanding. It remains to be hoped that corpus linguists will address these topics (more) soon and consider work already undertaken in computational linguistics (cf. Kita et al. 1993, 1994; Nagao and Mori 1994; Ikehara, Shirai, and Uchino 1996; Shimohata, Sugio, Nagata 1997; da Silva, Dias, Guilloré, and Pereira Lopes 1999; Mukherjee and Gries 2009).

3. Statistical evaluation of distributional data

In this section, I will discuss a few central statistical methods for the analysis of corpus data.

3.1. Correlations of interval/ordinal-scaled data

One frequent scenario involves the comparison of how two variables are related to each other, and such relations are sometimes, and should always, be explored graphically in a scatter plot of the kind exemplified in Figure 1, which uses a solid line to show the correlation between time (on the *x*-axis) and the relative frequency of the expression *just because* (on the *y*-axis) (from Hilpert and Gries 2009; we disregard the dashed line for now).

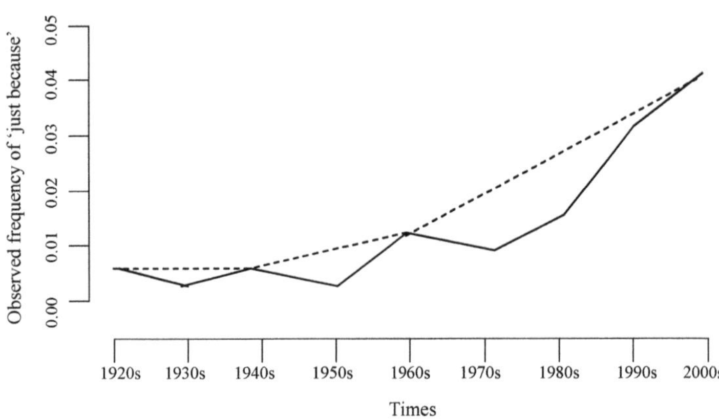

Figure 1. The development of the frequency of *just because* over time

It is obvious that there seems to be a positive trend, but of course this needs to be tested. The probably most frequently used correlation is Pearson's *r*, but the significance test for Pearson's *r* relies on distributional assumptions that corpus data often violate, so it is nearly always safer to use an alternative measure that does not, such as Kendall's *tau*. Like many correlation coefficients, *tau* is close to 1 when there is a strong positive correlation ('the more *a*, the more *b*'), it is close to -1 when there is a strong negative correlation ('the more *a*, the less *b*'), and it is close to zero in the absence of a correlation. Kendall's *tau* for the correlation between the time and the relative frequency is rather high and positive (τ=0.743; z=2.74; p=0.006), which means that, obviously, the frequency of *just because* increases significantly over time.

While Kendall's *tau* is often safer to use than Pearson's *r*, it can only be applied to scenarios in which two variables are correlated – for scenarios where more than one variable is involved in the prediction of a dependent variable, frequently the approach of *linear modeling* is used, which uses the same logic underlying Pearson's *r*. The mathematically simplest approach of linear models requires that all variables involved are interval-scaled, and the model selection process is typically performed in such a way that one begins to model the data with the most comprehensive model that one's data allow one to formulate, and then non-significant predictors are removed in a stepwise fashion (following Occam's razor), until only significant predictors remain. While corpus data often violate the assumptions of linear models, the logic of linear modeling and the model selection process helps to understand other statistical regression methods that can handle corpus data (cf. Section 3.2.2 below).

3.2. *(Cross-)Tabulation of frequency data*

3.2.1. Chi-square statistics

The simplest way of analyzing frequency data involves creating a one-dimensional frequency table of linguistic expressions and perform a test of whether the distribution of the observed frequencies of occurrence deviate significantly from an expected distribution, where that expected distribution may be just a random distribution or a distribution following from some other study or expectation.

For example, Table 2 above listed the frequencies of the inflectional forms of the lemma *give*, for which then also H and H_{rel} were computed. A *chi-square test* can now also show whether the observed frequencies differ significantly from a uniform distribution – i.e., the case where all inflectional forms are equally frequent. A chi-square test shows that the frequencies of the inflectional forms of *give* are not compatible with the assumption that they are equally frequent: χ^2=377.72; df=4; p<0.001.

Also, on the basis of a previous study one may believe that the frequencies of the five inflectional forms should be distributed as follows: 40% vs. 10% vs. 10% vs. 15% vs. 25%. Again, a chi-square test can show whether the observed frequencies fit that distribution, and they do not: χ^2=24.35; df=4; p<0.001.

The probably more frequent scenario is that one cross-tabulates two different variables with each other, to obtain tables of the kind exemplified in Table 3. For example, Hundt and Smith (2009) discuss the frequencies of the simple past and the present perfect in four corpora on the basis of the following data:

	LOB	**FLOB**	**BROWN**	**FROWN**	**Totals**
pres. perf.	4196	4073	3538	3499	15306
simple past	35821	35276	37223	36250	144570
Totals	40017	39349	40761	39749	159876

Table 5. Observed co-occurrence frequencies of two tenses in four corpora

Hundt and Smith (2009: 51) conclude that they are "dealing with stable regional variation rather than ongoing diachronic change." However, there are two potential problems. First, their way of representing the data is statistically speaking less than ideal; second, they do not provide a statistical test to support their interpretation. As for the second problem, a chi-square test shows that they are right: there is a significant correlation between the tenses and the corpus parts (χ^2=130.8; df=3; p<0.001), but the results also show that the two British and the two American varieties pattern together: BrE has more present perfects than expected, and AmE has less. This pattern can be very clearly seen in an *association plot* such as Figure 2, in which black and white bars indicate observed frequencies that are larger and smaller than expected by chance respectively.

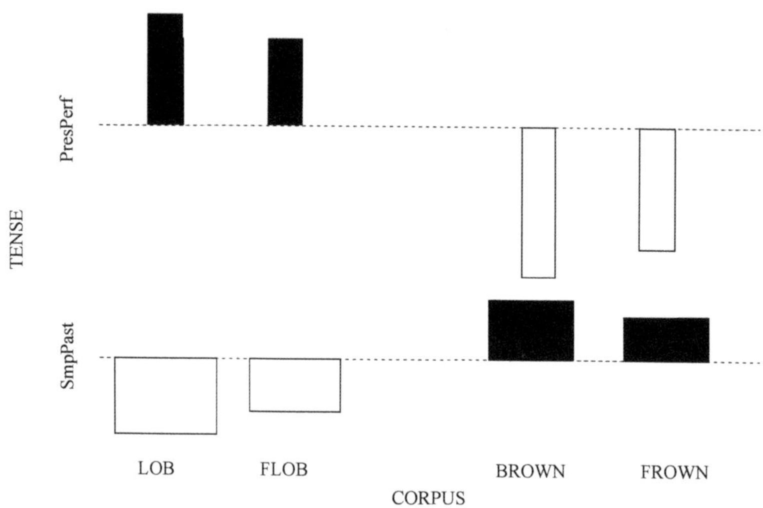

Figure 2. Association plot for the interaction TENSE:CORPUS

It should be noted, however, that the observed effect is also very small, as a standard *effect size* for *r*×*c* tables shows: Cramer's *V*=0.03. The highly significant result arises because of the large sample size.[2]

However, while the above computation exemplifies the use of the chi-square test (with the caveat of n. 2), there is still the first problem, which is somewhat more tricky and leads to the next section on multifactorial models. This problem is that one would normally actually not compute the above chi-square test on these data. Hundt and Smith represented the data as if it represents a two-dimensional data set: TENSE (present perfect vs. simple past) × CORPUS (LOB vs. Brown vs. FLOB vs. Frown) whereas in fact it is a three-dimensional data set: TENSE (present perfect vs. simple past) vs. VARIETY (BrE vs. AmE) vs. TIME (early (for LOB and Brown) vs. late (for FLOB and Frown)). Just because such data *can* be represented two-dimensionally does not mean they *are* two-dimensional. However, for such a three-dimensional data set, a chi-square test is not the most appropriate method – rather, a *generalized linear regression* is more appropriate here.

2 Note that the above kind of chi-square test assumes that all data points are independent of each other, a condition which is strictly speaking probably not met because all the data points provided by one and the same author are related to each other; cf. Baroni and Evert (2009) and Evert (2006, 2009a) for insightful discussion of this problem as well as suggestions for analysis (cf. also Gries 2006a, b).

3.2.2. Generalized linear models: logistic regression and Poisson regression

Just like the linear models mentioned above, generalized linear models try to predict the outcome of a dependent variable on the basis of one or more independent variables. Also, they involve the same kind of model selection process in which non-significant variables are successively eliminated. The main difference to simple linear models is that the dependent variable need not be a interval-scaled variable but can also be factors with two levels (*binary logistic regression*) or more levels (*multinomial logistic regression*) or frequencies (*Poisson regression*).

To at least briefly exemplify one application this approach, we can revisit Hundt and Smith's (2009) data from the previous section and, first, represent them in a way that makes the design of the study more obvious. In Table 6, the left three columns contain what may be considered the independent variables while the rightmost column contains the observed frequencies of the levels of the independent variables.

TENSE	VARIETY	TIME	**Frequency**
present perfect	BrE	early	4196
present perfect	BrE	late	4073
present perfect	AmE	early	3538
present perfect	AmE	late	3499
simple past	BrE	early	35821
simple past	BrE	late	35276
simple past	AmE	early	37223
simple past	AmE	late	36250

Table 6. Observed co-occurrence frequencies of two tenses in four corpora

The model selection process of, in this case, a Poisson regression begins with a completely saturated model, which contains the three variables, their three two-way interactions (TENSE:VARIETY, TENSE:TIME, and VARIETY:TIME), and their three-way interaction (TENSE:VARIETY:TIME). However, this first model shows that the three-way interaction is not needed, and subsequent elimination of interactions shows that TENSE:TIME and VARIETY:TIME can also be omitted. The final highly significant model contains the three independent variables and the interaction TENSE:VARIETY and this interaction shows the dispreference of BrE for simple past tense is significant.

In sum, Hundt and Smith's analysis has been on the right track. However, this must not distract from the fact that, especially in the case of multifactorial data sets, only a careful and statistically comprehensive analysis can ensure that all significant effects are discovered; for an example from the same journal where a more comprehensive analysis could find effects not discussed by the original authors, cf. Hommerberg and Tottie (2007) and Gries (2009b).

3.3. Further hints: useful and underutilized methods

It is impossible to provide a good overview of the many very useful aspects of the above tests and modeling methods, let alone discuss all other ways in which corpus data can be analyzed, so a few selected comments must suffice.

One important aspect has to do with non-linearity of data. Often, linear correlation measures and linear regression lines are among the first or even only statistics and graphics that are applied to data. However, a linear correlation may be significant even though the real underlying trend is not linear but curvilinear. One should therefore always plot the data – because particular relations or outliers cannot be seen from numbers alone – but also always try to summarize trends using non-parametric smoothers. These try to summarize data just like linear regression lines do, but they need not be a straight line and can therefore detect nonlinear (portions of) trends much better. One example is the dashed smoother in Figure 1.

One notion that is especially important in corpus linguistics is that of *effect sizes*. This is because the large sample sizes that many contemporary corpora provide basically guarantee that even minuscule effects will be highly significant. For example, the first analysis of Hundt and Smith's data in Section 3.2.1 returned an extremely significant result – $p<10^{-27}$ – but this is because of the sample size of nearly 160,000. The effect size, on the other hand, showed that the effect is in fact extremely small (0.03). Hence, one should always provide an effect size so that one's significant result can be better evaluated.

A second important point is concerned with Occam's razor. It is widely-known that Occam's razor dictates that non-significant predictors must be eliminated. What is less widely-known apparently is that this argument does not only apply to variables or factors, but also to levels of factors. For example, if one obtains a significant result from a table such as Table 5, then this does not mean that all four corpora differ significantly from each other. While the 'real' solution to this particular case was discussed in Section 3.2.2, such 2×*c* tables can also be analyzed using the so-called *Marascuilo procedure*. This procedure involves pairwise comparisons of all combinations of columns; its output can look like Table 7.

Comparisons	**Differences**	**Critical ranges**	**Decision**
LOB vs. FLOB	0.0013	0.0061	ns
LOB vs. Frown	0.0168	0.0058	*
LOB vs. Brown	0.0181	0.0058	*
FLOB vs. Frown	0.0155	0.0058	*
FLOB vs. Brown	0.0167	0.0058	*
Frown vs. Brown	0.0012	0.0056	ns

Table 7. Output of the Marascuilo procedure applied to Table 5

The central result is that the Marascuilo procedure shows that LOB and FLOB as well as Frown and Brown do not differ significantly from each other (and should thus be combined), but all other combinations of corpora are significantly different. This result corresponds to that of the Poisson regression from above, in which TENSE:VARIETY:TIME and TENSE:TIME were non-significant.

3.4. Exploratory methods

The final set of statistical methods to be discussed here briefly is different from most others mentioned so far. Most of the above statistics are *hypothesis-testing* in nature such that a particular *a priori* hypothesis about patterns and relations in data are tested. However, another very useful kind of methods is *exploratory* and/or *hypothesis-generating* in nature: instead of testing a hypothesis, these methods seek – in a bottom-up, data-driven fashion – patterns and relations in data sets that are too large, complex, and/or noisy to understand without such techniques. This kind of bottom-up approach is often very attractive because it relies less on any researcher's preconceptions of how the data will pattern but more on the data themselves. In fact, in corpus linguistics, where findings are often bound to be significant simply by virtue of the sample size, it is often a good idea to apply exploratory methods on top of a significance test to either test whether the variable or distinctions / variable levels tested for significance are in fact the ones most strongly supported in the data. One application of this kind was already exemplified above in Section 3.3: the Marascuilo procedure took as input four levels of the variable CORPUS and output the result that it would be better to distinguish only two kinds of corpora, which then corresponded to the variable VARIETY, whose interaction with TENSE turned out to be significant in the Poisson regression.

As usual, there is a large number of such methods: cluster analysis, principal component and factor analysis, multidimensional scaling, association rules, Bayesian classifiers, etc. The family of methods I discuss here is *hierarchical agglomerative cluster analysis*, which is one of the most versatile methods (in the sense that can handle many different kinds of input data – nominal, ordinal, interval data, raw data and distance matrices – and produces first results in the form of a tree diagram that is intuitively easy to understand. This kind of cluster analysis is typically applied to data sets consisting of n objects that are characterized by x characteristics, which may be binary, polytomous, or numeric; the main purpose is to find structure in the data set such that the n objects can be clustered into $m<n$ groups that are characterized by a large within-cluster similarity and a small between-cluster similarity.

As one example, consider Figure 3, which represents a dendrogram of nine Russian near synonyms meaning 'to try' (from Divjak and Gries 2006). The n objects clustered were the nine verbs, the x characteristics were relative frequencies for 87 morphological, syntactic, and semantic characteristics of how altogether 1585 instances of these verbs were used.

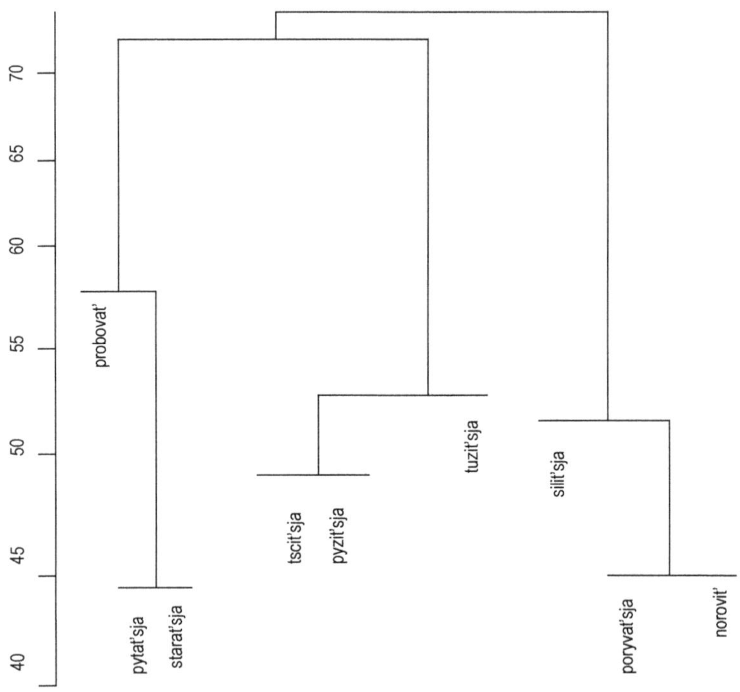

Figure 3. Clustering Russian verbs meaning 'to try'

In this case, the result is fairly clear: there are three clusters: {*silit'sja poryvat'sja norovit'*}, {*tuzit'sja tscit'sja pyzit'sja*}, and {*probovat' pytat'sja starat'sja*}, and these results can then be compared to semantic/lexicographic analyses.

While clustering methods are rather widespread in computational linguistics, their full potential has apparently not been recognized in corpus linguistics. This may be in part due to the seemingly contradictory facts that, on the one hand, cluster analyses are sometimes perceived as a mythical black box returning tree diagrams, but on the other hand, require not only statistically-informed decisions to create the tree, but also some experience and/or statistical know-how when it comes to interpreting a dendrogram in more detail than just stating the groups or when it comes to identifying groups in more ambiguous dendrograms.

The former kind of knowledge is necessary to define (i) how the *n* objects' similarities to each other are measured and (ii) how objects that are considered very similar are amalgamated into clusters. As for (i), the analyst can choose between measures that respond to distances or curvature; as for (ii) the analyst can choose between amalgamation rules that create small even-sized or elongated clusters, but the consequences of these decisions are rather well documented in the relevant introductory literature.

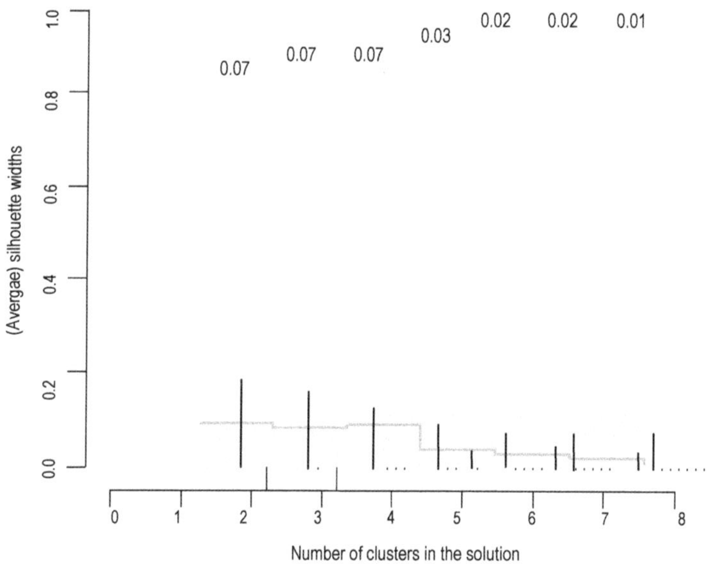

Figure 4. Average silhouette widths of different cluster solutions of Figure 3

What is much less well documented in one place is the latter kind of knowledge. One interesting way to determine the number of clusters when the dendrogram does not strongly suggest a number involves the notion of (average) silhouette widths. Simply speaking, average silhouette widths quantify the ratio between the cohesion of the elements (here, verbs) within a cluster and the cohesion of elements within a cluster to elements outside of it. The higher the average silhouette width of a cluster solution, the more discriminatory it is. This is interesting because it is then possible to compute all possible cluster solutions for a data set and determine which number of clusters results in the best discrimination. Figure 4 summarizes the results of this approach to the data of

Figure 3. The x-axis represents all possible and meaningful numbers of clusters for n=9 objects, this means testing 2, 3, …, 7, 8 clusters), and the y-axis portrays the silhouette width. The black vertical lines are silhouette widths of the clusters, and the grey step function as well as the numbers at the top represent the average silhouette widths for each number of clusters. Figure 4 shows that the intuitive assessment of three clusters is confirmed.

Not only are those comprehensive tests of how many clusters there are rare to find, but often there is also no further post hoc analysis of the clustering, although these are often very interesting. For example, one can compute F-values for each cluster to quantify its internal homogeneity. For example, one can compute t-scores for each characteristic in a cluster to determine which characteristics drive the cluster solution, and there are many other approaches like these which allow for a comprehensive study of data sets. Hopefully, the many ingenuous tools statisticians have provided will find their way into suitable corpus studies.

4. Concluding remarks

Given considerations of space, the above sections could only introduce a very small number of corpus-linguistically important statistics and caveats. I hope, however, to have illustrated a few relevant methods as well as arguments why a proper use of statistical methods in indispensable, and elsewhere (e.g., Gries 2003, 2009a) I have argued and exemplified the kinds of problems that can arise from the improper statistical analysis of linguistic data. It is therefore imperative that we as corpus linguists collectively increase the level of statistical sophistication of our analyses. Next to Oakes's (1998) slightly older introduction to statistics for corpus linguistics plus some short overview articles (e.g., Biber and Jones 2009), there are now several new introductions to statistics for linguists in general available (Baayen 2008, Johnson 2008, Gries 2009b), which help familiarize the reader with incredibly powerful software.

With regard to software, it is also worth pointing out that it is no coincidence that these new introductions all use a particular piece of software for their analysis, namely the open source software R (R Development Core Team 2009). R is now the leading programming environment for statistical applications, available for different operating systems, constantly updated, and incredibly powerful in terms of range of methods, graphical exploration, sizes of data sets, etc., and can in fact also be used as full-fledged corpus-linguistic retrieval software. Given the power and the free availability of this resource, contemporary corpus linguistics should seize the opportunity and help break new ground in making our discipline empirically more precise, comprehensive, and responsible.

References

Baayen, R. H. (2008): *Analyzing Linguistic Data: A Practical Introduction to Statistics Using R*, Cambridge, Cambridge University Press.

Baroni, M. and S. Evert. (2009): "Statistical methods for corpus exploitation," in A. Lüdeling and M. Kytö (eds.), *Corpus Linguistics: An International Handbook Vol. 2*, Berlin, New York, 777-803.

Biber, D. and J. K. Jones. (2009): "Quantitative methods in corpus linguistics," in A. Lüdeling and M. Kytö (eds.), *Corpus Linguistics: An International Handbook Vol. 2*, Berlin / New York, 1286-1304.

Damerau, F.J. (1993): "Generating and evaluating domain-oriented multi-word terms from texts," *Information Processing & Management*, 29, 433-447.

Daudaravičius, V. and R. Marcinkevičienė (2004): "Gravity counts for the boundaries of collocations," *International Journal of Corpus Linguistics*, 9, 2, 321-348.

Divjak, D.S. and St. Th. Gries. (2006): "Ways of trying in Russian: clustering behavioral profiles," *Corpus Linguistics and Linguistic Theory*, 2, 1, 23-60.

Evert, S. (2004): *The Statistics of Word Cooccurrences: Word Pairs and Collocations* (Unpublished doctoral dissertation, Institut für maschinelle Sprachverarbeitung, University of Stuttgart).

Evert, S. (2006): "How random is a corpus? The library metaphor," *Zeitschrift für Anglistik und Amerikanistik*, 54, 2, 177-190.

Evert, S. (2009a): "Rethinking corpus frequencies," paper presented at ICAME 2009.

Evert, S. (2009b): "Corpora and collocations," in A. Lüdeling and M. Kytö (eds.), *Corpus Linguistics: An International Handbook Vol. 2*, Berlin, New York, 1212-1248.

Gale, W. and G. Sampson. (1995): "Good-Turing smoothing without tears," *Journal of Quantitative Linguistics*, 2, 217-237.

Gries, St. Th. (2003): *Multifactorial Analysis in Corpus Linguistics: The Case of Particle Placement*, London / New York, Continuum.

Gries, St. Th. (2006a): "Some proposals towards more rigorous corpus linguistics," *Zeitschrift für Anglistik und Amerikanistik*, 54, 2, 191-202.

Gries, St. Th. (2006b): "Exploring variability within and between corpora: some methodological considerations," *Corpora*, 1, 2, 109-151.

Gries, St. Th. (2008): "Dispersions and adjusted frequencies in corpora," *International Journal of Corpus Linguistics*, 13, 4, 403-437.

Gries, St. Th. (2009a): *Quantitative Corpus Linguistics with R: A Practical Introduction*, London / New York, Routledge (Taylor Francis).

Gries, St. Th. (2009b): *Statistics for Linguists with R: A Practical Introduction*. Berlin / New York, Mouton de Gruyter.

Gries, St. Th. (2009c): "Dispersions and adjusted frequencies in corpora: further explorations," in St. Th. Gries, S. Wulff, and M. Davies (eds.), *Corpus Linguistic Applications: Current Studies, New Directions*, Amsterdam, Rodopi.

Gries, St. Th. (to appear): "Methodological skills in corpus linguistics: a polemic and some pointers towards quantitative methods …"

Hilpert, M. and St. Th. Gries. (2009): "Assessing frequency changes in multi-stage diachronic corpora: applications for historical corpus linguistics and the study of language acquisition," *Literary and Linguistic Computing*, 34, 4, 385-401.

Hommerberg, C. and G. Tottie. (2007): "*Try to* and *try and*? Verb complementation in British and American English," *ICAME Journal*, 31, 45-64.

Hundt, M. and N. Smith. (2009): "The present perfect in British and American English: has there been any change recently?" *ICAME Journal*, 32, 45-63.

Ikehara, S., S. Shirai, and H. Uchino. (1996): "A statistical method for extracting uninterrupted and interrupted collocations from very large corpora," *Proceedings of the 16th Conference on Computational linguistics (Vol. 1)*, 574-579.

Johnson, K. (2008): *Quantitative Methods in Linguistics*, Malden, MA: Blackwell.

Kita, K., K. Ogura, T. Morimoto, Y. Ueno, Y. (1993): "Automatically extracting frozen patterns from corpora using cost criteria," *Journal of Information Processing*, 34, 9, 1937-1943.

Kita, K., W. Kato, T. Omoto, and Y. Yano. (1994): "A comparative study of automatic extraction of collocations from corpora: mutual information vs. cost criteria," *Journal of Natural Language Processing*, 1, 1:21-33.

Mason, O. (1997): "The weight of words: an investigation of lexical gravity," *Proceedings of PALC'97*, 361-375.

Mason, Oliver (1999): "Parameters of collocation: the word in the centre of gravity," in J. M. Kirk (ed.), *Corpora Galore: Analyses and Techniques in Describing English*, Amsterdam, Rodopi, 267-280.

Mukherjee, J. and St. Th. Gries. (2009): "Lexical gravity across varieties of English: an ICE-based study of speech and writing in Asian Englishes," paper presented at ICAME 2009.

Nagao, M. and S. Mori. (1994): "A new method of *n*-gram statistics for large number of *n* and automatic extraction of words and phrases from large text data of Japanese," *Proceedings of the 15th Conference on Computational Linguistics*, 611-615.

Oakes, M. (1998): *Statistics for Corpus Linguistics*, Edinburgh, Edinburgh University Press.

R Development Core Team. (2009): *R: A Language and Environment for Statistical Computing*, Vienna, R Foundation for Statistical Computing, URL <http://www.R-project.org>.

Scott, M. (1997): "PC analysis of key words – and key key words," *System*, 25, 2, 233-245.

Shimohata, S., T. Sugio, and J. Nagata. (1997): "Retrieving collocations by co-occurrences and word order constraints," *Proceedings of the 35th Annual Meeting of the Association for Computational Linguistics*, 476-481.

da Silva, J. F., G. Dias, S. Guilloré, and J. G. Pereira Lopes. (1999): "Using *LocalMaxs* Algorithm for the extraction of contiguous and non-contiguous multiword lexical units," *Proceedings of the 9th Portuguese Conference on Artificial Intelligence: Progress in Artificial Intelligence*, 849-849.

Wiechmann, D. (2008): "On the computation of collostruction strength: testing measures of association as expressions of lexical bias", *Corpus Linguistics and Linguistic Theory*, 4, 2, 253-290.

Studien zur romanischen Sprachwissenschaft und interkulturellen Kommunikation

Herausgegeben von Gerd Wotjak

Band 1 Gerd Wotjak (ed.): Teoría del campo y semántica léxica. Théorie des champs et sémantique lexicale. 1998.

Band 2 Eva Martha Eckkrammer / Hildegund Maria Eder: (Cyber)Diskurs zwischen Konvention und Revolution. Eine multilinguale textlinguistische Analyse von Gebrauchstextsorten im realen und virtuellen Raum. 2000.

Band 3 Monika Gräfe: Untersuchungen zur Konstituentenabfolge spanischer Adverbiale auf Satz- und Textebene mit EDV-gestützter quantitativer Analyse. 2000.

Band 4 Juan Pablo Larreta Zulategui: Fraseología contrastiva del alemán y el español. Teoría y práctica a partir de un corpus bilingüe de somatismos. 2001.

Band 5 Catalina Jiménez Hurtado: Léxico y Pragmática. 2001.

Band 6 Félix Jiménez Ramírez: El español en la Suiza alemana. Estudio de las características lingüísticas e identitarias del español de la segunda generación en una situación de contacto de lenguas. 2001.

Band 7 Gerd Wotjak (Hrsg.): Studien zum romanisch-deutschen und innerromanischen Sprachvergleich. Akten der IV. Internationalen Tagung zum romanisch-deutschen und innerromanischen Sprachvergleich (Leipzig, 7.10.-9.10.1999). 2001.

Band 8 Romanische Sprachen in Amerika. Festschrift für Hans-Dieter Paufler zum 65. Geburtstag. Herausgegeben von Kerstin Störl und Johannes Klare. 2002.

Band 9 José-Antonio Calañas Continente: El dominio léxico *Existencia* en alemán. Diccionario lexemático-funcional alemán-español del lexicón verbal básico. 2002.

Band 10 Gabriele Blaikner-Hohenwart (Hrsg.): Portugiesisch, Papiamentu et al. Salzburger Beiträge zu Prozessen und Produkten der Translation in der Romania. 2003.

Band 11 Juan Cuartero Otal: Cosas que se hacen. Esquemas sintáctico-semánticos agentivos del español. 2003.

Band 12 Michael Schreiber: Vergleichende Studien zur romanischen und deutschen Grammatikographie. 2004.

Band 13 Carmen Mellado Blanco: Fraseologismos somáticos del alemán. Un estudio léxico-semántico. 2004.

Band 14 Henk Vanhoe: Aspectos de la sintaxis de los verbos psicológicos en español. Un análisis léxico funcional. 2004.

Band 15 Susana Azpiazu: Las estrategias de nominalización. Estudio contrastivo del estilo nominal. 2004.

Band 16 Meike Meliss: Recursos lingüísticos alemanes relativos a "GERÄUSCH" y sus posibles correspondencias en español. Un estudio lexicológico modular-integrativo. 2005.

Band 17 Marcial Morera: La Complementación Morfológica en Español. Ensayo de Interpretación Semántica. 2005.

Band 18 Alberto Bustos Plaza: Combinaciones verbonominales y lexicalización. 2005.

Band 19 Jean Peeters (ed.): On the Relationships between Translation Theory and Translation Practice. 2005.

Band 20 María José Domínguez Vázquez: Die Präpositivergänzung im Deutschen und im Spanischen. Zur Semantik der Präpositionen. 2005.

Band 21 Thomas J. C. Hüsgen: Vom getreuen Boten zum nachdichterischen Autor. Übersetzungskritische Analyse von Fernando Pessoas *Livro do Desassossego* in deutscher Sprache. 2005.

Band 22 Gerd Wotjak / Juan Cuartero Otal (eds.): Entre semántica léxica, teoría del léxico y sintaxis. 2005.

Band 23 Manuel Casado Velarde / Ramón González Ruiz / Óscar Loureda Lamas (eds.): Estudios sobre lo metalingüístico (en español). 2005.

Band 24 Celia Martín de León: Contenedores, recorridos y metas. Metáforas en la traductología funcionalista. 2005.

Band 25 Ulrike Oster: Las relaciones semánticas de términos polilexemáticos. Estudio contrastivo alemán-español. 2005.

Band 26 María Teresa Sánchez Nieto: Las construcciones perifrásticas españolas de significado evaluativo y sus equivalentes alemanes en la traducción. Con ejercicios para la clase de español como lengua extranjera. 2005.

Band 27 María Amparo Montaner Montava: Análisis cognitivo-perceptivo de la combinatoria de los verbos de transferencia. Se incluye CD-ROM con actividades para estudiantes de lingüística, lenguas y traducción. 2005.

Band 28 Clara Curell: Contribución al estudio de la interferencia lingüística. Los galicismos del español contemporáneo. 2005.

Band 29 Antonio Pamies / Francisca Rodríguez Simón: El lenguaje de los enfermos. Metáfora y fraseología en el habla espontánea de los pacientes. 2005.

Band 30 Gisela Marcelo Wirnitzer: Traducción de las referencias culturales en la literatura infantil y juvenil. 2007.

Band 31 Elena De Miguel/Azucena Palacios/Ana Serradilla (eds.): Estructuras Léxicas y Estructura del Léxico. 2006.

Band 32 Esteban Tomás Montoro del Arco: Teoría fraseológica de las *locuciones particulares*. Las locuciones prepositivas, conjuntivas y marcadoras en español. 2006.

Band 33 Nicola Matschke: Zeitgenössische französische Bibelübersetzungen: exemplarische textlinguistische und stilistische Übersetzungsprobleme. 2006.

Band 34 Mónica Aznárez Mauleón: La fraseología metalingüística con verbos de lengua en español actual. 2006.

Band 35 Moisés Almela Sánchez: From Word to Lexical Units. A Corpus-Driven Account of Collocation and Idiomatic Patterning in English and English-Spanish. 2006.

Band 36 Marta Albelda Marco: La intensificación como categoría pragmática: revisión y propuesta. Una aplicación al español coloquial. 2007.

Band 37 María del Carmen África Vidal Claramonte: Traducir entre culturas. Diferencias, poderes, identidades. 2007.

Band 38 Maria Eugênia Olímpio de Oliveira Silva: Fraseografía teórica y práctica. 2007.

Band 39 Catalina Jiménez Hurtado (ed.): Traducción y accesibilidad. Subtitulación para sordos y audiodescripción para ciegos: nuevas modalidades de Traducción Audiovisual. 2007.

Band 40 Emilio Ortega Arjonilla (ed.): El Giro Cultural de la Traducción. Reflexiones teóricas y aplicaciones didácticas. 2007.

Band 41 María Álvarez de la Granja (ed.): Lenguaje figurado y motivación. Una perspectiva desde la fraseología. 2008.

Band 42 Kathrin Siebold: Actos de habla y cortesía verbal en español y en alemán. Estudio pragmalingüístico e intercultural. 2008.

Band 43 Germán Conde Tarrío (ed.): Aspectos formales y discursivos de las expresiones fijas. 2008.

Band 44 Carmen Mellado Blanco (ed.): Colocaciones y fraseología en los diccionarios. 2008.

Band 45 Leonor Ruiz Gurillo / Xose A. Padilla García (eds.): *Dime cómo ironizas y te diré quién eres*. Una aproximación pragmática a la ironía. 2009.

Band 46 María Cecilia Ainciburu: Aspectos del aprendizaje del vocabulario. Tipo de palabra, método, contexto y grado de competencia en las lenguas afines. 2008.

Band 47 Susana Rodríguez Rosique: Pragmática y Gramática. Condicionales concesivas en español. 2008.

Band 48 Daniel Veith: Italienisch am Río de la Plata. Ein Beitrag zur Sprachkontaktforschung. 2008.

Babd 49 Gloria Corpas Pastor: Investigar con corpus en traducción: los retos de un nuevo paradigma. 2008.

Band 50 Maurício Cardozo / Werner Heidermann / Markus J. Weininger (eds.): A Escola Tradutológica de Leipzig. 2009.

Band 51 Luis Alexis Amador Rodríguez: La derivación nominal en español: nombres de agente, instrumento, lugar y acción. 2009.

Band 52 José-Luis Mendívil Giró: Origen, evolución y diversidad de las lenguas. Una aproximación biolingüística. 2009.

Band 53 Victòria Alsina / Gemma Andújar / Mercé Tricás (eds.): La representación del discurso individual en traducción. 2009.

Band 54 Sonia Bravo Utrera / Rosario García López (eds.): Estudios de Traducción: Perspectivas. Zinaida Lvóskaya in memoriam. 2009.

Band 55 Carlos Buján López / María José Domínguez Vázquez (eds.): Centros y periferias en España y Austria: Perspectivas lingüísticas y traductológicas. 2009.

Band 56 María Azucena Penas / Rosario González (eds.): Estudios sobre el texto. Nuevos enfoques y propuestas. 2009.

Band 57 Juan Pedro Monferrer-Sala / Àngel Urbán (eds.): Sacred Text. Explorations in Lexicography. 2009.

Band 58 Gerd Wotjak / Vessela Ivanova / Encarnación Tabares Plasencia (Hrsg./eds.): *Translatione via facienda*. Festschrift für Christiane Nord zum 65. Geburtstag / Homenaje a Christiane Nord en su 65 cumpleaños. Herausgegeben von Gerd Wotjak, Vessela Ivanova und Encarnación Tabares Placencia / Editado por Gerd Wotjak, Vessela Ivanova y Encarnación Tabares Placencia. 2009.

Band 59 M. Belén Alvarado Ortega: Las fórmulas rutinarias del español: teoría y aplicaciones. 2010.

Band 60 Louisa Buckingham: Las construcciones con verbo soporte en un corpus de especialidad. 2009.

Band 61 Martin Mehlberg: Weil man es so sagt. Wissenschaftstheoretische und valenzlexikographische Überlegungen zu ausgewählten Aspekten der lexikalischen Variation. 2010.

Band 62 Miguel Albi Aparicio: La valencia lógico-semántica de los verbos de movimiento y posición en alemán y español. 2010.

Band 63 Concepción Martínez Pasamar (ed.): Estrategias argumentativas en el discurso periodístico. 2010.

Band 64 Regina Gutiérrez Pérez: Estudio cognitivo-contrastivo de las metáforas del cuerpo. Análisis empírico del corazón como dominio fuente en inglés, francés, español, alemán e italiano. 2010.

Band 65 Dolores García Padrón / María del Carmen Fumero Pérez (eds.): Tendencias en lingüística general y aplicada. 2010.

Band 66 Aquilino Sánchez / Moisés Almela (eds.): A Mosaic of Corpus Linguistics. Selected Approaches. 2010.

www.peterlang.de

www.ingramcontent.com/pod-product-compliance
Ingram Content Group UK Ltd.
Pitfield, Milton Keynes, MK11 3LW, UK
UKHW021831100926
8556IPUK00004B/274

9 783631 587898